PART
5&6
READING

解きまくれ！
リーディングドリル
TOEIC® L&R TEST PART 5&6

TOEIC is a registered trademark of ETS.
This publication is not endorsed or approved by ETS.
＊L&R means LISTENING AND READING.

著：大里秀介

スリーエー
ネットワーク

Published by 3A Corporation
Trusty Kojimachi Bldg., 2F, 4, Kojimachi 3-Chome, Chiyoda-ku, Tokyo 102-0083, Japan

ISBN 978-4-88319-895-5 C0082

First published 2022
Printed in Japan

はじめに

　解きまくれ！リーディングドリル TOEIC® L&R TEST の Part 5&6 が完成しました。

　前作のシリーズでは、私自身が学習者の立場で相当お世話になり、ちょうどスコアが 900 点程度で、950 点、990 点とスコアを伸ばしていくときにとても役立ちました。そのため、今回は著者として相当気合を入れて作り込みました。

　Part 5&6 の問題は、とっつきやすいという特徴がありながら、2 択まで絞り込んで迷う、難しい語彙問題でどれが正解かわからない、といった問題に時間を取られ、時間を割く必要のある Part 7 への余裕もなくなり、結果的に『英語力はあるものの本来のスコアが取れなかった』という学習者が多いと感じています。また、Part 6 の文選択問題の文脈を意識して解くことが苦手な学習者も多く、スコアの伸び悩みの原因になっているかと思います。

　本書は『解きまくれ！』という冠にふさわしく、厳選した 8 セット分の問題が難易度、出題範囲共にバランスよく収録されています。順番に解いていきながら、自分の苦手なところを丁寧に復習するというやり方や、タイムトライアルとして、早く解いてリーディングセクションの時間管理に役立てるやり方など、目的に沿った学習をすることができます。

　私自身も苦手な問題を克服した後に、『自分が解ける問題をいかに早く解いて、Part 7 に余裕・余力を残すか』をテーマに 1 日 1 回すべての問題をやりきる（1 周する）というスタイルを継続して、950 点の壁を突破し、990 点に到達することができました。

　Part 5&6 で高得点を取るコツは、問題の種類を把握し、解き方のアプローチ（部分的に読むか、全部読むか、文脈を意識するかなど）を選択し、文の構造を把握しながら、いかにスピードを持って終えるかに尽きます。本書の問題量は、そのサイクルを回しやすく、かつ繰り返しやすいため、スピードを意識して『解きまくる』ことで実力もつき、目標とするスコアに到達しやすくなると思います。

　現代は、今まで以上にグローバリゼーションが意識される世の中になっているため、英語を学ぶということは皆さんが社会に出て、何かを成し遂げるための強力なツールになることは間違いありません。そしてその方法の 1 つとして Part 5&6 の問題をたくさんこなしてレベルアップすることで、英文を読んで理解することやメールなどの文字情報で発信していくことの基本を身に付けることができると思います。私自身、そういった学習をすることで、海外で活躍することができました。

　本書と共に学習をすることで、目標スコアを達成し、ひいてはアナタの夢が達成されますことを心より願っております。

2022 年 12 月　大里　秀介

目次

※ マークシート（解答用紙）は、一番最後のページに付いています。

本書の構成と使い方

本書は、問題ページ → 解説ページを繰り返す、ドリル形式の問題集です。テスト 8 回分の問題（368 問）が収録されており、学習者が繰り返し解きやすいように工夫をしています。また、300 頁以降にはドリル形式で解いた問題を模試形式で掲載していますので、用途に合わせてさまざまな解き方で問題に取り組むことができます。

【特長】

● 左ページには 3 回分のチェックボックスを設けています。間違えた問題にチェックを入れることで、復習の際に容易に探せるようになっています。

● 300 頁以降には、ドリル形式で解いた問題を模試形式でも解ける形で掲載しています（問題は同じです）。

● 巻末にはマークシートが収録されています。

PART 5

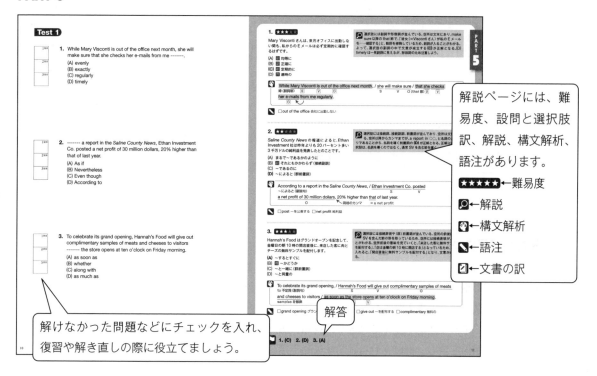

解説ページには、難易度、設問と選択肢訳、解説、構文解析、語注があります。

★★★★★ ←難易度
🔍 ←解説
🧩 ←構文解析
📖 ←語注
📝 ←文書の訳

解けなかった問題などにチェックを入れ、復習や解き直しの際に役立てましょう。

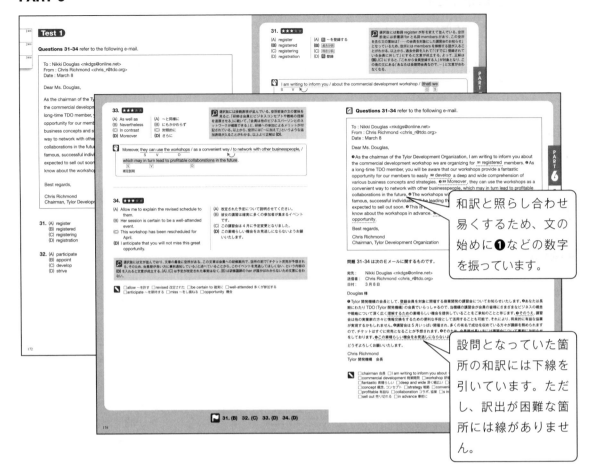

PART 6

〈構文解析の記号について〉

・S（主語）、V（動詞）、O（目的語）、C（補語）（アミカケした節では $\boxed{S}$ $\boxed{V}$ $\boxed{O}$ $\boxed{C}$）

・文の意味を素早く取るために、①句動詞や準動詞、熟語などを、まとめて V（ $\boxed{V}$ ）としたり、②意味や文構造の区切りでスラッシュを入れたりしています。

・副詞節や副詞句、イディオムや覚えておきたい語句・語法にはなるべく意味を入れました。

・破線で修飾する語句を表し、修飾される語句を矢印で示しました。

・文を理解するために、ここで挙げた以外の分析もできる限り示しました。

アプリのご利用

■ AI 英語教材 abceed

株式会社 Globee が提供する、マークシート連動型アプリで解答ができます。

abceed

https://www.abceed.com/

　アプリのダウンロード、その他アプリに関する不具合やご質問に関しましては、上記の配信先へお問い合わせください。弊社ではお答えいたしかねますので、ご了承ください。

TOKIMAKURE!

PART
5

1. While Mary Visconti is out of the office next month, she will make sure that she checks her e-mails from me -------.

(A) evenly
(B) exactly
(C) regularly
(D) timely

2. ------- a report in the *Saline County News*, Ethan Investment Co. posted a net profit of 30 million dollars, 20% higher than that of last year.

(A) As if
(B) Nevertheless
(C) Even though
(D) According to

3. To celebrate its grand opening, Hannah's Food will give out complimentary samples of meats and cheeses to visitors ------- the store opens at ten o'clock on Friday morning.

(A) as soon as
(B) whether
(C) along with
(D) as much as

1. ★★★★☆

Mary Visconti さんは、来月オフィスに出勤しない間も、私からの E メールは必ず定期的に確認するはずです。

(A) 副 均等に
(B) 副 正確に
(C) 副 定期的に
(D) 形 適時の

選択肢には副詞や形容詞が並んでいる。空所は文末にあり、make sure 以降の that 節で、「彼女（＝Visconti さん）が私の E メールを……確認する」と、動詞を修飾しているため、副詞が入ることがわかる。よって、選択肢の副詞の中で文意が成立する **(C)** が正解となる。(D) timely は一見副詞に見えるが、形容詞のため注意しよう。

While Mary Visconti is out of the office next month, / she will make sure / that she checks
（副詞節［時］） S   V   C   S   V   O   S   V
                                （that 節）
her e-mails from me regularly .
     O

□ out of the office 会社に出勤しない

---

2. ★★☆☆☆

Saline County News の報道によると、Ethan Investment 社は昨年よりも 20 パーセント多い 3 千万ドルの純利益を発表したとのことです。

(A) まるで～であるかのように
(B) 副 それにもかかわらず（接続副詞）
(C) ～であるのに
(D) ～によると（群前置詞）

選択肢には接続詞、接続副詞、前置詞が並んでおり、空所は文頭にある。空所以降からカンマまでが、a report in ○○, と名詞のカタマリであることから、名詞を導く前置詞の **(D)** が正解となる。正解以外の選択肢は、名詞を導くのではなく、通常 SV を含む節を導く。

According to a report in the *Saline County News*, / Ethan Investment Co. posted
～によると（副詞句）   S   V
a net profit of 30 million dollars, 20% higher than that of last year.
     O   同格のカンマ   = a net profit

□ post ～を公表する □ net profit 純利益

---

3. ★★★★☆

Hannah's Food はグランドオープンを記念して、金曜日の朝 10 時の開店直後に、来店した客に肉とチーズの無料サンプルを配付します。

(A) ～するとすぐに
(B) 接 ～かどうか
(C) ～と一緒に（群前置詞）
(D) ～と同量の

選択肢には接続表現や（群）前置詞が並んでいる。空所の前後は共に SV を含んだ節の形を取っているため、空所には接続表現が入ることがわかる。空所前後の意味を見ていくと、「来店した客に無料サンプルを配付する」、「店は金曜の朝 10 時に開店する」となっているため、**(A)** を入れると、「開店直後に無料サンプルを配付する」となり、文意が成立する。

To celebrate its grand opening, / Hannah's Food will give out complimentary samples of meats
to 不定詞（副詞句）   S   V   O
and cheeses to visitors / as soon as the store opens at ten o'clock on Friday morning.
                （副詞節［時］） S   V

□ grand opening グランドオープン、華々しい開店 □ give out ～を配布する □ complimentary 無料の

---

 1. (C) 2. (D) 3. (A)

4. There has been a lot of ------- that Mike Travel Magazine will go out of business at the end of the year because of its declining number of subscribers.

(A) speculation
(B) to speculate
(C) speculated
(D) speculators

5. You are cordially invited to stay for the ------- being held in honor of Courtney Woods, the retiring president.

(A) celebration
(B) progress
(C) approval
(D) encouragement

6. ------- employee interested in attending the workshop should contact Jacky Lee to reserve a seat in advance.

(A) All
(B) Any
(C) Both
(D) Few

4. ★★★★☆

購読者の減少のため、Mike Travel Magazine 社は年末に廃業するとの憶測が飛び交っています。

(A) 名 憶測
(B) 動 推測する　[to 不定詞]
(C) [過去分詞]
(D) 名 投機家（複数形）

選択肢には名詞 speculation の派生語などが並んでいる。空所の前後を見ると、形容表現の a lot of と節を導く接続詞 that があるため、修飾される名詞が入るとわかる。選択肢中に名詞は (A) と (D) があるが、「会社が廃業するかもしれないというたくさんの……」という意味に繋がるのは、**(A)** 憶測である。なお、冒頭に There has been... と has が使われていることから、単数名詞が入ることがわかるため、文法的にも (D) は当てはめられない。

〈There is 構文〉
There has been a lot of speculation / that Mike Travel Magazine will go out of business
　　V　　　　　　S　　　　　　　　同格　　　　　S　　　　　　　　V　　　　　　O
　　　　　　　　　　　　　　　　　　　（that 節）

at the end of the year / because of its declining number of subscribers.
　　　　　　　　　　　　　（副詞句 [原因・理由]）

□go out of business 廃業する　□declining 低下する　□subscriber (定期) 購読者

5. ★★★☆☆

社長を退任される Courtney Woods 氏に敬意を表して開催する祝賀会にぜひご招待したいと思います。

(A) 名 祝賀会
(B) 名 進捗
(C) 名 承認
(D) 名 奨励

選択肢には名詞が並んでいる。文の意味を取っていくと、「Courtney Woods 氏へ敬意を表して開催される……に招かれている」とある。敬意を表して開催されるものなので、**(A)** 祝賀会を入れると文意に合う。冒頭の You are cordially invited ... という表現は、通常公式的なイベントに招く際の常套句のため、イベントなどの招待に関する話題の目印として押さえておくとよい。

You are cordially invited to stay for the celebration / being held in honor of Courtney Woods,
　S　　　　　　V

the retiring president.
= Courtney Woods 氏

□cordinally 心から　□in honor of ～に敬意を表して　□retiring まもなく退任する

6. ★★★☆☆

講習会への参加を検討している従業員は、Jacky Lee さんに連絡をして事前に席を押さえてもらうようにしてください。

(A) すべての
(B) いかなる～でも
(C) 両方の
(D) ごく少数の

選択肢には不定代名詞が並んでいる。空所直後の employee を、その後の interested から workshop が修飾し、「講習会への参加に興味のある従業員」という意味になっている。この文の主語は employee であり、空所もこの語を修飾することがわかる。employee は単数のため、選択肢の中で単数と結びつくのは **(B)** となる。

Any employee interested in attending the workshop should contact Jacky Lee /
　　　S　　　　　　　　　　　　　　　　　　　　　　　　　　V　　　　　O

to reserve a seat in advance.
to 不定詞 (副詞句)

□interested in ～に興味のある　□workshop 研修　□in advance 事前に

 4. (A)　5. (A)　6. (B)

7. Ms. Moore is planning a conference ------- the customers to discuss their specific requests for the construction of new office space.

(A) above
(B) until
(C) around
(D) with

8. The first step that you have to take in preparing for an ------- presentation is to choose a proper topic.

(A) inform
(B) informer
(C) informative
(D) information

9. It is suggested that the general manager ------- the new workers with operating the cash registers.

(A) assist
(B) assists
(C) assisted
(D) assisting

7. ★★☆☆☆

Moore さんは新しい事務所スペースの建設に関する具体的な要望について話し合うために顧客との会議を計画しています。

(A) 前 ～より上に
(B) 前 ～まで
(C) 前 ～の周辺に
(D) 前 ～と一緒に

選択肢には前置詞が並んでいる。空所前後の意味を取っていくと「具体的な要望について話し合うために顧客……会議を計画中」とあるので、顧客と一緒に話し合うイベントだと考えられる。以上から、選択肢の中でこのような内容になるのは **(D)**。

 Ms. Moore is planning a conference with the customers /
    S   V   O

to discuss their specific requests for the construction of new office space.
to 不定詞（副詞句）

□specific 具体的な

---

8. ★★★★☆

有益な発表の準備をするために最初に行わなければならないことは、適切なテーマを選ぶことです。

(A) 動 ～に知らせる
(B) 名 情報提供者
(C) 形 有益な
(D) 名 情報

選択肢には動詞 inform とその派生語が並んでいる。空所前後には冠詞 an と名詞 presentation があるため、空所には名詞を修飾する語、つまり名詞もしくは形容詞が入る。次に意味を考えていくと、「……発表準備のために行うことは適切なテーマを選ぶことだ」とあるので、「適切なテーマを選ぶ」と結びつき、文意が成り立つ **(C)** が正解となる。(B)、(D) の名詞も複合名詞として捉えることはできるが、(B) 情報提供者の発表、(D) 情報に関する発表、では文意が通らないため、いずれも不正解。

The first step / that you have to take in preparing for an informative presentation / is
    S   O S   V   V

to choose a proper topic.
  C（to 不定詞の名詞的用法）

□a step that you have to take 取るべき手段　□in preparing for ～を準備する際に　□proper 適切な

---

9. ★★★★★

新人従業員のレジ操作は店長が補助したらどうかという提案が出されています。

(A) 動 ～を手伝う　原形
(B) 三人称単数現在形
(C) 過去形
(D) 現在分詞

選択肢には動詞 assist のさまざまな形が並んでいる。次にこの文の冒頭の It is suggested that（～のことを勧める）に着目しよう。この suggest のように、提案・要求・命令などの意味を持つ動詞の後に that 節がある場合、that 節の動詞は主語が何であっても原形を用いる、という仮定法現在のルールに従う必要がある。よって、正解は **(A)**。

〈It ... that 構文〉
It is suggested / that the general manager assist the new workers with operating
仮S   V   真S（that 節）   S   V   O

the cash registers.

□general manager 店長、部長　□assist A with B　A の B を補助する　□cash register レジ

---

 7. (D)　8. (C)　9. (A)

10. Jesse's Shoe Store is going to make ------- room for its new summer collection after the seasonal clearance sale ends on May 31.

(A) sufficient
(B) accurate
(C) communicative
(D) competent

11. During its repair, the untidy appearance of the May Housing Complex has not ------- potential renters from calling to inquire about the availability of units.

(A) argued
(B) interfered
(C) evaded
(D) discouraged

12. ------- setting up your new Rose Spring Office desk, please make sure you keep the instructions in the manual sent along with the product.

(A) When
(B) How
(C) In case
(D) Unless

10. ★★★☆☆

Jesse's 靴店は、5月31日に季節の在庫処分セールが終了した後、夏の新商品のために十分なスペースを確保する予定です。

(A) 形 十分な
(B) 形 正確な
(C) 形 話し好きな
(D) 形 有能な

選択肢には形容詞が並んでいる。空所を含む文の意味を取っていくと、「夏の新商品のために……なスペースを確保する」とあるので、「陳列のための在庫スペースを十分に確保する」という意味になる **(A)** を入れると文意が成立する。

Jesse's Shoe Store is going to make sufficient room for its new summer collection /
　　　　　S　　　　　　　　　V　　　　　　　O

after the seasonal clearance sale ends on May 31.
（副詞節［時］）　　　S　　　　　　V

□make room 場所を空ける　□collection 新商品　□seasonal 季節の　□clearance sale 在庫処分セール

11. ★★★★★

修繕の間、May Housing Complex については、外観がごちゃごちゃしているという理由で、賃貸希望者が空室の問い合わせの電話をかけるのをためらうということはなかった。

(A) 動 論じる　過去分詞
(B) 動 妨げる　過去分詞
(C) 動 ～を避ける　過去分詞
(D) 動 ～を思いとどまらせる　過去分詞

選択肢には動詞の過去分詞が並んでいる。空所を含む文の意味を取っていくと、「外観の不具合がお客様の問い合わせ電話を……ことはなかった」とあるので、「～を止める、思いとどまらせる」という意味の **(D)** を入れると文意が成立する。discourage 人 from doing で、「人が～するのを思いとどまらせる」という意味になる。(B) も類似の意味だが自動詞のためここでは不正解。

During its repair, / the untidy appearance of the May Housing Complex has not discouraged
～の間（副詞句）　　　　　　S　　　　　　　　　　　　　　　　　　V

potential renters from calling to inquire about the availability of units.
　　　O　　　　　　　　　　to 不定詞（副詞句）

□untidy 整えられていない　□appearance 外観　□potential renter 賃借人になる可能性のある人
□inquire 問い合わせる　□availability of unit 空室

12. ★★★★☆

新品の Rose Spring Office の机を設置する際には、製品と一緒にお送りした説明書の手順を必ず守ってください。

(A) 接 ～の時に
(B) 副 どのように
(C) ～の場合
(D) 接 ～でない限り

選択肢には接続表現などが並んでおり、空所後は setting up という現在分詞が続いている。空所を含む文の意味を取っていくと、「机を設置する……、説明書の手順を守るように」となっているため、分詞を導き、時を表す接続詞となる **(A)** を入れると文意が成立する。分詞構文の形でも表すことができるが、when を置くことで意味を明確にしている。(C)、(D) は意味的に合わないためいずれも不正解。

〈命令文〉

When (you are) setting up your new Rose Spring Office desk, / please make sure / (that)
　　副詞句　主語＋be 動詞の省略　　　　　　　　　　　　　　　　　V　　　O (that 節)

you keep the instructions in the manual sent along with the product.
S　V　　　　O

□set up ～を設置する　□instruction 手順　□manual 取扱説明書　□along with ～とともに

10. (A)　11. (D)　12. (A)

1 回目
2 回目
3 回目

13. Although Tera Nixon considered herself just a consultant, her coworkers were ------- more dependent on her intelligence than she had thought.

(A) highly
(B) so
(C) only
(D) somewhat

1 回目
2 回目
3 回目

14. Danny Smoltz ------- profound articles for many influential local newspapers until he retired.

(A) write
(B) writes
(C) wrote
(D) written

1 回目
2 回目
3 回目

15. Please keep in mind that you should ------- all safety regulations when using the pool and fitness facilities in this building.

(A) dedicate
(B) comply
(C) observe
(D) adhere

13. ★★★★★

Tera Nixon さんは自分自身を単なる相談役だと考えていましたが、同僚たちは彼女が思っていたよりも、幾分かはその知性を当てにしていました。

(A) 副 非常に
(B) 副 とても
(C) 副 ただ単に
(D) 副 幾分

Although Tera Nixon considered herself just a consultant, / her coworkers were
（副詞節［譲歩］） S   V   O   C   S   V

somewhat more dependent on her intelligence / than she had thought (they were dependent).
C   比較 S   V

□considered oneself A　自分のことを A だと考える　□consultant 相談役　□coworker 同僚
□dependent on ～を当てにする　□intelligence 知性

---

14. ★★★☆☆

Danny Smoltz さんは、引退するまでに、有力な地元の新聞の多くに有意義な記事を書いた。

(A) 動 ～を書く　[原 形]
(B) [三人称単数現在形]
(C) [過去形]
(D) [過去分詞]

Danny Smoltz wrote profound articles for many influential local newspapers / until
S   V   O   （副詞節［時］）

he retired.
S   V

□profound 有意義な　□influential 有力な、影響力のある

---

15. ★★★★☆

このビルのプールとフィットネス施設を利用する際には、すべての安全規則を遵守しなければならないことにご留意ください。

(A) 動 ～をささげる
(B) 動 従う
(C) 動 ～を遵守する
(D) 動 遵守する

〈命令文〉
Please keep in mind / that you should observe all safety regulations /
V   O（that 節）S   V   O

when using the pool and fitness facilities in this building.
副詞句

□keep in mind that ～のことに留意する　□safety regulation 安全規則

---

 13. (D)　14. (C)　15. (C)

16. To place your order, completely fill out the enclosed order form and return it, ------- your payment, in the response envelope provided.

(A) as long as
(B) otherwise
(C) not only
(D) along with

17. The antique fair in the commercial district, which the citizens are eagerly awaiting, is expected to ------- in April.

(A) commence
(B) transmit
(C) revolve
(D) prolong

18. The board of directors has finally reached a decision about ------- operations in Jacksonville.

(A) suspend
(B) suspends
(C) suspending
(D) to suspend

16. ★★★★☆

ご注文の際は同封の注文票に漏れなく記入し、お渡しした返信用封筒で代金とともに返送してください。

(A) 〜である限り
(B) 圖 さもなければ（接続副詞）
(C) 〜だけでなく
(D) 〜と一緒に（群前置詞）

選択肢には接続表現や群前置詞が並んでいる。空所を含む箇所の意味を取っていくと、「渡した返信用封筒に代金……、注文票を返送」とあるので、代金と一緒にという意味となる **(D)** を入れると文意が成立する。(A)、(B) は節 (SV) がないと文法的に当てはめられない。文末の provided は述語動詞ではなく、envelope を後置修飾していることに注意しよう。

〈命令文〉

To place your order, / completely fill out the enclosed order form and return it, /
to 不定詞（副詞句）　　　　　V¹　　　　　O　　　　　　V²　O

along with your payment, / in the response envelope provided.

□place an order 注文する　□completely 漏れなく、完全に　□fill out 〜に記入する　□enclosed 同封した
□order form 注文票　□payment 支払い (代金)　□response envelope 返信用封筒

17. ★★★☆☆

市民が心から待ち望んでいる商業地区の骨董市は、4月に始まる予定です。

(A) 動 始まる
(B) 動 送信する
(C) 動 回転する
(D) 動 〜を長引かせる

選択肢には動詞が並んでいる。空所を含む文の意味を取っていくと、「骨董市が4月に……予定だ」とあるので、自動詞として「始まる、開始する」という意味を持つ **(A)** を入れると文意が成立する。commence は start や begin の同義語として頻出の語彙なので押さえておこう。", which ...," は the antique fair を補足説明している部分だ。Part 5 では関係詞の部分をカットして、文の構造をシンプルにして解くようにしよう。

The antique fair in the commercial district, / which the citizens are eagerly awaiting, /
S　　　　　　　　　　　　　　　O　　S　　　V

is expected to commence in April.
V

□antique fair 骨董市　□commercial district 商業地区　□citizen 市民　□eagerly 心から　□await 〜を待ち望む
□be expected to do 〜する予定である

18. ★☆☆☆☆

取締役会はついに Jacksonville での事業の停止を決定するに至りました。

(A) 動 〜を一時中止する [原形]
(B) [三人称単数現在形]
(C) [動名詞]
(D) [to 不定詞]

選択肢には動詞 suspend が形を変えて並んでいる。空所の前後には前置詞 about と空所の目的語に相当する operation（事業、業務）という名詞がある。ここから、目的語を取り、前置詞 about に導かれる **(C)** を選ぶ必要がある。

The board of directors has finally reached a decision about suspending operations
S　　　　　　　　　V　　　　O

in Jacksonville.

□board of directors 取締役会　□finally 最終的に　□reach a decision 結論に至る

 **16. (D)　17. (A)　18. (C)**

19. Purchases that you bought in our shop can be returned or refunded ------- accompanied with an original receipt.

(A) since
(B) until
(C) only if
(D) in full

20. ------- you need any further help during your first year, please refer to your employee guide or visit the personnel office.

(A) Than
(B) Should
(C) What
(D) Having

21. Mr. Columbus, the director of the general affairs department, will forward an ------- from minutes of last month's meeting to board members.

(A) exertion
(B) excitement
(C) excerpt
(D) expedition

19. ★★★★★

当店で購入された商品はレシート原本を一緒にお持ちいただいた場合に限り、返品または返金が可能です。

(A) ～以来
(B) ～まで
(C) ～の場合に限り
(D) 金額

選択肢にはさまざまな表現が並んでいる。意味を取っていくと、「購入品はレシート原本を持ってきた……、返品か返金が可能になる」という意味なので、限定された条件を意味する接続表現の **(C)** を入れると文意が成立する。この文は ... only if (they are) accompanied with ... と、従属節以降で主語が重複しないように省略された形となっていることにも注目しておこう。

Purchases / that you bought in our shop / can be returned or refunded /
  S   O S V   V

only if (they are) accompanied with an original receipt.
（副詞句［条件］）

□accompanied with ～が添えられて、～を伴って　□original receipt 領収証原本

20. ★★★★★

入社 1 年目に何か困ったことがあったら、従業員の手引きを参照するか、人事部まで来てください。

(A) ～よりも
(B) もし～ならば
(C) ～すること
(D) 動 持っている　現在分詞

選択肢にはさまざまな表現が並んでおり、空所は文頭にある。文の構造と意味に着目すると、カンマ前後が節になっており、「困ったことがある」➡「手引書を参照するか人事部へ」となっていることから、仮定を表す **(B)** が正解となる。この文の元は If you should need any further ... という仮定法の形から If が省略され、should が倒置として文頭に来ている。

〈命令文〉

Should you need any further help during your first year, /
条件節＝ If you should need ... (If が省略されて倒置)

please refer to your employee guide or visit the personnel office.
     V¹   O   V²   O

□further さらなる　□first year 初年度　□refer to ～を参照する　□employee guide 従業員手引書
□personnel office 人事部

21. ★★★★☆

総務部長の Columbus さんが先月の会議からの議事録の抜粋を理事会のメンバーに転送します。

(A) 名 努力
(B) 名 興奮させるもの
(C) 名 抜粋
(D) 名 遠征

選択肢には ex- で始まる名詞が並んでいる。空所を含む箇所の意味を取っていくと、「会議議事録の……を理事会メンバーに送付する」となっているので、正解は「議事録を抜粋したもの」となる **(C)**. excerpt は少し難しめ（860 点以上レベル）の語だが、Part 4 の Question 71-73 refer to the following excerpt from a meeting（問題 71-73 は次の会議の抜粋に関するものです）というナレーション表現でも登場するので押さえておこう。

Mr. Columbus, the director of the general affairs department, / will forward
    S   S の同格   V

an excerpt from minutes of last month's meeting to board members.
                      O

□general affairs department 総務部　□forward ～を送付する、転送する　□board member 理事会メンバー

19. (C)　20. (B)　21. (C)

22. The Golden Prize will be granted to Mr. Damon, from
Northern New Zealand Morning Post, ------- photographs
leave a deep impression.

(A) that
(B) whose
(C) which
(D) who

23. It seems that the readers' response to the updated print
layout has been ------- negative.

(A) overwhelm
(B) overwhelmed
(C) overwhelming
(D) overwhelmingly

24. All workers have to shut down their computers before
leaving for the day unless instructed -------.

(A) meanwhile
(B) accordingly
(C) otherwise
(D) indeed

22. ★★★☆☆

The Golden 賞は、写真がとても印象深い、*Northern New Zealand Morning Post* の Damon さんに授与されます。

(A) ～ということは
(B) ～の
(C) それ
(D) その人は

The Golden Prize will be granted to Mr. Damon, / from Northern *New Zealand Morning Post*, /
S · V · O

whose photographs leave a deep impression.
S · V · O

 □grant ～を授与する □leave ～を残す □deep impression 深い印象

---

23. ★☆☆☆☆

新しくなった印刷レイアウトに対する読者の反応はひどく不評だったようです。

(A) 動 ～を圧倒する
(B) 過去分詞
(C) 現在分詞
(D) 副 圧倒的に

〈It seems that 構文〉

It seems that the readers' response to the updated print layout
S · V · · · S

has been overwhelmingly negative.
V · O

 □updated 新しくなった □negative 不評である

---

24. ★★★★★

特に指示がない限り、すべての作業員は退勤前にコンピューターを終了しなければなりません。

(A) 副 その間に
(B) 副 それに応じて
(C) 副 それとは別に
(D) 副 実のところは

All workers have to shut down their computers before leaving for the day /
S · V · O

unless (they are) instructed otherwise.
条件の副詞句

 □shut down ～の電源を落とす □leave for the day 退勤する □instruct ～に指示する

25. Hera's Fashion Shop can be found in five ------- in the city for the convenience of its customers.

(A) locations
(B) moments
(C) executives
(D) appointments

26. As per your request, I am writing to confirm that the briefcase left in bus number 615 on July 28 is -------.

(A) myself
(B) mine
(C) your
(D) yourselves

27. Excursions to the island's most celebrated historical sites should be reserved two weeks ------- your departure.

(A) because of
(B) together with
(C) prior to
(D) as for

25. ★★★☆☆

Hera's 洋品店は、顧客の利便性のため、市内5カ所に店舗があります。

(A) 名 場所
(B) 名 瞬間
(C) 名 幹部
(D) 名 約束

選択肢には名詞が並んでいる。意味を取っていくと、「Hera's 洋品店は市内の5つの……で発見できる」とあるため、市内で発見できる店舗数、つまり5つの場所で、という意味になると文意が通る。よって、正解は (A)。このような適切な語彙を選ぶ問題は、きちんと意味を取り、根拠を持って解くようにしよう。

 Hera's Fashion Shop can be found in five locations / in the city / for the convenience of
　　　　　S　　　　　　　 V

its customers.

□convenience 利便性

---

26. ★★★☆☆

ご指示いただいたとおり、7月28日に615番バスに残されたブリーフケースは私のものであることを確認しましたので、手紙を書いています。

(A) 私自身（再帰代名詞）
(B) 私のもの（所有代名詞）
(C) あなたの（所有格）
(D) あなた方自身（再帰代名詞）

選択肢には代名詞が並んでいる。空所を含め意味を取っていくと、「バスに置き忘れたブリーフケースは……です」とあるため、「○○のもの」という所有代名詞を入れると文意が通る。以上より正解は (B)。

As per your request, / I am writing to confirm / that
　～のとおり（副詞句）　　 S　　 V　　　　　　O（that 節）

the briefcase left in bus number 615 on July 28 is mine.
　　　S　　　　　　　　　　　　　　　　　 V　 C

□as per ～のとおり　□confirm ～を確認する

---

27. ★★★★☆

島で最も名高い史跡を訪問するツアーは出発日の2週間前までに予約する必要があります。

(A) ～のために（群前置詞）
(B) ～と一緒に（群前置詞）
(C) ～より前に（群前置詞）
(D) ～に関する限りでは（群前置詞）

選択肢には群前置詞が並んでいる。空所を含め意味を取っていくと、「ツアーは出発の2週間……予約が必要」とある。予約は出発より前に行うと考えられるので、「～より前に」を意味する (C) が正解となる。この問題は主述の関係がわかりづらいので、Excursions の修飾部分をカットして文の構造をシンプルにすると意味を取りやすい。

Excursions to the island's most celebrated historical sites should be reserved
　　S　　　　　　　　　　　　　　　　　　　　　　　　　　　　　　V

two weeks prior to your departure.

□excursion 小旅行、ツアー　□celebrated 著名な　□historical site 史跡　□departure 出発

---

25. (A)　26. (B)　27. (C)

28. Individuals who stay at our hotel will be given three-day ------- to the weight room and swimming pool.

(A) access
(B) accessed
(C) accessing
(D) accesses

29. Ms. Anderson was honored for ------- missing a day of work at Dally's Accounting Firm during the last three years.

(A) still
(B) even
(C) quite
(D) never

30. Savannah Inc. has endeavored to build partnerships with various companies ------- the nation.

(A) everywhere
(B) somewhat
(C) moreover
(D) throughout

28. ★★★★☆

当ホテルにご宿泊の方は、ウエートルームとプール を 3 日間ご利用になれます。

(A) 名 利用する権利
(B) 動 〜に接近する 〔過去分詞〕
(C) 〔現在分詞〕
(D) 名 通路 (複数形)

🔍 選択肢には名詞や動詞の意味を持つ access が形を変えて並んでいる。空所前後を見ていくと、be given three-day ------- to ... 「〜に対する 3 日間の……」という意味になっていることがわかる。ここから動詞 give が受け身となって第 4 文型の目的語として、「3 日間利用する権利」を意味する表現を入れれば文意が成立する。以上から、正解は (A)。名詞までは見抜けても、three-day が空所直前にあるので複数形が入るかと思ったかもしれないが、「利用」という意味の access は不可算名詞となるため、(D) は不正解。

🗣️ Individuals / who stay at our hotel / will be given three-day access to the weight room
　　　S 　　　　S 　V 　　　　　　　V 　　　　　　O
and swimming pool.

✏️ □individual 個人、人　□weight room ウエートトレーニング室

---

29. ★★★☆☆

Anderson さんは、過去 3 年間 Dally's 会計事務所で仕事を 1 日も休まなかったことを表彰されました。

(A) 副 いまだに
(B) 副 〜さえも
(C) 副 かなり
(D) 副 まったく〜することがない

🔍 選択肢には副詞が並んでいる。空所前後の意味を取っていくと、「仕事を 1 日休む……で表彰された」という意味になっている。休んで表彰されるとは考えにくいが、「欠勤がない」という意味にすれば文意は通じる。以上より、欠勤していないという意味になる (D) が正解となる。

🗣️ Ms. Anderson was honored for never missing a day of work
　　　　S 　　　　V 　　　　　　　O
at Dally's Accounting Firm / during the last three years.

✏️ □be honored for 〜で表彰される　□miss a day of work 仕事を 1 日休む

---

30. ★★★☆☆

Savannah 社は国中のさまざまな企業との協力関係の構築を試みてきた。

(A) 副 どこでも
(B) 副 多少
(C) 副 さらに
(D) 前 〜の隅から隅まで

🔍 選択肢には副詞や前置詞が並んでいる。空所前後は「国……さまざまな会社との関係の構築を試みてきた」という意味になるので、空所は the nation を受ける語が入ることがわかる。以上より、前置詞として機能し、「〜の隅から隅まで」を意味する (D) が正解。(A) は意味的に選びがちだが、副詞のため the nation と結びつけることができない (everywhere in the nation なら正解になる)。

🗣️ Savannah Inc. has endeavored to build partnerships with various companies
　　　S 　　　　　V 　　　　　　　　O
throughout the nation.

✏️ □endeavor 努力する　□build a partnership 関係を構築する　□various さまざまな

🚩 28. (A)　29. (D)　30. (D)

1☐☐ | 2☐☐ | 3☐☐

1. Starting next month, Ethan Institution ------- free lunches to all of its staff members to keep them motivated.

(A) has provided
(B) will be providing
(C) will have provided
(D) has been providing

1☐☐ | 2☐☐ | 3☐☐

2. ------- the repairperson come earlier this morning, the customer database server would now be fixed.

(A) If
(B) Had
(C) Should
(D) Did

1☐☐ | 2☐☐ | 3☐☐

3. The city has contracted Wales Design to ------- the historical Edison Museum to its original condition.

(A) restore
(B) regain
(C) resume
(D) replace

1. ★★★☆☆

来月から、Ethan Institution は、職員のやる気を維持するため、職員全員に対し無料で昼食を提供します。

(A) 動 ～を提供する 〔現在完了形〕
(B) 〔未来進行形〕
(C) 〔未来完了形〕
(D) 〔現在完了進行形〕

選択肢には動詞 provide が時制を変えて並んでいる。文頭に next month（来月）という未来のある時点を示す表現があり、空所後に provide の目的語に相当する free lunches があるため、能動態で未来を表す形が入ることがわかる。よって、未来進行形の **(B)** が正解となる。(C) の未来完了は、By the time SV（S が V するまでに）というような、未来の一定期間内に、という文脈なら当てはめることができるが、ここではある時点での未来の表現となるため、不正解。

Starting next month, / Ethan Institution will be providing free lunches to all of its staff members /
　　　　　　　　　　　　　　　S　　　　　　　　　V　　　　　　　O
to keep them motivated.
to 不定詞（副詞句）

□provide A to B　A を B に提供する　□keep＋O＋過去分詞　O を～の状態に保つ　□motivate ～に意欲を持たせる

2. ★★★★★

修理担当者が今朝もっと早く来ていたら、顧客データベースのサーバーは今ごろ復旧していたでしょう。

(A) 援 もしも～ならば
(B) 助動詞 have 〔過去形〕
(C) 助動詞 should
(D) 助動詞 do 〔過去形〕

選択肢には接続詞や助動詞が並んでいる。文全体を見ると、文中にカンマがあり、その前後に節がある。主節には助動詞 would があるため、従属節は「～であれば」という仮定法表現が入ることがわかる。ここから、倒置により仮定法過去完了形の形を取ることができる **(B)** が正解となる。If the repairperson had come ... の had が文頭に来ることで If を省略した形となっている。なお、(A) は、If the repairperson comes と、動詞の人称を変化させないと文法的に当てはまらない。(C) の場合は先の未来についての仮定となるため、過去の事実の反対を表していないことから不正解となる。

Had the repairperson come earlier this morning, /
（副詞節 [条件]）(If the repairperson had come ... から、倒置により If が省略されている)
　　　　　　　　　　　　S　　　　　　　　V
the customer database server would now be fixed.
　　　　　　S　　　　　　　　　V

□repairperson 修理工　□fix ～を修復する

3. ★★★☆☆

市は歴史のある Edison 博物館を元の状態に復元するにあたり、Wales Design を起用しました。

(A) 動 ～を復元する
(B) 動 ～を取り戻す
(C) 動 ～を再び始める
(D) 動 ～を交換する

選択肢には動詞が並んでいる。空所の周辺を中心に意味を取っていくと、「博物館を元の状態に……する」とある。ここから、最も適切な文意となる **(A)** が正解。(B) は失ってしまったものを取り戻すような意味になるため、ここでは文意に合わない。

The city has contracted Wales Design / to restore the historical Edison Museum /
　　　S　　　V　　　　　　O　　　　　to 不定詞（副詞句）
to its original condition.

□contract ～と契約する　□restore A to B　A を B に復元する　□historical 歴史的な
□original condition 元通りの状態

 1. (B)　2. (B)　3. (A)

31

4. Sales figures for the last quarter will be ------- to the public before the end of the week.

(A) assured
(B) requested
(C) convinced
(D) announced

5. We have encountered ------- problems such as system errors since installing the latest version of Saline Scheduling software.

(A) supportive
(B) numerous
(C) exclusive
(D) voluntary

6. Next week, the citizens ------- will take place in the convention center of the Stoltz Hotel.

(A) assembly
(B) assemble
(C) assembles
(D) assembled

4. ★★★☆☆

前四半期の売上高は週末までに公表されます。

(A) 動 ~であると保証する [過去分詞]
(B) 動 ~を要求する [過去分詞]
(C) 動 ~を納得させる [過去分詞]
(D) 動 ~を発表する [過去分詞]

> 選択肢には動詞の過去分詞が並んでいる。空所を含む文の意味を取っていくと、「前四半期の売上高は週末までに公に……される」となっており、「売上高」という情報が主語であることがわかる。選択肢の中で、意味が通るのは **(D)** で、「公に発表される」となる。

Sales figures for the last quarter will be announced to the public /
  S   V
before the end of the week.

□sales figures（通常複数形で）売上高 □to the public 公に、一般大衆に

---

5. ★★★★☆

Saline Scheduling 社のソフトの最新版をインストールして以来、システムエラーなどの多くの問題が発生しています。

(A) 形 協力的な
(B) 形 多くの
(C) 形 排他的な
(D) 形 自主的な

> 選択肢には形容詞が並んでいる。空所を含む箇所を中心に文の意味を取っていくと、「システムエラーといった……問題が発生している」となっている。ここでの problem は複数形になっており、問題がいくつか発生していることから、**(B)** を入れると、「多くの問題」となり意味が通じる。それ以外の選択肢は、システムエラーに通じるような形容詞の意味としてはいずれも考えにくいため、不正解。

We have encountered numerous problems such as system errors /
 S   V   O
since installing the latest version of Saline Scheduling software.
～以来（副詞句）

□encounter ~に遭遇する □such as~ たとえば~のような □error エラー □latest 最新の

---

6. ★★★★★

来週、市民集会が Stoltz ホテルの会議場で開催されます。

(A) 名 集会
(B) 動 ~を集める [原形]
(C) [三人称単数現在形]
(D) [過去形]

> 選択肢には動詞 assemble が形を変えているものや派生語が並んでいる。空所を含む箇所は、the citizens ------- で、will の直前にあり、後ろには take place「（催しが）開催される」という自動詞的な意味の述語動詞があることから、空所には動詞以外の要素が入るとわかる。よって、**(A)** を入れて「市民集会」とすると、開催されるイベントを意味することになり、文意が通る。(D) は、文法的には過去分詞として citizens を修飾すると考えることもできるが、「集められた市民」という意味では文意が通じないため不正解。

Next week, / the citizens assembly will take place in the convention center
               S   V
of the Stoltz Hotel.

□citizen 市民 □take place （~が）開催される □convention center 会議場

4. (D)　5. (B)　6. (A)

7. Columbus Motors' contract clearly stipulates that the final delivery of automotive components will be postponed ------- the remainder of the payment has been made.

(A) then
(B) next
(C) by
(D) until

8. Patrick Jackson will be the leader of the consulting team at Bonner Chemistry, ------- in April.

(A) begins
(B) beginning
(C) began
(D) begun

9. ------- the spring music festival is over, the temporary concession stands at the park will be packed up and taken away.

(A) Owing to
(B) In particular
(C) Even so
(D) Now that

34

7. ★★☆☆☆

Columbus Motors 社との契約書には、自動車部品の最終的な納品は残額の支払いが完了するまで延期されることがはっきりと明記されています。

(A) 副 その後
(B) 副 次に
(C) 前 ～によって
(D) 接 ～まで

選択肢には副詞や前置詞、接続詞が並んでいる。空所以降を見ると、○○ has been made という節の形を取っていることから、空所には接続詞が入ることがわかる。選択肢の中で接続詞は **(D)** のみのため、これが正解となる。空所後の文の構造を見極めると、選択肢が絞り込めるようになるので、しっかりチェックしよう。

Columbus Motors' contract clearly stipulates / that the final delivery of automotive components
S　　　　　　　　　　　V　　　O (that 節)　　　S

will be postponed / until the remainder of the payment has been made.
V　　　　　(副詞節 [時])　　　S　　　　　V

□contract 契約　□clearly はっきりと　□stipulate ～を規定 [明記] する　□automotive component 自動車構成部品
□remainder of the payment 支払い残額

8. ★★☆☆☆

Patrick Jackson さんは、4月より Bonner Chemistry 社のコンサルティングチームのリーダーになります。

(A) 動 始める　[三人称単数現在形]
(B) 動 [現在分詞]
(C) 動 [過去形]
(D) 動 [過去分詞]

選択肢には動詞 begin が形を変えて並んでいる。空所前にはカンマがあり、空所後には時を表す表現が来ている。ここから、空所以下をカンマの前に接続するために、現在分詞にして副詞句にすると文意が成立する。以上から、正解は **(B)**。beginning (starting)＋時を表す表現は、TOEIC では頻出表現となるため、言い回しとしても押さえておこう。

Patrick Jackson will be the leader of the consulting team at Bonner Chemistry, /
S　　　　　　V　　　　　　　C

beginning in April.

□consulting team コンサルティングチーム (専門的な助言を与える組織)

9. ★★★☆☆

春の音楽祭が終了してしまったため、公園の仮設店舗は、解体され、撤去されます。

(A) ～のせいで (群前置詞)
(B) とりわけ
(C) たとえそうでも
(D) 今や～なので

選択肢には群前置詞や副詞表現、接続表現が並んでいる。空所後には、節 (the spring music festival is over) とカンマがあるため、空所は接続表現が入ることがわかる。意味を見ていくと、「春の音楽祭が終了している➡公園の仮設店舗は撤去される」となっているため、空所には「今現在～なので」という順接の意味を持つ **(D)** が入ることがわかる。(A)、(B) は接続表現ではなく副詞表現なので、文法的に当てはめることができない。

Now that the spring music festival is over, / the temporary concession stands at the park
(副詞節 [時])　　　S　　　　　V C　　　　　　　　　　　S

will be packed up and taken away.
V¹　　　　　　V²

□temporary 一時的な、仮の　□concession stand 売店　□pack up and take away ～を梱包して撤収する

7. (D)　8. (B)　9. (D)

10. In an effort to expand its international presence, Demian Holdings, originally based in Macau, is planning to ------- foreign branches in Taipei and Singapore.

(A) grant
(B) demolish
(C) establish
(D) name

11. Due to a shortage of qualified graduates in San Remo City, we are having a hard time finding someone with suitable skills and ------- qualifications.

(A) similar
(B) appropriate
(C) relative
(D) alternative

12. Rainfall amounts in the northeastern region of the country this year have been ------- lower than those of last year.

(A) notices
(B) noticing
(C) notice
(D) noticeably

10. ★★★★☆

当初はマカオを拠点としていたDemian Holdingsは、国際的な存在感を高めるための取り組みとして、台北とシンガポールに海外支店を開設することを計画しています。

(A) 動 ～を承諾する
(B) 動 ～を解体撤去する
(C) 動 ～を開設する
(D) 動 ～に命名する

> 選択肢には動詞が並んでいる。空所を含む文の意味を取っていくと、「国際的な存在感を高めるために、マカオ拠点の会社が海外支店を……することを計画」とあるため、海外進出するという意味で、**(C)** を当てはめると文意が成立する。(A) は、嘆願や権利などに対して承諾するという意味であるため、ここでは文意に合わない。

> In an effort to expand its international presence, / Demian Holdings, originally based in Macau,
> ～するために (副詞句)　　　　　　　　　　　　　　　　　　　　　　　　S　　←
>
> is planning to establish foreign branches in Taipei and Singapore.
> 　　　V　　　　　　　　　O

> □in an effort to *do* ～するため　□expand ～を拡大する、高める　□presence 存在感　□originally もともと
> □based in ～を拠点として　□foreign branch 海外支店

---

11. ★★★☆☆

San Remo 市では、卒業資格を満たしている人が不足しているため、我々は十分な技術や適切な資格を持った人材を見つけるのに苦労しています。

(A) 形 似ている
(B) 形 適切な
(C) 形 相対的な
(D) 形 代わりの

> 選択肢には形容詞が並んでいる。空所の周辺の文の意味を取っていくと、「十分な技術や……資格を持った人材を見つける」とあるため、「十分な技術」と並列するポジティブな意味の **(B)** を入れると文意が通る。(C) は「関連の」という意味もあるが、主に名詞の後で、○○ relative to ...（…に関連した○○）、という用法を取る。今回は具体的に関連する資格の分野もないため、ここでは不正解。

> Due to a shortage of qualified graduates in San Remo City, /
> （前置詞句 [理由・原因]）
>
> we are having a hard time finding someone / with suitable skills and appropriate qualifications.
> S　　V　　　　　O　　　　　　　　　　　←

> □due to ～により　□shortage 不足　□qualified 資格のある　□have a hard time *doing* ～するのに苦労する
> □qualification 資格

---

12. ★★☆☆☆

国の北東部における今年の降雨量は、昨年よりも著しく少なくなっています。

(A) 動 ～に気が付く　[三人称単数現在形]
(B) [現在分詞]
(C) [原形]
(D) 副 著しく

> 選択肢には動詞 notice が形を変えたものやその派生語が並んでいる。空所は be 動詞と形容詞の比較級 lower に挟まれているため、形容詞を修飾する表現、つまり副詞が入ることがわかる。以上から、**(D)** が正解。このような品詞を見抜く問題は、文の構造を見れば正解が瞬時にわかるため、覚えておこう。

> Rainfall amounts in the northeastern region of the country this year have been
> 　　　　　　　　　　　S　　　　　　　　　　　　　　　　　V
>
> noticeably lower than those of last year.
> 　　　　C　　　　　= rainfall amounts in the northeastern region

> □rainfall amount 降雨量　□northeastern 北東の　□region 地域

13. -------, it was Dr. Judy Waters who was selected to serve as the new chief surgeon at Eugene General Hospital.

(A) Timely
(B) Ultimately
(C) Permanently
(D) Realistically

14. ------- who believe in the growth potential of solar power are increasingly investing in alternative energy sources.

(A) Ours
(B) Anyone
(C) These
(D) Those

15. The Mayor, Mr. Upton, was formerly an actor who had ------- major roles in various movies and TV series.

(A) made
(B) brought
(C) served
(D) had

13. ★★★★★

Eugene 総合病院で最終的に新しい主任外科医として選ばれたのは、Judy Waters 医師でした。

(A) 形 適切な
(B) 副 最終的に
(C) 副 恒久的に
(D) 副 現実的に

選択肢には形容詞や副詞が並んでおり、空所後はカンマがあるため、文全体を修飾していることがわかる。「Judy Waters 医師が、病院の新しい主任外科医に選ばれた」という内容であることから、選考プロセスを終え、「最終的に」選ばれたとすると文意が通る。よって、正解は**(B)**。決定した、という事実を伝える際に、(A)、(C)、(D) だと文意がつながらない。(A)、(C) は述語動詞や形容詞を修飾することが多く、(D) はまだ定まっていない際の推測などに用いられることが多い。

〈強調構文〉

Ultimately, / it was Dr. Judy Waters who was selected to serve as
         S   V

the new chief surgeon at Eugene General Hospital.

□serve as ~として勤務する　□chief 主任　□surgeon 外科医

---

14. ★★★☆☆

太陽光発電の成長の可能性を信じている人々は、代替エネルギー源にさらなる投資をしています。

(A) 私たちのもの
(B) どんな人でも
(C) これら
(D) 人々

選択肢には代名詞が並んでおり、空所後には空所に入る代名詞を先行詞とする関係詞 who があることがわかる。関係詞以降の動詞が believe と原形になっていることから、空所には三人称複数で「人々」を意味する **(D)** が入るとわかる。

Those who V（~する人々）

Those / who believe in the growth potential of solar power / are increasingly investing in
 S S V   O   V

alternative energy sources.
    O

□growth 成長　□potential 可能性　□solar power 太陽光発電　□increasingly さらに、増加して
□invest in ~に投資する　□alternative 代替の　□energy source エネルギー源

---

15. ★★★★☆

市長の Upton さんは、以前はさまざまな映画や連続テレビドラマで主要な登場人物を演じる俳優でした。

(A) 動 ~を作る　[過去分詞]
(B) 動 ~を持ってくる　[過去分詞]
(C) 動 ~に仕える　[過去分詞]
(D) 動 ~を経験する　[過去分詞]

選択肢には動詞の過去分詞が並んでおり、空所の直前が had となっていることから、過去完了形の述語動詞が入ることがわかる。空所を含む文の意味を取っていくと、「市長は、以前は映画やドラマで主要人物役を……俳優だった」という意味になっている。目的語に major roles を取って「主役を経験する」という意味になるのは、**(D)**。ほかは文意が通らない。(A) は role を目的語に取った場合、make someone's role clear（誰かの役割を明確にする）など、第 5 文型で用いられることがある。

The Mayor, Mr. Upton, was formerly an actor / who had had major roles
  S   V   C   S V   O

in various movies and TV series.

□formerly 以前　□major role 主要な役、主役　□various さまざまな

13. (B)　14. (D)　15. (D)

16. Some of the apartment complexes in the older neighborhoods of Tempa are in need of ------- remodeling.

(A) extend
(B) extension
(C) extensively
(D) extensive

17. The location of the ceremony was not decided officially, ------- was given oral approval by the chairperson of the planning board.

(A) nor
(B) but
(C) which
(D) or

18. All employees who work in the payroll office at the cosmetic company have been prevented from signing ------- paychecks.

(A) themselves
(B) them
(C) their own
(D) theirs

16. ★★★★☆

Tempa 内の古い地区にある集合住宅のいくつか
は、広範囲にわたる改装が必要です。

(A) 動 ～を拡張する
(B) 名 延長
(C) 副 広範囲にわたって
(D) 形 広範囲にわたる

🔍 選択肢には動詞 extend の派生語が並んでいる。空所の前後を見て
いくと、空所前に名詞(句)を導く群前置詞の in need of があり、
空所後は名詞の remodeling がある。ここから空所は名詞 remodeling
を修飾する形容詞が入ることがわかる。以上から、正解は **(D)**。remodel
(～を改装する)が動名詞だと思って (C) を選ばないようにしよう。動名
詞の場合は、目的語となる名詞(句)が remodeling 以降に必要となる。

🧠 Some of the apartment complexes in the older neighborhoods of Tempa are
　　　　　 S　　　　　　　　　　　　　　　　　　　　　　　　　　　 V

in need of extensive remodeling.
　　　　　 C

✏️ □apartment complex 集合住宅 □neighborhood 地区 □in need of ～を必要とする □remodeling 改装

---

17. ★★★★☆

式典の場所は公式には決定されませんでしたが、計
画委員会の委員長により口頭で承認されました。

(A) 接 ～もない
(B) 接 しかし
(C) ～する○○
(D) 接 または

🔍 選択肢には接続詞、関係詞などが並んでいる。空所を含む文の意味
を取っていくと、「式典の場所は公式に決定されなかった、……委員
長により承認された。」と、カンマ前後で逆接の関係となっていることが
わかる。以上から、逆接を意味する **(B)** が正解。not A, but B で、「A で
はなく B」という慣用表現となっているので押さえておこう。(A) の nor
が入り、〈not A, nor B〉と考えたかもしれないが、その場合は nor was
it given と倒置にする必要があるため、文法的に成り立たない。

🧠 The location of the ceremony was not decided officially, but was given
　　　 S　　　　　　　　　　　　 V¹　　　　　　　　　　　 V²

oral approval by the chairperson of the planning board.

✏️ □ceremony 式典 □officially 公式に □oral 口頭の □approval 承認 □chairperson 委員長
□planning board 計画委員会

---

18. ★☆☆☆☆

化粧品会社の給与課に勤務している従業員は全員
自分の給料小切手への署名を禁じられています。

(A) 彼ら自身 (再帰代名詞)
(B) 彼らを (目的格)
(C) 彼ら自身の
(D) 彼らのもの (所有代名詞)

🔍 選択肢には代名詞の格が並んでいる。空所後には paychecks と名
詞が来ているため、空所には所有格が入ることがわかる。選択肢の
中で、所有格に相当するのは **(C)**。their だけでも OK だが、their own
の形で、「彼ら自身の」と強調した表現となっている。

🧠 All employees / who work in the payroll office at the cosmetic company /
　　　 S　　　　 　 S　 V

have been prevented from signing their own paychecks.
　　　 V

✏️ □payroll office 給与課 □cosmetic company 化粧品会社 □prevent A from *doing* A が～するのを防ぐ
□paycheck 給与小切手

🚩 **16. (D)　17. (B)　18. (C)**

19. During her meeting at the corporate headquarters,
Ms. Yasmin said that the company would go bankrupt -------
cutting costs drastically.

(A) further
(B) without
(C) considering
(D) against

20. Information that we have collected over the last year will be
first categorized according to location and ------- in
alphabetical order.

(A) since
(B) there
(C) then
(D) largely

21. Student academic progress should be reviewed at the end
of each academic year for programs lasting ------- 4 years.

(A) as much
(B) by then
(C) at least
(D) in case

19. ★★★★☆

本社での会議の中で、Yasmin さんは、大胆な費用削減をしなければ、会社は倒産するかもしれないと発言しました。

(A) 副 さらなる
(B) 前 ~なしに
(C) 前 ~を考慮すると
(D) 前 ~に対して

選択肢には副詞、前置詞が並んでいる。空所の周辺の意味を取っていくと、「大胆な費用削減……、会社は倒産するかも」という意味になっており、費用削減するかしないかに、会社の倒産が懸かっていることがわかる。以上から、「費用削減しなければ、倒産するかも」という関係が成り立つ **(B)** が正解となる。(A) は副詞であり、空所に入れてもその後ろが文法的に合わないため不正解。

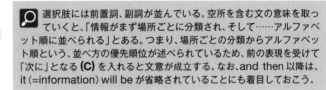

During her meeting at the corporate headquarters, / Ms. Yasmin said /
～の間に (副詞句)　　　　　　　　　　　　　　　S　　　　　V

that the company would go bankrupt without cutting costs drastically.
O (that 節) S　　　　　V　　　　C

□corporate headquarters 本社　□go bankrupt 倒産する　□drastically 大胆に

---

20. ★★★☆☆

昨年1年間に収集した情報はまず場所ごとに分類され、次にアルファベット順に並べられます。

(A) 前 ~以来
(B) 副 そこに
(C) 副 次に
(D) 副 大きく

選択肢には前置詞、副詞が並んでいる。空所を含む文の意味を取っていくと、「情報がまず場所ごとに分類され、そして……アルファベット順に並べられる」とある。つまり、場所ごとの分類からアルファベット順という、並べ方の優先順位が述べられているため、前の表現を受けて「次に」となる **(C)** を入れると文意が成立する。なお、and then 以降は、it (=information) will be が省略されていることにも着目しておこう。

Information / that we have collected over the last year / will be first categorized
　　S　　　　　　　O　S　　　　　　V　　　　　　　　　　　　V

according to location and then in alphabetical order.

□categorize ~を分類する　□according to ~に従って　□in alphabetical order アルファベット順に

---

21. ★★★☆☆

4年以上継続して実施しているプログラムについては、各学年の終わりに学生の到達度の確認を行う必要があります。

(A) 等しく
(B) それまでに
(C) 少なくとも
(D) 万一に備えて

選択肢には副詞などの表現が並んでいる。空所を含む文の意味を取っていくと、「4年……続いているプログラムに対して、学生の到達度を確認する必要がある」となっている。つまり、空所は「一定期間以上もしくは以下」といった期間にかかる表現が入ることがわかる。よって、「少なくとも」を意味する **(C)** を入れると文意に合う。(A) は期間ではなく、量を示す際に使用する表現で、(D) は in case (that) SV と、節を導く表現のため、いずれも文法的に当てはめることができない。

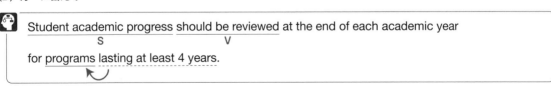

Student academic progress should be reviewed at the end of each academic year
　　　　S　　　　　　　　　V

for programs lasting at least 4 years.

□academic progress 学習習得度　□academic year 学年　□last 続く

22. The construction industry in Manila is experiencing substantial growth ------- the increasing number of newcomers.

(A) in that
(B) as for
(C) prior to
(D) due to

23. As discussed at today's conference, Richmond's newly elected mayor is taking a ------- fresh approach to improving the city's transit system.

(A) decided
(B) decision
(C) decidedly
(D) deciding

24. We are searching for trained actors who have the skills to communicate ------- with various kinds of audiences.

(A) effect
(B) effective
(C) effectiveness
(D) effectively

22. ★★★☆☆

マニラの建設業界は、新規参入事業者の増加により大幅な成長を遂げています。

(A) 〜という点で
(B) 〜に関して
(C) 〜より前に
(D) 〜により

選択肢には２語からなる接続表現が並んでいる。空所を含む箇所の意味を取っていくと、「新規参入事業者の増加……、大幅な成長を遂げている」となっている。ここから、新規参入事業者の増加により、成長を遂げた、という因果関係が成立するため、原因を導く群前置詞の **(D)** が正解となる。(B)、(C) もそれぞれよくでる表現なので、しっかり押さえておこう。

The construction industry in Manila is experiencing substantial growth /
         S   V   O

due to the increasing number of newcomers.
（前置詞句［原因・理由］）

□construction industry 建設業界　□substantial かなりの　□growth 成長　□increasing 増えつつある
□newcomer 新規参入者

---

23. ★★★★☆

本日の協議会で議論されたとおり、Richmond で新しく選出された市長は市の交通システムを改善するため、非常に斬新な取り組みを行います。

(A) 動 〜を決心する　［過去分詞］
(B) 名 決定
(C) 副 明らかに
(D) ［現在分詞］

選択肢には動詞 decide が形を変えているものや派生語が並んでいる。空所の前後を見ると、前が不定冠詞の a、後ろが形容詞＋名詞（fresh approach）となっている。ここから、空所直後の形容詞 fresh を修飾する副詞の **(C)** が入るとわかる。副詞の decidedly は「明らかに」という難語だが、語彙の意味がわからない場合でも、文の構造から副詞が入ると考えることができる。

As discussed at today's conference, / Richmond's newly elected mayor is taking
議論されたとおり（副詞句）   S   V

a decidedly fresh approach to improving the city's transit system.
             O

□as discussed 議論されたとおり　□newly elected 新たに選出された　□take approach to 〜に対する取り組みを行う
□transit system 交通システム

---

24. ★★★☆☆

さまざまなお客様と効果的に意思疎通を行うことができる熟練した俳優を求めています。

(A) 名 効果
(B) 形 効果的な
(C) 名 有効性
(D) 副 効果的に

選択肢には名詞 effect が形を変えているもの、あるいは派生語が並んでいる。空所の前後を見ると、前に不定詞を取る動詞 communicate があり、後ろには前置詞 with がある。ここから、空所は前置詞 with 以降の audience（聴衆）と共に、「効果的に」通じているとすると文意が通じる。以上より、正解は副詞である **(D)**。communicate は自動詞、他動詞両方の意味を持つが、今回他動詞として「〜をやりとりする」と考えると (A) や (C) も候補に上がるが、「聴衆と効果や有効性を伝える」というのは文意に合わないため、ここではいずれも不正解。

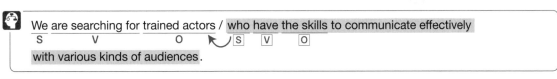

We are searching for trained actors / who have the skills to communicate effectively
   S   V   O   S V   O

with various kinds of audiences.

□communicate 意思疎通をはかる　□various さまざまな　□audience 聴衆

22. (D)　23. (C)　24. (D)

25. The main buildings of the state government are closed to the general public ------- Friday evening to Monday morning every week.

(A) of
(B) in
(C) from
(D) only

26. The ------- of the lease agreement with Dally Condominiums can be renegotiated every two years.

(A) locations
(B) records
(C) views
(D) terms

27. Successful applicants should have at least three years of relevant experience, ------- in the online advertising field.

(A) inclusively
(B) ideally
(C) completely
(D) mutually

25. ★☆☆☆☆

州政府の主要な建物には、毎週金曜日の夜から月曜日の朝まで一般の人は入場できません。

(A) 前 ~の
(B) 前 ~に
(C) 前 ~から
(D) 形 だけの

選択肢には前置詞や形容詞が並んでいる。空所を含む箇所の意味を見ていくと、「毎週金曜日の夜……月曜日の朝まで一般公開はされていない」となっているため、ある期間を指していることがわかる。よって、from A to B（A から B まで）となる **(C)** が正解。

The main buildings of the state government <u>are closed</u> <u>to the general public</u> /
　　　　　　　　　　　　　S　　　　　　　　　　　　　 V　　　　　　　　　　 O

from Friday evening to Monday morning every week.
from A to B（A から B まで）

□state government 州政府　□closed to the general public 一般公開されていない

---

26. ★★★☆☆

Dally Condominiums との賃貸借契約の条件は 2 年ごとに再交渉することができます。

(A) 名 所在地
(B) 名 記録
(C) 名 眺め
(D) 名 条件

選択肢には名詞が並んでいる。空所を含む箇所の意味を見ていくと、「賃貸借契約の……は 2 年ごとに再交渉できる」とあるため、空所には、2 年ごとに再交渉できるもの、が入る。以上より、正解は **(D)**。そのほかの選択肢では文意が通らない。

<u>The terms</u> of the lease agreement with Dally Condominiums <u>can be renegotiated</u>
　　 S　　　　　　　　　　　　　　　　　　　　　　　　　　　　　　　 V

every two years.

□lease agreement 賃貸借契約　□renegotiate ～を再交渉する

---

27. ★★★★★

選考に通るためには、応募者は最低 3 年間、関連分野、理想を言えば、インターネット広告の分野の職務経験を有する必要があります。

(A) 副 包括的に
(B) 副 理想的には
(C) 副 完全に
(D) 副 相互に

選択肢には副詞が並んでいる。空所を含む文の意味を見ていくと、「選考通過にあたり、応募者は、最低 3 年間の関連経験を有する必要があり、……インターネット広告分野だ」となっている。つまり、関連経験は必須だが、できればインターネット広告分野だとよい、という文脈であることがわかるため、「理想的には」を意味する **(B)** が正解となる。

<u>Successful applicants</u> <u>should have</u> at least three years of relevant <u>experience</u>,
　　　　　S　　　　　　　　　　 V　　　　　　　　　　　　　　　　　　 O

ideally in the online advertising field.

□successful applicant 選考通過者　□relevant experience 関連分野の経験　□field 分野

---

 25. (C)　26. (D)　27. (B)

28. Quantum Bank takes every ------- to protect your personal information by requiring all users to enter a unique login ID and password whenever they want to access their account.

(A) advice
(B) recommendation
(C) precaution
(D) suggestion

29. Staff members ------- reimbursement of travel expenses for their business trips must submit an expense report with the approval of their managers.

(A) seeking
(B) struggling
(C) returning
(D) aiming

30. ------- her dedication and commitment to trying to reach solutions, I am sure that Ms. Hartford will be a great asset to your company.

(A) Given
(B) Between
(C) Namely
(D) Regardless

28. ★★★★☆

Quantum Bank 社は、すべての利用者が、自身の口座にアクセスする際はいつでも、個別のログインID とパスワードの入力を要求することにより、個人情報を保護するためのあらゆる予防策を講じています。

(A) 名 助言
(B) 名 推奨
(C) 名 予防策
(D) 名 提案

選択肢には名詞が並んでいる。空所を含む箇所の意味を見ていくと、「Quantum Bank 社は、個人情報を保護するためのあらゆる……を講じている」となっている。以上から、個人情報保護のための、対策・予防策を講じている、とすると文意が成立する。よって、正解は **(C)**。take precaution で「予防策を講じる」というコロケーション（組み合わせのよい語と語）となっているので、ここでしっかり押さえておこう。なお、by 以下は、予防策の具体的な手段になっている。

Quantum Bank takes every precaution / to protect your personal information /
　　S　　　　V　　　　O　　　　　　　　　　to 不定詞（副詞句）
by requiring all users / to enter a unique login ID and password /
　　　　　　　　　　　　to 不定詞（副詞句）
whenever they want to access their account.
（副詞節［時］）　S　　　　V　　　　　O

□personal information 個人情報　□require A to *do*　A に〜するように要求する　□user 利用者　□unique 個別の
□whenever 〜するときはいつでも　□access 〜に接続する　□account 口座

29. ★★★☆☆

職員が出張にかかった旅費の精算を要請する場合、管理職の承認を得てから経費報告書を提出する必要があります。

(A) 動 〜を求める　[現在分詞]
(B) 動 もがく　[現在分詞]
(C) 動 〜を戻す　[現在分詞]
(D) 動 〜を向ける　[現在分詞]

選択肢には現在分詞が並んでいる。空所を含む箇所の意味を見ていくと、「出張旅費の精算を……する職員」となっている。ここから、空所には、この文の主語となる Staff members を修飾する語が入ることがわかるので「〜を求める」という意味の **(A)** を入れると文意が通じる。

Staff members seeking reimbursement of travel expenses for their business trips /
　　　S
must submit an expense report with the approval of their managers.
　　V　　　　O

□reimbursement 払い戻し　□travel expense 旅費　□business trip 出張　□expense report 経費報告

30. ★★★☆☆

解決に向けて努力する真摯な姿勢とひたむきさを考えれば、Hartford さんが貴社にとって貴重な財産になることは確実です。

(A) 前 〜を考慮すると
(B) 前 〜の間に
(C) 副 具体的に名前をあげると
(D) 副 かまわず

選択肢には前置詞や副詞が並んでいる。空所を含む箇所の意味を見ていくと、「解決に向けて努力する姿勢とひたむき……、Hartford さんは貴社にとって偉大な財産になる」となっている。つまり、前半は、Hartford さんが貴重な人財である、という内容の理由・根拠が書かれていることがわかる。以上から、「〜を考慮すると」という意味の **(A)** が正解。Given は、接続詞的に that 節 (SV) も導くことができるため、知識に入れておこう。

Given her dedication and commitment to trying to reach solutions, /
　〜を考慮に入れれば（前置詞句）
I am sure / that Ms. Hartford will be a great asset to your company.
〜だと確信している　　S　　　　　V　　　　　C

□dedication and commitment to 〜に対するひたむきさ、真剣さ　□reach a solution 解決に至る
□asset 財産（となる人）、人財

🚩 **28. (C)　29. (A)　30. (A)**

1㎜㎜

2㎜㎜

3㎜㎜

1. Since customer satisfaction is our number one priority, we
------- conduct a brief survey to learn more about our
customers' needs.

(A) routinely
(B) vastly
(C) approximately
(D) considerably

1㎜㎜

2㎜㎜

3㎜㎜

2. Today's staff meeting will begin late ------- some of the sales
department employees are meeting with a customer right
now.

(A) until
(B) because
(C) in case of
(D) so that

1㎜㎜

2㎜㎜

3㎜㎜

3. Candidates for accounting positions ------- to possess at
least five years of experience and three or more letters of
reference.

(A) require
(B) are required
(C) have required
(D) requiring

1. ★★★★★

私どもはお客様の満足が第一ですから、お客様のニーズをより深く理解するため、簡単なアンケートを定期的に実施しています。

(A) 副 定期的に
(B) 副 大いに
(C) 副 おおよそ
(D) 副 かなり

選択肢には副詞が並んでいる。空所を含む箇所の意味を見ていくと、「お客様のニーズをより深く理解するため、簡単なアンケートを……実施している」となっている。つまり、顧客のニーズを深く理解するために一定の頻度でアンケートなどを実施していることを意味する副詞が入ると文意が成立する。以上より、「定期的に」を意味する (A) が正解。(D) は感覚的に入りそうだが、この語は、形容詞 (considerably cold, かなり寒い)、や動詞 (improved considerably, かなり改善した) について程度を示すため、ここでは当てはめられない。

Since customer satisfaction is our number one priority, / we routinely conduct a brief survey /
（副詞節 [理由]）　S　　　　　V　　　　　C　　　　　S　　　　　V　　　　　O

to learn more about our customers' needs.
to 不定詞（副詞句）

□customer satisfaction 顧客の満足　□number one priority 最優先　□conduct ～を実施する　□brief 簡単な
□survey 調査

2. ★★★★☆

営業部の従業員がちょうどお客様と打ち合せをしているため、今日のスタッフミーティングは開始を遅らせます。

(A) 接 ～まで
(B) 接 なぜなら
(C) 前 ～の場合（群前置詞）
(D) そのため

選択肢には接続詞や前置詞表現が並んでいる。空所を含む箇所の意味を見ていくと、「本日のスタッフミーティングは遅れることになる……営業担当者がお客様と打ち合せ中である」となっており、前者が未来、後者が現在と時制が異なる。ここから後者の内容を原因、前者の内容を結果として接続表現で結ぶと、「営業担当者が今打ち合せ中のため、スタッフミーティングは遅れる」となり、文意が成立する。以上より、このような原因・理由を表す (B) が正解。(D) は、A so that B とした場合、「A だから B」「B をするために A する」となり、時系列的に A が B よりも前の情報ではないと成立しないため、ここでは不正解となる。

Today's staff meeting will begin late / because some of the sales department employees
　　　　　S　　　　　V　　　　　（副詞節 [理由]）　　　　　S

are meeting with a customer right now.
　V　　　　　O

□right now 今ちょうど

3. ★★☆☆☆

経理の求人に応募するには少なくとも 5 年の実務経験と 3 通以上の推薦状が必要です。

(A) 動 ～に要求する　原形
(B) 受動態
(C) 現在完了形
(D) 現在分詞

選択肢には動詞 require が形を変えて並んでいる。空所を含む文の構造を見ると、主語は複数形の candidates で、この文の述語動詞が見当たらないため、空所には述語動詞が入ることがわかる。動詞 require は他動詞であり、空所直後に目的語がないことから受動態にする必要がある。以上から、主語が三人称複数、動詞が受動態の形を満たす (B) が正解となる。

Candidates for accounting positions are required to possess at least five years of experience
　　　　　S　　　　　　　　　　　　　　　　　V　　　　　　　　　　　O

and three or more letters of reference.

□candidate 志願者　□accounting position 経理担当職　□possess ～を有している　□at least 少なくとも
□letter of reference 推薦状

 1. (A)　2. (B)　3. (B)

4. Mr. Russel said he will draft the yearly advertising budget proposal ------- because most of his colleagues are away attending a conference.

(A) he
(B) himself
(C) his
(D) him

5. Hexagon Industrial Support provides ------- workwear and full safety training to all employees.

(A) protection
(B) protective
(C) protectively
(D) protect

6. With annual rainfall decreasing substantially in the North Sydney area in recent years, the ------- of groundwater is now well below normal.

(A) reinforcement
(B) jeopardy
(C) accumulation
(D) consideration

4. ★★★★★

Russel さんは、同僚はほとんど全員が会議に出席するため不在なので、年間広告予算案を自分で作成すると言いました。

(A) 彼が（主格）
(B) 彼自身（再帰代名詞）
(C) 彼の（所有格）
(D) 彼に（目的格）

選択肢には代名詞が並んでいる。空所の前は、he will draft the yearly advertising budget proposal（彼が年間広告予算案を作成する）と完全な節となっていることから、空所は、強調表現として再帰代名詞を入れ、「Russel さん自身で」という意味になると、文法的にも文意も通じる。以上から、正解は **(B)**。この選択肢以外は、文法的に当てはめることができない。

Mr. Russel said / (that) he will draft the yearly advertising budget proposal himself /
　　S　　　V　　(that 節)　S　　V　　　　　　　　　　O

because most of his colleagues are away attending a conference .
（副詞節［理由］）　　　　　　S　　　　　　V　　C

□draft 〜の案を作成する　□yearly 1 年間　□advertising budget 広告予算　□proposal 提案

---

5. ★★★★★

Hexagon Industrial Support 社は、全従業員に対し、保護作業服を支給し、安全教育を十分に行います。

(A) 名 保護
(B) 形 保護のための
(C) 副 保護するように
(D) 動 保護する

選択肢には動詞 protect の派生語が並んでいる。空所を含む文の前後を見ると、述語動詞 provides と、その目的語に相当する workwear がある。ここから、空所は provides の目的語の workwear を修飾する形容詞が入ることがわかる。以上から、正解は **(B)** となる。

Hexagon Industrial Support provides protective workwear and full safety training
　　　　S　　　　　　　　　V　　　　　　　　O

to all employees.

□provide 〜を供給する、提供する　□workwear 作業服　□safety training 安全教育

---

6. ★★★★★

近年、ノースシドニー地区では年間降水量が大幅に減少しているため、地下水の貯水量が平年を大きく下回っています。

(A) 名 補強
(B) 名 危機
(C) 名 蓄積量
(D) 名 考慮

選択肢には意味の異なる名詞が並んでいる。文の意味を見ていくと、「ある地区の年間降水量が大幅に減少しているため、地下水の……が平年を大きく下回っている」となっている。年間降水量が減少したことにより平年を大きく下回るものとして考えられるのは、地下水の蓄積の量のため、正解は **(C)** となる。この問題は、理由を示す with からカンマまでの意味を取ることがカギ。

With annual rainfall decreasing substantially in the North Sydney area in recent years, /
（副詞句［付帯状況］）

the accumulation of groundwater is now well below normal.
　　　　S　　　　　　　　V　　　　C

□annual 年の　□rainfall 降水量　□substantially 大いに　□groundwater 地下水

---

 4. (B)　5. (B)　6. (C)

TEST 3

53

7. Nora Johns Express will be ------- its delivery operations into three more countries in April.

(A) choosing
(B) expanding
(C) reserving
(D) cooperating

8. The ------- employees at Gateway Ski Resort create a welcoming and comfortable atmosphere for its visitors.

(A) except
(B) exception
(C) exceptionally
(D) exceptional

9. Although staff members are satisfied with the proposed salary and benefits, some object to ------- to the new overseas branch at short notice.

(A) relocated
(B) relocate
(C) relocating
(D) relocates

7. ★★★☆☆

Nora Johns Express 社は 4 月からさらに 3 カ国に宅配事業を拡大する予定です。

(A) 動 ～を選択する 〔現在分詞〕
(B) 動 ～を拡張する 〔現在分詞〕
(C) 動 ～を予約する 〔現在分詞〕
(D) 動 協力する 〔現在分詞〕

選択肢には意味の異なる動詞の ing 形が並んでいる。空所を含む意味を見ていくと、「Nora Jones Express 社は 4 月からさらに 3 カ国に宅配事業を……する予定だ」となっている。ここから、3 カ国に対して宅配事業を拡大していくと考えられる。以上より、正解は **(B)**。

Nora Johns Express <u>will be expanding</u> its delivery operations
S   V   O

into three more countries in April.
expand A into B（A を B に発展させる）

□delivery operation 宅配事業

....

8. ★★★★★

Gateway Ski Resort 社の優秀な従業員は、滞在客にとって居心地がよく快適な雰囲気を作り出しています。

(A) 前 ～を除いて
(B) 名 例外
(C) 副 例外的に
(D) 形 優れた

選択肢には前置詞 except やその派生語が並んでいる。空所の前後を見ると、定冠詞 the＋空所＋employees ... となっている。ここから、空所には名詞 employees を修飾する形容詞が入ることが考えられる。以上から、**(D)** が正解。〈冠詞＋空所＋名詞〉の組み合わせの場合は、空所には形容詞が入ると第一に考えて解こう。

The exceptional employees at Gateway Ski Resort create
S   V

a welcoming and comfortable atmosphere for its visitors.
O

□create ～を作り出す □welcoming 居心地がいい □comfortable 心地よい □atmosphere 雰囲気 □visitor 訪問者

....

9. ★★★★☆

社員は提示された給与や福利厚生には満足していますが、何人かは新しい海外支店への急な転勤に抗議しています。

(A) 動 移転する 〔過去形〕
(B) 〔原 形〕
(C) 〔動名詞〕
(D) 〔三人称単数現在形〕

選択肢には動詞 relocate が形を変えて並んでいる。空所を含む文を見ると、カンマの後に some object to ------- to ... となっており、複数の人を意味する不定代名詞の some、述語動詞の object、前置詞 to があることから、空所には名詞が入ることがわかる。選択肢の中で名詞として機能するのは動名詞の **(C)** となる。この問題は、述語動詞 object は自動詞で前置詞 to を伴うという知識がないと、不定詞の to と勘違いして (B) を選んでしまうため、注意しよう。

Although staff members are satisfied with the proposed salary and benefits, /
（副詞節［譲歩］）　S　　　　　V　　　　　　　　　　　O

some object to relocating to the new overseas branch at short notice.
S   V   O

□proposed 提示された □benefit 福利厚生 □object to ～に不服である □at short notice 急に

....

 7. (B)　8. (D)　9. (C)

10. ------- printed on the label, these dairy products must not be sold after their expiration date.

(A) As
(B) Since
(C) Unless
(D) While

11. Some reviewers said Jessica Bradley's new drama was ------- boring because of its weak storyline.

(A) still
(B) rather
(C) worse
(D) merely

12. In Fulton County, the discount coupons of One Mart are mailed to participating customers on a monthly -------.

(A) base
(B) basis
(C) based
(D) basing

10. ★★★★☆

ラベルに印刷されているとおり、これらの乳製品は賞味期限を過ぎて販売してはいけません。

(A) 接 〜のとおり
(B) 前 〜以来
(C) 接 〜でない限り
(D) 接 〜なのに対し

選択肢には前置詞や接続詞が並んでいる。空所を含む意味は、「ラベルに印刷されている……、これらの乳製品は賞味期限を過ぎて販売してはいけない」となっている。ここから、賞味期限を超過した乳製品を販売してはいけないのは、ラベルにも書いているとおり周知している、という文意になるように考えると、接続表現で「〜のとおり」という意味になる (A) が正解となる。この従属節は、As (they are) printed on the label, と、主節と重複する主語の they (dairy products) と be 動詞が省略されていることにも注目しておこう。

 As (they are) printed on the label, these dairy products must not be sold /
〜のとおり（副詞句）　　　　　　　　　　　　　　S　　　　　　　　　　V

after their expiration date.

□dairy product 乳製品　□expiration date 賞味期限

---

11. ★★★★☆

Jessica Bradley さんの新しいドラマは話の筋に説得力がなく、むしろ退屈だという批評もありました。

(A) 副 それでもなお
(B) 副 やや
(C) 形 悪い（bad の比較級）
(D) 副 単に（…にすぎない）

選択肢には意味の異なる副詞、形容詞が並んでおり、空所を含む文の意味は、「新しいドラマは話の筋が弱いため、……退屈だという批評もあった」となっている。「話の筋が弱い」という箇所から、ネガティブな内容が来ることがわかるので、空所後の形容詞 boring（退屈な）を、「やや、いくぶん」と控えめに修飾した (B) が正解となる。副詞 rather は、今回のようにネガティブな形容詞を修飾することがあるので注意しよう。

 Some reviewers said / (that) Jessica Bradley's new drama was rather boring /
　　　　　　　S　　　　V　　O (that 節)　　　　　S　　　　　　　　V　　　　C

because of its weak storyline.
（副詞句 [原因・理由]）

□reviewer 批評家　□boring 退屈な　□storyline 話の展開、筋

---

12. ★★★☆☆

Fulton 地域では、One Mart 社の割引クーポンが、参加されるお客様に毎月郵送されます。

(A) 名 土台、基礎
(B) 名 基準
(C) 動 〜の基礎を置く　過去分詞
(D) 現在分詞

選択肢には名詞（動詞）base のさまざまな形などが並んでいる。空所は文末にあり、前置詞句である on a monthly ------- となっている。不定冠詞 a と形容詞 monthly が並んでいるので、空所には名詞が入る。ここから (A) と (B) に絞られるが、意味を考えると、「月単位で」という内容にすると文意が通じる。よって、正解は (B)。慣用表現として on a monthly (weekly, annual) basis で、頻度を表す表現として覚えておこう。

 In Fulton County, / the discount coupons of One Mart are mailed to
　　　　　　　　　　　　　　　S　　　　　　　　　　　　　V

participating customers on a monthly basis
　　　　　O

□discount coupon 割引クーポン　□mail 〜を郵送する　□participating 参加中の

1回目 2回目 3回目

13. As a benefit of being a newly registered member, any purchase of more than $500 ------- for free shipping within three months of registration.

(A) equips
(B) qualifies
(C) arranges
(D) schedules

1回目 2回目 3回目

14. Almost everyone considered Ms. Mogan's plan to be -------, but she believes it is simple to implement.

(A) inaudible
(B) unconcerned
(C) impractical
(D) unavoidable

1回目 2回目 3回目

15. ------- the shocking news that Mill Lane Investments had filed for bankruptcy aired, most of its stakeholders sold their stocks at a loss.

(A) Already
(B) So
(C) Once
(D) Along

13. ★★★★☆

新規会員登録の特典として、500 ドルを超えるお買い上げで、登録後 3 カ月以内は送料が無料になります。

(A) 動 ～に備え付ける 〔三人称単数現在形〕
(B) 動 権利を得る 〔三人称単数現在形〕
(C) 動 取り決める 〔三人称単数現在形〕
(D) 動 ～を予定する 〔三人称単数現在形〕

選択肢には意味の異なる動詞が並んでいる。空所を含む箇所の意味を取ると、「500 ドル以上の購入には登録後 3 カ月、送料無料の……」となっており、かつカンマ以前が「新規会員登録の特典として」とある。つまり、新規会員登録特典として、一定額の購入者にはある期間送料無料の資格が発生すると考えると文意が通る。以上から、正解は **(B)**。

As a benefit of being a newly registered member, / any purchase of more than $500 qualifies for
副詞句   S   V
free shipping within three months of registration.
O

□benefit 特典 □newly registered 新規登録された □free shipping 送料無料

---

14. ★★★★★

ほとんどの人が、Mogan さんの計画は非現実的だと考えていましたが、本人は簡単に実行できると考えています。

(A) 形 聞き取れない
(B) 形 気にしない
(C) 形 非現実的な
(D) 形 避けられない

選択肢には意味の異なる形容詞が並んでいる。空所を含む文の意味を取ると、「ほとんどの人が、Mogan さんの計画は……だと考えていたが、彼女は簡単にできると考えている」となっており、カンマ前後が逆接の関係である。つまり、カンマ以前は、多くの人は簡単にできない、実現できないと考えているといった内容であることがわかる。よって、**(C)** が正解となる。

Almost everyone considered Ms. Mogan's plan to be impractical, /
S   V   O   C
but she believes / (that) it is simple / to implement .
S   V   O   S V   C
(that 節)

□consider A to be B　A を B と考える　□implement ～を実行する

---

15. ★★★☆☆

Mill Lane Investments 社が破産を申請したという衝撃的なニュースがいったん流れると、ほとんどの関係者が株を売却して損切りしました。

(A) 副 すでに
(B) 接 では
(C) 接 いったん～すると
(D) 前 ～に沿って

選択肢にはさまざまな副詞、接続詞などが並んでいる。空所を含む文の意味を見ていくと、「Mill Lane Investments 社が破産申請したニュースが流れる……、関係者が株を売却した」となっている。カンマ前後はいずれも過去形で時制がそろっていることから、「ニュースが流れると➡株が売られた」という内容に合う接続表現を空所に入れると意味が通じる。選択肢の中でこのような接続表現が取れるのは **(C)** のみだ。この問題は、文の構造を単純化し、"Once the shocking news aired, most sold their stocks." とするとわかりやすい。air は「(ニュースなどが) 流れる」という意味の動詞。

Once the shocking news / that Mill Lane Investments had filed for bankruptcy / aired ,
(副詞節 [時])   S   同格の that (S)   (V)   (O)   V
most of its stakeholders sold their stocks at a loss.
S   V   O

□shocking 驚くべき □file for bankruptcy 破産申請する □air 放送される □stakeholder 利害関係者 □stock 株
□at a loss 損を出して

---

16. ------- up to twenty-four hours for our customer satisfaction center to reply to your e-mail before you send a new inquiry.

(A) Allowed
(B) Allow
(C) Allowing
(D) Allows

17. ------- a power failure, the crisis management department recommends that each state government should operate backup generators immediately.

(A) Only if
(B) For example
(C) In case of
(D) In contrast

18. With just five days remaining before Albam's annual festival, the coordinator has ------- to determine the parade route.

(A) finally
(B) yet
(C) seldom
(D) already

16. ★★★★☆

新たなお問い合わせの前に、当社カスタマーサービスセンターからのお客様のメールへのご返信は24時間までお待ちくださいますよう、お願いいたします。

(A) 動 ～を見込む　過去形
(B) 原形
(C) 現在分詞
(D) 三人称単数現在形

選択肢には動詞 allow がさまざまな形になって並んでいる。空所を含む文意は、「新規問合わせ前に、当社からの返信は最大24時間ほど……」となっている。この文には主語がなく、また空所の目的語の部分には時間が来ていることから、この allow は、（時間的な）余裕を見ておく、という意味だとわかる。以上より、空所に **(B)** の原形を入れ、命令文にすると、「最大で24時間みてほしい」となり、文意が通る。allow は、今回のように allow A for B の形で、TOEIC では頻出なのでしっかり押さえておこう。

〈命令文〉

Allow up to twenty-four hours for our customer satisfaction center to reply to your e-mail /
V　　　　　O　　　　　　　　　　　　to reply の意味上の主語

before you send a new inquiry.
（副詞節 [時]）S　V　　O

□allow A for B　B のために A（時間など）の余裕を見ておく　□up to 最大～まで　□customer satisfaction 顧客の満足
□inquiry 問い合わせ

---

17. ★★☆☆☆

停電が発生した場合、各州政府が直ちに予備の発電機を稼働させることを、危機管理部門は推奨します。

(A) ～する場合にのみ
(B) 例えば（接続副詞）
(C) ～の場合（群前置詞）
(D) 対照的に（接続副詞）

選択肢にはさまざまな接続表現が並んでいる。空所後に名詞句＋カンマがあることから、空所には名詞句を導く表現が入ることがわかる。よって、名詞句を導く **(C)** が正解となる。(A) は節を導くため文法的に当てはめられず、(B)、(D) は副詞表現として独立しているが、当てはめても文意が通らない。

In case of a power failure, / the crisis management department recommends /
～の場合に（副詞句）　　　　　　S　　　　　　　　　　　V

that each state government should operate backup generators immediately.
O (that 節)　　　S　　　　　V　　　　O

□power failure 停電　□crisis management 危機管理　□state government 州政府　□backup 予備の
□generator 発電機　□immediately 即座に

---

18. ★★★★☆

年に一度の Albam のお祭りまであと5日しかないにもかかわらず、主催者はまだパレードのルートを決めていません。

(A) 副 ついに
(B) 副 まだ
(C) 副 めったに～ない
(D) 副 すでに

選択肢にはさまざまな副詞が並んでいる。空所を含む文の意味を取ると、「年に一度のお祭りまであと5日だけあり、主催者はパレードルートを決め……」となっている。ここで、yet を入れると、慣用句として has yet to do「まだ～してない」という意味になり、「残り5日しかないのに、まだルートを決めていない」と文意が成立する。よって、**(B)** が正解。ほかの副詞も文法的には当てはめられないことはないが、文意が通らない。

With just five days remaining before Albam's annual festival, /
（副詞節 [付帯状況]）

the coordinator has yet to determine the parade route.
S　　　　V　　　　　　O

□remaining 残っている　□have yet to do まだ～していない　□coordinator 開催者、主催者
□determine ～を決定する　□parade パレード　□route ルート

16. (B)　17. (C)　18. (B)

19. The many ------- listed on her résumé suggest that no one
will be better qualified for the job than Audrey Breeding.

(A) accomplish
(B) accomplishes
(C) accomplishing
(D) accomplishments

20. The report that Mr. Stevenson has submitted does not only
contain a technical ------- of the problem, but also a possible
solution.

(A) attention
(B) intelligence
(C) information
(D) description

21. To ensure that your order is ------- efficiently, please fill in the
order form completely and return it in the envelope provided.

(A) provided
(B) processed
(C) promised
(D) persisted

19. ★★☆☆☆

Audrey Breeding さんの履歴書に記載された多くの功績が、彼女以外にその仕事に適した人物はいないことを示唆しています。

(A) 動 ～を達成する ［原形］
(B) ［三人称単数現在形］
(C) ［現在分詞］
(D) 名 業績

選択肢には動詞 accomplish がさまざまな形で並んでいる。空所を含む文の構造に着目すると、空所は主語に相当し、述語動詞は suggest（原形）であることから、空所には名詞かつ複数形が入ることがわかる。以上から、正解は **(D)**。文の構造からアプローチすると、意味を取らなくても文法的に当てはめられる選択肢が限定されるので、構造をしっかり把握できるようにしておこう。

The many accomplishments listed on her résumé suggest /
　　　　　S　　　　　　　　　　　　　　　　　V
that no one will be better qualified for the job than Audrey Breeding .
O (that節) S　　　　　　　　V　　　　　　　O

□résumé 履歴書　□suggest ～を示唆している　□be qualified for ～の資格がある

---

20. ★★★★★

Stevenson 氏が提出した報告書には、問題の技術的な説明だけでなく、実行可能な解決策も書かれています。

(A) 名 注意
(B) 名 知恵
(C) 名 情報
(D) 名 説明

選択肢には意味の異なる名詞が並んでいる。空所を含む文の意味を取っていくと、「報告書には、問題の技術的な……だけでなく、見込みある解決策が含まれている」となっている。選択肢を見ると、(C) か (D) に絞られるが、空所の前が a technical ------- と、冠詞がつくため、可算名詞だということがわかる。information は不可算名詞なので、**(D)** が正解となる。意味だけではなく、文法的に可算か不可算かも見ておくことが名詞の語彙問題では重要だ。

The report / that Mr. Stevenson has submitted / does not only contain
　　　S　　　　　　　S　　　　　　　　V　　　　　　V¹
a technical description of the problem, but also (contain) a possible solution.
　　　　　　O　　　　　　　　　　　　　　　　V²　　　　O

□submit ～を提出する　□contain ～を含む　□possible 可能な　□solution 解決法

---

21. ★★★★☆

ご注文が効率的に処理されるように、注文書に必要事項をすべてご記入の上、同封の封筒でご返送ください。

(A) 動 ～を供給する ［過去分詞］
(B) 動 ～を処理する ［過去分詞］
(C) 動 ～を約束する ［過去分詞］
(D) 動 ～と言い張る ［過去分詞］

選択肢には意味の異なる動詞の過去分詞が並んでいる。空所を含む文の意味を取っていくと、「注文が効率的に……されるために、注文書に必要事項をすべてご記入の上返送を」となっており、空所には、「注文を効率的に進める」という意味が入ることがわかる。よって、**(B)** が正解となる。process には「（書類など）を（決まった方法で）処理する」という意味がある。

〈命令文〉
To ensure / that your order is processed efficiently , / please fill in the order form completely
to 不定詞 (副詞句)　　S　　　　　V　　　　　　　　　　　　　　V¹　　　O
and return it in the envelope provided.
　　V²　O

□ensure ～を確実にする　□efficiently 効率的に　□fill in ～に書き入れる　□completely すべて
□envelope provided 同封の封筒

---

 19. (D)　20. (D)　21. (B)

22. People on the mailing list of Hampshire Shopping Mall receive text alerts ------- new sales promotions begin.

(A) whenever
(B) therefore
(C) unless
(D) whatever

23. To satisfy all our customers, every cup of coffee at Williams Restaurant is prepared with gourmet beans ------- from Columbia.

(A) imports
(B) imported
(C) import
(D) importing

24. The White Tiger Football team ended its season with a remarkable winning record ------- even the most ambitious goal of the coaching staff.

(A) into
(B) excluding
(C) beyond
(D) though

22. ★★★☆☆

Hampshire ショッピングモールのメーリングリストにご登録の方には、新しいセールが始まるたびに文字によるお知らせが送信されます。

(A) ～するときはいつでも
(B) そのため
(C) ～でない限り
(D) 何が～でも

選択肢にはさまざまな副詞や接続表現が並んでいる。空所を含む文の意味を取っていくと、「メーリングリスト登録者には、新しい販売促進活動が始まる……、文字通知が送信される」となっており、空所には、活動が始まるごとに、始まる時はいつでも、といったような通知頻度に関する表現が入ることが考えられる。以上から、正解は **(A)**。それ以外の選択肢では、文意が上手く通らない。

People on the mailing list of Hampshire Shopping Mall receive text alerts /
　　S　　　　　　　　　　　　　　　　　　　　　　V　　　　O

whenever new sales promotions begin .
（副詞節［時］）　　　　S　　　　　　V

□mailing list メーリングリスト □text alert メールなどの文字による通知 □sales promotion 販売促進

---

23. ★★☆☆☆

すべてのお客様にご満足いただけるよう、Williams レストランではコロンビアから輸入した高級豆を使用し、一杯一杯コーヒーを淹れています。

(A) 動 ～を輸入する ［三人称単数現在形］
(B) ［過去分詞］
(C) ［原 形］
(D) ［現在分詞］

選択肢には動詞 import のさまざまな形が並んでいる。空所を含む箇所を見ると、「レストランではコロンビアから……高級豆が用意されている」となっていることから、「輸入された～」という、過去分詞を当てはめると文意が成立することがわかる。よって、正解は **(B)**。

To satisfy all our customers, / every cup of coffee at Williams Restaurant is prepared
to 不定詞（副詞句）　　　　　　　　S　　　　　　　　　　　　　　　　　V

with gourmet beans imported from Columbia.

□satisfy ～を満足させる □gourmet 高級な

---

24. ★★★☆☆

White Tiger フットボールチームは、コーチングスタッフの最も高望みした目標をも超える、驚くべき勝利数でシーズンを終えました。

(A) 前 ～の中に
(B) 前 ～を除いて
(C) 前 ～を超えて
(D) 前 ～を通って

選択肢には前置詞などが並んでいる。空所を含む箇所の意味を取っていくと、「フットボールチームは、コーチングスタッフの目標さえも……驚くべき勝利数でシーズンを終えた」とある。ここから、コーチが立てた目標さえも超える、という意味が入ることがわかる。よって、正解は **(C)** となる。

The White Tiger Football team ended its season with a remarkable winning record /
　　　　　S　　　　　　　　　　V　　　　O

beyond even the most ambitious goal of the coaching staff.

□remarkable 素晴らしい □winning record 勝利の記録 □ambitious 野心的な

---

 22. (A)　23. (B)　24. (C)

25. Kirt Motors Co. has been using Sheena Promotions to increase the company's ------- in foreign markets.

(A) recognized
(B) recognizing
(C) recognition
(D) recognize

26. To confirm how capable you are at solving problems, the recruiter will ask you for an example of the ------- you showed in a past project.

(A) revision
(B) initiative
(C) requirement
(D) suspension

27. Melies Inc. is celebrating after being announced as one of the firms to ------- a government contract on the new highway construction.

(A) reserve
(B) order
(C) secure
(D) record

25. ★★☆☆☆

Kirt Motors 社は、Sheena Promotions 社を利用して、海外市場での認知度を高めています。

(A) 動 〜を認める　過去分詞
(B) 現在分詞
(C) 名 認知
(D) 原形

> 選択肢には動詞 recognize が形を変えて並んでいる。空所の前後を見ると、空所前が所有格 company's、空所後が前置詞 in となっていることから、空所には名詞が入ることがわかる。以上から、正解は **(C)**。(B) を動名詞として捉えることもできるが、recognize は他動詞なので、目的語に相当する語が後ろにないと文法的に当てはめられない。

Kirt Motors Co. has been using Sheena Promotions /
<u>S</u>　　　　<u>V</u>　　　　　<u>O</u>

to increase the company's recognition in foreign markets.
to 不定詞（副詞句）

□foreign market 海外市場

----

26. ★★★★☆

あなたの問題解決能力を審査するため、採用担当者からは過去のプロジェクトで主導権を握って進めた事例をお尋ねします。

(A) 名 改訂
(B) 名 主導権
(C) 名 要件
(D) 名 中止

> 選択肢には意味の異なる名詞が並んでいる。空所を含む文の意味を見ると、「問題解決能力の確認のため、採用担当者からあなたに過去のプロジェクトで発揮した……のある事例を尋ねる」とある。ここから、空所には前向きな意味になる語が入ると考えられるので、**(B)** を入れると文意が成立する。(A) revision は文書の修正等を意味するため、ここでは文意に合わない。

To confirm how capable you are at solving problems, / the recruiter will ask you for an example
to 不定詞（副詞句）　　　　　　　　　　　　　　　　　　S　　　　V　　O

of the initiative / (that) you showed in a past project.
　　　　　　　　S　　V

□confirm 〜を確認する　□capable 能力のある　□solve problems 問題を解決する　□recruiter 採用担当者
□past 過去の

----

27. ★★★★☆

Melies 社は新しい幹線道路の建設において、政府との契約を獲得した企業の1つであることが報じられ、お祝いをしています。

(A) 動 〜を予約する
(B) 動 〜を注文する
(C) 動 〜を獲得する
(D) 動 〜を記録する

> 選択肢には意味の異なる動詞が並んでいる。空所を含む文の意味を見ると、「Melies 社は幹線道路建設において、政府からの契約を……した企業の1つとして発表されたことを受け、お祝いをしている」とある。お祝いをするということから、契約を得た、ということが考えられる。以上から、**(C)** が正解。secure には get というような意味もあると覚えておこう。

Melies Inc. is celebrating / after being announced as one of the firms /
　　　S　　　　　V　　　　　　（副詞句［時］）

to secure a government contract on the new highway construction.
to 不定詞（形容詞句）

□firm 会社　□secure 〜を確保する　□contract 契約　□highway construction 幹線道路の建設

 25. (C)　26. (B)　27. (C)

28. The boss ------- disagrees with his financial advisor about the company's growth potential.

(A) thoroughness
(B) thorough
(C) thoroughly
(D) most thorough

29. ------- slow wage growth in the last year, consumer confidence is stronger than experts previously expected.

(A) Despite
(B) Nonetheless
(C) Although
(D) So

30. The Fall Concert Series this year features musical performances by ------- of the finest bands in the region.

(A) little
(B) some
(C) any
(D) every

28. ★☆☆☆☆

会社の成長の可能性について、社長はファイナンシャル・アドバイザーと徹底して意見が合いません。

(A) 名 徹底
(B) 形 徹底的な
(C) 副 徹底的に
(D) 形 徹底的な（最上級）

🔍 選択肢には形容詞で「徹底的な」を意味する thorough が形を変えて並んでおり、空所は、主語の boss と述語動詞 disagree に挟まれている。ここから、空所は動詞を修飾する副詞が入ることがわかる。以上から、正解は **(C)**。文の構造を見抜くと、自然とどの箇所にどの品詞が入るかわかるので、構文の分析はしっかりしておこう。

🎧 The boss <u>thoroughly</u> <u>disagrees with</u> <u>his financial advisor</u> about the company's growth potential.
　　　S　　　　　　　　V　　　　　　　　O

✏️ □disagree with ～に反対する　□financial advisor ファイナンシャルアドバイザー　□growth potential 成長の可能性

---

29. ★★★☆☆

昨年は賃金が伸び悩んだにもかかわらず、消費者信頼感の強さは専門家の事前予想を上回っています。

(A) 前 ～にもかかわらず
(B) 副 それでもなお
(C) 接 ～だけれども
(D) 接 だから

🔍 選択肢には前置詞や副詞、接続語が並んでいる。空所は文頭にあり、その後に名詞句とカンマが来ている。ここから、名詞句を導くことができる前置詞の **(A)** が正解となる。「賃金が伸び悩んだにもかかわらず、消費者信頼感は強い」と文意も通じる。ほかの選択肢は名詞句を導くことができず、文法的に当てはめることができない。

🎧 Despite slow wage growth in the last year, / <u>consumer confidence</u> is stronger /
　～にもかかわらず（副詞句）　　　　　　　　　　　　S　　　　　　V　C
than experts previously expected.

✏️ □slow wage growth 賃金の伸び悩み　□consumer confidence 消費者の信頼感　□expert 専門家
□previously 事前に、過去に

---

30. ★★★☆☆

今年の秋のコンサートシリーズは、地元の優れたバンドによる演奏を呼び物としています。

(A) 名 わずか
(B) 名 いくらか
(C) 名 だれでも
(D) 形 あらゆる

🔍 選択肢には数を表す代名詞や形容表現が並んでいる。問題の文は肯定文で、空所前に前置詞 by、空所後には of the finest bands と、可算名詞の複数形が来ていることから、空所には「数あるバンドのいくつか」を意味する **(B)** を入れると正解になる。(A) は程度や量が少量であること、(D) は原則単数の名詞を修飾する形容詞用法しかないので文法的に当てはまらない。(C) は、主に否定文などで用いられることが多い。肯定文で用いた場合、「いくらでも」と数を規定しない意味合いになるため文意に合わない。

🎧 The Fall Concert Series this year features musical performances /
　　　　　S　　　　　　　　　　　V　　　　　　O
by some of the finest bands in the region.

✏️ □feature ～を呼び物にする　□fine 優秀な　□region 地元

🚩 **28. (C)　29. (A)　30. (B)**

1. While Mr. Oliver's job application is -------, we are looking for someone with an accounting qualification.

(A) impresses
(B) impression
(C) impressive
(D) impressively

2. ------- the environmental organization has limited funds, it has managed to put together a number of informative seminars.

(A) Despite
(B) Meanwhile
(C) Whether
(D) Although

3. The food stands which operate on Patrick Street must be at least twenty feet -------.

(A) apart
(B) between
(C) beyond
(D) far

1. ★★☆☆☆

Oliver さんの応募書類は印象的ですが、私たちは会計の資格を持つ人を探しています。

(A) 動 ～に印象を与える 〔三人称単数現在形〕
(B) 名 印象
(C) 形 印象的な
(D) 副 印象的に

選択肢には名詞 impression の派生語が並んでいる。空所を含む箇所を見ていくと、空所前が接続詞 While＋主語＋be 動詞となっており、空所後にはカンマがあることから、空所は主語と be 動詞を補う語、つまり第 2 文型 (SVC) の C が来ることがわかる。文法的には名詞と形容詞が入るが、(B) を入れるためには冠詞が必要なので、正解は **(C)** となる。

While Mr. Oliver's job application is impressive , /
(副詞節 [譲歩])　　　　　S　　　　V　　C

we are looking for someone with an accounting qualification.
　S　　V　　　　O

□job application 求人の応募 (書類)　□accounting qualification 会計の資格

---

2. ★★★☆☆

この環境保護団体の資金には限りがありますが、多くの有益なセミナーを開催してきました。

(A) 前 ～にもかかわらず
(B) 副 その一方で
(C) 接 ～かどうか
(D) 接 ～ではあるが

選択肢には前置詞や副詞、接続詞が並んでいる。次に空所を含む文の構造を見ると、カンマの前後に節があることがわかる。意味を取っていくと、「この団体の資金は限られている……、たくさんセミナーを開催してきた」とあり、お金が無いのにもかかわらずイベント開催をした、という逆接の意味になっていることがわかる。以上から、逆接の意味をもつ接続語の **(D)** が正解となる。(A) も逆接の意味があるが前置詞のため節を導くことはできない。

Although the environmental organization has limited funds , /
(副詞節 [譲歩])　　　　　　　　　　S　　　　V　　O

it has managed to put together a number of informative seminars.
S　　　V　　　　　　　　　　O

□environmental 環境の　□organization 団体、組織　□limited 限りがある　□fund 資金
□manage to *do* 何とかして～する　□put together ～を取りまとめる　□a number of 多くの　□informative 有益な

---

3. ★★★★☆

Patrick 大通りで営業する屋台は、少なくとも 20 フィート間隔で設置する必要があります。

(A) 副 互いに距離を隔てて
(B) 前 ～の間に
(C) 副 向こうに
(D) 副 遠くに

選択肢には意味の異なる副詞や前置詞が並んでいる。文の意味を取っていくと、「営業する屋台は、少なくとも 20 フィート……でなければならない」となっている。空所直前には 20 フィートという距離を表す語が来ているため、それぞれの屋台が 20 フィート離れている状態となれば文意が成立する。以上から、正解は **(A)**。apart は、ある一定の距離を持って離れた様子を表す副詞として機能している。(D) も「遠くに」という距離的な意味合いがあるが、ある地点からどれくらい遠いか、というニュアンスを含むため、ここでは不正解となる。

The food stands / which operate on Patrick Street /
　　　S　　　　　　S　　V

must be at least twenty feet apart.
　V　　　　　　C

□food stand 屋台　□at least 少なくとも

---

 1. (C)　2. (D)　3. (A)

4. Mr. McGuire, spokesman of Sammy Electronics, said that it will establish one manufacturing plant in Queensland and ------- in Perth by the end of this year.

(A) each other
(B) one another
(C) another
(D) other

5. When ------- the protective film from the screen, be careful not to scratch the glass.

(A) removes
(B) removing
(C) remove
(D) removed

6. To succeed in today's highly competitive environment where online reviews have real influence, manufacturers must focus on the ------- of their products.

(A) reliability
(B) dependence
(C) obligation
(D) determination

4. ★★★★☆

Sammy Electronics 社の広報担当者である McGuire 氏は、今年中にクイーンズランドとパースにそれぞれ 1 棟ずつ製造工場を設立する予定だと述べました。

(A) 互いに
(B) 互いに
(C) もう 1 つのもの
(D) ほかのもの

選択肢には数を表す代名詞表現などが並んでいる。空所を含む箇所の意味を取っていくと、「Sammy Electronics 社が、クイーンズランドに製造工場を 1 棟、そしてパースに……設立する」となっている。以上から、「クイーンズランドのほかのもう 1 つの工場」を意味する another を入れると文意が成立する。よって、正解は **(C)**。another は「あるもののほかにもう 1 つ」という場合に用いると覚えておこう。(A)、(B) は、それぞれが交互に作用しあっている状況に使用し、(D) は主にほかに複数ある場合に用いる。

Mr. McGuire, spokesman of Sammy Electronics, said / that it will establish
　　　S　　　　　　　　　S の同格　　　　　　　　V　　O　S　　　V
　　　　　　　　　　　　　　　　　　　　　　　　　　　　　　(that 節)

one manufacturing plant in Queensland and another in Perth by the end of this year.
　　　　　　O　　　　　　　　　　　　　　　　　　　　　O

□spokesman 広報担当者　□establish ～を設立する　□manufacturing plant 製造工場
□by the end of this year 今年の年末までに

---

5. ★★★☆☆

画面の保護フィルムをはがすときは、ガラスに傷をつけないように注意してください。

(A) 動 ～を取り除く　[三人称単数現在形]
(B) [現在分詞]
(C) [原　形]
(D) [過去分詞]

選択肢には動詞 remove が形を変えて並んでいる。空所を含む文の構造を見てみると、接続詞 when があり主語がなく、カンマを挟んで命令形となっている。ここから主節、従属節共通の主語 (you) が省略されていると考えて現在分詞を入れると、分詞構文となり、文法的にも文意的にも合う。以上より、正解は **(B)**。remove は他動詞であり空所後に目的語があるため、ここでは過去分詞を用いることはできないことから (D) は不正解。

When (you are) removing the protective film from the screen, /
　　　(副詞句 [時])

be careful not to scratch the glass.
　　　　　　V　　　　　　O

□protective film 保護フィルム　□screen 画面　□careful not to *do* ～しないように注意して
□scratch ～に傷をつける

---

6. ★★★★☆

オンラインレビューが実質的な影響力を持っている今日の厳しい競争環境で成功するためには、メーカーは自社製品の信頼性を重視しなければなりません。

(A) 名 信頼性
(B) 名 依存性
(C) 名 義務
(D) 名 決意

選択肢には意味の異なる名詞が並んでいる。空所を含む文の意味を取っていくと、「今日の厳しい競争環境で成功するために、メーカーは自社製品の……を重視する必要がある」となっている。成功するためにメーカーが自社製品について重視するものを選択肢から見ていき、**(A)** を入れると意味が通るため、これが正解。

To succeed in today's highly competitive environment / where online reviews have real influence,
to 不定詞 (副詞句)　　　　　　　　　　　　　　　　　　　　　　S　　　　V　　　O

manufacturers must focus on the reliability of their products.
　　　S　　　　　V　　　　　　　O

□highly 大いに　□competitive environment 競争環境　□online review オンラインレビュー
□real influence 実質的な影響力　□manufacturer 製造業者　□focus on ～に集中する

---

4. (C)　5. (B)　6. (A)

7. Special meals can be ------- for passengers with food allergies when notified in advance.

(A) collected
(B) aligned
(C) compensated
(D) arranged

8. Classroom assistants at Simane Art School perform many routine tasks ------- teachers can give more attention to the students.

(A) just as
(B) rather than
(C) so that
(D) as if

9. Applicants are asked to send official transcripts ------- their degree from an accredited educational institution.

(A) verified
(B) verification
(C) verifiable
(D) verifying

7. ★★★★☆

食物アレルギーをお持ちの乗客には、事前にお申し出いただければ、特別食の手配をいたします。

(A) 動 ～を収集する　[過去分詞]
(B) 動 ～を一列に並べる　[過去分詞]
(C) 動 ～を補償する　[過去分詞]
(D) 動 ～を手配する　[過去分詞]

選択肢には意味の異なる動詞の過去分詞が並んでいる。空所を含む文の意味を取っていくと、「アレルギーのある乗客には、事前に申し出があれば特別食が……されることが可能。」となっている。ここから、事前に連絡すれば特別食を手配することができる、とすれば文意が成立する。以上より、正解は **(D)**。本文の when 以降は主語が省略されているが、ここには、食事をサービスとして提供する会社など（例：when (the airline is) notified）がある、と捉えると文の構造を理解できる。

Special meals can be arranged for passengers with food allergies /
　　　　　S　　　　　V　　　　　　　　　O

when (the airline is) notified in advance.
（副詞句［時］）

□special meal 特別食　□food allergies 食物アレルギー　□notify ～に知らせる　□in advance 事前に

---

8. ★★★☆☆

Simane 芸術学校の教室アシスタントは、教師が生徒により多くの注意を払えるように、多くの日常業務をこなしています。

(A) ちょうど～のときに
(B) ～よりむしろ
(C) ～するように
(D) まるで～かのように

選択肢には意味の異なる接続表現などが並んでいる。空所を含む文の意味を取っていくと、「学校の教室アシスタントは、教師が生徒により多くの注意を払える……、多くの日常業務をこなしている」となっている。ここから空所は、教師が注意を払えるために、という目的となる〈so that S can V〉という形にすると文意が成立する。よって、正解は **(C)**。今回のように so that 構文があった場合は、文頭から意味を取って「アシスタントが業務をこなす➡そうすれば教師が注意を払える」と因果関係が成立するかどうかを考えて当てはめることもできる。

Classroom assistants at Simane Art School perform many routine tasks /
　　　　　S　　　　　　　　　　　　V　　　　　O

so that teachers can give more attention to the students.
（副詞節［目的］）S　　　　V　　　　C

□routine task 日常の業務　□give attention to ～に集中する

---

9. ★★★☆☆

応募者は、認定された教育機関の学位を証明する正式な成績証明書を送付することが求められています。

(A) 動 ～を実証する　[過去分詞]
(B) 名 実証
(C) 形 確認できる
(D) 動 [現在分詞]

選択肢には動詞 verify が形を変えた形や派生語が並んでいる。空所を含む文の意味を取っていくと、「応募者は、認定教育機関の学位を……成績証明書を送付することが求められている」となっている。空所前の部分で文が成り立っているため、空所を含む文後半が transcripts を修飾していると判断できる。以上より、their degree を目的語に取り transcripts を修飾できる現在分詞の **(D)** が正解となる。

Applicants are asked to send official transcripts verifying their degree from an accredited
　　　S　　　　V　　　　　　　O

educational institution.

□applicant 応募者　□official 正式な、公式な　□transcript 成績証明書　□degree 学位　□accredited 認定された
□educational institution 教育機関

---

 7. (D)　8. (C)　9. (D)

10. ------- next week, the municipal library will lend newly released books to users for six days only.

(A) As of
(B) At
(C) Behind
(D) Since

11. All the software programs you see on this Web site are now ------- free of charge for both commercial and non-commercial use.

(A) completely
(B) extremely
(C) exclusively
(D) continually

12. A store gift card will be sent to you upon ------- of your customer questionnaire.

(A) receive
(B) receiving
(C) recipient
(D) receipt

10. ★★★☆☆

来週から、市立図書館では新発売の本を 6 日間だけ
利用者に貸し出すことになりました。

(A) ～をもって（群前置詞）
(B) 前 ～に
(C) 前 ～より遅れて
(D) 前 ～以降

選択肢には前置詞や群前置詞が並んでいる。文の意味を取っていく
と、「来週……、市立図書館で新刊を貸し出す」となっていることか
ら、来週を起点として未来に対して行われる予定を意味する語が入ると
わかる。以上から、正解は **(A)**。as of は前置詞 1 語だと from と同義語
になる。(D) もある時点を起点とすることがあるが、主に過去の時点を起
点とし、完了形で用いられるためここでは不正解。

As of next week, / the municipal library will lend newly released books to users
～以降（副詞句）　　　　　　　S　　　　　　V　　　　　　　　　O
for six days only.

□municipal 市営の　□newly released 新刊の　□users 利用者

---

11. ★★★★☆

このウェブサイトにあるすべてのソフトウェアプ
ログラムは、現在、商用と非商用の両方で完全に無
償でご利用いただけます。

(A) 副 完全に
(B) 副 きわめて
(C) 副 独占的に
(D) 副 継続的に

選択肢には意味の異なる副詞が並んでいる。空所を含む箇所の意味
を取っていくと、「現在……無料」となっている。ここから、「完全に
無料」とすると文意が成立するため、正解は **(A)**。完全に無料という表現
である completely free of charge はコロケーション（語の組み合わ
せ）で覚えておくとよい。(D) は文中に now とあり、現時点での話をして
いるため、文脈に合わない。

All the software programs / (that) you see on this Web site / are now completely free of charge
　　　　S　　　　　　　　　　S　V　　　　　　　　V　　　　　　　　　　　C
for both commercial and non-commercial use.
　　　both A and B

□commercial and non-commercial use 商用と非商用

---

12. ★★★★☆

お客様アンケートにお答えいただいた方にギフト
カードをお送りいたします。

(A) 動 ～を受け取る
(B) 動名詞
(C) 名 受納者
(D) 名 受け取り

選択肢には動詞 receive の形を変えたものや派生語が並んでいる。
空所は前置詞と前置詞に挟まれているため、前置詞 upon に導かれ
る名詞が入ることがわかるので、(B)、(C)、(D) が候補として挙げられる。
まず (B) は receive が他動詞のため目的語を伴って動名詞にする必要が
あるが、空所直後が of なので文法的に合わない。次に、意味を取っていく
と、「アンケート（受領後に）ギフトカードを送る」と受領を意味する語を
入れると文意が成立する。以上から、正解は **(D)**。

A store gift card will be sent to you / upon receipt of your customer questionnaire.
　　　　S　　　　　　V　　　　　　　～するとすぐに（副詞句）

□upon (on) ～するとすぐに　□questionnaire アンケート

13. The reception party will begin at 6:30 P.M. and will be ------- by the opening remarks of the CEO, Todd Critcher.

(A) advanced
(B) followed
(C) finalized
(D) permitted

14. The president of Macro World Iron attributed the recent success in developing new alloys ------- its hard-working and dedicated employees.

(A) to
(B) for
(C) as
(D) by

15. Due to overwhelming customer demand, orders for new office equipment ------- take at least five business days to process.

(A) quickly
(B) totally
(C) specially
(D) generally

13. ★★★★☆

レセプションパーティーは午後6時30分から始まり、次にCEOのTodd Critcher氏が開会の挨拶する予定です。

(A) 動 ～を前に進める [過去分詞]
(B) 動 ～の後に続く [過去分詞]
(C) 動 ～を決定的にする [過去分詞]
(D) 動 ～を許す [過去分詞]

The reception party will begin at 6:30 P.M. and will be followed /
  S   V¹   V²
by the opening remarks of the CEO, Todd Critcher.

□reception party 懇親会 □follow ～の次にくる □opening remarks 開会の挨拶

---

14. ★★★★☆

Macro World Iron 社の社長は、最近の新合金の開発の成功は、勤勉で熱心な従業員によるものだと考えています。

(A) 前 ～に
(B) 前 ～のために
(C) 前 ～として
(D) 前 ～によって

The president of Macro World Iron attributed the recent success in developing new alloys
   S   V   O
to its hard-working and dedicated employees.

□attribute A to B AはBの結果だと考える □develop ～を開発する □alloy 合金 □hard-working 勤勉な □dedicated 熱心な

---

15. ★★★★☆

お客様の需要が非常に多いため、新しい事務機器の注文の処理には通常少なくとも5営業日かかります。

(A) 副 すぐに
(B) 副 全く
(C) 副 特別に
(D) 副 普通、通例

Due to overwhelming customer demand, / orders for new office equipment generally take
（前置詞句 [原因・理由]）   S   V
at least five business days / to process.
     O

□due to ～のため □overwhelming 圧倒的な □demand 需要 □business day 営業日

13. (B) 14. (A) 15. (D)

16. This year's distinguished service award went to an individual ------- volunteer work totaled more than 200 hours.

(A) whom
(B) what
(C) who
(D) whose

17. EBS Airlines, which operates out of Taipei, canceled more flights ------- any other small-scale international airline.

(A) as
(B) to
(C) while
(D) than

18. Mr. Anderson, who ------- works part-time from 2 to 6 P.M. at the local public library, used to be a well-known graphic artist.

(A) precisely
(B) currently
(C) commonly
(D) academically

16. ★★★★☆

今年の功労賞は、ボランティア活動の合計が200時間以上に達した個人の方に授与されました。

(A) 目的格
(B) ～ (する) もの
(C) 主格
(D) 所有格

選択肢には関係代名詞が並んでいる。空所を含む文の構造を見ていくと、空所前には空所の先行詞となる individual があり、空所後には複合名詞 volunteer work、従属節の述語動詞 totaled がある。ここから、所有格の関係詞を入れると、「ボランティア活動の合計が200時間以上の個人」と文意が成立することがわかる。以上から、正解は **(D)**。

This year's distinguished service award went to an individual / whose volunteer work
　　　　　　　　S　　　　　　　　　　　　V　　　　O　　　　　　　　　S

totaled more than 200 hours.
　V　　　　　O

□distinguished service award 功労賞　□individual 個人、人　□volunteer work ボランティア活動
□total 合計～となる

---

17. ★★☆☆☆

台北を拠点とする EBS 航空は、ほかのどの小規模な国際航空会社よりも多くのフライトをキャンセルしました。

(A) 前 ～として
(B) 前 ～へ
(C) 接 ～する間に
(D) 前 ～よりも

選択肢には前置詞、接続詞が並んでいる。空所前の more flights から、フライトの数が何かと比べて多いことがわかり、空所後の any other ... airline (ほかのどの航空会社)、がその比較対象を指していると考えられる。よって、空所は「～より多い」という意味となる前置詞を入れると文意が成立する。以上より、正解は **(D)**。

EBS Airlines, / which operates out of Taipei, / canceled more flights
　　S　　　　　　S　　　V　　　　　O　　　　　　　V　　　　　O

than any other small-scale international airline.

□operate out of ～を拠点として活動する　□small-scale 小規模の

---

18. ★★☆☆☆

現在、地元の公立図書館で午後2時から6時までアルバイトをしている Anderson さんは、以前は有名なグラフィックアーティストだったそうです。

(A) 副 正確に
(B) 副 現在
(C) 副 一般に
(D) 副 学問的に

選択肢には異なる副詞が並んでいる。空所前に関係詞 who があるので、空所を含む関係詞節の部分は、Anderson さんについて書かれていることがわかる。who 以下の意味を取ると、「公立図書館でアルバイトをしている」という現在のことが書かれているため、**(B)** を入れると文意が通る。

Mr. Anderson, / who currently works part-time from 2 to 6 P.M. at the local public library,
　　S　　　　　　S　　　　　　　　V

used to be a well-known graphic artist.
　　V　　　　　　　　C

□part-time パートタイムで　□well-known 有名な　□graphic artist グラフィックアーティスト

---

16. (D)　17. (D)　18. (B)

19. Beginning next year, ------- to *Trinity Monthly Magazine* may sometimes include special offers from trusted partner companies.

(A) subscribe
(B) subscribed
(C) subscriber
(D) subscriptions

20. Viet-Jet Air's ------- is to make international air travel accessible to a large number of people through low fares.

(A) structure
(B) inquiry
(C) transfer
(D) objective

21. ------- did the items arrive two weeks late, but they also were in a severely damaged condition.

(A) Hardly
(B) Never
(C) Neither
(D) Not only

19. ★★★☆☆

来年から、Trinity Monthly Magazine を定期購読すると、信頼できるパートナー企業の特典をもらえる場合があります。

(A) 動 ～を定期購読する 　原形
(B) 過去分詞
(C) 名 購読者
(D) 名 定期購読

選択肢には動詞 subscribe が形を変えたものや派生語が並んでいる。空所を含む文の構造を見ると、------- to Trinity Monthly Magazine / may sometimes include /... で、空所は主語になるため、名詞が入ることがわかる。選択肢で名詞は (C) と (D) があるが、意味を取ると、「……には特典を含む」とあることから、特典を含むものは定期購読そのものであるので、正解は (D) となる。(C) は可算名詞でもあるため、文法的にも当てはめることはできない。

Beginning next year, / subscriptions to *Trinity Monthly Magazine* may sometimes include
　　　　　　　　　　　　　　S　　　　　　　　　　　　　　　　　　　　　V

special offers from trusted partner companies.
　　O

□trusted 信頼できる

20. ★★★☆☆

Viet-Jet Air 社の目標は、安い運賃によって海外旅行を多くの人にとって身近なものにすることです。

(A) 名 構造
(B) 名 調査
(C) 名 移動
(D) 名 目標

選択肢には意味の異なる名詞が並んでいる。空所を含む箇所の意味を取っていくと、「Viet-Jet Air 社の……は、多くの人にとって海外旅行が身近なものになるようにすることだ」となっている。ここから、将来に向けて達成すべき目的、目標のような語句が適当だと考えられる。以上より、正解は (D)。

Viet-Jet Air's objective is to make international air travel accessible
　　　S　　　　　　　V　　　　　　　　　　　　　C

to a large number of people through low fares.

□air travel 空の旅　□accessible to ～にとって身近な　□a large number of 大多数の　□low fare 低価格運賃

21. ★☆☆☆☆

商品の到着が 2 週間遅れただけでなく、ひどく破損した状態でした。

(A) 副 ほとんど～ない
(B) 副 決して～ない
(C) どちらも～ない
(D) ～だけでなく

選択肢には意味の異なる副詞や副詞表現が並んでいる。文の構造を見ると、カンマを挟み、"but they also ..." という表現がある。ここから、Not only 入れ、空所を含む箇所の意味を取っていくと、「商品の遅延だけではなく、破損も」となり、文意が成立する。以上より、正解は (D)。慣用表現として、Not only A, but also B という形を見抜けるようにしていこう。

Not only did the items arrive two weeks late, /
　　　　　　　S　　　 V

but they also were in a severely damaged condition.
　　　S　　　 V　　　　　　C

□severely damaged ひどく破損した

19. (D)　20. (D)　21. (D)

83

22. Before the merger deal was announced to the public, Kissmer Services ------- redesigning the company logo to reflect its new name, Kissmer-Musk, Inc.

(A) had begun
(B) will begin
(C) begins
(D) having begun

23. A government commission will be set up tasked with finding ways to minimize the time it takes ------- from economic recessions.

(A) to recover
(B) will recover
(C) be recovered
(D) has recovered

24. ------- other employees, front desk clerk Katie Weinberg has worked at the Joey Inn for more than ten years.

(A) Unlike
(B) Rather
(C) Similarly
(D) Altogether

22. ★★★★☆

この合併が公に発表される前から、Kissmer Services 社は、会社ロゴを新しい社名である Kissmer-Musk 社のロゴにするため、デザインの変更に取り掛かっていました。

(A) 動 ～を始める 　過去完了形
(B) 　未来表現
(C) 　三人称単数現在形
(D) 　現在完了形

PART 5

選択肢には動詞 begin が時制を変えて並んでいる。本文はカンマ前が、「この合併が公に発表された過去の時点よりも前に」となっていることから、カンマ以降は過去の時点より前の時制となることがわかる。次にカンマ以降は主語が Kissmer Services、目的語が redesigning the company なので、述語動詞が空所だとわかる。以上から、過去よりの前の時制、つまり過去完了形を当てはめると文意が成立するため、正解は **(A)**。

Before the merger deal was announced to the public, / Kissmer Services had begun
（副詞節【時】）　S　　　　　V　　　　　　　　　　　　　S　　　　　　　V

redesigning the company logo / to reflect its new name, / Kissmer-Musk, Inc.
　　　　　O　　　　　　　to 不定詞（副詞句）　　　←同格のカンマ

□merger deal 合併　□to the public 公に　□redesign ～のデザインを変更する　□company logo 会社のロゴ
□reflect ～を反映する

---

23. ★★★☆☆

景気後退からの回復にかかる時間を最小限にする方法を見つけることを任務とする政府委員会が設置されます。

(A) 動 回復する 　to 不定詞
(B) 　未来表現
(C) 動 ～を取り戻す 　受動態
(D) 　現在完了形

選択肢には動詞 recover が形を変えて並んでいる。空所を含む意味を取っていくと、「景気後退から……かかる時間を最小限にする方法」となっており、副詞句の不定詞として、「回復するために」とすると、文意が成立する。以上より、正解は **(A)**。この問題は、空所直前の it takes が the time を修飾している、という構造を理解して意味を取らないと不定詞が入ると判断するのが難しいので、しっかり構造を見抜いて解くようにしよう。

A government commission will be set up / tasked with finding ways to minimize the time /
　　　　　　S　　　　　　　　　V

it takes to recover from economic recessions.
time を修飾（形容詞節）

□commission 委員会　□set up ～を設置する　□task ～に任務を課す　□minimize ～を最小限にする
□economic recession 景気後退

---

24. ★★★☆☆

ほかの従業員とは違って、フロント係の Katie Weinberg さんは、Joey ホテルで 10 年以上働いてきました。

(A) 前 ～とは異なり
(B) 副 むしろ
(C) 副 同様に
(D) 副 全体で

選択肢には前置詞や副詞が並んでいる。空所を含む文の意味を取っていくと、「ほかの従業員……、Katie Weinberg さんは、Joey ホテルで 10 年以上働いてきた」となっている。つまり、ほかの従業員と Katie さんを比較したような表現が入ることが考えられる。ここから、「～のようではなく」と比較するような意味を持つ前置詞を入れると文意が成立する。以上より、正解は **(A)**。

Unlike other employees, / front desk clerk Katie Weinberg has worked
～と違って（副詞句）　　　　　S　　　　　　　S の補足説明　　　V

at the Joey Inn for more than ten years.

□front desk clerk フロントデスクの係員

---

 22. (A)　23. (A)　24. (A)

TEST 4

25. Mr. Simon was assigned to ------- the emergency exits during the next building maintenance.

(A) admit
(B) guarantee
(C) inspect
(D) extinguish

26. Every moment on an Addam Elegance Cruise is filled with ------- onboard events and activities.

(A) reimbursed
(B) amused
(C) stimulating
(D) exchanging

27. Hankins Studio spent more than ------- to enhance the quality of its recent design project, and the client was completely satisfied.

(A) particular
(B) ready
(C) probable
(D) usual

25. ★★★☆☆

Simon 氏は、次回のビルメンテナンスの際に非常口の点検をすることになりました。

(A) 動 ～を認める
(B) 動 ～を保証する
(C) 動 ～を点検する
(D) 動 ～を消す

選択肢には意味の異なる動詞が並んでいる。空所を含む文の意味を取っていくと、「Simon 氏は、次回のビルメンテナンスの際に非常口を……する」となっている。つまり、メンテナンスの際に行うこと、が問われているため、空所は点検を意味する (C) が入る。

Mr. Simon was assigned to inspect the emergency exits /
　　S　　　　V　　　　　　　O

during the next building maintenance.
～の間（副詞句）

□assign ～に割り当てる　□emergency exit 非常口

26. ★★★☆☆

Addam Elegance クルーズでのひとときは、刺激的な船内イベントやアクティビティで満たされています。

(A) 動 ～を払い戻す　過去分詞
(B) 動 ～をおもしろがらせる　過去分詞
(C) 動 ～を刺激する　現在分詞
(D) 動 ～を交換する　現在分詞

選択肢には意味の異なる動詞の現在分詞、過去分詞が並んでいる。空所は前置詞と複合名詞に挟まれているため、onboard event を修飾する語が入ることがわかる。これを踏まえて空所を含む意味を取っていくと、「クルーズ船でのひとときは、……船内イベントやアクティビティで満たされている」となっている。以上から最も文意が通る (C) が正解。(B) は「おもしろがった」対象、つまり、人を対象にした場合に用いる。amusing なら正解となった。

Every moment on an Addam Elegance Cruise is filled with
　　S　　　　　　　　　　　　　　　　　　　V

stimulating onboard events and activities.
　　　　　　　　　　O

□every moment すべての時間　□filled with ～で満たされる　□onboard 乗り物の中の

27. ★★★☆☆

Hankins Studio は、最近のデザインプロジェクトには、品質を高めるために通常より多くの費用をかけたので、顧客はとても満足しました。

(A) 形 特定の
(B) 形 用意のできた
(C) 形 見込みのある
(D) 形 通常の

選択肢には意味の異なる形容詞が並んでいる。空所を含む箇所の意味を取っていくと、「Hankins Studio は、品質を高めるために……より多くの費用をかけており、」となっているため、どういう状態よりお金をかけているか、というところがポイントとなっている。ここから、選択肢の中で「通常」という対象になる意味を入れると文意が通じる。以上より、正解は (D)。

Hankins Studio spent more than usual / to enhance the quality of its recent design project, /
　　S　　　　V　　　　　　　　　　　to 不定詞（副詞句）

and the client was completely satisfied.
　　S　　　V　　　　　C

□enhance ～を高める、強化する　□completely satisfied すっかり満足して

 25. (C)　26. (C)　27. (D)

28. In spite of the clear need to focus on long-term sustainability, most companies have been ------- concerned with short-term profits.

(A) excessive
(B) excess
(C) excessively
(D) excesses

29. Based on safety laws, green neon exit signs should be installed ------- every door of the movie theater.

(A) up
(B) until
(C) along
(D) above

30. ------- it may be difficult to avoid natural disasters such as earthquakes, the damage can be minimized by thorough preparation.

(A) Despite
(B) Since
(C) While
(D) However

28. ★☆☆☆☆

長期的な持続可能性を重視する必要があることは明らかであるにもかかわらず、多くの企業は短期的な利益に過度にこだわってきました。

(A) 形 過度の
(B) 名 過度であること
(C) 副 過度に
(D) 名 過度な行為（複数形）

選択肢には形容詞 excessive の派生語が並んでいる。空所は be 動詞と完了形の過去分詞の間に挟まれていることから、この述語動詞を修飾する副詞が入ることがわかる。以上より、正解は **(C)**。動詞を形容するのは副詞しかないため、文の構造を素早く把握してスピードを持って正解できるようになろう。

In spite of the clear need / to focus on long-term sustainability, /
　　〜にもかかわらず（副詞句）　　　to 不定詞（形容詞句）

most companies have been excessively concerned with short-term profits.
　　　　S　　　　　　　　　　V　　　　　　　　　　　　　　O

□in spite of 〜にもかかわらず　□clear need 明らかな必要性　□long-term 長期の　□sustainability 持続可能性
□concerned with 〜に関心を持つ　□short-term 短期の　□profit 利益

---

29. ★★★★★

安全法に基づき、映画館にあるすべてのドアの上に緑色のネオンの出口標識を設置する必要があります。

(A) 前 〜の上へ
(B) 前 〜になるまで
(C) 前 〜に沿って
(D) 前 〜より上に

選択肢には前置詞が並んでいる。空所を含む文の意味を取っていくと、「映画館にあるすべてのドア……緑色のネオンの出口標識が設置される必要がある」となっているため、ドアに対して上の位置に、という意味が来ると文意が成立する。以上より、正解は **(D)**。(A) は位置としての上ではなく、上昇しているイメージがあるため、ニュアンス的に合わない。(C) の場合は、ドアに沿って取り付けるイメージとなるため、これも文意に合わない。

Based on safety laws, / green neon exit signs should be installed
　　〜に基づき（副詞句）　　　　　　　S　　　　　　　　　　V

above every door of the movie theater.

---

30. ★★★★☆

地震などの自然災害を避けることは難しいかもしれませんが、十分な備えにより被害を最小限に抑えることはできます。

(A) 前 〜にもかかわらず
(B) 接 〜であるから
(C) 接 〜であるが
(D) 副 どんなに〜でも（接続副詞）

選択肢には前置詞や接続詞などが並んでいる。空所を含む文の意味を取っていくと、「地震などの自然災害を避けることは難しいかもしれない……、十分な準備により被害を最小限に抑えられる」となっている。ここから、「〜かもしれないが」と逆接の意味を持つ接続詞が入ると文意が成立する。以上より、正解は **(C)**。(A) も逆接の意味を持つが、前置詞のため節を導くことはできない。(D) は節を導いて、「たとえどれだけ〜しても」という意味の副詞節になれるが、However＋形容詞＋SV という語順でなければ文法的に当てはめることはできないため不正解。

While it may be difficult to avoid natural disasters such as earthquakes, /
　　仮S　V　　C　　　　　　　　　　　　真S
（副詞節［譲歩］）

the damage can be minimized by thorough preparation.
　　S　　　　　V

□avoid 〜を避ける　□natural disaster 自然災害　□such as 〜のような　□earthquake 地震
□minimize 〜を最小化する　□thorough 徹底的な、入念な　□preparation 準備

 28. (C)　29. (D)　30. (C)

1回目
2回目
3回目

1. The purpose of today's presentation is to show how ------- our advertising campaigns perform.

(A) effect
(B) effective
(C) effectively
(D) effectiveness

1回目
2回目
3回目

2. Any ------- payments must be received within two weeks of initial notice.

(A) prominent
(B) extraordinary
(C) tremendous
(D) outstanding

1回目
2回目
3回目

3. *Siobhan Magazine*'s revised guide to Prague has caused some confusion ------- the readers due to some wrong information.

(A) among
(B) after
(C) against
(D) besides

1. ★★★☆☆

本日のプレゼンの目的は、当社の広告キャンペーンがいかに効果的であるかを示すことです。

(A) 名 効果
(B) 形 効果のある
(C) 副 効果的に
(D) 名 効果のあること

選択肢には名詞 effect の派生語が並んでいる。空所を含む箇所を見ていくと、空所は to 不定詞 show の目的語である how 以下の名詞節の中にあることがわかる。空所以下を見てみると、SV と第 1 文型の節として完結しているので、空所はこの節を修飾する副詞が入る。以上から、正解は **(C)**。how＋形容詞(もしくは副詞)＋SV … の形の名詞節は、SV … の形を見て解くことが重要だ。また、ここでの perform は自動詞として使われていることにも注目しておこう。

The purpose of today's presentation is to show /
　　　　　　　S　　　　　　　　　　　V　　C
how effectively our advertising campaigns perform.
show の目的語(名詞節)　　　　　　　S　　　　　　V

□advertising campaign 広告キャンペーン

---

2. ★★★★☆

未払い金がある場合は、その最初の通知から 2 週間以内にお支払いください。

(A) 形 目立った
(B) 形 並外れた
(C) 形 巨大な
(D) 形 未払いの

選択肢には意味の異なる形容詞が並んでいる。空所を含む文の意味を見ていくと、「いかなる……支払いは、最初の通知から 2 週間以内に受領されていなくてはいけない」とあるため、この支払いは期限を要するもの、ということがわかる。以上より、選択肢で文意が成立するものは **(D)**。outstanding は形容詞で「目立つ、際立つ」の意味以外に「(支払いが)未払いである」という意味も持つ。

Any outstanding payments must be received within two weeks of initial notice.
　　　　　　　S　　　　　　　V

□initial notice 最初の通知

---

3. ★★★☆☆

Siobhan Magazine のプラハのガイドの改訂版に、一部誤った情報があったため、読者が混乱しています。

(A) 前 ～の中に(含まれて)
(B) 前 ～の後に
(C) 前 ～に反対して
(D) 前 ～のほかに

選択肢にはさまざまな前置詞が並んでいる。空所を含む文の意味を見ていくと、「ガイド改訂版は、一部誤った情報により、読者……混乱を引き起こしていた」という意味になっており、「読者」と「混乱」をつなげる前置詞が必要となる。ここから、「読者間での混乱」となる **(A)** を入れると文意が成立する。among は明確な人々など、可算名詞間で何かあった場合に用いることができる。

Siobhan Magazine's revised guide to Prague has caused some confusion
　　　　　　　S　　　　　　　　　　　　　　　　V　　　　O
among the readers / due to some wrong information.
　　　　　　～が原因で(前置詞句)

□revise ～を修正(改定)する

 1. (C) 2. (D) 3. (A)

4. If the items you purchased was defective, we will either send you a new one or refund you the ------- of the item.

(A) worthlessness
(B) fee
(C) fare
(D) value

5. Vicksburg Design Firm stated that it will ------- open a new branch office in Cleveland.

(A) soon
(B) recently
(C) once
(D) newly

6. The sales team event will be ------- until Wednesday afternoon at 5:00 in Indigo Banquet Hall.

(A) abbreviated
(B) postponed
(C) terminated
(D) scheduled

4. ★★★☆☆

万一、ご購入いただいた商品に不具合があった場合は、新しい商品をお送りするか、商品代金を返金いたします。

(A) 名 無価値
(B) 名 料金
(C) 名 運賃
(D) 名 価値

選択肢にはさまざまな名詞が並んでいる。空所を含む文の意味を見ていくと、「購入した商品に不具合があった場合、新品を送るか、商品の……に見合った返金をする」となっている。ここから、商品の価値に見合った返金、という文意が成立する **(D)** が正解。value は商品そのものの値打ち、金額的な価値を表す。

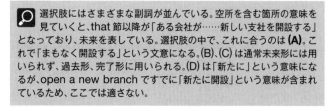

If the items (that) you purchased was defective, / we will either send you a new one /
（副詞節［条件］）　S　　　　　V　　C　　S　　　　V　O¹　O²
or (we) refund you the value of the item.
　　　V　O¹　　　O²

 □defective 不具合がある　□refund …に〜を払い戻す

---

5. ★★★☆☆

Vicksburg Design Firm 社は、近々クリーブランドに新しい支社を開設すると発表しました。

(A) 副 近いうちに
(B) 副 近ごろ
(C) 副 かつて
(D) 副 新しく

選択肢にはさまざまな副詞が並んでいる。空所を含む箇所の意味を見ていくと、that 節以降が「ある会社が……新しい支社を開設する」となっており、未来を表している。選択肢の中で、これに合うのは **(A)**。これで「まもなく開設する」という文意になる。(B)、(C) は通常未来形には用いられず、過去形、完了形に用いられる。(D) は「新たに」という意味になるが、open a new branch ですでに「新たに開設」という意味が含まれているため、ここでは適さない。

Vicksburg Design Firm stated / that it will soon open a new branch office in Cleveland.
　　　S　　　　　　V　O　S　　V　　　　　　O
　　　　　　　　　　　（that 節）

 □state 〜と述べる

---

6. ★★★☆☆

営業チームのイベントは、水曜日の午後 5 時から、Indigo Banquet Hall に延期されます。

(A) 動 〜を短縮する ［過去分詞］
(B) 動 〜を延期する ［過去分詞］
(C) 動 〜を終わらせる ［過去分詞］
(D) 動 〜を予定する ［過去分詞］

選択肢にはさまざまな動詞の過去分詞が並んでいる。空所を含む文の意味を見ていくと、「営業チームのイベントは、水曜日の午後 5 時まで……されることになった」とあるため、今の時点から水曜の午後 5 時まで継続している状況を表す動詞が来ることがわかる。この条件を満たすのは **(B)**。予定、イベントの類だと (C)、(D) も考えられるが、この問題のポイントは、前置詞 until が「ある一定期間までの継続性」を表しているところなので、その継続性を表すことのできる動詞を選ぶことがポイントとなる。

The sales team event will be postponed / until Wednesday afternoon at 5:00 in Indigo
　　S　　　　　V　　　　〜まで (副詞句)
Banquet Hall.

---

 4. (D)　5. (A)　6. (B)

7. In spite of the takeover, the new management has decided to ------- the former company's production line.

(A) practice
(B) persist
(C) cooperate
(D) retain

8. Waterfront Purifier Co. strongly recommends its customers to get their filters cleaned -------.

(A) frequently
(B) frequent
(C) frequency
(D) frequencies

9. Johnson Theater Group's ------- performances call attention to important social issues currently facing the people of this country.

(A) innovator
(B) innovative
(C) innovation
(D) innovated

7. ★★★☆☆

企業買収にもかかわらず、新たな経営陣は旧会社の生産ラインを維持することを決めました。

(A) 動 ～を実行する
(B) 動 言い張る
(C) 動 協力する
(D) 動 ～を保持する

選択肢には動詞が並んでいる。decide to＋空所という形であることから、不定詞を構成する部分であることがわかる。空所を含む文の意味を見ていくと、「買収にもかかわらず、新経営陣は旧会社の生産ラインを……することを決めた」とあるため、買収した旧会社のラインを引き続き保有、維持する、となると文意が成立する。以上より、正解は **(D)**。(A) は意味が通らず、(B)、(C) は自動詞で直接目的語を取ることができないため当てはまらない。

In spite of the takeover, / the new management has decided to retain
～にもかかわらず (副詞句)　　　　S　　　　　　　V

the former company's production line.
　　　　　　O

□in spite of ～にもかかわらず　□takeover 企業買収　□management 経営陣　□former 前の、以前の
□production line 生産ライン

---

8. ★★☆☆☆

Waterfront Purifier 株式会社では、お客様にこまめなフィルタークリーニングを強くお勧めしています。

(A) 副 頻繁に
(B) 形 頻繁な
(C) 名 頻度
(D) 名 頻度 (複数形)

選択肢には frequent の派生語が並んでいる。空所を含む文の構造を見ると、空所は不定詞以降の get (V) their filters (O) cleaned (C) という 5 文型が成立した後にあり、文自体が完成されていることがわかる。以上より、空所はこの部分を修飾する副詞の **(A)** が正解。空所がなくても文の構造が完全である場合は、副詞が入ることが多いと押さえておこう。

Waterfront Purifier Co. strongly recommends its customers to get their filters cleaned frequently.
　　　　　S　　　　　　　　　　　　　V　　　　　O　　　　　　　　　　C

□get＋O＋過去分詞　O を～してもらう

---

9. ★★★☆☆

Johnson Theater Group の革新的なパフォーマンスは、現在この国の人々が直面している重要な社会問題に注目を集めるものです。

(A) 名 革新者
(B) 形 革新的な
(C) 名 革新
(D) 動 ～を取り入れる 〔過去分詞〕

選択肢には innovate の派生語が並んでいる。空所前後の構造を見ると、所有格＋空所＋名詞となっており、空所はこの名詞を修飾することがわかる。以上から、形容詞に相当する (B) または (D) が入ると考えられるが、意味を考えると、「革新的な」パフォーマンスとなり、文意が成立する **(B)** が正解とわかる。(D) は、The performances innovated by Johnson Theater Group (～によって導入されたパフォーマンス) のように語順を変えないと意味が通じない。

Johnson Theater Group's innovative performances call attention to
　　　　　　　　S　　　　　　　　　　　　　V

important social issues / currently facing the people of this country.
　　　　O　　　　　　　　　(形容詞句)

□call attention to ～に注意を促す　□social issue 社会問題　□face ～に直面する

 7. (D)　8. (A)　9. (B)

10. Our expenses policy requires truck drivers to submit road toll receipts ------- were issued out of state.

(A) whether
(B) that
(C) if
(D) what

11. ------- surpassed the quarterly goal for lumber sales, all employees in Randy Harper's sales department received a bonus check.

(A) Having
(B) To have
(C) Being
(D) To be

12. Drysdale's Interior shelving units need to be fully assembled ------- delivery at your retail branch.

(A) next
(B) afterward
(C) about
(D) upon

10. ★★★☆☆

当社の経費規定では、トラックの運転手は州外で発行された道路通行料の領収書を提出しなければなりません。

(A) 接 ～かどうか
(B) that（関係詞）
(C) 接 もし～ならば
(D) what（関係詞）

選択肢には接続詞、関係詞が並んでいる。空所後は be 動詞＋過去分詞で受動態となっており、主語がないことがわかる。次に空所前が複合名詞（road toll receipts）となっていることから、これを先行詞とした主格の関係代名詞を入れると、「州外で発行された領収書」となり、文意が成立する。以上から、**(B)** が正解。(A)、(C) の接続詞は、空所後に主語のみ省略された形で be 動詞＋過去分詞を残すことはできないため当てはめられない。(D) も関係詞だが、what＝things which であり、この語はすでに先行詞が含まれている意味合いを持つため、不正解。

Our expenses policy requires truck drivers to submit road toll receipts / that were issued
      S   V   O   C   S   V

out of state .

□expenses policy 経費規定　□require …に～を要求する　□toll 通行料金　□receipt 領収書
□issue ～を発行する　□out of state 州外で

---

11. ★★★☆☆

木材の売り上げが四半期の目標を上回ったため、Randy Harper 社の営業部門の全従業員にボーナス小切手が贈られました。

(A) 動 have ［現在分詞］
(B) 動 have ［to 不定詞］
(C) 動 be ［現在分詞］
(D) 動 be ［to 不定詞］

選択肢には一般動詞 have、be 動詞の形を変えたものが並んでいる。空所は文頭にあり、文中にカンマ、その後ろに節が並んでいるため、カンマ以前は接続表現の意味合いを含むものだとわかる。次に文の意味を見ていくと、「木材の販売で四半期目標を上回った……、営業部門の全従業員はボーナスを受け取った」となっており、空所を含むカンマ以前の表現の時制が過去の事なので、因果関係が成立しているとわかる。以上から、理由を表し、かつ過去の事象として、surpassed the quarterly goal を導く、完了形の分詞構文となる **(A)** が正解となる。(C) も分詞構文となるが、動詞 surpassed は目的語をすでに伴っているため文法的に当てはめられない。

Having surpassed the quarterly goal for lumber sales, /
分詞構文（副詞句）

all employees in Randy Harper's sales department received a bonus check.
         S   V   O

□surpass ～を超える、上回る　□quarterly 四半期の　□lumber 木材　□bonus check 賞与の小切手

---

12. ★★★☆☆

Drysdale 社のインテリアシェルフユニットは、小売店に納品され次第、組み立ててしまう必要があります。

(A) 形 次の
(B) 副 その後に
(C) 前 ～について
(D) 前 ～と同時に

選択肢にはさまざまな品詞が並んでいる。空所を含む文の意味を取ると、「本ユニットは、納品……組み立てる必要がある」となっている。ここから、納品と組立についてのタイミングに関することが問われていることがわかる。以上より、**(D)** が正解。(A) だと、次回納品という、納品自体の順番を意味するため、ここでは不正解となる。

Drysdale's Interior shelving units need to be fully assembled /
                 S   V

upon delivery at your retail branch.
（副詞句）

□shelving unit 棚一式　□fully 完全に　□assemble ～を組み立てる　□retail 小売店　□branch 支店

---

 10. (B)　11. (A)　12. (D)

13. According to our new policy, thirty hours of training in machine operation is a ------- for new product assemblers at Butterfly Electronics.

(A) requirement
(B) require
(C) requiring
(D) required

14. The municipal housing authority announced that limited financial ------- would be given to first-time home buyers.

(A) assistance
(B) division
(C) association
(D) statement

15. A late fee is ------- for books and magazines returned after the date indicated on your library card.

(A) allotted
(B) gratified
(C) imposed
(D) dismissed

13. ★★☆☆☆

新しい方針では、Butterfly Electronics 社の新製品の組み立て担当者は、30 時間の機械操作のトレーニングを受けることが義務付けられています。

(A) 名 必要条件
(B) 動 ～を要求する　原形
(C) 現在分詞
(D) 過去分詞

選択肢には名詞 requirement と動詞 require の形を変えたものが並んでいる。空所前後は、冠詞＋空所＋前置詞となっているため、空所には名詞が入ることがわかる。以上より、正解は **(A)**。(C) は動名詞としても考えられるが、この動詞は他動詞の性質を持つため、目的語を伴わないと当てはめることができないので、ここでは不正解。

According to our new policy, / thirty hours of training in machine operation is a requirement /
～によると（副詞句）　　　　　　　　　　　S　　　　　　　　　　　　　　　　　V　　C
for new product assemblers at Butterfly Electronics.

□according to ～によると　□policy 方針　□machine operation 機械操作　□assembler 組み立て担当者

---

14. ★★★☆☆

市の住宅局は、初めて住宅を購入する人に対して、わずかな資金援助を行うと発表しました。

(A) 名 援助
(B) 名 部門
(C) 名 協会
(D) 名 取引明細

選択肢にはさまざまな意味の名詞が並んでいる。空所は that 節内にあり、その意味を見ていくと、「資金……が初めて住宅を購入する人に与えられる」とある。購入する人に与えられるものと考え、「支援・援助」という意味の **(A)** を入れると文意が成立する。(D) は financial statement で「財務諸表」という表現となるが、意味的に合わないため不正解。

The municipal housing authority announced / that limited financial assistance
　　　　　　　　S　　　　　　　　　　V　　O (that 節)　　　S
would be given to first-time home buyers.
　　V　　　　　　　　O

□municipal 市の　□housing authority 住宅局　□limited 限られた　□financial 財政の
□first-time（体験などが）初めての～

---

15. ★★★☆☆

図書カードに記載された期日より後に返却された本や雑誌には延滞料が課せられます。

(A) 動 ～を割り当てる　過去分詞
(B) 動 ～を喜ばせる　過去分詞
(C) 動 ～を課す　過去分詞
(D) 動 ～を解雇する　過去分詞

選択肢にはさまざまな意味の動詞の過去分詞が並んでいる。空所を含む箇所の意味を見ていくと、「期日後の返却には延滞料が……される」という意味になっているため、延滞料のようなペナルティのある料金が「発生する、課される」という意味が来ると文意が成立する。以上より、正解は **(C)**。(A) は、延滞料は割り当てるものではなく、ある条件のもとで発生するものなので、ここでは当てはまらない。

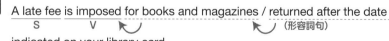

A late fee is imposed for books and magazines / returned after the date
　S　　　V　　　　　　　　　　　　　　　　　　　　　　　　　　　（形容詞句）
indicated on your library card.

□late fee 延滞料金　□indicate ～を示す、記載する

---

　13. (A)　14. (A)　15. (C)

| 1回目 |
| 2回目 |
| 3回目 |

16. In order to meet the demand for its products, Onomu Inc. will expand its international operations ------- by establishing a center in Singapore.

(A) over
(B) closely
(C) jointly
(D) further

| 1回目 |
| 2回目 |
| 3回目 |

17. After thorough investigation and analysis, Sheffield Property Services has decided to expand its business ------- the New Jersey market.

(A) include
(B) included
(C) to include
(D) includes

| 1回目 |
| 2回目 |
| 3回目 |

18. Every employee has scheduled appointments this week, so Ms. Vanderbilt has to travel by -------.

(A) she
(B) her
(C) hers
(D) herself

16. ★★★★☆

製品の需要に対応するため、Onomu 社はシンガポールにセンターを開設し、国際的な事業をさらに拡大する予定です。

(A) 副 一面に
(B) 副 密接に
(C) 副 共同で
(D) 副 さらに

選択肢にはさまざまな意味の副詞が並んでいる。空所を含む箇所の意味を見ていくと、「需要に対応するため、Onomu 社はシンガポールにセンターを設立し、国際事業を……拡大する予定だ」となっている。「需要に対応」、「事務所を新たに設置し事業拡大」というところに着目すると、「今まで以上に」という意味が入ると文意が成立することがわかる。よって、正解は **(D)**。副詞は動詞を修飾する、という観点で考えると正解にたどり着きやすくなる。

In order to meet the demand for its products, / Onomu Inc. will expand its international operations
（副詞句［目的］）　　　　　　　　　　　　　　　　S　　　　V　　　　　　O
further by establishing a center in Singapore.
V を修飾

□in order to *do* 〜するために　□meet 〜を満たす　□demand for 〜の需要　□expand 〜を拡張する
□international operation 国際事業　□establish 〜を設置する

17. ★☆☆☆☆

徹底的な調査と分析の結果、Sheffield Property Services 社はニュージャージー州の市場にも事業を拡大することを決定しました。

(A) 動 〜を含める　原形
(B) 過去形
(C) to 不定詞
(D) 三人称単数現在形

選択肢には動詞 include のさまざまな形が並んでいる。カンマより後の文構造を見ていくと、主語 (Sheffield Property Services)、述語動詞 (has decided)、目的語 (to expand its business) で、第3文型として成立している。ここから、不定詞の副詞的用法 (〜するために) とすると、文法上当てはめることができる。以上より、正解は **(C)**。それ以外の選択肢はすでに述語動詞が存在しているので、当てはめられない。

After thorough investigation and analysis, / Sheffield Property Services has decided
副詞句　　　　　　　　　　　　　　　　　　　　S　　　　　　　　　　V
to expand its business / to include the New Jersey market.
O　　　　　to 不定詞（副詞句）

□thorough 徹底的な　□investigation 調査　□analysis 分析　□expand 〜を拡大する

18. ★☆☆☆☆

今週は全従業員に予定が入っているため、Vanderbilt 氏は一人で外回りをしなければなりません。

(A) 彼女が（主格）
(B) 彼女に（所有格）
(C) 彼女のもの（所有代名詞）
(D) 彼女自身（再帰代名詞）

選択肢には格の異なる代名詞が並んでいる。空所は文末にあり、空所直前に前置詞 by がある。ここから〈by＋再帰代名詞〉の組み合わせで、「自分一人で」とすると文意が成立する。以上より、正解は **(D)**。

Every employee has scheduled appointments this week, /
S　　　　　　　V　　　　　　O
so Ms. Vanderbilt has to travel by herself.
だから　　S　　　　　V

□appointment 予定、約束

 16. (D)　17. (C)　18. (D)

19. The previous mayor, Ms. Franklin, believed that opening the Alabaster Hearts wholesale market was her ------- accomplishment.

(A) most gratifying
(B) more gratified
(C) gratify
(D) gratifyingly

20. Thomas Electronics' salespeople ------- skip any features when giving on-site product demonstrations.

(A) since
(B) seldom
(C) clearly
(D) afterward

21. Child care center workers are told to keep a first aid kit in every room in an ------- location in case of emergency.

(A) expert
(B) attentive
(C) extraordinary
(D) accessible

19. ★★★★☆

前市長の Franklin 氏は、Alabaster Hearts 卸売市場の開設が自身の最も満足の行く業績だと考えていました。

(A) 形 満足を与える（最上級）
(B) 形 満足した（比較級）
(C) 動 ～を喜ばせる
(D) 副 満足して

選択肢には動詞 gratify とその派生語が並んでいる。空所前後は所有格＋空所＋名詞という語順のため、空所には名詞 accomplishment を修飾する形容詞が入ることがわかる。形容詞 gratifying は人を喜ばせるもの、gratified は人が喜んでいる状態を意味するため、ここでは前者の (A) を入れるのが適切。上記以外に、所有格＋形容詞の場合は限定用法となり、形容詞は主に最上級を入れることから (A) を選ぶという考え方でも解法としては OK。

The previous mayor, Ms. Franklin, believed / that opening the Alabaster Hearts wholesale market
      S   S の同格   V   O（that 節）   S

was her most gratifying accomplishment.
 V   C

□previous 前の □mayor 市長 □wholesale market 卸売市場 □accomplishment 成果

---

20. ★★★☆☆

Thomas Electronics 社の販売員は現場で実演販売を行っているときに、製品の特徴の説明を省略することはめったにありません。

(A) 副 それ以来
(B) 副 めったに～ない
(C) 副 明確に
(D) 副 後で

選択肢には意味の異なる副詞が並んでいる。空所を含む文の意味を取っていくと、「ある会社の販売員は実演販売時に製品の特徴を……省略する」と動詞 skip（省略する）を修飾している。ここから、「めったにそのようなことはしない」という意味の (B) を入れると文意が成立する。以上から、正解は (B)。

Thomas Electronics' salespeople seldom skip any features /
             S   V   O

when (they are) giving on-site product demonstrations.
（副詞句［時］）

□salespeople 販売員、営業担当者 □skip ～を省略する □feature 特徴 □on-site 現場の
□product demonstration 商品の実演販売

---

21. ★★★★☆

保育所の職員は、緊急時に備えて、それぞれの部屋の手の届くところに救急箱を置いておくように言われています。

(A) 形 専門家による
(B) 形 注意深い
(C) 形 並はずれた
(D) 形 近づきやすい

選択肢には意味の異なる形容詞が並んでいる。空所を含む文の意味を取っていくと、「保育所職員は、緊急時に備え、各部屋の……位置に救急箱を置くように指示されている」となっており、緊急時に救急箱をすぐ取れるような場所が空所に入るとわかる。以上から、「手が届く範囲」とすると意味が通るため、正解は (D)。空所付近だけ見ると、どれも意味が当てはまる可能性があるため、文全体の意味から正解を選ぶ必要がある。

Child care center workers are told to keep a first aid kit / in every room /
             S   V   O

in an accessible location / in case of emergency.

□child care center 保育所 □first aid kit 救急箱 □in case of emergency 緊急時に備えて

---

 19. (A) 20. (B) 21. (D)

22. Those ------- office supplies should first obtain permission from their immediate supervisor.

(A) order
(B) ordered
(C) ordering
(D) will order

23. The maintenance crew will replace the air conditioning unit ------- cleaning out the air ducts throughout the building.

(A) as well as
(B) so that
(C) as for
(D) in order that

24. ------- you're purchasing or selling a house, be sure to contact Chicago Real Estate to receive the most competitive prices.

(A) That
(B) So
(C) If
(D) Due to

22. ★★★☆☆

事務用品を注文する人は、まず直属の上司の許可を得てください。

(A) 動 ～を注文する　原形
(B) 過去分詞
(C) 現在分詞
(D) 未来表現

選択肢には動詞 order が形を変えて並んでいる。文の構造を見ていくと、述部が should first obtain permission（最初に許可を得るべきだ）となっていることから、主語は文頭の Those から supplies までだとわかる。次に、「許可を得る」のは人であることから、文頭の those は複数の人を意味する代名詞だとわかる。以上から、office supplies を目的語とし、代名詞 those を修飾できる現在分詞の **(C)** が正解。人を表す those は the people（who are）と捉えると正解が導きやすくなる

<u>Those ordering office supplies</u> should first <u>obtain</u> <u>permission</u> from their immediate supervisor.
　　　　S　　　　　　　　　　　　　　　　　　V　　　　　O

□office supply 事務用品　□obtain ～を得る　□permission 許可　□immediate supervisor 直属の上司

---

23. ★★★★☆

整備スタッフは、建物全体の空気ダクトの清掃だけでなくエアコンの交換も行います。

(A) ～だけでなく
(B) そのため
(C) ～に関しては
(D) ～するために

選択肢にはさまざまな接続表現が並んでいる。文の意味を見ていくと、「整備スタッフは、エアコンの交換……建物全体の空気ダクトの清掃を行う」とある。エアコンの交換と建物全体のダクト清掃は別の作業なので、空所には「両方の作業を行う」という意味の語が入ると考えられる。以上より、前置詞句として「～も～も」と同様の作業という意味になるのは **(A)**。as well as は前置詞と同じように捉えることができるので、空所以降は動詞の clean が動名詞の形になっていることも押さえておこう。

<u>The maintenance crew</u> <u>will replace</u> <u>the air conditioning unit</u> /
　　　　S　　　　　　　　　V　　　　　　　O

as well as cleaning out the air ducts throughout the building.
～同様…も

□maintenance crew 整備担当者　□replace ～を交換する　□air conditioning unit エアコン一式
□air duct 空気ダクト

---

24. ★☆☆☆☆

家を購入または売却する際は、最も魅力的な価格を提示するシカゴ不動産にぜひご連絡ください。

(A) その
(B) だから
(C) もし～ならば
(D) ～のために

選択肢にはさまざまな接続表現が並んでいる。文の意味を見ていくと、「家を購入または売却する……、最も魅力的な価格を提供するシカゴ不動産にぜひご連絡を」とある。ここから、家の購入または売却はこれからすることであるため、「もし～」と進行形を使って、未来の時や条件を意味する副詞節を置くと文意が成立する。以上から、正解は **(C)**。(D) の後には名詞もしくは名詞句が続くため、文法的に当てはめることができない。

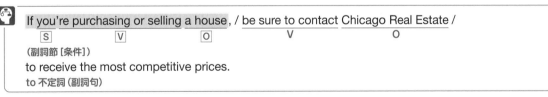

If you're purchasing or selling a house, / be sure to contact Chicago Real Estate /
　S　　　　　V　　　　　O　　　　　　　　　　V　　　　　　　　O
（副詞節［条件］）

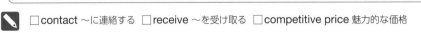

to receive the most competitive prices.
to 不定詞（副詞句）

□contact ～に連絡する　□receive ～を受け取る　□competitive price 魅力的な価格

---

25. If you have yet to turn in your self-evaluation form to your manager, please do ------- by the end of the week.

(A) one
(B) so
(C) which
(D) them

26. ------- displaying the time, the Delight watch is also a fashionable accessory that matches both casual and formal attire.

(A) Consisting of
(B) Aside from
(C) In view of
(D) Seeing that

27. Lynn Underwear is involved in the manufacture, sale, and ------- of its clothing products.

(A) distribution
(B) exception
(C) repetition
(D) accreditation

25. ★★★☆☆

自己評価書をまだ上司に提出していない方は、今週中に提出してください。

(A) 人
(B) そのように
(C) どれ
(D) それらを

選択肢には代名詞や接続詞、疑問詞（関係詞）などが並んでいる。文の意味を見ていくと、「自己評価書をまだ提出していない方は、今週中に……してください」となっている。ここで、カンマ以降の do は文意から turn in を重複しないように使われていると考えられるため、提出するもの＝自己評価書だとわかる。ここから、自己紹介書を提出、つまり「そうしてほしい」とすると文意が成立する。以上から正解は **(B)**。do so という表現は、今回のように接続詞で同じ表現が使用されている条件で、「そうする、そうしてほしい」という場面で用いられる。

If you have yet to turn in your self-evaluation form to your manager, /
   S   V   O
（副詞節 [時]）

please do so by the end of the week.
     V = turn in（命令文）

□have yet to *do* まだ〜していない　□turn in 〜を提出する　□self-evaluation form 自己評価書
□by the end of the week 週末までに

---

26. ★★★☆☆

時刻を表示するほかに、Delight ウォッチはカジュアルとフォーマルどちらの服装にもマッチするおしゃれなアクセサリーでもあるのです。

(A) 〜で構成されている
(B) 〜のほかに
(C) 〜を考慮して
(D) 〜を見ると

選択肢にはさまざまな意味の接続表現が並んでいる。文の意味を見ていくと、「時刻を表示する……、Delight ウォッチは服装を選ばないおしゃれなアクセサリーだ」となっている。つまり、この腕時計は機能性に加え、アクセサリーにもなる、ということを示したいと考えられるので、「〜に加え」という意味を持つ **(B)** が文意に合う、ここでの aside from は in addition to と同じ意味を持つ。(D) は後ろに節を導かなければならないため、ここでは文法的に当てはまらない。

Aside from displaying the time, / the Delight watch is also a fashionable accessory /
〜のほかに（副詞句）   S   V   C

that matches both casual and formal attire.
 S   V   O
that 節（形容詞節）

□attire 服装

---

27. ★★★★☆

Lynn Underwear 社は、自社の衣料品の製造、販売、そして流通を手掛けています。

(A) 名 流通
(B) 名 例外
(C) 名 繰り返し
(D) 名 認定

選択肢にはさまざまな意味の名詞が並んでいる。文の意味を見ていくと、「Lynn Underwear 社は、自社の衣料品の製造、販売、そして……を手掛けている」となっている。空所前に and という等位接続詞が来ていることから、述語動詞 be involved in の目的語となっている名詞と同じ性質の語が入ることがわかる。つまり、製造、販売、と商品が出荷されて販売されるまでのフローについての表現が入る、と考えることができるため、正解は **(A)** となる。

Lynn Underwear is involved in the manufacture, sale, and distribution of its clothing products.
       S   V   O

□be involved in 〜を手掛けている、〜に関与している　□manufacture 製造　□clothing product 衣料品

28. Due to unexpectedly high ------- for organic goods, we must quickly expand production.

(A) occurrence
(B) percentage
(C) demand
(D) amount

29. The main goal of the Austin Charity Foundation is to build a free medical clinic in ------- major city in the state of Texas.

(A) every
(B) all
(C) first
(D) many

30. Please enter another e-mail address ------- which you can be reached while you are away.

(A) at
(B) for
(C) in
(D) to

28. ★★★★☆

オーガニック商品の需要の予想外の高まりにより、早急に生産を拡大する必要があります。

(A) 名 発生
(B) 名 割合
(C) 名 需要
(D) 名 量

選択肢にはさまざまな意味の名詞が並んでいる。文の意味を見ていくと、「オーガニック商品への予想外に高い……により、早急に生産を拡大する必要がある」となっている。ここから、早急に生産を拡大する必要がある背景として、高い需要があると考えると文意が成立する。以上より、正解は **(C)**。(D) は意味的に選びがちだが、何に対する量なのかがわからないので、ここでは不正解。

Due to unexpectedly high demand for organic goods, / we must quickly expand production.
（前置詞句 [原因・理由]）　　　　　　　　　　　　　　S　　　　V　　　　　O

□due to 〜により　□unexpectedly 予想外に　□organic goods オーガニック商品
□expand production 生産を拡大する

---

29. ★★☆☆☆

Austin 慈善財団の主な目標は、テキサス州のすべての主要都市に無料の医療クリニックを開設することです。

(A) 形 すべての（単数形扱い）
(B) 形 すべての（複数形扱い）
(C) 形 最初の
(D) 形 多くの

選択肢にはさまざまな数に関わる形容詞が並んでいる。空所前後は、前置詞＋空所＋単数の名詞 (major city) となっていることから、空所には単数の名詞にかかる語が入ることがわかる。次に文の意味を見ていくと、「慈善財団の目標は……の主要都市に無料の医療クリニックを開設することだ」とあるので、それぞれの主要都市、とすると文意が成立する。以上から、正解は **(A)**。(B)、(D) は複数の名詞を受けるため、ここでは文法的に入らない。

The main goal of the Austin Charity Foundation is to build a free medical clinic /
　　　　　S　　　　　　　　　　　　　　　　V　　　C
in every major city in the state of Texas.

□main goal 主な目標　□medical clinic 医療クリニック　□state 州

---

30. ★★★☆☆

留守の間に連絡可能なメールアドレスをもう１つ入力してください。

(A) 前 〜で
(B) 前 〜のために
(C) 前 〜の中に
(D) 前 〜へ

選択肢にはさまざまな前置詞が並んでいる。空所前後は名詞 another e-mail address＋空所＋which となっていることから、前置詞＋関係詞の組み合わせで先行詞 another e-mail address を修飾していることがわかる。関係詞以降の述語動詞は、be reached なので、この述語動詞と another e-mail address をつなぐ **(A)** が正解となる。

〈命令文〉
Please enter another e-mail address / at which you can be reached / while you are away.
　　　　V　　　　　O　　　　　　　　　　　　　S　　　　V　　　　　　S V C
　　　　　　　　　　　　　　　　　　　　　　　　　　　　　　　　　　　（副詞節 [時]）

□be reach 人 at 〜で人に連絡する

28. (C)　29. (A)　30. (A)

1回目 2回目 3回目

1. The new payroll system for part-time workers was ------- than management had originally hoped.

(A) so efficiently
(B) as efficient
(C) most efficiently
(D) more efficient

1回目 2回目 3回目

2. It is essential to provide your outdoor pets with plenty of water to drink once summer -------.

(A) arrived
(B) arrives
(C) will arrive
(D) is arriving

1回目 2回目 3回目

3. Develyn Natural Cafe gives all visitors the chance to enjoy an exquisite ------- experience at a reasonable price.

(A) dine
(B) dines
(C) dined
(D) dining

1. ★☆☆☆☆

パートタイマー向けの新しい給与計算システムは、経営陣が当初期待していたよりも効率的でした。

(A) 非常に効率的に
(B) 同じくらい効率的な
(C) 副 効率的に（最上級）
(D) 形 効率的な（比較級）

選択肢には形容詞 efficient と副詞 efficiently が副詞などを伴った形が並んでいる。空所前後を見ると、be 動詞＋空所＋than … の形となっており、空所は be 動詞の補語に当たる。以上から、be 動詞の補語となる比較表現として適切なのは、形容詞の比較級の **(D)** である。

The new payroll system for part-time workers was more efficient /
　　　　S　　　　　　　　　　　　　　　　　　　　V　　　C
than management had originally hoped.
　　　　S　　　　　　V

□payroll system 給与計算システム　□part-time worker パートタイム従業員、アルバイト　□management 経営陣
□originally 当初

2. ★★★★☆

夏が来たら、屋外で飼っているペットにたっぷりと水を飲ませることが肝心です。

(A) 動 到来する　過去形
(B) 三人称単数現在形
(C) 未来表現
(D) 現在進行形

選択肢には動詞 arrive の異なる形が並んでいる。空所前は once summer という表現となっており、この once を時や条件の意味を表す副詞節の once（＝when）と考えると、「夏が来ると、ペットに水をたくさん飲ませることが重要」と文意が成立する。以上から、時や条件を表す副詞節の中では現在形を使うため **(B)** が正解となる。

〈形式主語〉
It is essential to provide your outdoor pets with plenty of water to drink /
仮 S V　C　　　　　　　　　　　　　　真 S
once summer arrives.
　　S　　　　　V
（副詞節 [時]）

□essential 不可欠な　□plenty of 多量の

3. ★★★★☆

Develyn Natural Cafe は、すべてのお客様に手ごろな価格で極上のお食事を楽しんでいただく機会を提供しています。

(A) 動 食事をする　原形
(B) 三人称単数現在形
(C) 過去形
(D) 名 食事

選択肢には動詞 dine の形を変えたものと派生語が並んでいる。空所前後を見ると、空所を含む名詞句が to 不定詞である enjoy の目的語となっていることがわかる。「極上の……経験を楽しむ」という内容には、複合名詞として dining experience「食事経験」とすると意味が成立する。以上から正解は **(D)**。(A)、(B) は動詞のため文法的に当てはめることができず、(C) は分詞として考えたとしても「食事された経験」となるため意味が通じない。

Develyn Natural Cafe gives all visitors the chance / to enjoy an exquisite dining experience
　　　　　　　　　　　S　　　　　V　　　O¹　　　　O²　　to 不定詞 (形容詞句)
at a reasonable price.

□visitor 訪問客　□exquisite 高級な　□at a reasonable price 手ごろな値段で

 1. (D)　2. (B)　3. (D)

4. In spite of the increased fares, analysts expect a rise in public transport use in Fort Worth ------- the next five years.

(A) upon
(B) over
(C) by
(D) against

5. All staff members who will attend this experiment should download and print laboratory handbooks for quick -------.

(A) reference
(B) procedure
(C) measure
(D) indication

6. The formal launch of the new comprehensive tax self-assessment program was postponed because of a problem that ------- when it was tested.

(A) connected
(B) emerged
(C) revealed
(D) reacted

4. ★★★☆☆

運賃が値上げされるにもかかわらず、アナリストは今後5年間でFort Worthの公共交通機関の利用が増加すると予想しています。

(A) 前 ～の上に
(B) 前 （時間が）～の間に
(C) 前 ～までには
(D) 前 ～に対して

In spite of the increased fares, / analysts expect a rise in public transport use in Fort Worth
～にもかかわらず（副詞句）　　　　　　S　　　V　　　O
over the next five years.

□in spite of ～にもかかわらず　□increased 増加した　□fare 運賃　□rise in ～の上昇
□public transport use 公共交通機関の利用

---

5. ★★★★☆

この実験に参加予定のすべてのスタッフは、実験室のハンドブックをすぐに参照できるようにダウンロードし、印刷しておいてください。

(A) 名 参照
(B) 名 手順
(C) 名 測定
(D) 名 表示

All staff members / who will attend this experiment / should download and print
　　　S　　　　　　　　S　　　V　　　　　O　　　　　　　　　　V
laboratory handbooks for quick reference.
　　　　　O

□experiment 実験　□laboratory 実験室　□handbook ハンドブック、手引書

---

6. ★★★★☆

新しい総合税務申告プログラムは、テスト時に問題が発生したため、正式な開始が延期されました。

(A) 動 つながる　[過去形]
(B) 動 発生する　[過去形]
(C) 動 ～を明らかにする　[過去形]
(D) 動 反応する　[過去形]

The formal launch of the new comprehensive tax self-assessment program was postponed /
　　　S　　　　　　　　　　　　　　　　　　　　　　　　　　　　V
because of a problem that emerged / when it was tested.
（副詞句[原因・理由]）　S　　V　　　　S　　V
　　　　　　　　　　　（副詞節[時]）

□launch 開始　□comprehensive 総合的な　□tax self-assessment program 税務申告プログラム
□test ～を試験する

---

 4. (B)　5. (A)　6. (B)

7. Maintenance records suggest that tools ordered from Granderson Products are more ------- than those ordered from Sanford's Wholesale Store.

(A) dependability
(B) depend
(C) dependably
(D) dependable

8. We have now realized that most tourists are ------- to reserve an unfamiliar hotel before consulting online reviews.

(A) reluctant
(B) detached
(C) sensitive
(D) provisional

9. A river cleanup campaign is one of the ------- activities that the NGO launched to fight pollution in their district.

(A) excessive
(B) voluntary
(C) competitive
(D) aggressive

7. ★★☆☆☆

メンテナンスの記録から、Granderson Products 社に発注した工具は、Sanford's Wholesale Store 社に発注した工具よりも信頼性が高いことが示唆されています。

(A) 名 信頼性
(B) 動 依存する
(C) 副 頼もしく
(D) 形 頼りになる

選択肢には名詞 dependability とその派生語が並んでいる。空所前後を見ると、be 動詞＋比較級＋空所＋than＋比較対象という構造になっていることから、空所は第2文型の補語として形容詞が入るとわかる。以上より、正解は **(D)**。

Maintenance records suggest / that tools ordered from Granderson Products are
　　　S　　　　　　　V　　　　O　　　　S　　　　　　　　　　　　　　　　　　V
　　　　　　　　　　　　　　　　(that 節)

more dependable than those ordered from Sanford's Wholesale Store .
　　　　C　　　　　　　　= tools

□maintenance record メンテナンスの記録　□tool 工具、用具

---

8. ★★★★★

多くの旅行者が、ネットのレビューを調べる前に、見知らぬホテルを予約しようとしないことに気づきました。

(A) 形 （人が）気が進まない
(B) 形 とらわれない
(C) 形 敏感な
(D) 形 仮の

選択肢には意味の異なる形容詞が並んでいる。空所を含む意味を見ていくと、「旅行者の多くは、ネットのレビューを参考にする前に見知らぬホテルを予約するのを……」となっていることから、「ためらう、渋る」を意味する **(A)** を入れると文意が成立する。be reluctant to 不定詞の形で、「～するのに気乗りしない、あまり～したくない」という意味になる（＝be unwilling to 不定詞）ので押さえておこう。(C) は be sensitive to で「～に敏感である」という意味になるが、to 以降は名詞を導くため、文法的にも当てはまらず、また意味も通じない。

We have now realized / that most tourists are reluctant to reserve an unfamiliar hotel /
　　S　　　　　V　　　　　O (that 節) S　　　　　　　V　　　　　　　　　O

before consulting online reviews .
～の前に (副詞句)

□realize ～を認識する　□unfamiliar よく知られていない　□consult ～を調べてみる　□review 感想、意見

---

9. ★★★★☆

河川の清掃活動は、地域の汚染を解消するために NGO が始めた自主的な活動の一つです。

(A) 形 過度の
(B) 形 自主的な
(C) 形 競争の
(D) 形 積極的な

選択肢には意味の異なる形容詞が並んでいる。文の意味を見ていくと、「河川の清掃活動は、地域の汚染を解消するために NGO が始めた……活動の一つだ」となっている。活動の性質や、NGO という非営利組織が始めたことから、**(B)** を入れると文意が成立する。この活動に競争性や積極性が伴うかどうかはこの文からわからないため、(C)、(D) は不正解。

A river cleanup campaign is one of the voluntary activities / that the NGO launched /
　　　　　　S　　　　　　　　V　　　　　　　C　　　　　　　　　　　　O　　S　　　V

to fight pollution in their district .
to 不定詞 (副詞句)

□activity 活動　□NGO (nongovernmental organization) 非政府組織　□launch ～を開始する　□fight ～に立ち向かう
□pollution 汚染　□district 地区

🚩 7. **(D)**　8. **(A)**　9. **(B)**

1回目

2回目

3回目

10. Ms. Turner and her colleagues are planning to give a presentation on consumer patterns, but outside consultants should join ------- to add in-depth knowledge.

(A) they
(B) their
(C) them
(D) themselves

1回目

2回目

3回目

11. In light of new safety regulations, you must refrain from using your cellular phone while ------- the aircraft.

(A) across
(B) into
(C) beyond
(D) aboard

1回目

2回目

3回目

12. Ms. Timber will represent Marybell Homes at the local real estate conference since she knows commercial property law better than -------.

(A) most
(B) whichever
(C) usual
(D) each

10. ★★★☆☆

Turner さんとその同僚たちは、消費者のパターンに関するプレゼンテーションを行う予定ですが、細かい知識を得るために外部のコンサルタントに参加してもらうべきです。

(A) 彼らが（主格）
(B) 彼らの（所有格）
(C) 彼らに（目的格）
(D) 彼ら自身（再帰代名詞）

🔍 選択肢には三人称複数の格の異なる代名詞が並んでいる。文の意味を見ていくと、「Turner さんと同僚たちは、プレゼンテーションを行う予定だが、より深い知識を加えるために外部のコンサルタントが……に加わるべきだ」となっている。ここから、主語の外部コンサルタントが「Turner さんと同僚たち」に加わるべきだ、とすると文意に合う。以上から、正解は目的格の **(C)** となる。(D) が入る場合は、主語と同じものとして入れる必要があるが、ここでは文意上入れることができないため不正解。

Ms. Turner and her colleagues are planning to give a presentation on consumer patterns, /
　　　　　S　　　　　　　　　　V　　　　　　　　　O
but outside consultants should join them / to add in-depth knowledge.
　　　　　S　　　　　　V　　　　O　　to 不定詞（副詞句）

✎ □consumer patterns 消費者の動向　□outside consultant 外部のコンサルタント　□in-depth 詳細な

---

11. ★★★☆☆

新しい安全規制に基づき、ご搭乗中は携帯電話のご使用をお控えください。

(A) 前 ～を横切って
(B) 前 ～の中に
(C) 前 ～を超えて
(D) 前 ～に乗って

🔍 選択肢には前置詞が並んでいる。文の意味を見ていくと、「飛行機……間は携帯電話の使用を控えるように」とあるため、飛行機に乗っている最中は、という内容にすると文意が成立する。以上から、正解は **(D)**。なお、空所前は、while (you are) aboard the aircraft と SV が省略されているので補うと意味が取りやすい。

In light of new safety regulations, / you must refrain from using your cellular phone /
　　　　　　　　　　　　　　　　　　　S　　　V　　　　　　　　　O

while (you are) aboard the aircraft.
～の間（副詞句）

✎ □in light of ～を考慮し、～に基づき　□safety regulation 安全規則　□ refrain from ～をやめる
□cellular phone 携帯電話

---

12. ★★★★☆

Timber さんは、商業用不動産の法律にたいていの人より詳しいので、地域の不動産会議に Marybell Homes 社を代表して参加することになりました。

(A) ほとんどの人
(B) どちらでも
(C) 通常の
(D) それぞれ

🔍 選択肢には代名詞などが並んでいる。空所前が better than となっていることから、空所は何かの比較対象であるとわかる。文の意味が、「彼女（Timber さん）は……よりも商業用不動産の法律を知っている」であるため、比較対象は人であることがわかる。よって、**(A)** が正解。better than most で、「たいていの（モノ・人）よりも」という意味になる。ここでは主語が人であるため、better than most (people) と補って考えると理解しやすい。

Ms. Timber will represent Marybell Homes at the local real estate conference / since
　　S　　　　　V　　　　　　O　　　　　　　　　　　　　　　　　　　（副詞節［理由］）

she knows commercial property law better than most.
　S　　V　　　　　　O

✎ □represent ～を代表する　□real estate 不動産　□commercial property 商業用不動産

🚩 **10. (C)　11. (D)　12. (A)**

13. Employees in the sales department are required to -------
regular meetings every Wednesday.

(A) register
(B) enroll
(C) attend
(D) participate

14. The area manager told Mr. Mathers that the accounting
figures from the Kanemone branch office need to be
regularly verified for -------.

(A) requirement
(B) complaint
(C) suggestion
(D) accuracy

15. The selection committee of the Auckland Writing
Competition created detailed evaluation criteria, and all the
submissions will be judged -------.

(A) purposely
(B) chiefly
(C) persistently
(D) accordingly

13. ★★★☆☆

営業部門の社員は、毎週水曜日の定例会議に出席することが義務付けられています。

(A) 動 登録する
(B) 動 名前を登録する
(C) 動 ～に出席する
(D) 動 参加する

選択肢には意味の異なる動詞が並んでいる。文の意味を見ていくと、「営業部門の社員は、定例会議に……する必要がある」となっている。ここから、目的語 regular meetings を伴って「～に出席する」という内容にすると文意が成立する。以上より、正解は **(C)**。(C) 以外は自動詞の場合に、参加・登録する、という意味になるため、(A) は register for、(B) は enroll in、(D) は participate in というように前置詞を補う必要がある。

Employees in the sales department are required to attend regular meetings every Wednesday.
S　　　　　　　　　　　　　　　V　　　　　　　O

□require ～に (…するように) 要求する

14. ★★★★☆

エリアマネジャーは Mathers 氏に、Kanemone 支店の会計の数字が正確かどうか、定期的に検証する必要があると言いました。

(A) 名 要件
(B) 名 苦情
(C) 名 提案
(D) 名 正確さ

選択肢には意味の異なる名詞が並んでいる。文の意味を見ていくと、「会計の数字は……のために定期的に検証する必要がある」となっており、会計の数字という性質から「正確さのために」とすると文意が成立する。よって、正解は **(D)**。

The area manager told Mr. Mathers / that the accounting figures from the Kanemone branch office
S　　　　　　V　　　O¹　　O²(that 節)　　S　　　　　　　　(形容詞句)
need to be regularly verified for accuracy.
V

□accounting figures 会計の数字　□verify ～を検証する

15. ★★★★☆

Auckland 文筆コンテストの選考委員会は詳細な評価基準を作成しました。そして、すべての応募作品はそれに従って審査されます。

(A) 副 意図的に
(B) 副 主として
(C) 副 しつこく
(D) 副 それに応じて

選択肢には意味の異なる副詞が並んでいる。文の意味を見ていくと、「選考委員会は詳細な評価基準を作成し、すべての応募作品は……審査される」とある。ここから、前の内容を受けて、「それに従って」を意味する **(D)** を入れると、それ（＝作成した評価基準）に従って、となり文意が成立する。

The selection committee of the Auckland Writing Competition created detailed evaluation criteria, /
S　　　　　　　　　　　　　　　　　　　　　　　V　　　　　　　　O
and all the submissions will be judged accordingly.
S　　　　　V

□detailed 詳細な　□evaluation criteria 評価基準　□submission 提出物　□judge ～を審査する

 13. (C)　14. (D)　15. (D)

16. A new location for Sakae Bakery is under construction at the corner of Bingham Avenue and Machado Street, ------- the old courthouse used to be.

(A) where
(B) next to
(C) when
(D) across

17. ------- accommodations in the small town of Bakersfield, there are only two bed-and-breakfasts and a mountain lodge.

(A) For example
(B) Because
(C) In terms of
(D) Whereas

18. ------- those interns who perform well in their assigned tasks will be permitted to apply for permanent positions.

(A) Ever
(B) If
(C) Only
(D) When

16. ★★★☆☆

Bingham 通りと Machado 通りの角の、旧裁判所があった場所に、Sakae ベーカリーの新店舗が建設中です。

(A) where（関係副詞）
(B) ～の隣に（群前置詞）
(C) when（関係副詞）
(D) 前 ～を横切って

A new location for Sakae Bakery is under construction at the corner of Bingham Avenue
　　S　　　　　　　　　　　　　　　　V　　C
and Machado Street, / where the old courthouse used to be.
　　　　　　　　　　　　　　　　　　S　　　　　V

□under construction 建設中 □courthouse 裁判所

17. ★★★☆☆

Bakersfield という小さな町の宿泊施設といえば、朝食付きの民宿が 2 軒と山小屋が 1 軒あるだけです。

(A) たとえば（接続副詞）
(B) 接 なぜなら
(C) ～に関して（群前置詞）
(D) 接 ～であるのに対して

In terms of accommodations in the small town of Bakersfield, /
～に関しては（副詞句）
there are only two bed-and-breakfasts and a mountain lodge.
　　　V　　　　　　　　　　　　S

□accommodation 宿泊施設 □mountain lodge 山小屋

18. ★☆☆☆☆

与えられた仕事をきちんとこなしたインターン生だけが、正社員への応募を許可されます。

(A) 副 いつか
(B) 接 もし～であれば
(C) 副 ただ～だけ
(D) 接 ～する時

Only those interns / who perform well in their assigned tasks / will be permitted to apply for
　　　　　S　　　　　S　　V　　　　　　　　　　　　　　　　V
permanent positions.
　　　　O

□intern インターン、実務研修生 □assigned 割り当てられた □task 任務 □permit ～を許可する
□apply for ～に応募する □permanent position 常勤の職

 16. (A)　17. (C)　18. (C)

1回目 2回目 3回目

19. After ------- considering the options, Ms. Craig was finally ready to resign from her job and run her own business.

(A) care
(B) caring
(C) careful
(D) carefully

1回目 2回目 3回目

20. Newly elected mayor Clara Hightower expressed her ------- to everyone who supported her campaign.

(A) publicity
(B) gratitude
(C) abundance
(D) replication

1回目 2回目 3回目

21. Emergency exit signs and maps of fire escape routes are ------- posted in every guest room at the Clint Hotel.

(A) harshly
(B) prominently
(C) forcefully
(D) cooperatively

19. ★★★★★

選択肢を慎重に検討した結果、Craig さんはつい
に、会社を辞めて自分でビジネスを手がける決意を
固めたのです。

(A) 名 世話
(B) 形 思いやりのある
(C) 形 注意深い
(D) 副 注意深く

選択肢には名詞 care とその派生語が並んでいる。空所前後を見ると、前置詞 after が文頭にあり、空所を挟んで considering the options という形で、「選択肢を考えた後で」と、ひととおりの前置詞句を完成させていることから、空所には動名詞 considering を修飾する副詞が入ることが考えられる。以上から、正解は **(D)**。

After carefully considering the options, / Ms. Craig was finally ready to resign from her job /
（副詞節 [時]）   S   V   O

and run her own business.
    V   O

□resign from ～を辞任する　□run one's own business 自分でビジネスを手がける

20. ★★★★★

新たに市長に当選した Clara Hightower 氏は、選
挙運動を支えてくれたすべての人に感謝の意を表
しました。

(A) 名 宣伝
(B) 名 感謝
(C) 名 豊かさ
(D) 名 複製

選択肢には意味の異なる名詞が並んでいる。文の意味を見ていくと、「新市長は、選挙運動を支えた人に……を表した」となっており、支えてくれた人に対する気持ちなどが入ることがわかる。以上から、正解は **(B)**。

Newly elected mayor Clara Hightower expressed her gratitude to everyone / who supported
     S   V   O   S   V

her campaign.
    O

□newly elected 新たに当選した　□express ～を表す

21. ★★★★★

Clint ホテルのすべての客室には、非常口の表示と
避難経路の図が目立つように掲示されています。

(A) 副 厳しく
(B) 副 目立って
(C) 副 力強く
(D) 副 協力的に

選択肢には意味の異なる副詞が並んでいる。文の意味を見ていくと、「ホテルのすべての客室には、非常口の表示と避難経路の図が……掲示されている」とあるので、「目立って」掲示されている、という意味を入れると文意が成立する。よって、正解は **(B)**。prominently は難語だが、何かが目立っているような状況で用いられる副詞で、リーディングセクションにはよく登場するのでしっかり押さえておこう。

Emergency exit signs and maps of fire escape routes are prominently posted /
     S   V

in every guest room at the Clint Hotel.

□emergency exit 非常口　□escape route 避難経路　□post ～を掲示する

 19. (D)　20. (B)　21. (B)

22. Ms. Hilton has to use public transportation to get to the airport ------- her car is being repaired.

(A) neither
(B) why
(C) that
(D) as

23. Mr. O'Reilly intends ------- his laptop computer from his office before leaving for the business trip.

(A) retrieve
(B) retrieved
(C) to retrieve
(D) being retrieved

24. Even mileage club members will need to pay almost double the normal fare for flying ------- peak times.

(A) while
(B) during
(C) when
(D) about

22. ★★★★☆

Hilton さんは車を修理に出しているため、空港に行くのに公共交通機関を利用しなければなりません。

(A) 副 どちらも～しない
(B) 副 ～である（理由）
(C) 接 ～ということ
(D) 接 ～なので

選択肢には疑問詞、接続詞などが並んでいる。文の意味を見ていくと、「Hilton さんは車を修理に出している……、空港に行くのに公共交通機関を利用する必要がある」となっていることから、理由を意味する接続表現を入れると文意が成立する。よって、理由を示す接続詞の **(D)** が正解。接続詞 as はさまざまな意味があるが、ここでは because と同じ意味として捉えておこう。

 Ms. Hilton has to use public transportation / to get to the airport / as her car is being repaired .
　　　　　　 S　　　 V　　　　　　 O　　　　　 to 不定詞（副詞句）　　　　 S　　　 V
　　　　　　　　　　　　　　　　　　　　　　　　　　　　　　　　 （副詞節 [原因・理由]）

□public transportation 公共交通機関

---

23. ★★☆☆☆

O'Reilly 氏は出張に出る前に会社からノートパソコンを回収するつもりである。

(A) 動 ～を回収する 　原形
(B) 過去分詞
(C) to 不定詞
(D) 動名詞（受動態）

選択肢には動詞 retrieve のさまざまな形が並んでおり、空所前には動詞 intend がある。この動詞は、将来の計画や目的に対して「意図する」という意味で用いられ、目的語に不定詞や動名詞を伴う。(D) は動名詞だが、受け身になっているため文意が通らない。よって、正解は **(C)**。

Mr. O'Reilly intends to retrieve his laptop computer from his office /
　　 S　　　　 V　　　　　　　　 O

before leaving for the business trip.

□intend to *do* ～するつもりである　□business trip 出張

---

24. ★★★★☆

マイレージクラブ会員でも、ピーク時のフライトには通常運賃のほぼ倍額を払う必要があります。

(A) 接 ～する間に
(B) 前 ～の間ずっと
(C) 接 ～する時
(D) 前 ～について

選択肢には接続詞や前置詞が並んでいる。空所以降は peak times という名詞句になっているため、空所には前置詞が入ることがわかる。次に、文の意味を取っていくと、「マイレージクラブ会員でも、ピーク……フライトは通常運賃のほぼ倍額を支払う必要がある」とあることから、ピークの間、といった一定の期間を意味する語が入ることがわかる。以上から、正解は **(B)**。

 Even mileage club members will need to pay almost double the normal fare
　　　　　　　　　　 S　　　　　　　 V　　　　　 O

for flying during peak times.

□mileage club member マイレージ会員　□normal fare 通常運賃　□peak times 最高に達する時、ピーク時

25. Our employees, in ------- with management, have identified ways to reduce costs by 10 percent.

(A) cooperate
(B) cooperated
(C) cooperation
(D) cooperates

26. The director of the human resource department made a ------- presentation on features of the newly announced employee benefits package.

(A) deserved
(B) subtle
(C) brief
(D) strict

27. The 19th Annual Accounting Conference was the highest attended conference ever ------- in Hong Kong.

(A) stayed
(B) referred
(C) gone
(D) held

25. ★☆☆☆☆

当社の従業員は、経営陣と協力して、10%のコスト削減を実現する方法を見つけました。

(A) 動 協力する 　原形

(B) 過去分詞

(C) 名 協力

(D) 三人称単数現在形

選択肢には動詞 cooperate の形を変えたものや派生語が並んでいる。空所前後を見ると前置詞に挟まれていることがわかる。ここから、空所は前置詞に導かれる名詞が入ることがわかる。以上から、正解は **(C)**。文法ルールで解く問題だが、in cooperation with（～と協力して）という決まり文句としても押さえておこう。

Our employees, / in cooperation with management, / have identified ways / to reduce costs by
　　　S　　　　　　　～と協力して（副詞句）　　　　　　　　　　V　　　　　O　　　 to 不定詞（形容詞句）

10 percent.

□identify ～を突き止める

---

26. ★★★☆☆

新しく発表された福利厚生の特徴について、人事部長から簡単な説明がありました。

(A) 形 当然の

(B) 形 微妙な

(C) 形 簡潔な

(D) 形 厳しい

選択肢には意味の異なる形容詞が並んでいる。文の意味を見ていくと、「人事部長が新しく発表された福利厚生の特徴について……説明した」となっていることから、「説明」を形容し、文意が通る **(C)** が正解となる。(B) は subtle difference（微妙な違い）といった、よく見分けがつきにくい場合などに用いる形容詞で、ここでは文意に合わないため不正解。

The director of the human resource department made a brief presentation on features
　　　　　　S　　　　　　　　　　　　　　　　　　　V　　　　　　O

of the newly announced employee benefits package.
features を修飾（形容詞句）

□feature 特徴　□benefits package 福利厚生

---

27. ★★★☆☆

第 19 回年次会計会議は、香港で開催された会議としては過去最高の参加者数を記録しました。

(A) 動 ～を延期する 　過去分詞

(B) 動 ～を差し向ける 　過去分詞

(C) 動 なくなる 　過去分詞

(D) 動 ～を開催する 　過去分詞

選択肢には意味の異なる動詞の過去分詞が並んでいる。空所を含む文の意味を見ていくと、「年次会計会議は、香港で……会議として過去最高の参加者数を記録した」となっており、空所は conference を修飾していることがわかる。空所以降は都市名になっていることから、「香港で開催された会議」とすると意味が通る。以上から、正解は **(D)**。

The 19th Annual Accounting Conference was the highest attended conference / (that was)
　　　　　　S　　　　　　　　　　　　V　　　　　　C

ever held in Hong Kong.

28. The heads of the marketing division ------- endorsed Mr. Blackstone's innovative advertising approach.

(A) enthusiastic
(B) enthusiast
(C) enthusiasm
(D) enthusiastically

29. Ziozia Conference Center is ------- larger than the Ozawa Auditorium, making it more appropriate for big events.

(A) such
(B) still
(C) very
(D) fairly

30. Please submit any questions or concerns in writing to the office of admissions, and then ------- fax or mail them using the contact details below.

(A) either
(B) neither
(C) both
(D) whether

28. ★☆☆☆☆

マーケティング部門の責任者たちは、Blackstone 氏の革新的な広告の手法に熱烈に賛同しました。

(A) 形 熱心な
(B) 名 熱中している人
(C) 名 熱狂
(D) 副 熱烈に

選択肢には形容詞 enthusiastic の派生語が並んでいる。空所前後を見ていくと、空所は主語と述語動詞に挟まれており、すでに文の形を構成していることがわかる。以上から、空所には述語動詞 endorsed を修飾する副詞の **(D)** が入るとわかる。

The heads of the marketing division enthusiastically endorsed
　　　　　　　　　S　　　　　　　　　　　　　　　　V
Mr. Blackstone's innovative advertising approach.
　　　　　　　　　　　　　　　O

□endorse 〜に賛同する　□innovative 革新的な　□approach 手法

---

29. ★★★★☆

Ziozia 会議場は、Ozawa 公会堂よりもずっと大きいので、大きなイベントに適しています。

(A) 形 そのような
(B) 副 ずっと
(C) 副 とても
(D) 副 かなり

空所には形容詞や意味の異なる副詞が並んでいる。空所は be 動詞と形容詞の比較級の間にあり、「A は B より大きい」という意味になっている。ここから、比較級を強調する副詞の **(B)** still が入る。比較級を強調する語は still のほかに much、a lot、even、far などがあり、いずれも TOEIC に出題されるので押さえておこう。

Ziozia Conference Center is still larger than the Ozawa Auditorium, /
　　　　　　　S　　　　　　　　　　V　　　　　　　　　　　　　C
making it more appropriate for big events.
分詞構文 (副詞句)

□auditorium 公会堂　□appropriate 適切な

---

30. ★★★★☆

ご質問やご相談は書面にて入試課までご提出いただきますので、下記の連絡先まで FAX または郵送にてお願いします。

(A) どちらか
(B) どちらでもない
(C) 両方
(D) 〜かどうか

選択肢には形容詞などが並んでいる。文の構造を見ると、Please submit ...、and then ------- fax or mail ... となっており、動詞 fax と mail が等位接続詞 or でつながっていることから、either A or B のように当てはめると、「FAX もしくは郵送してほしい」と文意が通じることがわかる。以上より、正解は **(A)**。(D) も A or B を導くが、either の場合は「A か B のいずれか」という選択のニュアンスがある一方で、whether A or B は「A であろうと B であろうと」と譲歩の意味を表す副詞節で、どちらであってもある方向が決まっているようなニュアンスとなるため、ここでは当てはまらない。

〈命令文〉
Please submit any questions or concerns in writing to the office of admissions, /
　　　　V¹　　　　O
and then either fax or mail them / using the contact details below.
　　　　　　　　　V²　　　　O　　　(副詞句)

□concern 関心事　□in writing 書面で　□office of admissions 入試課　□contact details 連絡先の詳細

---

 28. (D)　29. (B)　30. (A)

Test 7

1. Ms. Alves ------- her employees that the Dancer-S1 music player will be discontinued because of poor sales.

   (A) announced
   (B) informed
   (C) complied
   (D) verified

2. ------- for the work efficiency seminars have been sent at regular intervals throughout the year to all workers.

   (A) Invitations
   (B) Invitation
   (C) Invite
   (D) Inviting

3. To make our new textbook easier to understand, we eliminated some illustrations that we thought were too -------.

   (A) distract
   (B) distracting
   (C) distraction
   (D) distractedly

1. ★★★☆☆

Alves さんは、音楽プレーヤー Dancer-S1 が、販売不振のため、生産中止となることを社員に伝えました。

(A) 動 ～を発表する [過去形]
(B) 動 ～に通知 [過去形]
(C) 動 応じる [過去形]
(D) 動 ～を確認する [過去形]

選択肢には意味の異なる動詞が並んでいる。文の意味を見ていくと、「Alves さんは、音楽プレーヤーが販売不振のため、生産中止となることを社員に……」となっているので、「連絡した、知らせた」という意味の語が入ることがわかる。選択肢の中では (A)、(B) が意味として入りそうだが、人を目的語にとって「人に that 以下のことを知らせる」という第 4 文型を取るのは (B) のみなので、これが正解となる。

Ms. Alves informed her employees / that the Dancer-S1 music player will be discontinued /
　　S　　　V　　　O¹　　　　O²(that 節)　　　　S　　　　　　　V
because of poor sales.
（副詞句 [原因・理由]）

□discontinue ～を生産中止にする　□poor sales 販売不振

2. ★☆☆☆☆

仕事の効率化セミナーの招待状は、年間を通じて定期的に全労働者に送付されています。

(A) 名 招待状（複数形）
(B) 名 招待状
(C) 動 ～を招待する
(D) [動名詞]

選択肢には動詞 invite の派生語が並んでいる。空所は文頭にあり、後ろに述語動詞 have been sent があるため、この主語になることがわかる。また述語動詞が have been のため、主語は複数の形を持つということがわかる。以上より、名詞の複数形である (A) が正解。

Invitations for the work efficiency seminars have been sent at regular intervals throughout the year
　　S　　　　　　　　　　　　　　　　　　　V
to all workers.

□at regular intervals 時々

3. ★★★★☆

新しい教科書をよりわかりやすくするために、邪魔だと思われるイラストを削除しました。

(A) 動 ～の気を散らす
(B) 形 気を散らすような
(C) 名 気を散らすもの
(D) 副 上の空で

選択肢には動詞 distract の派生語が並んでいる。空所は文末で、illustrations を先行詞とする関係詞 that 節内の修飾表現となっている。以上から、illustrations were too -------. という関係が成り立つため、空所には形容詞が入ることがわかる。よって、正解は (B)。that 以降を 1 つの文にすると、We thought (that) some illustrations were too distracting. という構造になる。このカタマリが関係詞として文の後半に組み込まれていると考えよう。

To make our new textbook easier to understand, /
to 不定詞（副詞句）
we eliminated some illustrations / that we thought were too distracting.
　　S　　　V　　　　O　　　　　　S　　　　　　V　　　C

□eliminate ～を削除する　□illustration イラスト、挿絵

 1. (B)　2. (A)　3. (B)

4. The survey will determine ------- the new manufacturing plant in Bay Canou will have a significant impact on energy consumption.

(A) whatever
(B) whether
(C) whichever
(D) what

5. Valley Spring City Authority announced that Highway 12 will be temporarily closed ------- flooding from the nearby Redcliff River.

(A) owing to
(B) instead of
(C) ahead of
(D) besides

6. Shine Airline is planning to upgrade its fleet of aircraft over the next ------- years.

(A) of
(B) each
(C) some
(D) few

4. ★★★☆☆

この調査によって、Bay Canou の新しい製造工場がエネルギー消費に大きな影響を与えるかどうかを判断します。

(A) 〜するものは何でも
(B) 〜かどうか
(C) 〜するものはどちらでも
(D) 〜(する)もの

The survey will determine / whether the new manufacturing plant in Bay Canou will have
　　S　　　V　　　O (whether 節)　　　S　　　　　　　　　　　　　V
a significant impact on energy consumption.
　　　　　　O

□determine 〜を判断する　□significant 大きな　□impact on 〜への影響　□energy consumption エネルギー消費

---

5. ★★★☆☆

Valley Spring 市は、近隣の Redcliff 川の氾濫により、12 号線道路が一時的に閉鎖されると発表しました。

(A) 〜のために(群前置詞)
(B) 〜の代わりに(群前置詞)
(C) 〜に先行して(群前置詞)
(D) 前 〜を除いて

Valley Spring City Authority announced / that Highway 12 will be temporarily closed /
　　　　　　S　　　　　　　V　　　　O (that 節)　S　　　　　　　V
owing to flooding from the nearby Redcliff River.
〜が原因で(副詞句)

□temporarily closed 一時的に閉鎖されて　□flooding (川などの)氾濫

---

6. ★★★★☆

Shine Airline 社は、今後数年間で航空機のアップグレードを計画しています。

(A) 前 〜の
(B) 形 それぞれ
(C) 形 いくつかの
(D) 形 多少の

Shine Airline is planning to upgrade its fleet of aircraft over the next few years.
　　　S　　　　　　V　　　　　　　O

□upgrade 〜をアップグレードする　□one's fleet of aircraft 所有する飛行機

 4. (B)　5. (A)　6. (D)

7. Housing associations and construction firms in partnership with the city planning committee will host a state conference on new affordable housing -------.

(A) develop
(B) developers
(C) developmental
(D) development

8. Putting his own ------- aside, Bradley Plummer agreed to approve the office redesign favored by the majority of his staff.

(A) compensation
(B) preference
(C) reminder
(D) permission

9. Over the last two decades, there has been ------- little change in the gender balance in some of the most common occupations.

(A) remark
(B) remarkably
(C) remarking
(D) remarked

7. ★★☆☆☆

住宅協会と建設会社が、都市計画委員会と協力して、手ごろな価格の新しい住宅開発に関する州議会を開催します。

(A) 動 〜を開発する
(B) 名 開発者
(C) 形 開発的な
(D) 名 開発

> 選択肢には動詞 develop とその派生語が並んでいる。空所は文末にあり、前置詞 on を伴った前置詞句の中にある。空所を含む箇所は「手ごろな新しい住宅……について」という意味になっている。以上から、空所には名詞を入れ「住宅開発」とすると文意が通るので、正解は **(D)** となる。

Housing associations and construction firms in partnership with the city planning committee
              S

will host a state conference on new affordable housing development.
     V   O

□association 協会　□construction firm 建設会社　□in partnership with 〜と提携して
□city planning committee 都市計画委員会　□host 〜を開催する　□state conference 州議会
□affordable 手ごろな　□housing 住宅

---

8. ★★★☆☆

自分の好みは脇に置いて、Bradley Plummer 氏は、部下の大半が支持するオフィスの再設計を承認することに同意した。

(A) 名 報酬
(B) 名 好み
(C) 名 思い出させるためのもの
(D) 名 許可

> 選択肢には意味の異なる名詞が並んでいる。空所を含む箇所の意味は「自分の……は置いておき、Bradley Plummer 氏がオフィス再設計の承認に同意した」となっている。ここから、同意したことに対する自分自身の好みは別として、という内容にすると文意が成立するので、**(B)** が正解となる。

Putting his own preference aside, / Bradley Plummer agreed to approve the office redesign
分詞構文   S   V   O

favored by the majority of his staff.
redesign を修飾（形容詞句）

□put aside 〜を脇に置いておく　□approve 〜を承認する　□redesign 再設計　□favor 〜を支持する
□majority 大多数

---

9. ★★★☆☆

過去 20 年間で、最も一般的な職業のいくつかでは、男女のバランスに驚くほど変化がありませんでした。

(A) 名 批評、意見
(B) 副 著しく
(C) 動 〜と言う 〔現在分詞〕
(D) 〔過去分詞〕

> 選択肢には名詞 remark の派生語が並んでいる。空所前後には完了形 has been と名詞のかたまりである little change があり、「ほとんど変化がなかった」という意味になっている。ここから、形容詞で「ほとんどない」を意味する little を修飾する副詞が入る。以上から、正解は **(B)**。形容詞を修飾するのは副詞、と理解しておこう。

〈There is 構文〉

Over the last two decades, / there has been remarkably little change in the gender balance
                          V   S

in some of the most common occupations.

□decade 10 年　□gender balance 男女間のバランス　□common 一般的な　□occupation 職業

7. (D)　8. (B)　9. (B)

10. To ensure quality service is provided, Danson Satellite Ltd. reviews all technical support calls ------- the customer requests that the call not be recorded.

(A) unless
(B) without
(C) against
(D) despite

11. The director of the Personnel Department recommended that all employees should regularly ------- basic medical checkups.

(A) postpone
(B) undergo
(C) dissolve
(D) display

12. As Mr. Steinbeck had already been through the programming course, he offered to help his colleague finish -------.

(A) she
(B) her
(C) hers
(D) herself

10. ★★★☆☆

Danson Satellite 社では、質の高いサービスを提供するために、お客様から通話を録音しないでほしいという要請がない限り、すべてのテクニカルサポートの通話内容をチェックしています。

(A) 接 〜でない限り
(B) 前 〜なしに
(C) 前 〜に対して
(D) 前 〜にもかかわらず

選択肢には接続詞や前置詞が並んでいる。空所を含む文の意味を見ていくと、「Danson Satellite 社は、お客様から通話を録音しないよう要請する……、すべての通話内容を確認する」となっている。ここから、「要請することがなければ」という否定の形の条件を表す副詞節を入れると文意が成立することがわかる。以上より、正解は (A)。この問題は、unless 以降の従属節の述語動詞が request であるため、that 節の中の動詞 が the call not be recorded と原形になっている。これは request が仮定法現在を導く動詞だからで、the call (should) not be recorded のように should が省略された形になっていることも理解しておこう。

To ensure / (that) quality service is provided, / Danson Satellite Ltd. reviews
to 不定詞（副詞句）　　S　　　V　　　　　　　　　S　　　　　　V

all technical support calls / unless the customer requests / that the call not be recorded.
　　　　O　　　　　（副詞節［条件］）S　　　V　　　　　　O (that 節)

□ensure 〜を確実にする　□quality 質の高い　□review 〜をチェックする

---

11. ★★★☆☆

人事部長は、全従業員が定期的に基本的な健康診断を受けることを推奨しました。

(A) 動 〜を延期する
(B) 動 〜を受ける
(C) 動 〜を解散する
(D) 動 〜を表示する

選択肢には意味の異なる動詞が並んでいる。空所を含む文の意味を見ていくと、「人事部長は、全従業員が定期的に健康診断を……ことを推奨した」とあるので、ここから、「健康診断を受ける」という内容にすると文意が成立する。以上より、(B) が正解。undergo は「〜を経験する」という意味で TOEIC によく登場するが、目的語に medical checkup（健康診断）などを伴い、「（診断等）を受ける」という意味もあるので押さえておこう。

The director of the Personnel Department recommended / that all employees
　　　　　S　　　　　　　　　　　　　　　　　　　　V　　　　O (that 節) S

should regularly undergo basic medical checkups.
　　　　　　V　　　　　　　　　O

□medical checkup 健康診断

---

12. ★★★☆☆

Steinbeck 氏はすでにプログラミングの講座を修了していたので、同僚が講座を修了するのを手伝うと申し出ました。

(A) 彼女が（主格）
(B) 彼女の（所有格）
(C) 彼女のもの（所有代名詞）
(D) 彼女自身（再帰代名詞）

選択肢には代名詞のさまざまな格が並んでいる。空所は文末にあり、「彼（Steinbeck 氏）は、同僚が講座を修了するのを手伝うことを申し出た」という内容にすると文意が成立することがわかる。以上から、正解は所有代名詞の (C)。ここで注意したいのは、his colleague が女性であるため、選択肢が she や her などになっていること。空所は her programming course が hers に置き換えられていると考えるとよい。

As Mr. Steinbeck had already been through the programming course, /
（副詞節［理由］）S　　　　　V　　　　　　　　　C

he offered to help his colleague finish hers.
S　　V　　　　　O　　　　　C

□be through 〜を終了（修了）する

---

13. The new security guidelines mean users who ------- installed
unapproved software will be punished.

(A) know
(B) knowledge
(C) knowingly
(D) knowledgeable

14. The magazine's readership has risen almost 30 percent
------- its online promotion.

(A) aboard
(B) quickly
(C) straight
(D) through

15. College clerical staff need to ------- their parking permits on
their front windshields when using campus parking.

(A) display
(B) print
(C) commit
(D) state

13. ★★★★★

新しいセキュリティガイドラインでは、未承認のソフトウェアを故意にインストールしたユーザーは処罰されることになっています。

(A) 動 ～を知っている
(B) 名 知識
(C) 副 故意に
(D) 形 知識のある

選択肢には動詞 know の派生語が並んでいる。空所前後を見ると、先行詞 users に導かれる関係詞 who とその述語動詞 installed、目的語の unapproved software が並んでおり、すでに節の形が成立している。以上より、副詞として述語動詞 installed を修飾し、「意図的・故意にインストールした」とすると文意が成立する。よって、正解は **(C)**。

The new security guidelines mean / (that) users who knowingly installed unapproved software
　　　　　　　　　　　　　　　S　　　　　　　V　　　　O　　　S
　　　　　　　　　　　　　　　　　　　　　　　　　　　　(that 節)
will be punished.
　　V

□install ～をインストールする　□unapproved 未承認の　□punish ～を罰する

14. ★★★★★

この雑誌の読者数は、オンラインでの販促によって、30%近くも増加したそうです。

(A) 前 ～に乗って
(B) 副 すばやく
(C) 副 まっすぐに
(D) 前 ～により

選択肢には前置詞、副詞が並んでいる。文の意味を見ていくと、「この雑誌の読者数は、オンラインでの販促……30%近くも増加した」となっている。ここからオンライン販促は読者数を増やす手段であることがわかる。よって、「～により」と手段を意味する前置詞の **(D)** が正解となる。

The magazine's readership has risen / almost 30 percent through its online promotion.
　　　　　　　　　S　　　　　　　　V

□promotion 販売促進

15. ★★★★★

大学の事務員は、構内駐車場を利用する際、フロントガラスに駐車許可証を掲示する必要があります。

(A) 動 ～を表示する
(B) 動 ～を印刷する
(C) 動 （人）に～を約束する
(D) 動 ～を述べる

選択肢には意味の異なる動詞が並んでいる。文の意味を見ていくと、「構内駐車場を利用する際、フロントガラスに駐車許可証を……する必要がある」となっている。以上から、正解は **(A)**。

College clerical staff need to display their parking permits on their front windshields /
　　　　　S　　　　　　V　　　　　　　　O

when using campus parking.
（副詞句［時］）

□parking permit 駐車許可証　□front windshield （車の）フロントガラス

13. (C)　14. (D)　15. (A)

16. The price of Cavendar watermelons is ------- according to the size of that year's harvest.

(A) empathetic
(B) variable
(C) portable
(D) infrequent

17. ------- himself with new working practices and overcoming difficulties in communication were Mr. Rumelos' priorities in Korea.

(A) Familiarize
(B) Being familiarized
(C) Familiarizes
(D) Familiarizing

18. ------- the difficulty the event planners initially had with the sound system, the concert was a huge success.

(A) On the other hand
(B) As a matter of fact
(C) Although
(D) Notwithstanding

16. ★★★★☆

Cavendar 社のスイカは、その年の収穫量によって価格が変動します。

(A) 形 感情移入の
(B) 形 変動する
(C) 形 携帯用の
(D) 形 まれな

選択肢には意味の異なる形容詞が並んでいる。文の意味を見ていくと、「その年の収穫量により、Cavendar 社のスイカの価格は……」となっている。ここから、収穫量が変わる➡価格が変動する可能性があると考えると文意が成立する。以上より、正解は **(B)**。ほかの選択肢では、文意が通らないため、いずれも不正解。

The price of Cavendar watermelons is variable / according to the size of that year's harvest.
　　S　　　　　　　　　　　　　　　　　V　　C　　　　　　〜に応じて（副詞句）

□watermelon スイカ　□according to 〜により　□harvest 収穫（量）

---

17. ★★★☆☆

新しい仕事のやり方に慣れること、コミュニケーションの難しさを克服することが、Rumelos さんの韓国での優先課題でした。

(A) 動 〜を親しませる　[原形]
(B) [動名詞]（受動態）
(C) [三人称単数現在形]
(D) [動名詞]

選択肢には動詞 familiarize が形を変えて並んでいる。空所は文頭にあり、述語動詞 were まで長い主語が続いている。等位接続詞 and 以降が、overcoming difficulties in communication（コミュニケーションの難しさを克服すること）と並列になっていることから、同様に文頭も動名詞の形とし、「自分自身を新しい仕事に慣れ親しむこと」と主語を形成すれば文意が成立する。よって、正解は **(D)**。(B) は受け身のため文意が通らない。familiarize A with B で「A に B を慣れさせる」という意味になることも押さえておこう。

Familiarizing himself with new working practices / and overcoming difficulties in communication /
　　　　　　　　　　　　　　　　　　　　　　S

were Mr. Rumelos' priorities in Korea.
　V　　　　　　　　C

□working practices 仕事のやり方　□overcome 〜を克服する　□priority 優先事項

---

18. ★★★★★

当初、イベント企画担当者は音響設備に苦労していましたが、コンサートは大成功でした。

(A) 他方では
(B) 実のところ
(C) 接 〜だけれども
(D) 前 〜にもかかわらず

選択肢には接続表現や前置詞などが並んでいる。空所を含む文の意味を見ていくと、「イベント企画担当者は音響設備に苦労していた……、コンサートは大成功した」となっている。つまりカンマの前と後で、「苦労した」➡（けれども）➡「成功した」と、逆接の関係になっていることがわかる。空所の後からカンマまでは、the difficulty という名詞を the event planners 以降が修飾した形になっていることから、この名詞を逆接の意味でつなげる前置詞の **(D)** が正解となる。Notwithstanding は Despite や In spite of と同様の意味を持つ。(A) はこの表現の前に逆接の前提情報が必要であり、(B)、(C) は後ろが節ではないと文法上当てはめることができないため、不正解。

Notwithstanding the difficulty / (that) the event planners initially had with the sound system, /
〜にもかかわらず（副詞句）　　　　　　　O　　　　　　　　S　　　　　　　　　V

the concert was a huge success.
　　S　　　V　　C

□initially 当初　□sound system 音響設備　□huge success 大成功

16. (B)　17. (D)　18. (D)

1回目

2回目

3回目

19. Anyone working on site must return their identification badge
------- leaving the office building.

(A) upon
(B) to
(C) than
(D) among

1回目

2回目

3回目

20. All restaurant wait staff are required to wear uniforms for the
entire duration of their ------- unless instructed otherwise.

(A) challenge
(B) position
(C) shift
(D) gathering

1回目

2回目

3回目

21. ------- Fregonea Castle is twenty miles outside of the city, it
is one of the most visited tourist attractions in the area.

(A) For
(B) Until
(C) How
(D) Although

19. ★★★☆☆

現場で働く人は、事務所のビルを出るときに ID バッジを返却しなければなりません。

(A) 前 ～のとき
(B) 前 ～に
(C) 前 ～よりも
(D) 前 ～の間で

選択肢には前置詞が並んでいる。文の意味を見ていくと、「事務所のビルを出る……ID バッジを返却する必要がある」となっている。事務所ビルを出る、というある時点をもとにしていることから **(A)** が正解となる。

Anyone working on site must return their identification badge / upon leaving the office building.
　　　　S　　　　　　　　　　　 V　　　　　　　　 O　　　　　　　　　　～と同時に、～するとすぐに

□on site 現場で　□identification 身分証明

20. ★☆☆☆☆

レストランのホールスタッフは全員、特に指示がない限り、シフト中はユニフォームを着用することが義務付けられています。

(A) 名 挑戦
(B) 名 職
(C) 名 （交替制の）勤務時間
(D) 名 集まり

選択肢には意味の異なる名詞が並んでいる。文の意味を見ていくと、「スタッフは全員、特に指示がない限り、……の間中はユニフォーム着用が義務付けられている」となっていることから、「勤務中は」とすると文意が成立する。よって、勤務に関係する名詞である **(C)** が正解。(D) は、公私問わず集まっている間、という意味になってしまうため不正解。

All restaurant wait staff are required to wear uniforms / for the entire duration of their shift /
　　　　　　S　　　　　　　 V　　　　　　 O　　　（副詞句）

unless instructed otherwise.
（副詞句 [条件]）

□be required to *do* ～することが求められる　□entire duration 全期間
□unless instructed otherwise 特に指示のない限りは

21. ★★★☆☆

Fregonea 城は市から 20 マイルほど離れていますが、この地域で最も訪問者の多い観光名所のひとつです。

(A) 前 ～のために
(B) 接 ～の時まで
(C) どうにでも～するように（関係副詞）
(D) 接 ～であるが

選択肢には前置詞、接続詞などが並んでいる。空所を含む文の意味を見ていくと、「Fregonea 城は市から 20 マイルほど離れている……、この地域で最も訪問者の多い観光名所だ」となっており、「距離が離れている」➡「けれども」➡「観光名所だ」と逆接の関係になっていることがわかる。以上より、正解は **(D)**。(B) も接続詞だが、20 マイルほど「離れるまで」という継続の意味になるため、文意に合わない。

Although Fregonea Castle is twenty miles outside of the city , /
（副詞節 [譲歩]）　　 S　　　 V　　　　　　 C

it is one of the most visited tourist attractions in the area.
S V　　　　　　　　　　　　　　 C

□tourist attraction 観光名所

🚩 **19. (A)　20. (C)　21. (D)**

22. The appointment of Dr. Jim Trump as director will ------- Walterson Trust's position as one of the finest research institutions in Canada.

(A) administer
(B) solidify
(C) accomplish
(D) incline

23. The attached document details ------- changes to the existing billing procedure that all staff members should be aware of as soon as possible.

(A) proposed
(B) proposes
(C) to proposing
(D) propose

24. The flight reservations ------- Mr. Campbell's trip to Tokyo have just been confirmed by Peach Fly.

(A) by
(B) about
(C) in
(D) for

22. ★★★★★

Jim Trump 博士を所長に任命することによって、Walterson Trust はカナダで最も優れた研究機関の1つとしての地位を確固たるものにするでしょう。

(A) 動 ～を管理する
(B) 動 ～を堅固にする
(C) 動 ～を達成する
(D) 動 ～を傾ける

選択肢には意味の異なる動詞が並んでいる。文の意味を見ていくと、「Trump 博士を所長に任命することで、Walterson Trust はカナダで最も優れた研究機関の1つとしての地位を……するだろう」となっている。ここから、その地位を強固なものにする、という内容にすると文意が成立することがわかる。よって、正解は **(B)**。solidify は、「～を強化する、強固にする」という意味で、strengthen と同義語である。

The appointment of Dr. Jim Trump as director will solidify Walterson Trust's position /
　　　　　　 S 　　　　　　　　　　　　　　　　 V 　　　　　 O
as one of the finest research institutions in Canada.
position を修飾（形容詞句）

□position 地位　□fine 優れた　□research institution 研究機関

---

23. ★★★☆☆

添付の文書には、すべてのスタッフができるだけ早く知っておいたほうがよい、現行の請求手続きの変更案が詳しく書かれています。

(A) 動 ～を提案する　過去分詞
(B) 三人称単数現在形
(C) 提案することに
(D) 原形

選択肢には動詞 propose が形を変えて並んでいる。空所は述語動詞 details と目的語 changes の間にあるため、この目的語を修飾する形容表現だとわかる。以上から、形容詞として当てはめることができる **(A)** が正解。proposed change で「提案された変更」、つまり「変更案」という意味になる。決まり文句として覚えておこう。

The attached document details proposed changes to the existing billing procedure /
　　　　　 S 　　　　　　 V 　　　　　　　 O 　形容詞句
that all staff members should be aware of as soon as possible.
 O 　　　　　 S 　　　　　 V
= changes

□detail ～を詳細に述べる　□existing 既存の　□billing procedure 請求手続き　□be aware of ～を知っている

---

24. ★★☆☆☆

Campbell 氏の東京行きのフライトの予約が Peach Fly で確約されたところです。

(A) 前 ～によって
(B) 前 ～について
(C) 前 ～で
(D) 前 ～のために

選択肢には前置詞が並んでいる。空所を含む箇所の意味は「Campbell 氏の東京行き……フライト予約」となっており、この後に述語動詞 have been confirmed があることから「Campbell 氏のためのフライト予約」とすると文意が成立する。以上から、正解は **(D)**。

The flight reservations for Mr. Campbell's trip to Tokyo have just been confirmed by Peach Fly.
　　　　　 S 　　　　　　　　　　　　　　　　　　　　　　 V

□confirm ～を確定する、確認する

---

 22. (B)　23. (A)　24. (D)

25. Had Gaspa Television not hired Ms. Lucas as a general manager, we ------- her the same position with us.

(A) should offer
(B) will be offering
(C) would have offered
(D) has offered

26. At Greyhaven Mall, business owners will likely see an ------- in sales shortly after the completion of the second parking lot.

(A) array
(B) effort
(C) increase
(D) insert

27. Whether shopping for an economy car or a luxury vehicle, every customer who visits Kovac Auto Sales ------- high quality service.

(A) deserves
(B) awards
(C) manages
(D) relates

25. ★★★☆☆

もし、Gaspa Television 社が Lucas さんをジェネラル・マネジャーとして採用していなかったら、当社は Lucas さんに同じポジションを提案したことでしょう。

(A) 提案すべきだ
(B) 動 ～を提案する [未来進行形]
(C) 提案しただろう
(D) [現在完了形]

> 🔍 選択肢には動詞 offer のさまざまな形が時制を変えて並んでいる。空所を含む節はカンマの後にあり、カンマ前は過去完了で「Lucas さんをジェネラル・マネジャーとして採用していなかったら」となっている。ここから、仮定法の過去完了形として、カンマ以降を「Lucas さんに同じポジションを提案しただろうに」とすると文意が成立する。以上より、正解は **(C)**。この文は If Gaspa Television had not hired Ms. Lucas ... の if が省略されることで倒置され、had が文頭に置かれていることも押さえておこう。

> 🧠 Had Gaspa Television not hired Ms. Lucas as a general manager, /
> 仮定法 S V O
> (if 省略と倒置)
>
> we would have offered her the same position with us.
> S V O¹ O²

---

26. ★★★☆☆

Greyhaven Mall において、店舗のオーナーたちは第2駐車場の完成直後から売上が増加すると見込んでいるようです。

(A) 名 配置（ずらりと並んだもの）
(B) 名 努力
(C) 名 増加
(D) 名 挿入物

> 🔍 選択肢には意味の異なる名詞が並んでいる。空所を含む箇所の意味は「店舗のオーナーは第2駐車場の完成直後から売上の……を見込んでいる」となっている。ここから「売上増加を見込んでいる」とすると文意が成立する。以上から、正解は **(C)**。see an increase in で「～が増加する、～の増加が見込まれる」という意味。

> 🧠 At Greyhaven Mall, / business owners will likely see an increase in sales /
> S V O
>
> shortly after the completion of the second parking lot.
> ～の直後に（副詞句）

> ✏️ □shortly after ～の直後に □completion 完成 □parking lot 駐車場

---

27. ★★★★☆

大衆車をお求めの方から高級車をお求めの方まで、Kovac Auto Sales にご来店のすべてのお客さまに、質の高いサービスを提供します。

(A) 動 ～を受けるに値する
(B) 動 （賞など）を与える
(C) 動 ～を管理する
(D) 動 ～を関係づける

> 🔍 選択肢には意味の異なる動詞が並んでいる。空所を含む箇所の意味は「Kovac Auto Sales にご来店のすべてのお客さまは、質の高いサービスを……」、となっている。ここから「お客様」＝「質の高いサービスを受ける価値がある、受けるに値する」という内容にすると文意が成立する。以上より、**(A)** が正解。

> 🧠 Whether shopping for an economy car / or a luxury vehicle, /
> （副詞句［譲歩］）
>
> every customer who visits Kovac Auto Sales / deserves high quality service.
> S S V O V O

> ✏️ □economy car 大衆車 □luxury vehicle 高級車

🚩 **25. (C) 26. (C) 27. (A)**

28. After weeks of research, Kalama Presence Analysts reported that consumers reacted ------- to how content was presented on Murphy Coffee House's Web site.

(A) unlikely
(B) potentially
(C) unfavorably
(D) probably

29. To promote healthy living, Moop Beverages creates its products using all-natural ingredients ------- food additives.

(A) on account of
(B) rather than
(C) in that
(D) however

30. The number of entrants to the Delmonse Fitness Competition was expected to be lower than last year, but it was ------- much higher.

(A) strongly
(B) broadly
(C) actually
(D) particularly

28. ★★★★☆

数週間の調査の後、Kalama Presence Analysts 社は、Murphy Coffee House 社のウェブサイトでのコンテンツの見せ方に消費者が否定的な反応を示したと報告しました。

(A) 形 ありそうにない
(B) 副 潜在的に
(C) 副 否定的に
(D) 副 おそらく

PART 5

選択肢には形容詞、副詞が並んでいる。空所を含む箇所の意味を見ていくと、「Murphy Coffee House 社のウェブサイトでのコンテンツの見せ方に消費者が……反応を示した」とある。ここから、消費者が示す反応に関わる表現が入るとわかる。以上から、文意の通る **(C)** が正解。(A) は形容詞のため、文法的に当てはめることができず、(B)、(D) は文意に合わないため、ここでは不正解。

After weeks of research, / Kalama Presence Analysts reported / that consumers
　　　　　　　　　　　　　　　　　S　　　　　　　　　　　　　V　　O（that 節）　[S]
reacted unfavorably to / how content was presented on Murphy Coffee House's Web site.
　　[V]　　　　　　　　　　　[O]（how 節）

☐weeks of 数週間の　☐consumer 消費者　☐react to ～に対して反応する　☐content 内容、コンテンツ
☐present ～を提示する

---

29. ★★★☆☆

健康的な生活を促進するために、Moop Beverages 社は、食品添加物ではなく、天然素材のみを使用して製品を製造しています。

(A) ～のために
(B) ～よりむしろ
(C) ～であるから、～という点で
(D) しかしながら

選択肢には接続表現が並んでいる。文の意味を見ていくと、「Moop Beverages 社は、食品添加物……天然素材のみを使用して製品を製造している」とあることから、「食品添加物ではなく、天然素材を使用」とすると文意が通る。よって、**(B)** が正解。A rather than B で、「B よりはむしろ A を」という意味になるので覚えておこう。

To promote healthy living, / Moop Beverages creates its products /
to 不定詞（副詞句）　　　　　　　　S　　　　　　　　V　　　O
using all-natural ingredients rather than food additives.
　　　　　　　　　　　　A rather than B

☐promote ～を促進する　☐healthy living 健康的な生活　☐natural ingredient 天然素材　☐food additive 食品添加物

---

30. ★★★★☆

Delmonse フィットネス大会の参加者数は昨年より少なくなると予想されていましたが、実際にはずっと多かったです。

(A) 副 強く
(B) 副 大まかに
(C) 副 実際に
(D) 副 特に

選択肢には意味の異なる副詞が並んでいる。文の意味を見ていくと、「大会の参加者数は昨年より少なくなると予想されたが、……かなり多かった」となっており、当初は少ないと思ったが、予想とは違ったという内容になると文意が成立する。以上から、正解は **(C)**。

TEST 7

The number of entrants to the Delmonse Fitness Competition was expected to be lower than
　　　　　　　　　　　　S　　　　　　　　　　　　　　　　　　　　　　　V　　　　　　C
last year, / but it was actually much higher.
　　　　　　　　　　S　V　　　　　C

☐entrant （大会等の）参加者　☐competition 大会

---

 28. (C)　29. (B)　30. (C)

1回目

2回目

3回目

1. Savings accounts are gaining ------- with many individuals as interest rates continue to rise.

(A) elevation
(B) mobility
(C) risk
(D) popularity

1回目

2回目

3回目

2. After receiving favorable feedback from customers, Presley Carpet Cleaning Service is justifiably ------- about its business outlook.

(A) optimistic
(B) exciting
(C) sufficient
(D) dedicated

1回目

2回目

3回目

3. Some canned dog food made by Navi Pet Supply is formulated ------- for large adult dogs over 20 kg, so please avoid feeding it to small dogs.

(A) incompletely
(B) jointly
(C) exclusively
(D) alternatively

1. ★★★☆☆

金利が上昇し続けるにつれ、貯蓄預金が多くの人の人気を集めています。

(A) 名 昇進
(B) 名 流動性
(C) 名 危険性
(D) 名 人気

> 選択肢には意味の異なる名詞が並んでいる。文の意味は「金利上昇につれ、貯蓄預金が多くの人の……を集めている」となっていることから、多くの人が貯蓄に魅力を感じていると考えられる。以上から、正解は **(D)**。gain popularity with で「〜の人気を集める」という意味。(C) の危険を伴う場合は carry a risk of と表現する。

Savings accounts are gaining popularity with many individuals / as interest rates continue to rise .
S　　　　　　V　　　　　O　　　　　　　　　　（副詞節 [比例]）S　　　　　　V

□savings accounts 普通預金口座　□gain 〜を集める　□individual 個人　□interest rate 金利　□rise 上昇する

---

2. ★★★☆☆

顧客から好評を博して以降、Presley Carpet Cleaning 社は、当然のように事業の見通しを楽観視しています。

(A) 形 楽観的な
(B) 形 刺激的な
(C) 形 十分な
(D) 形 ひたむきな

> 選択肢には意味の異なる形容詞が並んでいる。空所を含む文の意味は「顧客から好評を得て、Presley Carpet Cleaning 社は、当然のように事業の見通しを……している」となっている。ここから、事業の見通しについてどう思っているかを形容できる **(A)** が正解となる。ほかの選択肢ではいずれも意味が通らなくなってしまうので不正解。

After receiving favorable feedback from customers, / Presley Carpet Cleaning Service is
（副詞句 [時]）　　　　　　　　　　　　　　　　　　　　S　　　　　　　　　V

justifiably optimistic about its business outlook.
　　　　　　　C

□favorable feedback 好評　□justifiably 当然のように　□business outlook 事業の見通し

---

3. ★★★★☆

Navi Pet Supply 社製のドッグフードの缶詰の中には、20kg を超える大型成犬専用に配合されているものがありますので、小型犬には与えないようにしてください。

(A) 副 不完全に
(B) 副 共同で
(C) 副 全く〜のみ、独占的に
(D) 副 代わりに

> 選択肢には意味の異なる副詞が並んでいる。文の意味を見ていくと、「ドッグフード缶詰の中には、大型成犬のため……配合されているものがあるので、小型犬には与えないように」となっている。以上から、文意が成立する **(C)** が正解。ここでの exclusively は only の同義語と捉えておこう。

Some canned dog food made by Navi Pet Supply is formulated exclusively for
　　　S　　　　　　　　　　　　　　　　　　　V

large adult dogs over 20 kg, / so please avoid feeding it to small dogs.
　　　　　　　　　　　命令文　　　V　　　=dog food

□canned 缶入りの　□formulated 配合されている　□avoid 〜を避ける　□feed A to B　A（食料など）を B に与える

 1. (D)　2. (A)　3. (C)

4. Our warehouse staff all agree that the HG-5 bar code scanner is more reliable than ------- they have used.

(A) last
(B) others
(C) who
(D) ever

5. For your convenience, Sally-B's Web site lists prices of products and gives information ------- shipping options in our place.

(A) on
(B) into
(C) until
(D) along

6. Most residents who attended the municipal conference shared some ------- that were related to traffic problems in the downtown area.

(A) worries
(B) worried
(C) worrying
(D) worrisome

4. ★★★★★

当社の倉庫スタッフは皆、HG-5 バーコードスキャナーは、これまで使ってきたほかのスキャナーよりも信頼性が高いと考えています。

(A) 名 最後のもの
(B) ほかのもの
(C) 誰
(D) 副 今までに

選択肢にはいろいろな品詞の語が並んでいる。空所前は more reliable than と比較表現になっているため、空所には比較対象となるものが入ることがわかる。この比較表現の主語を見ていくと、HG-5 bar code scanner という製品であるので、比較対象として「複数の他製品」を意味する others を入れると文意が成立する。以上より、正解は **(B)**。

Our warehouse staff all agree / that the HG-5 bar code scanner is more reliable than others /
　　　 S　　　　　　 V　　 O (that 節)　　　　 S　　　　　　　 V　　　　　 C

they have used .
others を修飾 (形容詞節)

□warehouse 倉庫　□bar code scanner バーコードスキャナー　□reliable 信頼できる

---

5. ★★★★★

ご参考までに、Sally-B 社のウェブサイトでは、商品の価格を表示し、配送方法についてもご案内しています。

(A) 前 ～について
(B) 前 ～の中に
(C) 前 ～まで (ずっと)
(D) 前 ～に沿って

選択肢には前置詞が並んでいる。空所を含む箇所の意味は「Sally-B 社のウェブサイトでは、配送方法……案内している」とある。以上より、正解は **(A)**。前置詞 on は about と同じように「～に関する」という意味を持つことを押さえておこう。

For your convenience, / Sally-B's Web site lists prices of products and gives
　　　　　　　　　　　 S　　　 V¹　　 O　　　　　　　 V²

information on shipping options in our place.
　　 O

□for your convenience 参考までに、便宜を図るために　□shipping option 配送方法

---

6. ★★★★★

自治体会議に参加した住民のほとんどが、繁華街の交通の問題に関する悩みを共有していました。

(A) 名 心配事
(B) 動 ～を心配させる　過去分詞
(C) 動名詞
(D) 形 気がかりな

選択肢には worry の形を変えたものが並んでいる。空所を含めた文の構造を見てみると、主語が Most residents、述語動詞が shared で、空所は share の目的語に当たる箇所だとわかる。空所以降には関係詞 that があり、その後に were が続いていることから、空所には複数の意味を持つ名詞が入る。以上から、**(A)** が正解。

Most residents / who attended the municipal conference / shared some worries /
　 S　　　　　　 S　　 V　　　　 O　　　　　　　 V　　 O

that were related to traffic problems in the downtown area.
 S　　 V　　　　　　 O
(=worries)

□municipal conference 自治体会議　□related to ～に関連した

4. **(B)**　5. **(A)**　6. **(A)**

7. Lindon Bistro Co. is joining the organizers of Dextra Automobile Expo ------- an official catering partner.

(A) against
(B) during
(C) as
(D) below

8. The Wilpont Associate Council is now ------- applications for the position of program director to begin in August.

(A) accepting
(B) advising
(C) renovating
(D) running

9. The company's policy regarding the salary payment schedule and health benefits is ------- outlined in the staff handbook.

(A) passionately
(B) elusively
(C) equally
(D) explicitly

7. ★★☆☆☆

Lindon Bistro 社は、公式ケータリングパートナーとして Dextra 自動車博覧会の主催者に加わってます。

選択肢には意味の異なる前置詞が並んでいる。文の意味を見ていくと、「Lindon Bistro 社は、Dextra 自動車博覧会の主催者に公式ケータリングパートナー……加わっている」となっている。ここから、文意が成立する (C) が正解となる。

(A) 前 ～に対して
(B) 前 ～の間ずっと
(C) 前 ～として
(D) 前 ～より下に

Lindon Bistro Co. is joining the organizers of Dextra Automobile Expo as an official
  S   V   O

catering partner.

□catering ケータリングの、飲食物を提供する

---

8. ★★★☆☆

Wilpont Associate Council では現在、8月入社のプログラムディレクターの求人の応募を受け付けています。

選択肢には意味の異なる動詞の現在分詞が並んでいる。空所を含む箇所の意味を見ていくと「Wilpont Associate Council は現在プログラムディレクターの応募を……している」となっている。以上から、「応募を受け付けている」という内容にすると文意が成立するので、正解は (A)。

(A) 動 ～を受け入れる [現在分詞]
(B) 動 ～に助言する [現在分詞]
(C) 動 ～を改修する [現在分詞]
(D) 動 ～を行う [現在分詞]

The Wilpont Associate Council is now accepting applications for the position of program director /
  S   V   O

to begin in August.
to 不定詞（形容詞句）

□application for ～への応募

---

9. ★★★★★

給与の支給予定日や傷病手当に関する会社の方針は、社員ハンドブックに明示されています。

選択肢には意味の異なる副詞が並んでいる。文の意味を見ていくと、「会社の方針は、社員ハンドブックに……説明されている」とある。ここから、outlined「～の説明をする」という動詞を修飾する表現として文意が成立するものを選ぶ。以上から、正解は (D)。

(A) 副 熱心に
(B) 副 捉えようのない
(C) 副 等しく
(D) 副 明確に

The company's policy regarding the salary payment schedule and health benefits /
   S   （形容詞句）

is explicitly outlined in the staff handbook.
 V   （副詞句）

□regarding ～に関する □salary payment 給与の支払い □health benefit 傷病手当 □outline ～の説明をする
□handbook ハンドブック、手引書

⚑ **7. (C)　8. (A)　9. (D)**

10. The ------- document should be signed and returned to Mallory Business Publishers before a manuscript can be considered for publication.

(A) surrounded
(B) confined
(C) stationed
(D) enclosed

11. Every survey respondent is required ------- to the guidelines listed in the manual, and failure to do so may invalidate the survey.

(A) adhere
(B) adhering
(C) have adhered
(D) to adhere

12. Murdoch Electronics is closely following the trend ------- interactive games, which allow users to play and chat together.

(A) onto
(B) beside
(C) toward
(D) along

10. ★★★☆☆

同封の書類は、原稿の出版を検討できるようになる前に、署名して Mallory Business Publishers に返送する必要があります。

(A) 動 ～を囲む [過去分詞]
(B) 動 ～を閉じ込める [過去分詞]
(C) 動 ～を配置する [過去分詞]
(D) 動 ～を同封する [過去分詞]

🔍 選択肢にはさまざまな動詞の過去分詞が並んでいる。空所を含む箇所の意味は「……の書類は署名して返送の必要がある」となっている。ここから、同封された文書、とすると文意が成立するので (D) が正解。

The enclosed document should be signed and returned to Mallory Business Publishers /
　　　　S　　　　　　　　V¹　　　　　　　　V²

before a manuscript can be considered for publication .
(副詞節 [時])　S　　　　　　　　V

✏ □manuscript 原稿　□publication 出版

---

11. ★★☆☆☆

すべての調査回答者は、マニュアルに記載されているガイドラインを遵守する必要があり、遵守されない場合は調査が無効となる場合があります。

(A) 動 遵守する [原形]
(B) [動名詞]
(C) [現在完了形]
(D) [to 不定詞]

🔍 選択肢には動詞 adhere が形を変えて並んでいる。空所前に be required という動詞があることから、require every survey respondent to do が受け身になった文だと考えられる。以上より、正解は (D)。require は be required to 不定詞の形で覚えておこう。また adhere to は、「～を遵守する」という TOEIC 頻出の動詞でもあるため、これもチェックしておこう。

Every survey respondent is required to adhere to the guidelines listed in the manual, / and
　　　　　　S　　　　　　　　　V　　　　　　　　　O

failure to do so may invalidate the survey.
　　　S　　　　　　V　　　　O

✏ □respondent 回答者　□require ～を必要とする　□guideline ガイドライン、指針
□failure to do so may そうしなかった場合は～となることもある　□invalidate ～を無効にする

---

12. ★★★☆☆

Murdoch Electronics 社は、ユーザー同士が一緒にゲームをしたり、チャットしたりできる、対話型ゲームの流行をしっかり押さえています。

(A) 前 ～の上に
(B) 前 ～のそばに
(C) 前 ～に向かって
(D) 前 ～に沿って

🔍 選択肢には前置詞が並んでいる。文の意味を見ていくと、「Murdoch Electronics 社は、対話型ゲーム……流行をしっかり押さえている」という意味になっている。ここから「対話型ゲームに対する流行、対話型ゲームに向いた流行」という内容にすると文意が成立する。以上より、正解は (C)。trend toward ... で「～に対する流行・傾向」という表現になるので、押さえておこう。

Murdoch Electronics is closely following the trend toward interactive games, / which allow users
　　　　S　　　　　　　V　　　　　　　　O　　　　　　　　　　　　　S　　V　　O

to play and chat together .
　　C

✏ □closely しっかりと　□follow ～についていく　□interactive 相互に行う　□allow 人 to do　人が～できるようにする
□chat チャットする、話す

🚩 **10. (D)　11. (D)　12. (C)**

13. Remington General Hospital has been meeting the health care ------- of the greater Fosberg area for nearly fifteen years.

(A) to need
(B) has needed
(C) needing
(D) needs

14. Watson Studios of Hampton is seeking a marketing agent to ------- publicity campaigns for three new movies that will premiere this spring.

(A) inform
(B) participate
(C) emerge
(D) launch

15. The task of restructuring the finance and administration should take ------- over all other work in the coming weeks.

(A) resolve
(B) priority
(C) credit
(D) standard

13. ★★☆☆☆

Remington 総合病院は、15年近くにわたり、Fosberg 広域の医療ニーズに応えてきました。

(A) 動 ～を必要とする　[to 不定詞]
(B) [現在完了形]
(C) [動名詞]
(D) 名 必要性

選択肢には動詞 need の形を変えたものや派生語が並んでいる。文の意味を見ていくと、「Remington 総合病院は、長きにわたり、この広域の医療……に応えてきた」とある。ここから、「～に応える、～を満たす」という動詞 meet を充足させる目的語として適切な名詞が入ることがわかる。以上から、正解は **(D)**。

Remington General Hospital has been meeting the health care needs of the greater Fosberg area
　　　　　　S　　　　　　　　　V　　　　　　　　O　　　　　　　（形容詞句）
for nearly fifteen years.

□health care 医療

---

14. ★★★☆☆

Hampton 市の Watson Studios 社が、今春公開の新作映画3本の宣伝活動を開始するため、マーケティング担当者を募集しています。

(A) 動 ～に報告する
(B) 動 参加する
(C) 動 現れる
(D) 動 ～を開始する

選択肢には意味の異なる動詞が並んでいる。文の意味を見ていくと、「Watson Studios 社が、今春公開の新作映画3本の宣伝活動を……ためマーケティング担当者を募集している」とある。ここから、「宣伝活動を行う、始める」という内容にすると文意が成立することがわかる。以上から、正解は **(D)**。(B)、(C) は自動詞であり、文法的に当てはめることができないため不正解。

Watson Studios of Hampton is seeking a marketing agent / to launch publicity campaigns
　　　　　S　　　　　　　　V　　　　　O　　　　to 不定詞（副詞句）
for three new movies / that will premiere this spring.
　　　　　　　　　　　　S　　　V

□seek ～を募集する　□agent 担当者　□publicity campaign 宣伝活動　□premiere 初めて公開される

---

15. ★★★★☆

財務・管理部門の再編成の仕事は、今後数週間のうち、ほかのどの仕事より優先するべきです。

(A) 名 決心
(B) 名 優先
(C) 名 信用
(D) 名 標準

選択肢には意味の異なる名詞が並んでいる。文の意味を見ていくと、「財務・管理部門の再編成の仕事は、ほかのすべての仕事から……すべきものだ」となっている。ここから、優先すべきとすると文意が成立するとわかる。よって、**(B)** が正解。take priority over で「～より優先度が高い」という決まり文句なので押さえておこう。

The task of restructuring the finance and administration should take priority over all other work
　　S　　　　　　　　　　　　　　　　　　　　　　　　　　　　V　　　O
in the coming weeks.

□task タスク、任務　□restructuring 再編成　□administration 管理部門　□in the coming weeks 今後数週間で

---

 13. (D)　14. (D)　15. (B)

16. Chase Foodmarkets has seen only ------- profit growth and so may start an expansion program.

(A) margin
(B) marginal
(C) marginally
(D) marginalize

17. Salespeople who will be involved in the sales campaign targeting senior citizens must take the training course on effective -------.

(A) communication
(B) communicate
(C) communicated
(D) communicatively

18. The report by Roseville City on population growth strategies ------- data from the past forty years.

(A) observes
(B) arrives
(C) believes
(D) contains

16. ★★★☆☆

Chase Foodmarkets 社は利益がわずかしか伸びていないため、拡張計画を開始することになりそうです。

(A) 名 粗利益
(B) 形 わずかな
(C) 副 わずかに
(D) 動 ～を軽視する

> 選択肢には名詞 margin とその派生語が並んでいる。空所の前後は述語動詞 has seen と名詞句 profit growth（利益成長）がある。ここから「利益成長」を修飾する形容詞「わずかな」を当てはめると文意が成立するとわかる。以上より、正解は **(B)**。

Chase Foodmarkets has seen only marginal profit growth / and so (it) may start an expansion program.
　　　　S　　　　　　　V　　　　　　　　　O　　　　　　　 S　　 V　　　　　O

□profit growth 利益の伸び　□expansion program 拡張計画

---

17. ★☆☆☆☆

高齢者を対象とした販売キャンペーンに携わる営業担当者は、効果的なコミュニケーションに関する研修コースを受講する必要があります。

(A) 名 コミュニケーション
(B) 動 ～を伝える　[原形]
(C) [過去分詞]
(D) 副 話し好きで

> 選択肢には名詞 communication の派生語が並んでいる。空所は on から始まる前置詞句の中にあり、前には形容詞 effective があることから、ここには effective に修飾される名詞が入るとわかる。以上から、正解は **(A)**。

Salespeople / who will be involved in the sales campaign targeting senior citizens / must take
　　S　　　　　S　　　　　V　　　　　　　　　O　　　　　　　　　　　　　　　V
the training course on effective communication.
　　　　　O

□be involved in ～に関わる　□target ～を対象とする　□senior citizen 高齢者　□effective 効果的な

---

18. ★★★☆☆

Roseville 市によって作られた人口増加戦略に関する報告書には、過去 40 年間のデータが掲載されています。

(A) 動 ～を観察する
(B) 動 到着する
(C) 動 ～を信じる
(D) 動 ～を含む

> 選択肢には意味の異なる動詞が並んでいる。文の意味を見ていくと、「Roseville 市によって作られた人口増加戦略に関する報告書は、過去 40 年間のデータを……」とある。よって、「報告書の中にはデータが含まれている」と考えると文意が成立する。以上より、正解は **(D)**。

The report by Roseville City on population growth strategies contains
　　S　　　　　　　　　　　　　　　　　　　　　　　　　　　V
data from the past forty years.
　O

□population growth 人口増加　□strategy 戦略

16. (B)　17. (A)　18. (D)

19. Advancements in the field of agriculture over the last decade have increased ------- to such an extent that surplus produce is now exported abroad.

(A) location
(B) preparation
(C) output
(D) rules

20. Larson's new range features cell phone cases that are both ------- and heat resistant.

(A) durably
(B) durability
(C) durable
(D) durableness

21. Although the latest software is expensive, its implementation will greatly ------- the performance of the company's accounting system.

(A) adapt
(B) improve
(C) reimburse
(D) reward

19. ★★★☆☆

ここ 10 年の農業分野の進歩により、余剰生産物を海外に輸出するくらい、生産量が増加しています。

(A) 名 場所
(B) 名 準備
(C) 名 生産量
(D) 名 ルール

🔍 選択肢には意味の異なる名詞が並んでいる。文の意味を見ていくと、「ここ 10 年の農業分野の進歩が、余剰生産物を海外に輸出するくらい、……が増加している」となっている。ここから、輸出されるほど多くなっているものとして適切な **(C)** が正解となる。

🎧 Advancements in the field of agriculture over the last decade have increased
　　　　S　　　　　　　　　　　　　　　　　　　　　　　　　　　　　　　　　　V

output to such an extent / that surplus produce is now exported abroad .
　O　　　such ... that 〜　　　　　　S　　　　　　V
　　　　　（〜ほどの…）

✏️ □advancement in 〜における進歩　□field 分野　□agriculture 農業
□to such an extent that SV　S が V するほどまでに　□surplus 過剰な　□produce 農作物　□export 〜を輸出する

....

20. ★★☆☆☆

Larson の新製品は、耐久性と耐熱性を両立させた携帯電話ケースです。

(A) 副 耐久的に
(B) 名 耐久性
(C) 形 耐久性のある
(D) 名 耐久性のあること

🔍 選択肢には形容詞 durable の派生語が並んでいる。空所の前後を見ると、決まり文句である both A and B（A も B も両方とも）という表現の中に、空所と形容表現の heat resistant があることがわかる。つまり、空所には並列の品詞となる形容詞が入ることがわかるので、正解は **(C)**。等位接続詞 and は、品詞や句、節、同じ性質のものを並列すると覚えておこう。

🎧 Larson's new range features cell phone cases / that are both durable and heat resistant .
　　　　S　　　　　　　V　　　　　　O　　　　　S　V　　　　　　　　C

✏️ □range 製品　□feature 〜を主力商品とする　□cell phone 携帯電話　□heat resistant 耐熱性のある

....

21. ★★★☆☆

最新のソフトウェアは高価ですが、導入すれば会社の会計システムの性能は大きく向上するでしょう。

(A) 動 〜を適応させる
(B) 動 〜を改善する
(C) 動 〜を払い戻す
(D) 動 〜に報いる

🔍 選択肢には意味の異なる動詞が並んでいる。文の意味を見ていくと、「最新のソフトウェアは高価だが、その導入は会社の会計システムの性能を大きく……だろう」なっている。ここから「高価だが、性能を上げる」といった内容にすると文意が成立することがわかる。以上から、正解は **(B)**。

🎧 Although the latest software is expensive , / its implementation will greatly improve
（副詞節 [譲歩]）　　S　　　　V　　C　　　　　　S　　　　　　　V

the performance of the company's accounting system.
　　　　O

✏️ □latest 最新の　□implementation 導入、実行　□greatly 大きく

🚩 **19. (C)　20. (C)　21. (B)**

22. Oscar Copeland's job appraisal stated that he is more efficient when working ------- than as a team member.

(A) substantially
(B) independently
(C) jointly
(D) dramatically

23. Food items containing milk or eggs are more ------- to spoiling when there is an increase in temperature.

(A) obtainable
(B) sensational
(C) vulnerable
(D) compatible

24. Last month, ------- of the new workers was officially invited to participate in the welcome reception held by the company's president.

(A) most
(B) all
(C) every
(D) each

22. ★★★★☆

Oscar Copeland さんの職務評価書には、チームの一員としてよりも単独で仕事をした方が効率がいいと書かれていました。

(A) 副 大いに
(B) 副 独立して
(C) 副 共同で
(D) 副 劇的に

選択肢には意味の異なる副詞が並んでいる。文の意味を見ていくと、「Oscar Copeland さんの職務評価書には、チームの一員としてよりも……仕事をする方が効率的であると書かれていた」とある。ここから「チームメンバーという語と対比する関係となる意味の語が入ると考えられる。よって、**(B)** が正解。この問題は空所前後だけを見てしまうと、どれも当てはまると思えてしまうため、文全体の内容（＝文脈）を意識して解く必要がある。

Oscar Copeland's job appraisal stated / that he is more efficient / when working independently
　　　　　　S　　　　　　　　V　　　　O　S V　　　　C　　　（副詞句）
than as a team member.　　　　　　　　　　　（that 節）

□job appraisal 職務評価 □state that 〜と記載されている □efficient 効率的な

---

23. ★★★★★

牛乳や卵を含む食品は、温度が上がると傷みやすくなります。

(A) 形 入手できる
(B) 形 人騒がせな
(C) 形 傷つきやすい
(D) 形 互換性のある

選択肢には意味の異なる形容詞が並んでいる。文の意味を見ていくと、「牛乳や卵を含む食品は、温度が上がると……となる」となっている。ここから、「卵・乳製品の温度が上がる➡それが原因で起こる現象」という内容にすると文意が成立する。以上から、**(C)** が正解となる。全体的に選択肢の単語の意味が少し難しかったと思うので不明なものがあればしっかり復習しておこう。

Food items containing milk or eggs are more vulnerable to spoiling /
　　　　S　　　　　　　　　　　　　V　　　　　　　O
when there is an increase in temperature.
（副詞節 [時]） V　　　　　S

□contain 〜を含む □spoil ダメになる、傷む □increase in 〜の増加

---

24. ★★★☆☆

先月、新入社員は全員、社長主催の歓迎会に正式に招待されました。

(A) 大部分
(B) すべて
(C) すべての
(D) それぞれ

選択肢には名詞の数を表す語が並んでいる。空所の後ろに述語動詞の was があることから、主語は単数を受けるものだとわかる。そして空所後の of 以降に workers と複数の名詞が来ている。以上から、正解の条件を満たすのは **(D)**。each of the 可算名詞で、「〇〇のひとりひとり」という意味となる。all も空所の前後を見ると当てはめることができそうだが、この場合は「〇〇すべて」と述語動詞を were にする必要があるため、ここでは当てはめられない。

Last month, / each of the new workers was officially invited to participate in
　　　　　　　　S　　　　　　　　　　　　V
the welcome reception / (that was) held by the company's president.
　　　　　O

□welcome reception 歓迎会

 22. (B) 23. (C) 24. (D)

25. At the tourist information counter, officials hand out guide maps and brochures featuring regional attractions to ------- requests them.

(A) whoever
(B) whatsoever
(C) whenever
(D) whichever

26. Our company ------- its overall sales grow by 20 percent since Sylvia Ritter joined the sales force.

(A) sees
(B) can see
(C) seeing
(D) has seen

27. The more Ann Ruiz's clients dealt with her, the more ------- they became with her customer service and attention to detail.

(A) impressed
(B) impression
(C) impress
(D) impresses

25. ★★★☆☆

観光案内所では、地域の観光スポットを紹介するガイドマップやパンフレットを職員が希望者全員に配布しています。

(A) ～する人は誰でも
(B) どんなものであれ
(C) ～するときはいつでも
(D) どちらの～でも

選択肢には異なる意味の複合関係代名詞が並んでいる。空所を含む箇所の意味は「地域の観光スポットを紹介するガイドマップなどを希望する……に配布している」であることから、空所には目的格が入り、かつ配布される対象であることがわかる。以上から、正解は **(A)**。whoever は (to) anyone who に置き換えると理解しやすい。

At the tourist information counter, / officials hand out guide maps and brochures / (that are) featuring
　　　　　　　　　　　　　　　　　　　　　S　　　V　　　　　　　　O　　　　　　　　　　　　　　（形容詞句）

regional attractions to whoever requests them.
　　　　　　　　　　　　　S　　　　　V　　　　O
　　　　　　　　　　　　　（名詞節）

□hand out ～を配布する　□brochure パンフレット　□feature ～を特集する
□regional attraction 地域の観光スポット

---

26. ★★☆☆☆

Silvia Ritter 氏が営業に加わってから、私たちの会社は全体の売上が 20%伸びました。

(A) 動 ～を見る 三人称単数現在形
(B) 見ることができる
(C) 動 ～を見る 動名詞
(D) 動 ～を見る 現在完了形

選択肢には動詞 see が形を変えたものが並んでいる。文の意味を見ていくと、「Silvia Ritter 氏が営業に加わってから、私たちの会社は全体の売上が 20%伸びるのを……」とある。ここから、Silvia Ritter 氏が会社に入った時点から売上が 20%成長して現在に至ったという継続された内容になっているため、空所には現在完了の時制が入ることがわかる。以上から、正解は **(D)**。

Our company has seen its overall sales grow by 20 percent /
　　　　S　　　　V　　　　　O　　　　　　C

since Sylvia Ritter joined the sales force.
（副詞節［時］）S　　　　　V　　　　O

□overall sales 売り上げ全体　□sales force 営業チーム

---

27. ★★★☆☆

Ann Ruiz さんの顧客は、取引すればするほど、彼女の顧客サービスや細やかな配慮に感銘を受けました。

(A) 動 ～に感銘を与える 過去分詞
(B) 名 印象
(C) 原 形
(D) 三人称単数現在形

選択肢には動詞 impress が形を変えた語やその派生語が並んでいる。文の構造を見ると、the more ..., the more ...「～すればするほど、～」という構文になっていることがわかる。ここから空所の前後は、比較表現である more、かつ倒置となっている主語 they (Ann Ruiz's clients)、述語動詞 became という関係であることがわかる。よって空所には形容詞として考えられる impressed を入れて、「顧客がますます感銘を受ける」とすると文意が成立する。以上より、正解は **(A)**。

The more Ann Ruiz's clients dealt with her, /
　　　　　　　　S　　　　　　V　　　O

the more impressed they became with her customer service and attention to detail.
　　　　　　C　　　　S　　　V

□deal with ～と取引する　□attention to detail 細部への配慮

---

25. **(A)**　26. **(D)**　27. **(A)**

28. The sign warns that ------- is allowed to enter Stevenage Forest without written permission from its owner.

(A) anything
(B) somebody
(C) each other
(D) no one

29. The findings from new research show that in most industries, novice workers spend at least twice ------- hours as experienced workers finishing the same tasks.

(A) much more
(B) more than
(C) as many
(D) very long

30. According to market analysts, the price of gasoline is expected to increase -------, so drivers are encouraged to fill up their gas tanks now.

(A) mainly
(B) ever
(C) anxiously
(D) soon

28. ★★☆☆☆

この看板は、所有者の書面による許可なくして、誰も Stevenage の森に入ることは許可されないと警告しています。

(A) 何でも
(B) 誰か
(C) 互いに
(D) 誰も～ない

> 選択肢にはさまざまな代名詞が並んでいる。空所は that 節の主語に当たる箇所で、文は「所有者の書面による許可なく、……森に入ることを許されてはいない」という意味になっている。以上から、肯定文で「誰も～ない」という意味になる **(D)** が正解。

The sign warns / that no one is allowed to enter Stevenage Forest without written
　　S　　　V　　O（that 節） S　　　　　　V　　　　　　　　　O
permission / from its owner.

□sign 看板、標識　□allow to enter ～の立ち入りを許可する　□written permission 書面による許可

---

29. ★★★★☆

新しい研究の結果、ほとんどの産業で、新規の労働者は同じ仕事を終わらせるのに、経験豊富な労働者の少なくとも2倍の時間がかかることがわかりました。

(A) はるかに多い
(B) ～より多く
(C) 同じぐらい長い
(D) 非常に長い

> 選択肢にはさまざまな形容表現が並んでいる。文の意味を見ていくと、「新しい研究結果では、ほとんどの産業で、新規労働者は同じ仕事を終えるのに、経験豊富な労働者の少なくとも2倍の……時間を費やしていることがわかった」という意味になっている。空所以降には hours as experienced workers と、比較対象の「経験豊富な労働者」の前に as があるため、「新人が経験豊富な労働者の相当する時間から2倍くらいかかる」という意味になるよう、as many hours as... を当てはめると文意が成立する。以上より、正解は **(C)**。「～倍」を表す表現（twice, three times）+as many hours as で「～の時間の～倍」という意味になる。文中に as が含まれているので、ほかの比較表現 (A)、(B) は文法上当てはめることができない。

The findings from new research show that in most industries, novice workers spend
　　　S　　　　　　　　　　　　　V　　O（that 節）　　　　　　S　　　　　V
at least twice as many hours as experienced workers finishing the same tasks.
　　　　　　　　　　　　　　　　　O

□finding 発見、成果　□novice worker 初心者の労働者　□spend＋O＋doing ○ を～して過ごす
□experienced 経験のある　□task タスク、業務

---

30. ★★☆☆☆

市場アナリストによると、ガソリンの価格はまもなく上昇すると予想されているので、ドライバーは今のうちにガソリンを満タンにしておくことを推奨されています。

(A) 副 主に
(B) 副 今までに
(C) 副 心配して
(D) 副 近いうちに

> 選択肢には意味の異なる副詞が並んでいる。文の意味を見ていくと、「ガソリンの価格は……上昇する見込みのため、ドライバーは今のうちにガソリンを満タンにしておくべき」となっている。以上から、「すぐに、まもなく」を意味する **(D)** が正解。

According to market analysts, / the price of gasoline is expected to increase soon, /
　　　　　　　　　　　　　　　　　　S　　　　　　　　　V
so drivers are encouraged to fill up their gas tanks now.
だから S　　　V　　　　　　　　O

□according to ～によると　□be encouraged to do ～することを奨励される
□fill up one's gas tanks ガソリンを満タンに入れる

🚩 **28. (D)　29. (C)　30. (D)**

TOKIMAKURE!

PART

6

Test 1

Questions 31-34 refer to the following e-mail.

To: Nikki Douglas <nkdgs@online.net>
From: Chris Richmond <chris_r@tdo.org>
Date: March 8
Subject: Workshop

Dear Ms. Douglas,

As the chairman of the Tylor Development Organization, I am writing to inform you about the commercial development workshop we are organizing for ------- members. As a long-time TDO member, you will be aware that our workshops provide a fantastic opportunity for our members to easily ------- a deep and wide comprehension of various business concepts and strategies. -------, they can use the workshops as a convenient way to network with other businesspeople, which may in turn lead to profitable collaborations in the future. The workshops will take place throughout May, and many famous, successful individuals will be leading the sessions, so the tickets for the events are expected to sell out soon. This is why I am contacting our long-time members to let them know about the workshops in advance. -------.

Best regards,

Chris Richmond
Chairman, Tylor Development Organization

31. (A) register
(B) registered
(C) registering
(D) registration

32. (A) participate
(B) appoint
(C) develop
(D) strive

33. (A) As well as
(B) Nevertheless
(C) In contrast
(D) Moreover

34. (A) Allow me to explain the revised schedule to them.
(B) Her session is certain to be a well-attended event.
(C) This workshop has been rescheduled for April.
(D) I anticipate that you will not miss this great opportunity.

31. ★★★☆☆

(A) register
(B) registered
(C) registering
(D) registration

(A) 動 ～を登録する
(B) 過去分詞
(C) 現在分詞
(D) 名 登録

選択肢には動詞 register が形を変えて並んでいる。空所前後には前置詞 for と名詞 members があり、この空所を含む文の意味は「……の会員を対象にした講習会についてお知らせする」となっているため、空所には members を修飾する語が入ることがわかる。以上から、過去分詞を入れて「(すでに) 登録されている会員に対して」とすると文意が成立する。よって、正解は (B)。(C) にすると、「これから会員登録する人」が対象となり、この後の文にある「あなたは長期にわたり会員なので、…」と文意が合わなくなる。

 I am writing to inform you / about the commercial development workshop / (that) we
　　S　　V　　　　　　　　　　　　　　　　　　　　　　　　　　　　O　　S
are organizing for registered members.
　　V

---

32. ★★★★☆

(A) participate
(B) appoint
(C) develop
(D) strive

(A) 動 参加する
(B) 動 ～を任命する
(C) 動 ～を進展させる
(D) 動 励む

選択肢には動詞が並んでいる。空所を含む文の意味を見ると「会員が深く広い理解を容易に……する機会」とあるため、目的語を導き、「あることに対する理解を～する」という文意に当てはまる語が空所に入るとわかる。以上からその条件に当てはまる (C) が正解となる。(A)、(D) は自動詞なので文法的に当てはまらず、(B) は主に、任命する人や役割などを目的語として導くため、文意が通らない。

As a long-time TDO members, /
～として
you will be aware that our workshops provide a fantastic opportunity for our members /
　S　　V　　　　O (that 節)　S　　　　V　　　　　　　O
to easily develop a deep and wide comprehension / of various business concepts and strategies.
理解を深めるという (機会)

33. ★★★☆☆

(A) As well as
(B) Nevertheless
(C) In contrast
(D) Moreover

(A) 〜と同様に
(B) にもかかわらず
(C) 対照的に
(D) さらに

Moreover, they can use the workshops / as a convenient way / to network with other businesspeople, /
          S   V   O

which may in turn lead to profitable collaborations in the future.
 S   V   O

補足説明

---

34. ★★★☆☆

(A) Allow me to explain the revised schedule to them.
(B) Her session is certain to be a well-attended event.
(C) This workshop has been rescheduled for April.
(D) I anticipate that you will not miss this great opportunity.

(A) 改定された予定について説明させてください。
(B) 彼女の講習は確実に多くの参加者が集まるイベントです。
(C) この講習会は4月に予定変更となりました。
(D) この素晴らしい機会をお見逃しにならないようお願いいたします。

□allow 人 to *do* 人が〜するのを許す　□revised 改定された　□be certain to *do* 確実に〜する
□well-attended 多くが参加する　□anticipate 〜を期待する　□miss 〜を逃す　□opportunity 機会

Questions 31-34 refer to the following e-mail.

To: Nikki Douglas <nkdgs@online.net>
From: Chris Richmond <chris_r@tdo.org>
Date: March 8
Subject: Workshop

Dear Ms. Douglas,

❶ As the chairman of the Tylor Development Organization, I am writing to inform you about the commercial development workshop we are organizing for __31 registered__ members. ❷ As a long-time TDO member, you will be aware that our workshops provide a fantastic opportunity for our members to easily __32 develop__ a deep and wide comprehension of various business concepts and strategies. ❸ __33 Moreover__, they can use the workshops as a convenient way to network with other businesspeople, which may in turn lead to profitable collaborations in the future. ❹ The workshops will take place throughout May, and many famous, successful individuals will be leading the sessions, so the tickets for the events are expected to sell out soon. ❺ This is why I am contacting our long-time members to let them know about the workshops in advance. ❻ __34 I anticipate that you will not miss this great opportunity.__

Best regards,

Chris Richmond
Chairman, Tylor Development Organization

問題 **31-34** は次のEメールに関するものです。

宛先： Nikki Douglas <nkdgs@online.net>
送信者： Chris Richmond <chris_r@tdo.org>
日付： 3月8日
件名： 講習会

Douglas 様

❶ Tylor 開発機構の会長として、登録会員を対象に開催する商業開発の講習会についてお知らせいたします。❷ あなたは長期にわたり TDO (Tylor 開発機構) の会員でいらっしゃるので、当機構の講習会が会員の皆さまに、さまざまなビジネスの概念や戦略について深く広い理解を容易に伸ばすための素晴らしい機会を提供していることをご承知のことと存じます。❸ そのうえ、講習会はほかの実業家の方々と情報交換をするための便利な手段として活用することも可能で、それにより、将来的に有益な協業が実現するかもしれません。❹ 講習会は5月いっぱい開催され、多くの有名で成功を収めている方々が講師を務められますので、チケットはすぐに完売となることが予想されます。❺ そのため、会員歴が長い方には講習会について事前にお知らせをしております。❻ この素晴らしい機会をお見逃しにならないようお願いいたします。

どうぞよろしくお願いいたします。

Chris Richmond
Tylor 開発機構 会長

□chairman 会長 □I am writing to inform you about 〜についてお知らせする
□commercial development 商業開発 □workshop 講習会、研修 □organize 〜を主催する、開催する
□long-time 長きにわたる □fantastic 素晴らしい □deep and wide 深く幅広い □comprehension 理解
□various さまざまな □concept 概念、コンセプト □strategy 戦略 □convenient 便利な □in turn 今度は
□lead to 〜につながる □profitable 有益な □collaboration 共同事業、協業 □in the future 将来
□take place 開催される □individual 個人 □sell out 売り切れる □in advance 事前に

Questions 35-38 refer to the following article.

Dr. Eva Wilson -------- the visiting professor at the Maple Ocean Institute of Technology.
35
After completing a Bachelor's degree in engineering, Dr. Wilson went on to pursue a Ph.D. in
physics at the prestigious Notty University of Applied Sciences. --------. She then spent
36
twelve years as a Roswell University Professor. During her -------- there, she authored five
37
books on the physical changes undergone by rockets in space.

Her invitation was a delightful surprise to many in the institute's science department. Some
even suggest that she might be asked to stay on permanently after her term is up, due to
the -------- retirement of the Science Chair, Professor Anderson.
38

Anything is possible with her impressive credentials. We look forward to seeing what kind of
a contribution Dr. Wilson will make during her time at the institute.

35. (A) has named
(B) is naming
(C) has been named
(D) will have named

36. (A) Many ideas and concepts were
developed into prototypes.
(B) After that she spent six years working
at the Jumbo Propulsion Institute in
Germany.
(C) There was a long negotiation between
her and the university.
(D) She is operating her own company
which supplies various chemicals.

37. (A) tenure
(B) status
(C) consultation
(D) appearance

38. (A) plan
(B) planned
(C) planning
(D) planner

35. ★★★★☆

(A) has named
(B) is naming
(C) has been named
(D) will have named

(A) 現在完了形
(B) 現在進行形
(C) 現在完了受身形
(D) 未来完了形

🔍 選択肢には動詞 name（〜を任命する）が形を変えて並んでいる。name は、name A B で、「A を B に任命する」という意味になる。空所の目的語が「客員教授」と任命される役職になっていることから、受動態にすると、「Eva Wilson 博士が客員教授に任命された」という意味になり、その後の Wilson 博士の経歴を紹介していることとも文意が通じる。よって、正解は **(C)**。動詞の形を問う問題は、文の中から主語の数、時制、態の要素を考え、正解を導いていこう。

Dr. Eva Wilson has been named the visiting professor / at the Maple Ocean Institute of Technology.
　　　S　　　　　　V　　　　　　　　C

36. ★★★☆☆

(A) Many ideas and concepts were developed into prototypes.
(B) After that she spent six years working at the Jumbo Propulsion Institute in Germany.
(C) There was a long negotiation between her and the university.
(D) She is operating her own company which supplies various chemicals.

(A) 多くのアイデアやコンセプトから試作品になった。
(B) その後、6 年間はドイツの Jumbo Propulsion 研究所で働くことに費やした。
(C) 大学との間で長期間にわたる交渉があった。
(D) さまざまな化学製品を供給する自身の会社を運営している。

🔍 選択肢には文が並んでいる。空所の前後には、Wilson 博士の経歴に関する記載があり、「Notty 応用科学大学で物理学の博士課程に進学」➡「それから、Roswell 大学の教授を 12 年間務めた」と、学生時代から教授を務めるまでの経歴となっていることから、この間にも何か経歴にかかわる内容が書かれていると考えられる。以上から、**(B)** が正解。(A) 試作品について、(C) 大学との交渉、(D) 会社運営について、は文脈とは関連がなく、ここでは不正解。

✏️ □develop into 〜に発展する　□prototype 試作品　□negotiation 交渉
　□operate one's own company 自身の会社を経営する　□supply 〜を供給する　□various さまざまな
　□chemical 化学製品

P A R T 6

TEST 1

177

37. ★★★★★

(A) tenure
(B) status
(C) consultation
(D) appearance

(A) 名 在籍期間
(B) 名 地位
(C) 名 相談
(D) 名 外観

選択肢にはさまざまな名詞が並んでいる。空所を含む文は「Wlison 博士の……中、本を執筆した。」とあるため、ここには期間を表す語が入ることがわかる。以上から、「在籍している期間」を意味する (A) が正解となる。(B) は大学教授のような地位を指すが、ここで問われているのは「～する期間」のため、不正解となる。

During her tenure there, /
～の間 (副詞句)

she authored five books / on the physical changes / undergone by rockets in space.
S   V   O   ～に関する (形容詞句)

---

38. ★★★☆☆

(A) plan
(B) planned
(C) planning
(D) planner

(A) 名 計画
(B) 動 ～を計画する　過去分詞
(C) 現在分詞
(D) 名 立案者

選択肢には plan が形を変えて並んでいる。空所を含む箇所は due to the ------- retirement と冠詞と名詞の間にあることから retirement を修飾する語が入ることが推測される。次にこの文の意味は、「Anderson 教授の……引退のため、Wilson 博士が任期満了後も残るよう求められるのでは」であることから、Anderson 教授の引退はすでに予定されているものであることがわかる。よって、過去分詞の planned を入れると文意が成立する。以上から、正解は (B)。

Some even suggest / that she might be asked to stay on permanently / after her term is up,
S   V   S   V   (副詞節 [時])
                 O (that 節)

due to the planned retirement of the Science Chair, Professor Anderson.
(前置詞句 [原因・理由])

35. (C)　36. (B)　37. (A)　38. (B)

Questions 35-38 refer to the following article.

❶ Dr. Eva Wilson ___35__ has been named___ the visiting professor at the Maple Ocean Institute of Technology. ❷ After completing a Bachelor's degree in engineering, Dr. Wilson went on to pursue a Ph.D. in physics at the prestigious Notty University of Applied Sciences. ❸ __36__ After that she spent six years working at the Jumbo Propulsion Institute in Germany. ❹ She then spent twelve years as a Roswell University Professor. ❺ During her __37__ tenure___ there, she authored five books on the physical changes undergone by rockets in space.

❻ Her invitation was a delightful surprise to many in the institute's science department. ❼ Some even suggest that she might be asked to stay on permanently after her term is up, due to the __38__ planned___ retirement of the Science Chair, Professor Anderson.

❽ Anything is possible with her impressive credentials. ❾ We look forward to seeing what kind of a contribution Dr. Wilson will make during her time at the institute.

問題 35-38 は次の記事に関するものです。

❶ Eva Wilson 博士は Maple Ocean 工科大学の客員教授に任命された。❷工学の学士号を取得した後、Wilson 博士は名門である Notty 応用科学大学で物理学の博士課程に進学した。❸その後、6 年間はドイツの Jumbo Propulsion 研究所で働くことに費やした。❹それから、Roswell 大学の教授を 12 年間務めた。❺その在籍中、宇宙空間でロケットに起こる物理的変化に関する 5 冊の本を執筆した。

❻彼女の招聘は同大学の科学部に在籍する多くの人にとってうれしい驚きであった。❼科学部長である Anderson 教授が引退する予定であるため、任期満了後も無期限に残るよう求められるのではと考える者さえいた。

❽彼女の素晴らしい経歴を見れば何が起きてもおかしくない。❾ Wilson 博士が大学での任期中にどのような実績を残すか楽しみである。

□professor 教授　□complete 〜を修了する　□Bachelor's degree in 〜の学士号　□go on to *do* 続いて〜する
□pursue 〜を追求する　□physics 物理学　□prestigious 権威ある、名門の　□Applied Sciences 応用科学
□author 〜を著作する　□physical change 物理的変化　□undergo (変化など) を受ける　□in space 宇宙空間で
□delightful うれしい　□institute 教育機関、学校　□permanently 永久に、無期限に　□term 期間
□up (期間などが) 終了して、満了して　□due to 〜が原因で　□impressive 素晴らしい　□credentials 経歴
□contribution 貢献、実績

Questions 39-42 refer to the following letter.

Zelda's Coat Factory
153 Ford Drive
Saskatoon, SK S8M

Dear regular customer,

Are you ready for winter? Meteorologists are predicting one of the ------- winters we've
                                                                         39
ever seen in this region. At Zelda's Coat Factory, we don't want you to freeze! We ------- a
                                                                                    40
special sale throughout the month of November this year. Come to see us for a new coat.
With discounts of up to 50% off, you can't miss this great opportunity! -------. Thank you
                                                                         41
for your ------- and we look forward to welcoming you back in our store this November.
          42

Your Neighborhood Coat Store,
Zelda's Coat Factory
Marketing Team

39. (A) cold
(B) colder
(C) coldest
(D) coldly

40. (A) held
(B) are held
(C) are holding
(D) will have held

41. (A) You will receive your order in five
business days.
(B) This is our last big sale to make room
for the spring collection.
(C) You deserve to enjoy being warm
inside and cool outside.
(D) Many celebrities have endorsed our
products.

42. (A) patience
(B) contribution
(C) donation
(D) patronage

39. ★★☆☆☆

(A) cold
(B) colder
(C) **coldest**
(D) coldly

(A) 形 寒い 　原級
(B) 比較級
(C) 最上級
(D) 副 冷たく

 選択肢には形容詞 cold が形を変えて並んでいる。空所を含む箇所は one of the ------- winters we've ever seen（かつて経験した中で、……の冬の一つ）となっている。定冠詞 the を伴い寒さの程度を示すことができるのは最上級のため、正解は **(C)** となる。そのほかはすべて文法的に当てはめることができず、不正解。

 Meteorologists are predicting one of the coldest winters / (that) we've ever seen in this region.
　　　　S　　　　　　V　　　　　　　　O　　　　　　　　　　　　　O　S　　V

---

40. ★★★☆☆

(A) held
(B) are held
(C) **are holding**
(D) will have held

(A) 過去形
(B) 受動態
(C) 現在進行形
(D) 未来完了形

 選択肢には動詞 hold（～を催す）が形を変えて並んでいる。空所を含む文は、「今年は 11 月いっぱい特別セールを……」と述べられており、その後に対象製品を見に来るように誘導している。ここから、セール自体はこれから実施することがわかるため、**(C)** が正解となる。(D) も未来のニュアンスはあるが、「11 月中」と一定の期間を表す際に、「完了してしまっている」というのは文法的に当てはめられず、不正解。

 We are holding a special sale / throughout the month of November this year.
　　　　S　　V　　　　O　　　　　　　～の間ずっと（副詞句）

41. ★★★☆☆

(A) You will receive your order in five business days.
(B) This is our last big sale to make room for the spring collection.
(C) You deserve to enjoy being warm inside and cool outside.
(D) Many celebrities have endorsed our products.

(A) 注文品は5営業日で届きます。
(B) 今回は春の新作の売り場を作るための当店最後の大型セールです。
(C) 外が寒くてもコートの中は暖かくなさってください。
(D) 多くの有名人が当社の製品を推薦してくださっています。

選択肢には文が並んでいる。空所前後の内容は、「今年このエリアはすごく寒くなる予報」「特別セールを実施するので見逃してほしくない」➡（空所）➡「11月に是非お越しを」となっている。つまり、この寒い冬を乗り切るために、セールを活用して快適な冬を過ごしてほしい、という文脈であることがわかるため、それに合致する **(C)** が正解となる。

□business day 営業日　□make room for ～の場を作る、確保する　□deserve to ～に値する　□celebrity 有名人
□endorse ～を推奨する

---

42. ★★★★☆

(A) patience
(B) contribution
(C) donation
(D) patronage

(A) 名 忍耐
(B) 名 貢献
(C) 名 寄付
(D) 名 愛顧

選択肢には名詞が並んでいる。空所を含む文は、お礼に加え、「11月にまたお迎えすることを楽しみにしている」と、日ごろのご愛顧を伝える内容になっている。また、この文書冒頭にある regular customer という宛先から、お得意様に宛てた内容ということがわかる。以上から、正解は **(D)**。文法的にはほかの選択肢も空所に当てはめることができるため、今回は空所以外の情報から「常連のお客様に宛てている」という文意がくみ取れるかが正解の決め手となる。

Thank you for your patronage /

and <u>we</u> <u>look forward to</u> <u>welcoming you back</u> / in our store / this November.
　　 S　　　　V　　　　　　O（動名詞）

39. (C)　40. (C)　41. (C)　42. (D)

182

Questions 39-42 refer to the following letter.

Zelda's Coat Factory
153 Ford Drive
Saskatoon, SK S8M

Dear regular customer,

❶ Are you ready for winter? ❷ Meteorologists are predicting one of the ₃₉ coldest winters we've ever seen in this region. ❸ At Zelda's Coat Factory, we don't want you to freeze! ❹ We ₄₀ are holding a special sale throughout the month of November this year. ❺ Come to see us for a new coat. ❻ With discounts of up to 50% off, you can't miss this great opportunity! ❼ ₄₁ You deserve to enjoy being warm inside and cool outside . ❽ Thank you for your ₄₂ patronage and we look forward to welcoming you back in our store this November.

Your Neighborhood Coat Store,
Zelda's Coat Factory
Marketing Team

問題 **39-42** は次の手紙に関するものです。

Zelda's コート工場
153 Ford Drive
Saskatoon、SK S8M

お得意様へ

❶冬の準備はお済みですか。❷気象専門家はこの地域でこれまでに経験した中で最も寒い冬の一つとなると予想しています。❸Zelda's コート工場では、皆さまに寒い思いをしていただきたくありません。❹今年は 11 月いっぱい特別セールを開催いたします。❺新作のコートを見にご来店ください。❻最大 50 パーセント割引になる、この素晴らしい機会をお見逃しなく。❼外が寒くてもコートの中は暖かくなさってください。❽皆さまのご愛顧に感謝するとともに、11 月のご来店を心よりお待ちしております。

皆さまのお近くのコートの店
Zelda's コート工場
マーケティング担当

✎ □regular customer 常連のお客様、お得意様 □meteorologist 気象予報専門家 □predict ～を予測する □region 地域 □freeze 凍える □up to 最大～まで □miss ～を逃す

Questions 43-46 refer to the following notice.

Attention!!!

Sweeney Apartments Residents:

Please, note that the annual cleaning of the central air conditioning system and ventilation shafts has been rescheduled from June 24 to June 26. The maintenance will start at 10:00 A.M. and will end by 4:00 P.M., if no complex problem is ------. We prohibit the use of water during this time. ------. We apologize for any inconvenience this may ------ you.
                        43   44   45
It will help maintain good indoor air quality through adequate ventilation and provide a comfortable environment during the ------ summer.
                                    46

Thank you for your cooperation.

Karen Hicks, Manager

---

43. (A) solved
(B) happened
(C) detected
(D) brought

44. (A) Moreover, there will be coin laundries around the area.
(B) Therefore, you can't have access to the laundry equipment in the basement.
(C) Consequently, you can purchase drinking water from the local shops.
(D) Nevertheless, average water usage has risen a lot.

45. (A) cause
(B) include
(C) bear
(D) contain

46. (A) impulsive
(B) previous
(C) advisory
(D) upcoming

43. ★★★☆☆

(A) solved
(B) happened
(C) detected
(D) brought

(A) 動 ～を解決する 過去分詞
(B) 動 起こる 過去分詞
(C) 動 ～を発見する 過去分詞
(D) 動 ～を持ってくる 過去分詞

選択肢には動詞の過去分詞が並んでいる。この文書自体は、空調などのメンテナンスに関するお知らせで、空所を含む文は、「メンテナンスは午前10時に開始し、複雑な問題が1つも……なければ、午後4時までには終了する」となっている。ここから、複雑な問題がなければ予定通り終了、という文意だとわかるので、**(C)** が正解となる。一見、(A) を入れると「問題が解決」となり、しっくりくるように思えるが、ここでの主語が no complex problem となっているため、「もし何も複雑な問題が解決されないと」という意味になり、文意が通らなくなってしまう。

The maintenance will start at 10:00 A.M. / and will end by 4:00 P.M., /
　　　　　　S　　　　　　V¹　　　　　　　　　　　V²
if no complex problem is detected .
(副詞節［条件］) S　　　　　　　　V

---

44. ★★★★☆

(A) Moreover, there will be coin laundries around the area.
(B) Therefore, you can't have access to the laundry equipment in the basement.
(C) Consequently, you can purchase drinking water from the local shops.
(D) Nevertheless, average water usage has risen a lot.

(A) さらに、この地域にはコインランドリーができる予定です。
(B) そのため、地下室の洗濯機を利用することはできません。
(C) したがって、飲料水は近所のお店で購入することができます。
(D) それにもかかわらず、平均的な水の使用量は大幅に増加しています。

選択肢には文が並んでおり、空所前後は「この時間帯は水の使用が禁止となる」➡「ご不便をおかけし申し訳ない」となっている。つまり、水が使えないことに関連する不便な内容が入ると考えられるので、**(B)** が正解となる。(C)、(D) も水に関する内容だが、飲み水の購入や平均使用量はこの文脈と関連がない。

□coin laundry コインランドリー □access to ～を利用する権利 □basement 地下室 □consequently したがって □drinking water 飲料水 □water usage 水の使用量 □rise 上昇する

45. ★★★★☆

(A) cause
(B) include
(C) bear
(D) contain

(A) 動 ～に（面倒）をかける
(B) 動 ～を含む
(C) 動 ～を産む
(D) 動 ～を含む

選択肢には動詞が並んでいる。空所を含む表現は、any inconvenience this may ------ you で、「これ（水が使えないこと）があなた……不便」という意味になっている。文の構造を見ると、inconvenience を先行詞として this 以下が関係詞となっていることがわかる。以上より、目的語を2語取って、先行詞にかかる関係詞となるような動詞は **(A)** のみなので、これが正解。cause は、〈cause 人 ～〉で、人に何かを引き起こす、という意味になる。今回の inconvenience this may cause you のような表現は定型表現としてよく用いられるので、しっかり押さえておこう。

We apologize for any inconvenience / (that) this may cause you .
　　　S　　　V　　　　　　O　　　　　　　　　O² 　S　　　V　　　O¹

......

46. ★★★☆☆

(A) impulsive
(B) previous
(C) advisory
(D) upcoming

(A) 形 衝動的な
(B) 形 以前の
(C) 形 勧告の
(D) 形 今度の

選択肢には形容詞が並んでいる。空所を含む文の意味を取っていくと、「今回のメンテナンスが良好な空気環境を維持し、……の夏を快適に過ごせるだろう」となっている。これを時間軸で考えると、清掃作業は次の夏に備えて行われることがわかる。以上から、**(D)** が正解となる。

It will help maintain good indoor air quality / through adequate ventilation /
　S　　　V¹　　　　　　　　O　　　　　　　（副詞句［手段］）

and provide a comfortable environment / during the upcoming summer.
　　　V²　　　　　　　O　　　　　　　　　　～の間
　　　　　　　　　　　　　　　　　　　　（副詞句）

Questions 43-46 refer to the following notice.

Attention!!!

Sweeney Apartments Residents:

❶ Please, note that the annual cleaning of the central air conditioning system and ventilation shafts has been rescheduled from June 24 to June 26. ❷ The maintenance will start at 10:00 A.M. and will end by 4:00 P.M., if no complex problem is <u>**43** detected</u>. ❸ We prohibit the use of water during this time. ❹ <u>**44** Therefore, you can't have access to the laundry equipment in the basement.</u> ❺ We apologize for any inconvenience this may <u>**45** cause</u> you. ❻ It will help maintain good indoor air quality through adequate ventilation and provide a comfortable environment during the <u>**46** upcoming</u> summer.

Thank you for your cooperation.

Karen Hicks, Manager

問題 43-46 は次のお知らせに関するものです。

ご注意ください !!!

Sweeney Apartments の住民の皆さま：

❶全空調制御システムと換気シャフトの年次清掃の日程は 6 月 24 日から 6 月 26 日に変更となりました。❷メンテナンスは午前 10 時に開始し、複雑な問題が見つからなければ、午後 4 時までには終了いたします。❸この間、水の使用は禁止いたします。❹そのため、地下室の洗濯機を利用することはできません。❺ご不便をおかけし、申し訳ございません。❻十分な換気を通じて室内の良好な空気環境を維持し、これからの夏を快適に過ごすことができるようになります。

ご協力よろしくお願いいたします。
Karen Hicks, 管理者

□Attention!（冒頭に用いて）ご注意ください！ □resident 住民 □note that 〜について留意する
□central air conditioning system 全空調システム □ventilation shaft 換気シャフト □complex 複雑な
□prohibit 〜を禁じる □use 使用 □inconvenience 不便 □maintain 〜を維持する □adequate 十分な
□comfortable 快適な □environment 環境

Test 2

Questions 31-34 refer to the following e-mail.

To: Jesse Lundgard
From: Martin Kerr
Date: 20 October
Subject: Resignation Notice

Dear Ms. Lundgard

This e-mail is to ------- notify you that I will resign from my position as an assistant
31
accountant with Rydell Pharmaceuticals. -------. I think that one month will be sufficient
32
time for you to find and train my successor. I really appreciate the opportunity I have been
given at such a wonderful company. I worked for five years in the general administration
department before receiving accounting training and being placed in my current
department. There is no proper way to thank you for the knowledge and experience I have
gained while ------- for you.
33

If there is anything I can do to help you during this -------, then please don't hesitate to ask.
34
I wish you and Rydell Pharmaceuticals every success in the future.

Best regards,

Martin Kerr

---

31. (A) form
(B) forming
(C) formal
(D) formally

33. (A) work
(B) works
(C) working
(D) worked

32. (A) You are responsible for a full-time
position.
(B) November 23 should be my last day at
the company.
(C) According to the contract, I should
work until next year.
(D) Kindly tell me what steps you have
taken.

34. (A) transition
(B) conference
(C) promotion
(D) session

31. ★★☆☆☆

(A) form
(B) forming
(C) formal
(D) **formally**

(A) 動 ～を形成する
(B) 現在分詞
(C) 形 正式の
(D) 副 正式に

This e-mail is to formally notify you /
　　S　　　V to 不定詞（目的）　　notify+O（人）+that 節「人に～を知らせる」
that I will resign from my position / as an assistant accountant / with Rydell Pharmaceuticals.
　S　　　　V　　　　　　O

---

32. ★★★☆☆

(A) You are responsible for a full-time position.
(B) **November 23 should be my last day at the company.**
(C) According to the contract, I should work until next year.
(D) Kindly tell me what steps you have taken.

(A) あなたは常勤の仕事の担当です。
(B) **11 月 23 日が最後の勤務日となる予定です。**
(C) 契約によれば、来年まで働く予定です。
(D) どのような手順を踏んだか教えてください。

□full-time position 常勤の仕事　□according to ～によると　□kindly どうか～

PART 6

TEST 2

33. ★★★☆

(A) work
(B) works
(C) working
(D) worked

(A) 動 働く
(B) 三人称単数現在形
(C) 現在分詞
(D) 過去分詞

There is no proper way / to thank you for the knowledge and experience / (that) I have gained /
　　V　　S　　　　　　　　　　　　　　　　　　　　　　　　　　　　　　　　　　　　O　S　　V

while working for you.
（副詞句［時］）

---

34. ★★★★☆

(A) transition
(B) conference
(C) promotion
(D) session

(A) 名 移行
(B) 名 協議会
(C) 名 昇進
(D) 名 集い

If there is anything / (that) I can do / to help you / during this transition, /
　　　V　　　S　　　　O　S　V　　　　　　　　　　　　　（副詞句［時］）
（副詞節［条件］）
then please don't hesitate to ask.

Questions 31-34 refer to the following e-mail.

To: Jesse Lundgard
From: Martin Kerr
Date: 20 October
Subject: Resignation Notice

Dear Ms. Lundgard

❶ This e-mail is to **31** formally notify you that I will resign from my position as an assistant accountant with Rydell Pharmaceuticals. ❷ **32** November 23 should be my last day at the company. ❸ I think that one month will be sufficient time for you to find and train my successor. ❹ I really appreciate the opportunity I have been given at such a wonderful company. ❺ I worked for five years in the general administration department before receiving accounting training and being placed in my current department. ❻ There is no proper way to thank you for the knowledge and experience I have gained while **33** working for you.

❼ If there is anything I can do to help you during this **34** transition, then please don't hesitate to ask. ❽ I wish you and Rydell Pharmaceuticals every success in the future.

Best regards,

Martin Kerr

問題 31-34 は次の E メールに関するものです。

宛先： Jesse Lundgard
送信者： Martin Kerr
日付： 10 月 20 日
件名： 退職のお知らせ

Lundgard 様

❶ Rydell Pharmaceuticals 社の会計士補佐の仕事を退職することを正式にお知らせするために E メールを書いています。❷ 11 月 23 日が最後の勤務日となる予定です。❸ 私の後任を選定し研修を行うには 1 カ月あれば十分であると思います。❹ このような素晴らしい会社でチャンスを与えていただき、本当に感謝をしています。❺ 私は総務部で 5 年間働いたのち、経理のトレーニングを受けて現在の部に配属されました。❻ あなたと働く中で得られた知識と経験についてどのように感謝をすればいいのかわかりません。

❼ この移行期間中に私にできることがあれば、遠慮なくお知らせください。❽ 今後とも、Rydell Pharmaceuticals 社のご成功をお祈り申し上げます。

どうぞよろしくお願いいたします。

Martin Kerr

□resignation notice 退職のお知らせ □notify ～に知らせる □resign from ～を辞める □pharmaceuticals 製薬会社 □sufficient 十分な □successor 後任 □appreciate ～を感謝している □opportunity 機会 □general administration 総務 □proper way 正しい方法 □gain ～を得る □in the future 将来の

Questions 35-38 refer to the following memo.

To: All staff members
From: Kelly Douglas, Employee Training Manager
Date: April 5
Subject: Spreadsheet Software Training Classes

Many staff members have expressed an interest in ------- more skilled in the use of our
                                                35
spreadsheet software. So next week we will hold four training classes given by software

specialists from the Richmond Tech Advisory Group. They will provide a simple yet effective

training program for users at different ------- of ability.
                                        36

-------. Participants in this class are ------- to have some prior experience in using the
  37   38
spreadsheet software as well as basic knowledge of all its features. For staff members who

are not familiar with or have had little practice in using the spreadsheet software, a class for

beginners will be held next Tuesday, April 13.

35. (A) becoming
(B) to become
(C) become
(D) have become

36. (A) levels
(B) ideas
(C) plans
(D) actions

37. (A) New software will be installed within
the next month.
(B) The company will not provide private
classes.
(C) Please contact me if you wish to
cancel your appointment.
(D) The first class is designed for those of
medium ability.

38. (A) expect
(B) expects
(C) expected
(D) expecting

35.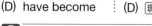

(A) becoming
(B) to become
(C) become
(D) have become

(A) 動名詞
(B) to 不定詞
(C) 動 〜になる
(D) 現在完了形

選択肢には動詞 become が形を変えて並んでいる。空所の前は an interest in で、後ろには more skilled という空所の補語に当たる語が来ている。よって、前置詞 in の後に入り後ろに補語を取る動名詞の **(A)** が正解となる。

 Many staff members have expressed an interest / in becoming more skilled in
　　　　　　　　 S　　　　　　 V　　　　　 O　　　　　　 〜にもっと熟練する

the use of our spreadsheet software.

---

36. ★★★★★

(A) levels
(B) ideas
(C) plans
(D) actions

(A) 名 レベル
(B) 名 アイデア
(C) 名 計画
(D) 名 行為

選択肢には意味の異なる名詞が並んでいる。空所を含むパラグラフ全体を見ると、表計算ソフトウェアに関するトレーニング講座を 4 回開催するとあり、その内容は基本的でありながら効果的な研修だ、と述べられている。ここから効果的＝4 つのそれぞれの講座は参加者にとって異なる技能のレベルで、という内容にすると文意が成立することがわかる。以上から、段階、レベルを意味する **(A)** が正解となる。

They will provide a simple yet effective training program for users at different levels of ability.
　　 S　　 V　　　　　　　　　　　　　　　　　　 O

PART 6

TEST 2

37. ★★★★☆

(A) New software will be installed within the next month.
(B) The company will not provide private classes.
(C) Please contact me if you wish to cancel your appointment.
(D) The first class is designed for those of medium ability.

(A) 新しいソフトウェアは今後 1 カ月以内にインストールされます。
(B) 会社は個人向けクラスの開講はいたしません。
(C) 予約のキャンセルをご希望の場合は、ご連絡ください。
(D) 一つ目のクラスは中級者向けの内容となっています。

選択肢には文が並んでおり、空所は第 2 パラグラフの冒頭にある。空所前後の文を読んでいくと、「表計算ソフトウェア研修案内」➡（空所）➡「このクラスはソフトウェアについてのある程度の経験が必要」となっている。ここから、空所後の文にある this class に着目し、ある程度経験が必要なクラス、に対応する内容が空所に入ると考えられる。よって、それについて言及している **(D)** が正解。

□private class 個人向けクラス　□contact 〜に連絡する　□be designed for 〜向けの　□medium ability 中級

---

38. ★★☆☆☆

(A) expect
(B) expects
(C) expected
(D) expecting

(A) 動 〜を期待する
(B) 三人称単数現在形
(C) 過去分詞
(D) 現在分詞

選択肢には動詞 expect が形を変えて並んでいる。空所を含む文を見ると、主語が人 (participants) であり、空所以降が to 不定詞となっているため、be expected to do の形で、「〜すると見込まれる、〜することになっている」という意味にすると文意が成立することがわかる。以上より、正解は **(C)**。

Participants in this class are expected to have some prior experience /
　　　　S　　　　　　　　　　V　　　　　　　　　O
in using the spreadsheet software as well as basic knowledge of all its features.
　　　　　　　　　　　　　　　　〜はもちろん…も

Questions 35-38 refer to the following memo.

To: All staff members
From: Kelly Douglas, Employee Training Manager
Date: April 5
Subject: Spreadsheet Software Training Classes

❶ Many staff members have expressed an interest in **35** becoming more skilled in the use of our spreadsheet software. ❷ So next week we will hold four training classes given by software specialists from the Richmond Tech Advisory Group. ❸ They will provide a simple yet effective training program for users at different **36** levels of ability.

❹ **37** The first class is designed for those of medium ability. ❺ Participants in this class are **38** expected to have some prior experience in using the spreadsheet software as well as basic knowledge of all its features. ❻ For staff members who are not familiar with or have had little practice in using the spreadsheet software, a class for beginners will be held next Tuesday, April 13.

問題 35-38 は次のメモ書きに関するものです。

宛先： 全スタッフ
送信者： Kelly Douglas 従業員研修部長
日付： 4月5日
件名： 表計算ソフトウェア実務講習

❶当社の表計算ソフトウェアをさらに使えるようになることを希望している職員が大勢います。❷そのため来週、Richmond Tech Advisory Group のソフトウェアの専門家によるトレーニング講座を4回開催いたします。❸さまざまな技能レベルの使用者に向けて、基本的でありながらも効果的な研修プログラムを提供いたします。

❹一つ目のクラスは中級者向けの内容となっています。❺このクラスの参加者は、表計算ソフトウェアの使用経験と、そのすべての機能について基本的な知識を持っていることを前提として行います。❻表計算ソフトの使用に慣れていない、又は、経験がほとんどない職員については、来週4月13日火曜日に初級者向けのクラスを開催いたします。

□spreadsheet スプレッドシート、表計算シート □express an interest in ～に関心を表す
□(be) skilled in ～に精通している □specialist 専門家 □simple yet effective 単純だが効果のある □ability 能力
□prior 事前の □feature 機能、内容

Questions 39-42 refer to the following article.

Reaching the Masses in the Digital Age

"I think that the best route to success in business is to enter the online market and use Web advertisements," says Garry Ford. He is a businessman who has been operating a jewelry shop on Main Street for almost fifteen years. As he was starting his business, he believed that having eye-catching print advertisements and an ------- packaging style was enough
                                                                                                                                      39
to ensure product marketability and exposure.

However, his ------- changed considerably a few years ago. "An increasing number of
                          40
customers suggested that I make my merchandise available online and advertise it on popular local Web sites. -------, I decided that an online store was becoming necessary."
                                            41
Mr. Ford now makes over 50 percent of his sales through his Web site. -------.
                                                                                                      42

39. (A) attracts
(B) attracted
(C) attraction
(D) attractive

40. (A) location
(B) outlook
(C) income
(D) appearance

41. (A) Eventually
(B) Typically
(C) Likewise
(D) Comparatively

42. (A) Market analysts suggest that online shopping statistics are wrong.
(B) He is trying to launch a massive sales campaign in major jewelry shops.
(C) Lower prices have attracted more customers to his business.
(D) His story shows the power of Internet marketing.

39. ★★★★★

(A) attracts
(B) attracted
(C) attraction
(D) attractive

(A) 動 〜を引きつける 〔現在形〕
(B) 〔過去分詞〕
(C) 名 魅力
(D) 形 魅力的な

🔍 選択肢には動詞 attract の派生語が並んでいる。空所は不定冠詞 an と名詞句 packaging style に挟まれていることから、この空所には packaging style を修飾する形容表現が入ることがわかる。以上から、正解は **(D)**。(B) も分詞の形容表現として考えられるが、packaging style は人を魅了「させる」ものなので、ここでは不正解。

As he was starting his business, / he believed / that having eye-catching print advertisements /
　Ｓ　　　Ｖ　　　　　　　　　Ｏ　　　Ｓ　　Ｖ　　Ｏ (that 節)　　　　　　　　　　　Ｓ¹
（副詞節［時］）

and an attractive packaging style was enough to ensure product marketability and exposure.
　　　　　　　　Ｓ²　　　　　　　　Ｖ　enough to *do*（〜するのに十分な）　Ｃ

---

40. ★★★★★

(A) location
(B) outlook
(C) income
(D) appearance

(A) 名 所在地
(B) 名 見解
(C) 名 収入
(D) 名 外観

🔍 選択肢には意味の異なる名詞が並んでいる。空所を含む文だけでは正解を選べないため、前後の内容を見ていくと、第 1 パラグラフの後半で、ビジネスマンの Garry Ford さんが「以前は、人目を引く印刷広告と魅力的な梱包さえあれば、十分だと信じていた」と述べた後、「彼の……が数年前にかなり変わった」と空所を含む文で述べられている。ここから、Garry Ford さんの見解や考え方が変わった、といった語が入ると考えられる。以上より、**(B)** が正解となる。

However, his outlook changed considerably / a few years ago.
　　　　　　Ｓ　　　　Ｖ

PART **6**

TEST **2**

41. ★★★☆☆

(A) Eventually
(B) Typically
(C) Likewise
(D) Comparatively

(A) 副 最終的に
(B) 副 典型的に
(C) 副 同様に
(D) 副 かなり

選択肢には意味の異なる（接続）副詞が並んでいる。空所は文頭にあって、直後にカンマがあるので、前の文も含めて見ていくと、「顧客がネット購入できるようにしたり、地元で人気のウェブサイトで宣伝することを提案した」➡「……、ネットショップが必要と判断した」となっている。つまり、顧客からの要望が多くなってきたため、最終的に判断した、ということがわかるので、**(A)** が正解となる。(C) は空所前後の内容が同様の内容ではないため不正解。

Eventually, / I decided that an online store was becoming necessary.
　　　　　　　　　S　　V　　O (that 節) ⑤　　　　　　Ⓥ　　　　Ⓒ

42. ★★★★☆

(A) Market analysts suggest that online shopping statistics are wrong.
(B) He is trying to launch a massive sales campaign in major jewelry shops.
(C) Lower prices have attracted more customers to his business.
(D) His story shows the power of Internet marketing.

(A) 市場アナリストは、インターネットショッピングの統計が間違っていることを示唆している。
(B) 主要な宝石店で大規模な販促キャンペーンを開始しようとしている。
(C) 低価格によりお店に引きつけられる顧客が増えてきた。
(D) 彼の話はインターネットマーケティングの力を示している。

選択肢には文が並んでおり、空所は文章の最後にある。空所前の文を読むと、「現在では、Ford さんの売上の 50% 以上はウェブサイトでのものだ」となっている。Ford さんは、これより前の 5 文目でもインターネット上での宣伝や店舗の必要性を語っていることから、これに関連した内容の **(D)** がこの文章を締めるにふさわしい内容となる。

□statistics 統計　□launch 〜を開始する　□massive 大規模な

39. (D)　40. (B)　41. (A)　42. (D)

Questions 39-42 refer to the following article.

Reaching the Masses in the Digital Age

❶ "I think that the best route to success in business is to enter the online market and use Web advertisements," says Garry Ford. ❷ He is a businessman who has been operating a jewelry shop on Main Street for almost fifteen years. ❸ As he was starting his business, he believed that having eye-catching print advertisements and an <u>**39** attractive</u> packaging style was enough to ensure product marketability and exposure.

❹ However, his <u>**40** outlook</u> changed considerably a few years ago. ❺ "An increasing number of customers suggested that I make my merchandise available online and advertise it on popular local Web sites. ❻ **41** <u>Eventually</u>, I decided that an online store was becoming necessary." Mr. Ford now makes over 50 percent of his sales through his Web site. ❼ **42** <u>His story shows the power of Internet marketing.</u>

問題 39-42 は次の記事に関するものです。

デジタル時代の大衆の心を動かす

❶「ビジネスで成功するための最良の方法は、インターネット市場に参入し、ウェブ広告を使用することだと思います。」と Garry Ford さんは言っている。❷ Ford さんは Main Street で 15 年近く宝石店を経営しているビジネスマンだ。❸ 開業当時は、人目を引く印刷広告と<u>魅力的な梱包</u>さえあれば、製品がよく売れて、多くの人に知られるようにするには十分であると信じていた。

❹ しかし、<u>彼の見解</u>は数年前にがらりと変化した。❺「当店の商品をインターネットで購入できるようにしたり、地元で人気のウェブサイトで宣伝したりしたらどうかというご提案を、お客様から頂くことが増えてきました。最終的に、インターネット上の店舗が必要であると判断しました。」❻ 現在では、Ford さんの売上の 50 パーセント以上を占めるのはウェブサイトでのものである。❼ <u>彼の話はインターネットマーケティングの力を示している。</u>

□reach ～の心を動かす □mass 大衆 □digital age デジタル時代、デジタル世代
□the best route to *do* ～する最善の方法 □eye-catching 人目を引く □print advertisement 印刷広告
□packaging style 梱包 □marketability 市場性 □exposure 露出 □considerably かなり
□an increasing number of ますます多数の □merchandise 商品

Questions 43-46 refer to the following letter.

September 12

Mr. Howard King
428 Cleary Avenue
Brownsburg, IN 46112

Dear Mr. King,

Thank you for contacting us about the vacant Head Computer Programmer position here at Double Gate Games Inc. ------- our evaluation of your skills and experience, we believe you are a strong candidate for the position. We would like to talk with you in person about the job. If it is convenient for you, we would like you to visit our headquarters at 2 P.M. on Wednesday, September 17.

43

At the meeting, you ------- to go into further detail about your strengths, and to describe your contributions to projects you have worked on in the past. If we feel that you would fit well into our team here at Double Gate Games Inc., we will then place ------- on a shortlist for the final round of interviews. Please call me at 999-5637 to let me know if the meeting date and time are agreeable to you. -------.

44

45

46

Sincerely,

Doug Goertz
Human Resources Manager
Double Gate Games Inc.

---

43. (A) Accordingly
(B) So that
(C) Based on
(D) Prior to

44. (A) would have asked
(B) were asked
(C) will be asked
(D) had asked

45. (A) us
(B) you
(C) him
(D) myself

46. (A) Thank you for your interest in our company.
(B) I'm very pleased to work with you.
(C) I'm so sorry that the meeting will be postponed.
(D) I'd like to put you on our waiting list for future positions.

43. ★★★☆☆

(A) Accordingly
(B) So that
(C) Based on
(D) Prior to

(A) したがって
(B) そのため
(C) ～に基づいて
(D) ～より前に

選択肢にはさまざまな接続表現が並んでいる。空所を含む文を見ていくと、冒頭で求人への応募に対するお礼を述べた後に、「技量と経験の評価……、この仕事の有力候補者だ」と書かれている。つまり、採用候補としての技量や経験を持っていると評価したということが理由になっているので、空所には「～に基づいて」という表現が入ることがわかる。以上より、正解は(C)。

Based on our evaluation of your skills and experience, /
～を根拠にして (副詞句)

we believe (that) you are a strong candidate / for the position.
S   V   O   S V   C
(that 節)

---

44. ★★★☆☆

(A) would have asked
(B) were asked
(C) will be asked
(D) had asked

(A) 仮定法過去完了形
(B) 受動態 (過去形)
(C) 受動態 (未来)
(D) 過去完了形

選択肢には動詞 ask (尋ねる) が時制を変えたものが並んでいる。空所前後を見ていくと、第1段落で求人への応募の有力候補と判断されて面接をお願いされた後、第2段落の空所を含む文で、面接の時には強みを深掘りすることについて述べられている。ここから、面接で強みを深掘りされるのは応募者だとわかる。以上より、受け身の関係で、これから行う面接 (未来のこと) について表す(C)が正解となる。

At the meeting, / you will be asked to go into further detail about your strengths, /
              S   V   O

and (you will be asked) to describe your contributions to projects / you have worked on in the past.
    S   V   O   S   V

---

45. ★★☆☆☆

(A) us
(B) you
(C) him
(D) myself

(A) 私たちを
(B) あなたを
(C) 彼を
(D) 私自身

選択肢にはさまざまな代名詞が並んでいる。空所を含む文は「我が社にしっかりと適合できると判断した場合は、……を最終面接の候補者リストに入れる」となっている。この空所前の文で面接対象となっているのはこの手紙の宛先の King さんであることから、空所に入るのは(B)だとわかる。

If we feel / that you would fit well into our team / here at Double Gate Games Inc., /
S V   O   (S)   (V)   (O)
(副詞節 [条件]) (that 節)

we will then place you / on a shortlist / for the final round of interviews.
S   V   O

46. ★★★☆☆

(A) Thank you for your interest in our company.
(B) I'm very pleased to work with you.
(C) I'm so sorry that the meeting will be postponed.
(D) I'd like to put you on our waiting list for future positions.

(A) 当社にご関心をお寄せいただきありがとうございます。
(B) 一緒にお仕事をさせていただくことができ、とてもうれしく思います。
(C) 面接が延期となりそうなことをお詫びいたします。
(D) 将来の求人の候補者リストに入れさせていただきます。

選択肢には文が並んでおり、空所は文章の最後にある。空所より前の文を読んでいくと、面接の詳細や、この面接後の流れについて述べられている。この手紙の結びの文としては、応募してくれたお礼で締めくくるのが文脈上自然と考えられることから、正解は **(A)**。面接の結果、面接の延期などについては述べられていないため、ほかの選択肢は不正解。

□interest in ~への関心　□waiting list 順番待ちリスト　□future position 将来の欠員

Questions 43-46 refer to the following letter.

September 12

Mr. Howard King
428 Cleary Avenue
Brownsburg, IN 46112

Dear Mr. King,

❶ Thank you for contacting us about the vacant Head Computer Programmer position here at Double Gate Games Inc. ❷ 43 Based on our evaluation of your skills and experience, we believe you are a strong candidate for the position. ❸ We would like to talk with you in person about the job. ❹ If it is convenient for you, we would like you to visit our headquarters at 2 P.M. on Wednesday, September 17.

❺ At the meeting, you 44 will be asked to go into further detail about your strengths, and to describe your contributions to projects you have worked on in the past. ❻ If we feel that you would fit well into our team here at Double Gate Games Inc., we will then place 45 you on a shortlist for the final round of interviews. ❼ Please call me at 999-5637 to let me know if the meeting date and time are agreeable to you. ❽ 46 Thank you for your interest in our company.

Sincerely,

Doug Goertz
Human Resources Manager
Double Gate Games Inc.

🚩 **43. (C)   44. (C)   45. (B)   46. (A)**

問題 43-46 は次の手紙に関するものです。

9 月 12 日

Howard King 様
428 Cleary Avenue
Brownsburg 市 , インディアナ州 46112

King 様

❶ Double Gate Games Inc. で欠員となっている主任コンピュータープログラマーの仕事についてお問い合わせいただきありがとうございます。❷技量と経験の審査の結果、King 様は弊社の求人の有力候補であると判断いたしました。❸ぜひ仕事について面接を行いたいと思います。❹もしご都合がよければ、9 月 17 日（水）の午後 2 時に本社にいらしていただけませんか。

❺面接では、ご自身の強みについてさらに詳しく掘り下げてお聞かせいただき、また過去に取り組んだプロジェクトへの貢献について説明していただきます。❻ Double Gate Games Inc. のチームで一緒にやっていけそうだと判断した場合、King 様を最終面接の候補者リストに入れます。❼ご都合のよろしい面談の日時をお知らせいただくため、999-5637 までお電話ください。❽当社にご関心をお寄せいただきありがとうございます。

どうぞよろしくお願いいたします。

Doug Goertz
人事マネジャー
Double Gate Games Inc.

□contact ～に連絡する　□evaluation 評価　□strong candidate 有力な候補　□in person 直接会って
□convenient 都合がよい　□headquarters 本社　□go into ～を詳細に述べる　□strength 強み
□describe ～を述べる、記載する　□contribution to ～に対する貢献　□in the past 過去に
□fit well into ～によく適応する、なじむ　□shortlist 最終候補者リスト　□the final round of interviews 最終面接
□agreeable 合意／同意できるものである

Test 3

Questions 31-34 refer to the following letter.

August 16

Ross Swan
Order Fulfillment Manager

Reynard Distribution, Ltd.
887 Sawyer Street
Boston, MA 02205

Dear Mr. Swan,

Thank you for enrolling in the 8th Logistics in Action Conference. In my ------- as chairman
                                                                          31
of the conference, I make every effort to contact those who might add significant value to

the discussion on areas of logistics at the conference. I would like you ------- in one of our
                                                                          32
discussion panels on either September 10 or 11. I will try to contact you by phone next

week. -------.
      33

I would also appreciate it if you could e-mail me some details about yourself such as your

full name, department, educational background and ------- companies so that I can place
                                                    34
this information on our conference Web site.

Sincerely,

Chairman, Logistics in Action Conference
Yann Koeman

---

31. (A) demonstration
(B) capacity
(C) guidance
(D) origin

32. (A) participation
(B) participating
(C) for participators
(D) to participate

33. (A) Committee members will vote on who
should speak.
(B) You do not need to pay until after the
conference.
(C) We will send the information to your
mailing address.
(D) I hope to hear soon which day is more
convenient for you.

34. (A) affiliated
(B) competed
(C) altered
(D) detect

31. ★★★★☆

(A) demonstration
(B) capacity
(C) guidance
(D) origin

(A) 名 実演
(B) 名 立場
(C) 名 指導
(D) 名 起源

選択肢には意味の異なる名詞が並んでいる。空所を含む文の意味を見ていくと、「この会議の議長としての私の……において、会議の討論に大きく寄与してくれそうな方と連絡を取るよう努めている」と、自分の役割の中で努力していることを述べている。ここから、自分の役割、立場に相当する語が入ると文意が成立する。以上より、正解は **(B)**。

In my capacity as chairman of the conference, / I make every effort to contact
副詞句　　　　　　　　　　　　　　　　　　　　　　S　　V　　　O　　　to 不定詞（副詞句）
those who might add significant value / to the discussion / on areas of logistics / at the conference.
S ～する人々　V　　　　　O

---

32. ★★☆☆☆

(A) participation
(B) participating
(C) for participators
(D) to participate

(A) 名 参加
(B) 動 参加する　現在分詞
(C) 関係者のために
(D) 不定詞

選択肢には名詞 participation の派生語が並んでいる。空所の前は I would like you、空所の後は in one of our discussion panels となっている。ここから、不定詞 to participate を入れると、「あなたに参加してほしい」という意味になり、文意も成立する。以上から、正解は **(D)**。would like you to do は第5文型の形で「あなたに～してほしい」という意味になる。

I would like you to participate in one of our discussion panels / on either September 10 or 11.
S　　　V　　O　　　C

---

33. ★★★☆☆

(A) Committee members will vote on who should speak.
(B) You do not need to pay until after the conference.
(C) We will send the information to your mailing address.
(D) I hope to hear soon which day is more convenient for you.

(A) 委員会のメンバーの投票により、発言者を決定します。
(B) 会議の終了まで、お支払いの必要はありません。
(C) あなたのご住所に情報を郵送いたします。
(D) どちらの日がご都合が良いか、近日中にお伺いできればと思います。

選択肢には文が並んでおり、空所は第1パラグラフの最後にある。空所前の文を読んでいくと、「9月10日または11日の討論会に参加してほしいので、来週電話連絡する」➡（空所）というつながりになっている。ここから、どちらの日にしてほしいか、という旨を聞きたいことが意図としてわかるので **(D)** が正解。

 □mailing address 郵送先住所

34. ★★★★★

(A) affiliated
(B) competed
(C) altered
(D) detect

(A) 動 〜と提携する 　過去分詞
(B) 動 競争する 　過去分詞
(C) 動 〜を変える 　過去分詞
(D) 動 〜を見つける 　過去分詞

選択肢には意味の異なる動詞の過去分詞が並んでいる。空所前には等位接続詞 and があり、「お名前、部署、学歴、……会社などの情報」とある。ここから空所は、後ろの companies を 修飾 し、name、department、educational background と同等の扱いになる名詞を導くものが入ることがわかる。以上より、「提携している会社」となる (A) が正解。

I would (also) appreciate it if you could e-mail me some details about yourself /
決まり文句（〜ならばありがたい）　S　V　O¹　O²

such as your full name, department, educational background and affiliated companies /
例えば〜など

so that I can place this information on our conference Web site.
　　　　　　　S　V　　　O
（副詞節 [目的]）

....

Questions 31-34 refer to the following letter.

August 16

Ross Swan
Order Fulfillment Manager

Reynard Distribution, Ltd.
887 Sawyer Street
Boston, MA 02205

Dear Mr. Swan,

❶ Thank you for enrolling in the 8th Logistics in Action Conference. ❷ In my **31** capacity as chairman of the conference, I make every effort to contact those who might add significant value to the discussion on areas of logistics at the conference. ❸ I would like you **32** to participate in one of our discussion panels on either September 10 or 11. ❹ I will try to contact you by phone next week. ❺ **33** I hope to hear soon which day is more convenient for you.

❻ I would also appreciate it if you could e-mail me some details about yourself such as your full name, department, educational background and **34** affiliated companies so that I can place this information on our conference Web site.

Sincerely,

Chairman, Logistics in Action Conference
Yann Koeman

🚩 **31. (B)　32. (D)　33. (D)　34. (A)**

問題 31-34 は次の手紙に関するものです。

8月16日

Ross Swan 様
受注・発送業務マネジャー

Reynard Distribution 社
887 Sawyer Street
ボストン、マサチューセッツ州 02205

Swan 様

❶この度は、第8回物流活動会議にご参加いただきありがとうございます。❷私はこの会議の議長としての立場で、会議で行われる物流分野の討論に大きく寄与していただけそうな方と連絡を取るよう努めております。❸9月10日または11日のいずれかの討論会にご参加いただけないでしょうか。❹来週、お電話でご連絡いたします。❺どちらの日がご都合が良いか、近日中にお伺いできればと思います。

❻また、Swan 様のフルネーム、部署、学歴、所属会社などの情報を E メールでお送りいただければ、当会議のウェブサイトに掲載させていただきます。

敬具

物流活動会議議長
Yann Koeman

Questions 35-38 refer to the following memo.

To: Evans Industries Staff Members
From: Ryan Fabian
Subject: Next month's training

I am pleased to invite you to our next training session ------- will show how to improve your
_35_
communication skills in the business world. Evans Industries' products and brand names
are well known all over the world. But our success is measured not just by our presence in
the business market but also by the ------- process of developing professional
_36_
relationships. Liam Baird, senior executive of business partnerships, is an authority in the
area of business communication.

This training session will address a crucial point of how to communicate ------- with other
_37_
professionals. -------. You can learn about many cases, from training new staff members to
_38_
working with other corporations.

Lunch will be served to all who attend.

---

35. (A) what
    (B) whose
    (C) so
    (D) which

36. (A) extensive
    (B) extend
    (C) extensively
    (D) extension

37. (A) confidently
    (B) alternatively
    (C) immaturely
    (D) handsomely

38. (A) It may be moved indoors depending
       on the weather.
    (B) Mr. Baird has worked for the company
       for fifteen years.
    (C) Please send your completed feedback
       forms to my inbox.
    (D) He will share his own experience of
       various types of problems and
       solutions.

35. ★★☆☆☆

(A) what
(B) whose
(C) so
(D) which

(A) 関係代名詞
(B) 関係代名詞（所有格）
(C) 接 そこで
(D) 関係代名詞

 選択肢には関係詞や接続詞が並んでいる。空所を含む文を見てみると、1つの文の中に述語動詞が2つある（am pleased to、will show）ことから、これらをつなげる表現が必要となる。ここから空所前の training session を先行詞とする主格の関係詞を入れると文法的に当てはめることができる。以上から、正解は **(D)**。

I am pleased to invite you / to our next training session / which will show
S   V   O   invite A to B   S   V

how to improve your communication skills / in the business world.
O

---

36. ★★☆☆☆

(A) extensive
(B) extend
(C) extensively
(D) extension

(A) 形 広範な
(B) 動 広がる
(C) 副 広く
(D) 名 延長

 選択肢には形容詞 extensive とその派生語が並んでいる。空所前後が定冠詞 the と名詞 process となっていることから、空所はこの名詞 process を修飾するものが入るとわかる。以上から、名詞を修飾する形容詞の **(A)** が正解。

But our success is measured / not just by our presence in the business market /
     S   V   not just A but also B（A のみならず B も）

but also by the extensive process of developing professional relationships.

37. ★★★★☆

(A) confidently
(B) alternatively
(C) immaturely
(D) handsomely

(A) 副 自信を持って
(B) 副 その代わりに
(C) 副 未熟に
(D) 副 立派に

This training session will address a crucial point of / how to communicate confidently /
　　　　　　　S　　　　　　V　　　　　O　　　　　　　　　名詞句
with other professionals.

38. ★★★☆☆

(A) It may be moved indoors depending on the weather.
(B) Mr. Baird has worked for the company for fifteen years.
(C) Please send your completed feedback forms to my inbox.
(D) He will share his own experience of various types of problems and solutions.

(A) 天候によっては、室内に移動することがあります。
(B) Baird 氏は 15 年間会社で働いてきました。
(C) 入力が終わった感想フォームは私の受信トレイへお送りください。
(D) さまざまなタイプの問題とその解決策について、ご自身の経験を交えて話してくださいます。

□move indoors ～を室内に移動する　□depending on ～により　□completed 記載した　□feedback 感想、意見
□inbox（E メールなどの）受信トレイ　□solution 解決策

Questions 35-38 refer to the following memo.

To: Evans Industries Staff Members
From: Ryan Fabian
Subject: Next month's training

❶ I am pleased to invite you to our next training session 35 which will show how to improve your communication skills in the business world. ❷ Evans Industries' products and brand names are well known all over the world. ❸ But our success is measured not just by our presence in the business market but also by the 36 extensive process of developing professional relationships. ❹ Liam Baird, senior executive of business partnerships, is an authority in the area of business communication.

❺ This training session will address a crucial point of how to communicate 37 confidently with other professionals. ❻ 38 He will share his own experience of various types of problems and solutions. ❼ You can learn about many cases, from training new staff members to working with other corporations.

Lunch will be served to all who attend.

問題 35-38 は次のメモ書きに関するものです。

宛先： Evans Industries 社スタッフ
差出人： Ryan Fabian
件名： 来月の研修について

❶ビジネスシーンにおけるコミュニケーション能力を高める方法を紹介する、次回の研修を皆さんにご案内します。❷Evans Industries 社の製品やブランド名は、世界中でよく知られています。❸しかし、私たちの成功の度合いは、ビジネス市場での存在感だけでなく、プロとしての人間関係を構築する広範なプロセスによって判断されるのです。❹ビジネスパートナーシップの上級管理職である Liam Baird 氏は、ビジネスコミュニケーションの分野での権威です。

❺この研修会では、いかにしてほかのプロの方たちと自信を持ってコミュニケーションをとるかという重要なポイントに触れます。❻さまざまなタイプの問題とその解決策について、ご自身の経験を交えて話してください。❼新入社員の教育から他企業との連携まで、多くの事例を学ぶことができます。

参加された方全員に、昼食をご用意します。

□brand name ブランド名 □measure 〜を測定する □presence 存在 □authority 権威 □address 〜に取り組む
□crucial 決定的な □other corporations 他企業

Questions 39-42 refer to the following e-mail.

To: All plant workers
From: Jolene Ratzenberger
Date: November 26
Sub: Trouble with the Equipment

Yesterday it was reported that a pressure regulation button on the machinery we use to

attach lids to our sauce jars was not working -------. The capping machine was applying a
                                              39
lower force than ------- the regulation button setting was showing. -------.
                    40   **41**

An engineer is scheduled to come by this morning to examine the button and pump of the

machine. -------, please inspect all the jars extra carefully before transferring them to the
         42
labeling department. If you notice any loosely sealed jars or other errors, please remove

them from the assembly line and place them in the rejection bin.

Sincerely,

Jolene Ratzenberger, Production Supervisor

39. (A) appropriately
(B) currently
(C) faithfully
(D) tightly

40. (A) that
(B) what
(C) how
(D) why

41. (A) Employees are asked to attend the training seminar to become familiar with the new machine.
(B) The instruction manual we have is very old.
(C) The expert suggested that we revise the safety guidelines.
(D) However, the equipment had been operating without issue for many years.

42. (A) Furthermore
(B) Conversely
(C) Besides
(D) Meanwhile

39. ★★★★☆

(A) appropriately
(B) currently
(C) faithfully
(D) tightly

(A) 副 正しく
(B) 副 現在
(C) 副 忠実に
(D) 副 しっかりと

選択肢には意味の異なる副詞が並んでいる。空所を含む文の意味を見ていくと、「昨日、ソースのビンに蓋をする機械の圧力調整ボタンが……作動していないとの報告があった」とあり、その後で「調節ボタンの設定値よりも低い力で作動していた」と不具合を述べていることから、機械自体が正しく作動していなかった可能性があるとわかる。以上より、**(A)** が正解。

Yesterday / it was reported / that a pressure regulation button / on the machinery / we use /
　　　　　　　仮 S　　V　　　真 S (that 節)　　　　　S　　　　　　　　　　　　　　　　(S) (V)

to attach lids to our sauce jars / was not working appropriately .
to 不定詞 (副詞句)　　　　　　　　　V

---

40. ★★★☆☆

(A) that
(B) what
(C) how
(D) why

(A) 関係代名詞
(B) 関係代名詞
(C) 関係副詞
(D) 関係副詞

選択肢には関係詞が並んでいる。空所前は a lower force than … と、「～よりも低い力」となっていることから、空所以下は比較対象を意味するとわかる。よって、空所には「調節ボタン設定が示していたもの」となる関係詞 what を入れると、文法的にも意味的にも成立することがわかる。以上より、正解は **(B)**。関係詞の what は先行詞も含むため、the things which と置き換えて考えてもよい。

The capping machine was applying a lower force / than
　　　　　S　　　　　　　V　　　　　　O　　　　　比較

what (= the thing which) the regulation button setting was showing
名詞節　　　　　O　　　　　　　　　　　　　　S　　　　　　　　　V

41. ★★★★☆

(A) Employees are asked to attend the training seminar to become familiar with the new machine.
(B) The instruction manual we have is very old.
(C) The expert suggested that we revise the safety guidelines.
(D) However, the equipment had been operating without issue for many years.

(A) 従業員は新しい機械に慣れるため、この研修会に参加するようお願いします。
(B) 私たちが持っている取扱説明書は大変古いです。
(C) 専門家は安全のためのガイドラインを改訂することを提案しました。
(D) ただ、この装置は何年もの間、問題なく動いてはいました。

選択肢には文が並んでおり、空所は第1パラグラフの最後にある。空所より前の文を読んでいくと、「昨日、ソースのビンに蓋をする機械が正しく作動していなかった」「調節ボタンの設定値よりも低い力で作動していた」➡（空所）➡（次のパラグラフの）「今日の午前中に技術者が来て検査する」というつながりになっている。これらは故障に関する内容について述べられていることから、故障や誤作動に関わる記載が入ると考えられる。以上から、これまでの故障状況の有無について触れている **(D)** が正解となる。

□familiar with ～に慣れて、精通して　□instruction manual 取扱説明書　□safety guideline 安全のためのガイドライン
□operate 作動する

42. ★★★★☆

(A) Furthermore
(B) Conversely
(C) Besides
(D) Meanwhile

(A) 副 なお
(B) 副 逆に
(C) 前 ～のほかに
(D) 副 その間

選択肢には接続副詞が並んでいる。空所は文頭にあることから、前の文のつながりを含めて意味を見ていくと、「今日の午前中に技術者が機械のボタンとポンプを検査する」「……、ラベル付け部門に移す前に、すべてのビンを特に注意して点検してほしい」と検査の間に行うべきことを指示していることがわかる。以上から、**(D)** が正解となる。

〈命令文〉
Meanwhile, please inspect all the jars extra carefully / before transferring them to the labeling
　　　　　　　　 V　　　 O　　　　　　　　 （副詞句［時］）transfer A to B
department.

To: All plant workers
From: Jolene Ratzenberger
Date: November 26
Sub: Trouble with the Equipment

❶ Yesterday it was reported that a pressure regulation button on the machinery we use to attach lids to our sauce jars was not working **39** appropriately . ❷ The capping machine was applying a lower force than **40** what the regulation button setting was showing. ❸ **41** However, the equipment had been operating without issue for many years .

❹ An engineer is scheduled to come by this morning to examine the button and pump of the machine. ❺ **42** Meanwhile , please inspect all the jars extra carefully before transferring them to the labeling department. ❻ If you notice any loosely sealed jars or other errors, please remove them from the assembly line and place them in the rejection bin.

Sincerely,

Jolene Ratzenberger, Production Supervisor

問題 39-42 は次の E メールに関するものです。

宛先： すべての工場関係者
差出人： Jolene Ratzenberger
日付： 11 月 26 日
件名： 装置の不具合について

❶昨日、ソースのビンに蓋をする機械の圧力調整ボタンが正しく作動していないとの報告がありました。❷蓋をする機械が、調節ボタンの設定値よりも低い力で作動していたのです。❸ただ、この装置は何年もの間、問題なく動いてはいました。

❹今日の午前中に技術者が来て、機械のボタンとポンプを検査する予定です。❺それまでの間に、すべてのビンを特に注意して点検してから、ラベル付けの部門に送ってください。❻もし、密封がゆるいビンやそのほかの欠陥に気づいた場合は、生産ラインから外し、不良品箱に入れるようお願いします。

よろしくお願いします。

Jolene Ratzenberger, 生産管理者

□pressure regulation 圧力調整 □attach a lid 蓋をする □sauce (食用) ソース □jar 広口びん
□capping machine キャッピングマシン (容器に蓋をする機械) □apply ～を作動する □pump ポンプ
□inspect ～を点検する □label ～にラベルを付ける □notice ～に気づく □loosely sealed ゆるく密閉された
□rejection bin 不良品用の箱、置き場

Questions 43-46 refer to the following letter.

11 April
3877 Pen Street
Jefferson City, MO 65109

Dear Mr. Routhier,

-------. These sessions are designed to help companies to cut down on absenteeism
       43
resulting from high levels of stress and to maintain efficient productivity. Seminar

participants learn to ------- the latest stress reduction and relaxation techniques. Our
                        44
sessions will teach the staff members of your organization practical and simple methods to

minimize and stop the stress response before it has a chance to build up.

Our seminars are run at our downtown location, ------- we can also arrange for them to be
                                                45
conducted at your place of business if you prefer. I have enclosed some information -------
                                                                                    46
available seminars and dates for you to review at your convenience.

For more details, please contact me directly at 777-4338.

Best regards,

Ken Gupta
Stress Control Seminars

43. (A) We are planning to sign up for your
           new series of seminars.
       (B) We are sure that you will hold our
           workplace safety seminar.
       (C) We have decided to offer our staff
           members free medical help for
           job-related stress.
       (D) Thank you for your keen interest in our
           stress control seminar.

44. (A) apply
       (B) appeal
       (C) resist
       (D) partition

45. (A) so
       (B) even
       (C) however
       (D) but

46. (A) at
       (B) in
       (C) on
       (D) to

43. ★★★☆☆

(A) We are planning to sign up for your new series of seminars.

(B) We are sure that you will hold our workplace safety seminar.

(C) We have decided to offer our staff members free medical help for job-related stress.

(D) Thank you for your keen interest in our stress control seminar.

(A) 御社の新しいセミナーシリーズに申し込むつもりです。

(B) あなたが私たちの職場安全セミナーを開催することを確信しています。

(C) 業務上のストレスに対する医療支援を当社のスタッフに無償で提供することを決定しました。

(D) 当社のストレスコントロールセミナーにご関心をお寄せいただき、誠にありがとうございます。

選択肢には文が並んでおり、空所は第1パラグラフの冒頭にある。空所後の文を読んでいくと、(空所) ➡「この講座ができた理由の説明」➡「参加者が学べること」という流れになっている。以上から、(A) は立場が逆であり、(B) は異なるセミナーについての内容、(C) は後の内容と文意が合わないため、セミナーに興味を持っていただいたことに関するお礼から切り出し、流れとしても自然である (D) が正解となる。

□sign up for 〜に申し込む □new series of 新たなシリーズの □workplace safety seminar 職場安全講習会
□medical help 医療支援 □keen interest in 〜への強い関心

44. ★★★★★

(A) apply
(B) appeal
(C) resist
(D) partition

(A) 動 〜を応用する
(B) 動 求める
(C) 動 〜に抵抗する
(D) 動 〜を仕切る

選択肢には意味の異なる動詞が並んでいる。空所を含む文の意味を見ていくと、「セミナー参加者は、最新のストレス解消法やリラックス法を……することを学ぶことができる」とある。この文の前にはセミナーの説明があり、「欠勤を繰り返す社員を減らし、効率的な生産性を維持することを支援するため」と述べられている。ここから、セミナーで教える方法論を実際に参加者が「適用する」ことを学ぶと考えられる。以上より、正解は (A)。

 Seminar participants learn to apply the latest stress reduction and relaxation techniques.
　　　　　　　 S 　　　　　　　　　　 V 　　　　　　　　　　　　 O

45. ★★★★☆

(A) so
(B) even
(C) however
(D) but

(A) 副 そのため
(B) 副 ～でさえ
(C) 副 しかしながら（接続副詞）
(D) 接 しかし

選択肢には副詞や接続詞が並んでいる。空所を含む文の意味を見ていくと、「セミナーはビジネス街にある弊社の会場で開催している、……希望であればお客様の会社で開催することも可能」となっている。ここから、セミナーの開催場所は弊社（だが）貴社でも開催は可能、と逆接の接続詞を入れると文意が成立する。以上から、正解は **(D)**。(C) も逆接の機能を持つ接続副詞だが、however は前の文を受けて、文頭に入れることで機能するため、文中にカンマを挟んで入れることはできない。

Our seminars are run / at our downtown location,
　　　　S　　　　　V

but we can also arrange for them to be conducted / at your place of business / if you prefer .
　　 S　　　　 V　　　　　　　 O (= seminars)　　　　　　　　　　　　　　　　　　（副詞節 [条件]）
　　　　　 arrange for O to *do*（O を～するよう手配する）　　　　　　　　　　　 もしよろしければ

---

46. ★★★☆☆

(A) at
(B) in
(C) on
(D) to

(A) 前 ～で
(B) 前 ～の中に
(C) 前 ～に関する
(D) 前 ～へ

選択肢には前置詞が並んでいる。空所を含む文の意味は「都合のよいときに確認できるように、開催可能なセミナーと日程……情報を同封している」という意味になっている。以上から、「開催可能なセミナーと日程に関する情報」とつなげると文意が成立することがわかる。よって、正解は **(C)**。

I have enclosed some information on available seminars and dates /
S　　　 V　　　　　　　　 O　　　　　 on (～に関する)

for you to review / at your convenience.
to review の意味上の主語

Questions 43-46 refer to the following letter.

11 April
3877 Pen Street
Jefferson City, MO 65109

Dear Mr. Routhier,

❶ **43** Thank you for your keen interest in our stress control seminar . ❷ These sessions are designed to help companies to cut down on absenteeism resulting from high levels of stress and to maintain efficient productivity. ❸ Seminar participants learn to **44** apply the latest stress reduction and relaxation techniques. ❹ Our sessions will teach the staff members of your organization practical and simple methods to minimize and stop the stress response before it has a chance to build up.

❺ Our seminars are run at our downtown location, **45** but we can also arrange for them to be conducted at your place of business if you prefer. ❻ I have enclosed some information **46** on available seminars and dates for you to review at your convenience.

❼ For more details, please contact me directly at 777-4338.

Best regards,

Ken Gupta
Stress Control Seminars

問題 43-46 は次の手紙に関するものです。

4月11日
3877 Pen Street
Jefferson City, MO 65109

Routhier 様

❶この度は、ストレスコントロールセミナーにご関心をお寄せいただき、誠にありがとうございます。❷この講座は、企業が、強いストレスのために欠勤を繰り返す社員を減らし、効率的な生産性を維持することを支援するために企画されたものです。❸セミナー参加者は、最新のストレス解消法やリラックス法の適用を学ぶことができます。❹このセミナーでは、ストレス反応が激しくなる前に、最小化して止めるための実用的でシンプルな方法を、貴社のスタッフの方々にお教えします。

❺セミナーはビジネス街にある弊社の会場で開催していますが、ご希望であれば、お客様の会社で開催することも可能です。❻ご都合のよいときにご覧いただけるよう、開催可能なセミナーとその日程に関する情報を同封しています。

❼詳細については、直接私 (777-4338) までご連絡ください。

よろしくお願いします。

Ken Gupta
ストレスコントロールセミナー

□cut down on ～を削減する　□absenteeism 欠勤を繰り返すこと　□result from ～が原因となる
□high levels of stress 高ストレス　□maintain ～を維持する　□efficient 効率的な　□productivity 生産性
□learn to *do* ～できるようになる　□latest 最新の　□reduction 減少　□relaxation technique リラックス法
□practical 実践的な　□minimize ～を最低限にする　□stress response ストレス反応　□build up 激しくなる
□run ～を行う　□conduct ～を実施する　□enclose ～を同封する　□review ～を閲覧する
□at your convenience 都合のよいときに　□detail 詳細　□contact ～に連絡する　□directly 直接

Test 4

Questions 31-34 refer to the following letter.

Kidman Utility Services

401 Minto Avenue
Cleveland, OH 44115

Dear Mr. Beltram,

Thank you for using our services. We issued a bill for your monthly utilities on November 3. And, according to our records, you have not paid the bill. The amount due is $57.69. If you have already sent your payment, then please ------- this part of the letter. But, if you have
                                                                            31
not yet made a payment, then please send it as soon as possible.

Kidman Utility Services would also like to make you ------- of some other resources which
                                                                  32
may be useful to you. If you are having trouble paying your bill, then you can call our

customer service hotline, 777-0573. -------. For those who need more convenience, we
                                            33
offer automatic withdrawal from your bank account with your written consent.

Please be advised that if we do not receive your payment by December 3, then you may experience an interruption in your utility services.

Thank you again for ------- Kidman Utility Services.
                          34

---

31. (A) modify
(B) discontinue
(C) complain
(D) disregard

32. (A) obvious
(B) impressed
(C) aware
(D) satisfied

33. (A) You can get more information about our services on our Web site.
(B) A late fee will be added to your next bill.
(C) Please contain your account number in the e-mail.
(D) Our representatives will explain the various payment options available.

34. (A) choosing
(B) chosen
(C) choice
(D) to choose

31. ★★★☆☆

(A) modify
(B) discontinue
(C) complain
(D) disregard

(A) 動 ～を修正する
(B) 動 ～を中断する
(C) 動 ～と不満を言う
(D) 動 ～を無視する

選択肢には意味の異なる動詞が並んでいる。空所を含む文の意味は「もしすでに支払いを済ませているのであれば、この手紙のこの部分は……してください」となっている。これより前に、未払いの公共料金に関する内容が述べられていることから、「もし支払っているのであれば、(読み捨てる、無視する)」という意味になると文意が成立する。以上から、正解は **(D)**。

If you have already sent your payment, / then please disregard this part of the letter.
S   V   O   (命令文)   V   O
(副詞節 [条件])

 PART 6

32. ★★★★☆

(A) obvious
(B) impressed
(C) aware
(D) satisfied

(A) 形 明らかな
(B) 形 感銘を受けた
(C) 形 気がついて
(D) 形 満足した

選択肢には意味の異なる形容詞が並んでいる。空所を含む文の意味は「Kidman Utility Services 社では、お客様に役立つそのほかの情報源を……している」となっている。ここからこの手紙はサービス会社からお客様宛の手紙とわかるため、情報源を「お知らせしている」とすると文意が成立する。以上から、使役動詞 make を使い、第 5 文型で「お知らせする」という意味になる **(C)** が正解。make 人 aware of で、「人に～を知らせる」という意味になる。

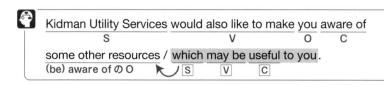

Kidman Utility Services would also like to make you aware of
          S   V   O   C
some other resources / which may be useful to you.
(be) aware of の O   ↰ S   V   C

TEST 4

33. ★★★★☆

(A) You can get more information about our services on our Web site.
(B) A late fee will be added to your next bill.
(C) Please contain your account number in the e-mail.
(D) Our representatives will explain the various payment options available.

(A) 弊社のサービスに関する詳しい情報は、ウェブサイトでご覧いただけます。
(B) 次回の請求書には延滞料が加算されます。
(C) Eメールにはあなたの口座番号を記載してください。
(D) 弊社の担当者が、さまざまなお支払い方法についてご説明いたします。

選択肢には文が並んでいる。空所前後の文を読んでいくと、「請求書の支払いに問題がある場合は、ホットラインにお電話ください」➡（空所）➡「より便利な銀行自動引き落としも行っている」というつながりになっている。空所後の「より便利な（more convenience）」から、空所にはこれ以外の支払い方法に関する内容が書かれていると考えられる。以上から、正解は **(D)**。

□late fee 延滞金　□contain 〜を含める　□representative 代表者、担当者　□various さまざまな
□payment option 支払方法

---

34. ★☆☆☆☆

(A) choosing
(B) chosen
(C) choice
(D) to choose

(A) 動 〜を選ぶ　動名詞
(B) 過去分詞
(C) 名 選択
(D) to 不定詞

選択肢には動詞 choose が形を変えたものや派生語が並んでいる。空所の前には前置詞 for、後ろにはこの手紙を出した会社名である Kidman Utility Services 社があるため、この前置詞 for に導かれ、目的語を取る動名詞が入るとわかる。よって、**(A)** が正解となる。Thank you for choosing＋会社名というフレーズは決まり文句の一つなので、覚えておこう。

Thank you again for choosing Kidman Utility Services.
　　　　　　　　　　　　動名詞　　　　　choose の O

Kidman Utility Services

401 Minto Avenue
Cleveland, OH 44115

Dear Mr. Beltram,

❶ Thank you for using our services. ❷ We issued a bill for your monthly utilities on November 3. ❸ And, according to our records, you have not paid the bill. ❹ The amount due is $57.69. ❺ If you have already sent your payment, then please **31 disregard** this part of the letter. ❻ But, if you have not yet made a payment, then please send it as soon as possible.

❼ Kidman Utility Services would also like to make you **32 aware** of some other resources which may be useful to you. ❽ If you are having trouble paying your bill, then you can call our customer service hotline, 777-0573. ❾ **33 Our representatives will explain the various payment options available.** ❿ For those who need more convenience, we offer automatic withdrawal from your bank account with your written consent.

⓫ Please be advised that if we do not receive your payment by December 3, then you may experience an interruption in your utility services.

⓬ Thank you again for **34 choosing** Kidman Utility Services.

PART 6

TEST 4

問題 **31-34** は次の手紙に関するものです。

Kidman Utility Services 社

401 Minto Avenue
Cleveland, オハイオ州 44115

Beltram 様

❶この度は弊社のサービスをご利用いただきありがとうございます。❷弊社は、11 月 3 日に、お客様のひと月分の光熱費の請求書を発行しました。❸しかし、弊社の記録によると、お客様よりご請求額のお支払いを頂いておりません。❹お支払いの金額は 57.69 ドルです。❺もしすでにお支払いを済まされているのであれば、この手紙のこの部分は無視してください。❻しかし、まだお支払いをされていない場合は、できるだけ早くご送金ください。

❼Kidman Utility Services 社では、お客様のお役に立つそのほかの情報源をお知らせしています。❽請求書のお支払いに問題が発生した場合は、カスタマーサービスのホットライン (777-0573) にお電話ください。❾弊社の担当者がさまざまなお支払い方法についてご説明いたします。❿また、さらに便利にご利用いただくために、ご本人様からの文書による同意を得たうえで、銀行口座からの自動引き落としも行っております。

⓫12 月 3 日までにお支払いがない場合、お客様への公共サービスの提供が停止する可能性がありますことをご了承ください。

⓬Kidman Utility Services 社をご利用いただき、重ねてお礼申し上げます。

□issue 〜を発行する □bill 請求書 □utility 光熱費、公共サービス □according to 〜によると
□amount due 支払予定金額 □as soon as possible 早急に □useful 役立つ
□have trouble doing 〜するのが難しい □hotline ホットライン、(緊急) 直通電話サービス □those who 〜する人
□automatic withdrawal from one's bank account 銀行口座からの自動引き落とし
□written consent 書面による同意 □Please be advised that 〜をご承知おきください
□experience an interruption 中断する

Questions 35-38 refer to the following letter.

August 22

Dear Valued Clients,

Dantona Crafts was established with the vision to offer our clients the means to sell their handmade goods in a secure online environment. Through our continued efforts ------- our **35** clients, we are pleased to announce a revamped Web site to facilitate your trading.

Up to now, the service was only available in the U.S., but we have now made it available worldwide. -------. In addition to this, customers can also perform ------- in their native **36** **37** languages.

Simply choose the language you want in the setting menu and the site will do the rest. Of course, you can return to the menu and ------- your language preference at any time. The **38** Web site will always remember your choice. This is just another example of how we are trying to satisfy our clients.

Annalise Woods
President
Dantona Crafts

---

35. (A) on behalf of
  (B) in honor of
  (C) by means of
  (D) with regard to

36. (A) An instruction manual was sent to you by e-mail.
  (B) We ask you to set up an online account.
  (C) You will be charged $100 every month.
  (D) Now five languages are available including Spanish, Chinese, and Korean.

37. (A) advertisements
  (B) presentations
  (C) options
  (D) transactions

38. (A) compare
  (B) alter
  (C) repeat
  (D) continue

35. ★★★☆☆

(A) on behalf of
(B) in honor of
(C) by means of
(D) with regard to

(A) ～のために
(B) ～に敬意を表して
(C) ～によって
(D) ～に関しては

選択肢にはさまざまな接続表現が並んでいる。空所を含む文の意味は「お客様……継続的な努力を重ね、簡単にビジネスをしていただけるよう、ウェブサイトをリニューアルしたので通知する」という内容になっている。努力を重ねたのは、お客様のためなので、正解は (A)。on behalf of は「～を代表して、～の代わりに」という意味もあるが、今回は「～のために、～の利益となるように」という意味で使われていることにも注目しよう。

Through our continued efforts on behalf of our clients, /
～を通して（副詞句）　　　　～の利益のために

we are pleased to announce a revamped Web site / to facilitate your trading.
S　　　V　　　　　　　O　　　　　to 不定詞（形容詞句）

PART 6

---

36. ★★★★☆

(A) An instruction manual was sent to you by e-mail.
(B) We ask you to set up an online account.
(C) You will be charged $100 every month.
(D) Now five languages are available including Spanish, Chinese, and Korean.

(A) 取扱説明書はメールでお送りいたしました。
(B) オンライン口座の開設をお願いします。
(C) 毎月 100 ドル請求されます。
(D) 現在は、スペイン語、中国語、韓国語など 5 つの言語に対応しています。

選択肢には文が並んでいる。空所前後の文を読んでいくと、「これまでは米国内のみだったが、今後は全世界で使える」➡（空所）➡「これに加えて母国語使用……」となっている。つまり、全世界で使用できるようになったことから、使用言語の選択の可能性について言及していると考えることができる。よって、(D) が正解となる

□instruction manual 取扱説明書　□charge（金額等）を課す　□include ～を含む

TEST 4

37. ★★★★☆

(A) advertisements
(B) presentations
(C) options
(D) transactions

(A) 名 広告
(B) 名 発表
(C) 名 選択肢
(D) 名 取引

 選択肢にはさまざまな意味の名詞が並んでいる。空所を含む文は、「これに加え、お客様は母国語でも……を行うことができる」という内容になっている。このサービスは手作りの商品の販売に関するものだと第1パラグラフで触れられていたので、ここで行うことができるのは取引だとわかる。以上より、正解は **(D)**。perform transactions で「商取引を行う」という意味になる。このサービスが広告を行っているかどうかは記載がなくわからないので、(A) は不正解。

In addition to this, / customers can also perform transactions / in their native languages.
～に加えて (副詞句)　　　　　S　　　　　V　　　　　O

---

38. ★★★☆☆

(A) compare
(B) alter
(C) repeat
(D) continue

(A) 動 ～を比較する
(B) 動 ～を変更する
(C) 動 ～を繰り返し行う
(D) 動 ～を継続する

 選択肢には意味の異なる動詞が並んでいる。空所を含む文は「もちろん、いつでも設定メニューに戻り、言語を……することができる」という内容になっている。この文の前には「設定メニューで好きな言語を選べばあとはサイトがやってくれる」とあることから、設定に戻れば言語を「変更できる」とすると、文意が通る。以上より、正解は **(B)**。空所後の文で、「選択した言語を記憶している」とあるので、(D) の「～を継続する」はここでは文意に合わず不正解。

Of course, you can return to the menu /
　　　　　S　　　V　　　　O

and (you can) alter your language preference / at any time.
　　　S　　V　　　　　　O　　　　　　いつでも (副詞句)

📝 **Questions 35-38** refer to the following letter.

August 22

Dear Valued Clients,

❶ Dantona Crafts was established with the vision to offer our clients the means to sell their handmade goods in a secure online environment. ❷ Through our continued efforts **35** on behalf of our clients, we are pleased to announce a revamped Web site to facilitate your trading.

❸ Up to now, the service was only available in the U.S., but we have now made it available worldwide. ❹ **36** Now five languages are available including Spanish, Chinese, and Korean. ❺ In addition to this, customers can also perform **37** transactions in their native languages.

❻ Simply choose the language you want in the setting menu and the site will do the rest. ❼ Of course, you can return to the menu and **38** alter your language preference at any time. ❽ The Web site will always remember your choice. ❾ This is just another example of how we are trying to satisfy our clients.

Annalise Woods
President
Dantona Crafts

問題 35-38 は次の手紙に関するものです。

8月22日

大切なお客様へ

❶ Dantona Crafts 社は、お客様が安全なオンライン環境で手作りの商品を販売する手段を提供する目的で設立されました。❷ この度、お客様のために継続的な努力を重ね、簡単にビジネスをしていただけるよう、ウェブサイトをリニューアルいたしましたので、お知らせいたします。

❸ これまでは米国内のみのサービスでしたが、この度、全世界でご利用いただけるようになりました。❹ 現在は、スペイン語、中国語、韓国語など5つの言語に対応しています。❺ これに加えて、お客様の母国語でも取引を行うことができます。

❻ 設定メニューで好きな言語を選ぶだけで、あとはサイトがすべて行います。❼ もちろん、いつでも設定メニューに戻り、言語を変更することができます。❽ ウェブサイトは常にお客様が選択された言語を記憶しています。❾ ただ、これはお客様に満足していただくために行っていることの一例に過ぎません。

Annalise Woods
社長
Dantona Crafts 社

✏️ □valued client お得意様　□establish 〜を設立する　□vision ビジョン、目的　□means 手段
□handmade goods 手作りの製品　□secure 安全な　□environment 環境　□continued effort 継続的な努力
□revamped 改修された　□facilitate 〜を容易にする　□trading 取引　□up to now これまで　□worldwide 世界中で
□in addition to 〜に加え　□native language 母国語　□setting menu 設定メニュー　□do the rest 残りの作業をやる
□language preference お好みの言語　□satisfy 〜を満足させる

Questions 39-42 refer to the following article.

Doubts Over Keyboard Benefits

TORONTO (September 1)— -------. The computer keyboards and mice in the latest MM5
                  39
series are advertised as preventing tiredness and pain. However, their benefits may be much
fewer than the manufacturers claim on television and in newspapers. According to a
recently published study, these specially designed devices do little to alleviate muscle or
joint pain.

Dr. Norman Johnson conducted a six-month study involving one hundred office workers
who regularly experience pain in their hands or wrists when typing. Half of the participants
used a standard keyboard and mouse for the first three months, ------- the other half used
                                  40
MM5 models. After three months, the groups switched devices. At the end of the study,
neither group reported any notable changes after switching models.

This news may be useful to consumers who are considering buying MM5 models. This
series of keyboards ------- cost around 80 dollars, which is about 1.5 times higher than
                  41
their standard counterparts. Now that Dr. Johnson's findings have been made public,
keyboard manufacturers may find it difficult to ------- such a high retail price.
                                         42

39. (A) Specially designed devices are to be
     recalled because of a design fault.
  (B) A survey show a decrease in demand
     for computer accessories.
  (C) New technology has improved the
     health of office employees.
  (D) Consumers are recommended to think
     again when buying new computer
     gadgets.

40. (A) while
  (B) during
  (C) as
  (D) in order to

41. (A) individually
  (B) typically
  (C) exclusively
  (D) particularly

42. (A) pay
  (B) allow
  (C) justify
  (D) advertise

39. ★★★★☆

(A) Specially designed devices are to be recalled because of a design fault.
(B) A survey show a decrease in demand for computer accessories.
(C) New technology has improved the health of office employees.
(D) Consumers are recommended to think again when buying new computer gadgets.

(A) 特別に設計された機器が、設計上の不具合で回収されることになった。
(B) ある調査の結果がコンピューターの付属品の需要が減少していることを示している。
(C) 新しい技術によって、会社員の健康が改善された。
(D) 消費者には、新しいコンピューター機器を購入する際に、よく考えることをお勧めする。

🔍 選択肢には文が並んでおり、空所は第1パラグラフの冒頭にある。空所の後を読んでいくと、「最新のコンピューター用キーボードとマウスは、疲れや痛みを防ぐと宣伝されているが、その効果はテレビや新聞でメーカーが主張するよりもずっと少ないかもしれない。というのも、最近発表された研究で、効果がほとんどないという結果が出た」と述べられている。以上より、宣伝されている効果が疑わしいため、購入に関して一考を求める、ということを伝えている **(D)** が正解。

✎ □recall ～を回収する □design fault 設計上の不具合 □decrease in ～の減少 □demand for ～の需要
□gadget 機器

---

40. ★★★☆☆

(A) while
(B) during
(C) as
(D) in order to

(A) 接 ～する一方で
(B) 前 ～の間
(C) 接 ～なので
(D) ～するために

🔍 空所には接続詞や前置詞などが並んでいる。空所を含む文の意味は「最初の3カ月は半数の被験者が標準的なキーボードとマウスを使い、……残りの半数は MM5 モデルを使った」となっている。ここから、別のキーボードを使った対比的な実験を行っていることがわかり、かつ空所の前後は節を形成していることから、空所には節を導く接続詞が入ることがわかる。以上から、正解は **(A)**。

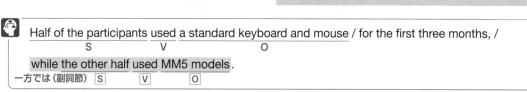

Half of the participants used a standard keyboard and mouse / for the first three months, /
     S   V   O

while the other half used MM5 models.
一方では（副詞節） S   V   O

41. ★★★☆☆

(A) individually
(B) typically
(C) exclusively
(D) particularly

(A) 副 個々に
(B) 副 通常は
(C) 副 独占的に
(D) 副 特に

🔍 空所には意味の異なる副詞が並んでいる。空所を含む文の意味は「このシリーズのキーボードは……約80ドルで、標準的なキーボードに比べて約1.5倍も高い」とMM5シリーズと標準的なキーボードの価格を比較している。以上から、「通常」を意味する **(B)** が正解。空所前後にキャンペーンや割引などの価格変動に関する内容があれば (C)、(D) が正解の候補になる可能性があるが、今回そのようなキーワードは見当たらないことから、この記載は通常の価格との比較であることがわかる。

🧠
This series of keyboards typically cost around 80 dollars, /
　　　　　S　　　　　　　　　　V　　　　　O

which is about 1.5 times higher / than their standard counterparts.
S　V　　　　　　C　　　　　　比較
(80 dollars の補足説明)

---

42. ★★★★★

(A) pay
(B) allow
(C) justify
(D) advertise

(A) 動 ～を支払う
(B) 動 ～を認める
(C) 動 ～が正当であることを説明する
(D) 動 ～を広告する

🔍 空所には意味の異なる動詞が並んでいる。空所を含む文は「Johnson博士の調査結果が公表された今、キーボードメーカーはこのような高い小売価格……することが難しくなるかもしれない」となっている。ここまでの文章の内容から、高い小売価格に見合った効果があると言いづらい状況であることから、正解は **(C)** となる。justify cost (price) はコロケーション（組み合わせの良い語）で、「かかっているコストを正当化する、正当だと説明する」という意味になる。(B) は、キーボードメーカー自体が高い価格を容認する、となり、文意に合わないため不正解。

🧠
Now that Dr. Johnson's findings have been made public, /
今や～だから（副詞節）　S　　　　　　　　V　　　　　　C

keyboard manufacturers may find it difficult to justify / such a high retail price.
　　　S　　　　　　　　V　仮O　C　　　真O　　　⤴ justify の O

🚩 **39. (D)　40. (A)　41. (B)　42. (C)**

Doubts Over Keyboard Benefits

TORONTO (September 1)— ❶ **39** Consumers are recommended to think again when buying new computer gadgets. ❷ The computer keyboards and mice in the latest MM5 series are advertised as preventing tiredness and pain. ❸ However, their benefits may be much fewer than the manufacturers claim on television and in newspapers. ❹ According to a recently published study, these specially designed devices do little to alleviate muscle or joint pain.

❺ Dr. Norman Johnson conducted a six-month study involving one hundred office workers who regularly experience pain in their hands or wrists when typing. ❻ Half of the participants used a standard keyboard and mouse for the first three months, **40** while the other half used MM5 models. ❼ After three months, the groups switched devices. ❽ At the end of the study, neither group reported any notable changes after switching models.

❾ This news may be useful to consumers who are considering buying MM5 models. ❿ This series of keyboards **41** typically cost around 80 dollars, which is about 1.5 times higher than their standard counterparts. ⓫ Now that Dr. Johnson's findings have been made public, keyboard manufacturers may find it difficult to **42** justify such a high retail price.

問題 39-42 は次の記事に関するものです。

キーボードの利点に疑問の声

トロント（9 月 1 日）—❶消費者には、新しいコンピューター機器を購入する際に、よく考えることをお勧めする。❷最新のMM5 シリーズのコンピューター用キーボードとマウスは、疲れや痛みを防ぐと宣伝されている。❸しかし、その効果は、テレビや新聞でメーカーが主張するよりもずっと少ないかもしれない。❹最近発表された研究によると、これらの特別に設計された機器には、筋肉や関節の痛みを緩和する効果はほとんどないというのだ。

❺ Norman Johnson 博士は、タイピングの際にたいてい手や手首に痛みを感じている 100 人の会社員を対象に、6 カ月間の研究を行った。❻最初の 3 カ月は半数の被験者が標準的なキーボードとマウスを使い、その一方で残りの半数は MM5 モデルを使った。❼3 カ月後、両グループは機器を交換した。❽研究終了時には、どちらのグループにも機種変更後の目立った変化は報告されなかった。

❾このニュースは、MM5 モデルの購入を検討している消費者にとって有益な情報かもしれない。❿このシリーズのキーボードは通常約 80 ドルで、標準的なキーボードに比べて約 1.5 倍も高い。⓫Johnson 博士の調査結果が公表された今、キーボードメーカーはこのような高い小売価格の理由を説明することが難しくなるかもしれない。

□latest 最新の □prevent 〜を防ぐ □tiredness 疲労 □pain 痛み □benefit メリット □manufacturer 製造業者
□claim 〜を主張する □according to 〜によると □recently published 最近発表された □study 研究
□specially designed device 特別に設計された装置 □muscle 筋肉 □alleviate pain 痛みを緩和する
□conduct 〜を行う □involve 〜を含む □wrist 手首 □switch 〜を交換する □useful 役立つ
□counterpart 同等のもの □finding 発見、調査結果 □retail price 小売価格

Questions 43-46 refer to the following letter.

14 Snyder Court
Winnipeg R3C 0H8

Dear Mr. Jake Warren,

We are writing to inform you that our insurance rates have recently been ------- to keep up

    43

with current market levels. This means that there will be an increase of $5.00 in your

monthly bill. These changes are necessary ------- we can continue to provide you with the

                    44

best coverage on the market. If you have any ------- inquiries about our prices or policies,

                    45

please do not hesitate to contact us. We will strive to continue to provide you with

high-quality insurance. -------.

                46

Best regards,

Kevin Qualls
Reva Insurance Customer Services

43. (A) adjusted
(B) waived
(C) exchanged
(D) omitted

44. (A) only if
(B) because
(C) so that
(D) whenever

45. (A) specify
(B) specific
(C) specifically
(D) specification

46. (A) Your car will be fully insured beginning
on January 1 next year.
(B) We would appreciate your
understanding of this change.
(C) Thank you for reporting this billing
error promptly.
(D) Please make use of this perfect
opportunity for your family.

43. ★★★☆☆

(A) adjusted
(B) waived
(C) exchanged
(D) omitted

(A) 動 ～を調整する 過去分詞
(B) 動 ～を放棄する 過去分詞
(C) 動 ～を交換する 過去分詞
(D) 動 ～を省く 過去分詞

 空所には意味の異なる動詞の過去分詞が並んでいる。空所を含む文の意味は「弊社の保険料率が現在の市場の水準に合わせて……されましたので、お知らせする」となっている。ここから、市場水準に合わせて対応するもの➡価格調整、と考えられるので、正解は **(A)** となる。

We are writing to inform you /
　S　　　V　　　to 不定詞　inform＋O（人）＋（that 節）「人に～を知らせる」
　　　　　　　　　　（副詞句）

that our insurance rates have (recently) been adjusted / to keep up with current market levels.
（that 節）　　　S　　　　　　　　　　　　V　　　　　　　　　　to 不定詞 (副詞句)

---

44. ★★★☆☆

(A) only if
(B) because
(C) so that
(D) whenever

(A) ～する場合に限り
(B) なぜなら
(C) ～するため
(D) ～するときはいつでも

 空所にはさまざまな接続表現が並んでいる。空所を含む文の意味は「この改訂は必要なもの……、お客様への最高の補償の提供を続けることができる」とある。ここから、空所前後の関係が「変更は必要➡そうすればお客様に最高の補償を提供できる」となることがわかる。以上より、so that S can V「SがV できるために」という形にすると文意が通るため、**(C)** が正解。

These changes are necessary /
　　　S　　　V　　　C

so that we can continue to provide you / with the best coverage / on the market.
　　　　S　　　　　V　　　　　　　　O　　　provide A with B (A に B を提供する)
（副詞節 [目的]）

45. ★★☆☆☆

(A) specify
(B) specific
(C) specifically
(D) specification

(A) 動 〜を詳しく言う
(B) 形 具体的な
(C) 副 具体的に言えば
(D) 名 詳述

If you have any specific inquiries / about our prices or policies, /
　　　S　　V　　　　　　　O
（副詞節［条件］）

please do not hesitate to contact us.
命令文　　　　　　　V　　　　　O

---

46. ★★★★☆

(A) Your car will be fully insured beginning on January 1 next year.
(B) We would appreciate your understanding of this change.
(C) Thank you for reporting this billing error promptly.
(D) Please make use of this perfect opportunity for your family.

(A) お客様の車に一式かけられた保険は来年の1月1日から保険期間が始まります。
(B) 今回の改訂について、何卒ご理解を賜りますようお願い申し上げます。
(C) 今回の誤請求を迅速にご報告いただき、ありがとうございました。
(D) この絶好の機会をご家族でご活用ください。

□fully 完全に　□insure 〜に保険をかける　□understanding 理解　□billing error 請求上の誤り　□promptly 直ちに
□make use of 〜を最大限利用する

Questions 43-46 refer to the following letter.

14 Snyder Court
Winnipeg R3C 0H8

Dear Mr. Jake Warren,

❶ We are writing to inform you that our insurance rates have recently been **43** adjusted to keep up with current market levels. ❷ This means that there will be an increase of $5.00 in your monthly bill. ❸ These changes are necessary **44** so that we can continue to provide you with the best coverage on the market. ❹ If you have any **45** specific inquiries about our prices or policies, please do not hesitate to contact us. ❺ We will strive to continue to provide you with high-quality insurance. ❻ **46** We would appreciate your understanding of this change.

Best regards,

Kevin Qualls
Reva Insurance Customer Services

問題 43-46 は次の手紙に関するものです。

14 Snyder Court
Winnipeg R3C 0H8

Jake Warren 様

❶この度、弊社の保険料率を現在の市場の水準に合わせて調整いたしましたので、お知らせいたします。❷このため、Warren 様への毎月の請求額が 5 ドル増えることになります。❸この改訂は、お客様への最高の補償の提供を続けるために必要なものです。❹当社の料金やポリシーについて具体的なご質問がありましたら、お気軽にお問い合わせください。❺今後も質の高い保険を提供できるよう努力してまいります。❻今回の改訂について、何卒ご理解を賜りますようお願い申し上げます。

よろしくお願いします。
Kevin Qualls
Reva Insurance 社 カスタマーサービス

□insurance rate 保険料率 □keep up with ～に追従して、合わせて □current market level 現在の市場の水準
□bill 請求 □coverage (保険等の) 補償 □on the market 市場での □inquiry 問い合わせ
□do not hesitate to contact ～に遠慮なく問い合わせる □strive to do ～しようとする

Test 5

Questions 31-34 refer to the following e-mail.

To: All employees <employees@westernvirginia.org>
From: Dana Ausbrook, Senior Manager <dnab@westernvirginia.org>
Date: May 15
Subject: A New Office

To all Western Virginia employees,

The purpose of this e-mail is to remind you of our upcoming relocation. As you know, in order to cut costs Western Virginia Law Firm will be moving ------- a new office building
31
next week. Employees need to be aware that there will be some disruptions in work schedules on May 20 because of this -------. The move is expected to last about eight
32
hours. Beginning at 9:00 A.M., we ask that you clean out your desks and place your documents and items in the cardboard boxes -------. -------.
33   **34**

Thank you,

Dana Ausbrook
Senior Manager
Western Virginia Law Firm

31. (A) into
(B) onto
(C) toward
(D) forward

32. (A) renovation
(B) change
(C) absence
(D) mistake

33. (A) provide
(B) provision
(C) providing
(D) provided

34. (A) Some movers are waiting on the first floor, so please hurry up.
(B) Take special care with important items such as contracts and keys.
(C) The moving company came last week to estimate costs.
(D) We will attempt to solve some scheduling conflicts before the weekend.

31. ★★★☆☆

(A) into
(B) onto
(C) toward
(D) forward

(A) 前 ～の中へ
(B) 前 ～の上に
(C) 前 ～に対して
(D) 副 前方へ

 選択肢には前置詞や副詞が並んでいる。空所を含む文の意味は「事務所は来週、新しいオフィスビル……移転する」となっている。ここから、ある地点から移動してビルの中に入る、という意味になる前置詞を入れると文意が成立することがわかる。以上より、正解は **(A)**。前置詞 into はある外の地点から中に入り込むイメージとして捉えておこう。

 As you know, / in order to cut costs /
ご存じのように　　　（副詞句［目的］）
（副詞節）

Western Virginia Law Firm will be moving into a new office building next week.
　　　　　　S　　　　　　　　　　V　　　　　　　O

---

32. ★★★★☆

(A) renovation
(B) change
(C) absence
(D) mistake

(A) 名 改修
(B) 名 変更
(C) 名 欠席
(D) 名 間違い

選択肢には意味の異なる名詞が並んでいる。空所を含む文の意味は「従業員は、この……のために5月20日の仕事のスケジュールが多少予定通りにならないことを認識しておいてください」となっている。次に、空所を含む前の文で「オフィスの移転」について記載されていることから、移転という「変更」があったことで仕事に支障をきたす可能性がある、とすると文意が成立する。以上より、正解は **(B)**。移転と改修は異なるため **(A)** は不正解。

Employees need to be aware /
　　S　　　　　　V

that there will be some disruptions / in work schedules on May 20 / because of this change.
O（that 節）　V　　　　S　　　　　　　　　　　　　　　　　　　　　（副詞句［理由］）

33. ★★★★☆

(A) provide   (A) 動 ～を与える
(B) provision   (B) 名 供給
(C) providing   (C) 現在分詞
(D) **provided**   (D) 過去分詞

選択肢には動詞 provide が形を変えて並んでいる。空所前に名詞句 the cardboard boxes があり、空所を含む文は「……段ボール箱に書類や物品を収納するように」という意味で、clean out という述語動詞が存在していることから、空所は直前の名詞句を修飾しているとわかる。以上から、分詞の形で「配布された（段ボール）」となる **(D)** が正解。

Beginning at 9:00 A.M., /
朝 9 時より

we ask / that you clean out your desks / and (you) place your documents and items
S   V   S   V   O   S   V   O
      O (that 節)

in the cardboard boxes provided .
place A in B

---

34. ★★★★☆

(A) Some movers are waiting on the first floor, so please hurry up.
(B) **Take special care with important items such as contracts and keys.**
(C) The moving company came last week to estimate costs.
(D) We will attempt to solve some scheduling conflicts before the weekend.

(A) 1 階で引っ越し業者が待っていますので、お急ぎください。
(B) **契約書や鍵など、大切なものには特に気をつけてください。**
(C) 引っ越し業者は先週、費用の見積もりに来ました。
(D) 私たちは週末までにいくつかのスケジュールの重複を解決しようと思っています。

選択肢には文が並んでおり、空所は文章の最後にある。空所前の文を読んでいくと、「引っ越しは約 8 時間かかり、午前 9 時から机の上の片付けや、書類や物品を用意された段ボール箱に入れるように」➡（空所）、というつながりになっている。ここから、空所には引っ越しでの片付け作業に関連する内容が入ると考えられる。以上から、片付けの際に特に紛失に気を付けてほしいものを述べている **(B)** が正解となる。

☐hurry up 急ぐ ☐take care with ～に気をつける ☐such as ～といったような ☐contract 契約書
☐estimate ～を見積もる ☐attempt to *do* ～しようとする ☐solve ～を解決する
☐scheduling conflict スケジュールの重複

Questions 31-34 refer to the following e-mail.

To: All employees <employees@westernvirginia.org>
From: Dana Ausbrook, Senior Manager <dnab@westernvirginia.org>
Date: May 15
Subject: A New Office

To all Western Virginia employees,

❶ The purpose of this e-mail is to remind you of our upcoming relocation. ❷ As you know, in order to cut costs Western Virginia Law Firm will be moving __31 into__ a new office building next week. ❸ Employees need to be aware that there will be some disruptions in work schedules on May 20 because of this __32 change__. ❹ The move is expected to last about eight hours. ❺ Beginning at 9:00 A.M., we ask that you clean out your desks and place your documents and items in the cardboard boxes __33 provided__. ❻ __34 Take special care with important items such as contracts and keys.__

Thank you,

Dana Ausbrook
Senior Manager
Western Virginia Law Firm

問題 31-34 は次の E メールに関するものです。

宛先： 全社員 <employees@westernvirginia.org>
差出人： Dana Ausbrook、部長 <dnab@westernvirginia.org>
日付： 5 月 15 日
件名： 新しいオフィス

Western Virginia 社の社員の皆さまへ。

❶このメールは、近々行う移転についてお知らせするためのものです。❷ご存じのように、コスト削減のため、Western Virginia 法律事務所は来週、新しいオフィスビルに移転します。❸従業員は、この移転のために 5 月 20 日の仕事のスケジュールが多少予定通りにならないことを認識しておいてください。❹引っ越しには約 8 時間かかると予想されます。❺午前 9 時より、机の中を片付け、書類や物品を用意された段ボール箱に入れてください。❻契約書や鍵などの重要なものには、特に注意してください。

よろしくお願いします。

Dana Ausbrook
部長
Western Virginia 法律事務所

☐ The purpose of this e-mail is to remind you of このメールは～をお知らせするものである ☐ upcoming きたるべき ☐ relocation 引っ越し ☐ in order to *do* ～するために ☐ be aware that ～ということを知っている ☐ disruption 混乱 ☐ be expected to *do* ～する見込みである ☐ last 続く ☐ cardboard box 段ボール箱

Questions 35-38 refer to the following e-mail.

To: John Principle
From: Nancy Arnott
Date: October 14
Re: Inquiries

Dear Mr. Principle,

Thank you for your e-mail inquiring about the estate listing number #76412, which is a two-bedroom bungalow on Halbrooke Lane. To answer your questions, you are very welcome to come and ------- the house. In line with the owner's request, the house can be
      35
entered only at certain times. Please call me to arrange an -------, which I will then confirm
                                                            36
with the owner. I usually work from 9 A.M. to 6 P.M. on weekdays. -------.
                                                                    37

Additionally, the asking price for this property is fixed. It is not -------. If there are any other
                                                                 38
questions, please call our office or my cellular phone at 0202-555-0347.

Kindly,

Nancy Arnott
Patel Solutions, Inc.

35. (A) repair
    (B) purchase
    (C) remodel
    (D) view

36. (A) interview
    (B) expansion
    (C) appointment
    (D) adjustment

37. (A) If needed, I could make myself
        available on weekends.
    (B) It is only for rent, not for sale.
    (C) It is well-furnished, including a
        king-sized bed.
    (D) The owner is absent for business
        purposes.

38. (A) transferable
    (B) comparable
    (C) negotiable
    (D) reasonable

35.

(A) repair
(B) purchase
(C) remodel
(D) view

(A) 動 〜を修繕する
(B) 動 〜を購入する
(C) 動 〜を改築する
(D) 動 〜を検分する

 選択肢には意味の異なる動詞が並んでいる。空所を含む文の意味は「質問への回答として、……に来ることは歓迎」となっている。次に空所前後を読むと、「お問い合わせいただいた不動産物件」、「特定の時間帯に入室可」という情報があるため、この質問は、物件の中を見たいことだとわかる。以上から、正解は **(D)**。

To answer your questions, /
to 不定詞 (副詞句)

you are very welcome to come / and view the house.
S   V¹   V²   O

36.

(A) interview
(B) expansion
(C) appointment
(D) adjustment

(A) 名 面談
(B) 名 拡張
(C) 名 アポイント
(D) 名 調整

選択肢には意味の異なる名詞が並んでいる。空所を含む文の意味は「電話で……を手配すれば、私がオーナーに確認する」となっている。次にこの前の文を見ると、「特定の時間で内覧が可能」という内容になっていることから、予約の手配、つまりアポイントをとれば、メールの差出人である Nancy さんが物件のオーナーに確認する、とすると文意が成立する。以上から、正解は **(C)**。arrange an appointment でアポイントを取り付ける、という意味になる。

〈命令文〉
Please call me / to arrange an appointment, / which I will then confirm with the owner.
       V   O   to 不定詞 (副詞句)   O S   V
                                              (補足説明)

PART **6**

37. ★★★★☆

(A) If needed, I could make myself available on weekends.
(B) It is only for rent, not for sale.
(C) It is well-furnished, including a king-sized bed.
(D) The owner is absent for business purposes.

(A) ご希望であれば、週末も対応可能です。
(B) レンタルのみで、販売はしておりません。
(C) キングサイズのベッドを含め、家具は十分に揃っています。
(D) オーナーは仕事の都合で不在です。

 選択肢には文が並んでおり、空所は第1パラグラフの最後にあることがわかる。空所前の文を読んでいくと、「私は通常、平日の午前9時から午後6時まで勤務している」➡（空所）、というつながりになっている。それより前で、アポイントメントを取ってもらえば、と伝えていることから、メール差出人の Nancy さんに連絡できる時間を伝えていることがわかるため、柔軟に対応できるような内容の (A) を入れると文意が通る。オーナー自身はメール差出人が調整する相手であって、一緒に仕事をしている同僚などではないので (D) は不正解。

□if needed 必要であれば □make oneself available 対応できるようにする □for rent 貸出用 □not for sale 非売品
□well-furnished 十分に家具が備え付けられている □king-sized 特大の、キングサイズの □absent 不在で
□for business purposes 商用で

38. ★★★★☆

(A) transferable
(B) comparable
(C) negotiable
(D) reasonable

(A) 形 移すことのできる
(B) 形 比較できる
(C) 形 交渉の余地のある
(D) 形 手ごろな

選択肢には意味の異なる形容詞が並んでいる。空所を含む文は「〜ではない」と否定文になっている。次にこの前の文を見ると、「物件の提示価格は固定されている」とあり、価格が変更できないような旨が書かれていることから、価格が固定で変更できない＝交渉の余地がない、という意味の (C) が正解となる。

※空所文が平易なため、その後の文を取り上げています。

If there are any other questions, /
     V   S
（副詞節［条件］）
please call our office or my cellular phone at 0202-555-0347.
命令文   V   O

Questions 35-38 refer to the following e-mail.

To: John Principle
From: Nancy Arnott
Date: October 14
Re: Inquiries

Dear Mr. Principle,

❶ Thank you for your e-mail inquiring about the estate listing number #76412, which is a two-bedroom bungalow on Halbrooke Lane. ❷ To answer your questions, you are very welcome to come and __35 view__ the house. ❸ In line with the owner's request, the house can be entered only at certain times. ❹ Please call me to arrange an __36 appointment__, which I will then confirm with the owner. ❺ I usually work from 9 A.M. to 6 P.M. on weekdays. ❻__37 If__ needed, I could make myself available on weekends.

❼ Additionally, the asking price for this property is fixed. ❽ It is not __38 negotiable__. ❾ If there are any other questions, please call our office or my cellular phone at 0202-555-0347.

Kindly,

Nancy Arnott
Patel Solutions, Inc.

問題 35-38 は次の E メールに関するものです。

宛先： John Principle
差出人： Nancy Arnott
日付： 10 月 14 日
件名： お問い合わせ

Principle 様

❶Halbrooke Lane にある不動産物件番号 #76412 の 2 部屋のバンガローについて、メールにてお問い合わせいただき、ありがとうございました。❷ご質問への回答ですが、ぜひ内覧にお越しください。❸ (ただし、) 所有者の要望により、特定の時間帯のみ入室が可能です。❹電話でアポイントをとっていただければ、私がオーナーに確認いたします。❺私は通常、平日の午前 9 時から午後 6 時まで勤務しております。❻ご希望であれば、週末も対応可能です。

❼また、この物件の提示価格は固定されております。❽交渉には応じかねます。❾そのほか、ご不明な点がございましたら、弊社または私の携帯電話 (0202-555-0347) にご連絡ください。

よろしくお願いします。
Nancy Arnott
Patel Solutions, Inc.

□inquire about ～について問い合わせる □estate 不動産 □listing number 一覧表の番号 □bedroom 寝室
□bungalow 平屋住宅、バンガロー □in line with ～により、～に沿って □at certain times 特定の時間帯で
□additionally 加えて □asking price 提示価格 □property 不動産物件 □fixed 固定された
□cellular phone 携帯電話

Questions 39-42 refer to the following letter.

June 7

Ms. Felizia Wolfmeier
31 Maylor Hill Road
Buckley CH7 3PL

Dear Ms. Wolfmeier,

Thank you for contacting Prescott School of Art & Design to inquire about our evening classes. Allow me to give you details of our courses, specifically ones that we run every week on Mondays and Wednesdays, ------- you requested. First, there is our Beginner Oil
                                                                                           39
Painting class, which provides instruction on basic techniques and emphasizes the importance of color. Second, there is our Technical Drawing class, which is designed for those interested in engineering and architecture. -------, these are the only weekday
                                                                     40
classes that we currently run in the evenings. However, we do offer various online classes for individuals who have particularly busy schedules. ------- who enroll in such courses will
                                                                    41
still have direct access to our team of instructors. -------.
                                                       42

Yours sincerely,

David Gadhavy, Student Services Manager
Prescott School of Art & Design

39. (A) so
(B) would
(C) what
(D) as

40. (A) Suddenly
(B) Unfortunately
(C) Alternatively
(D) Finally

41. (A) Ours
(B) Those
(C) He
(D) They

42. (A) There is more detailed information about the options on our Web site.
(B) Thank you for your interest in employment opportunities at our institution.
(C) Please contact me if you wish to withdraw from any of these classes.
(D) Your application for enrollment in the class is now being processed.

39. ★★★☆☆

(A) so
(B) would
(C) what
(D) as

(A) 接 だから
(B) よく～した
(C) ～であるもの
(D) 接 ～の通り

 〈命令文〉

Allow me to give you details of our courses, /
  V   O   C   O¹   O² give＋O（人）＋O
allow＋O（人）＋to *do*

specifically ones / that we run every week on Mondays and Wednesdays, / as you requested.
    =courses   O S V   要望通りに

---

40. ★★★☆☆

(A) Suddenly
(B) Unfortunately
(C) Alternatively
(D) Finally

(A) 副 突然に
(B) 副 不運にも
(C) 副 その代わりに
(D) 副 最終的に

 Unfortunately, these are the only weekday classes / that we currently run / in the evenings.
               S   V   C   O S   V

41. ★★★☆

(A) Ours
(B) Those
(C) He
(D) They

(A) 私たちのもの
(B) (〜である) 人たち
(C) 彼
(D) 彼ら

選択肢には代名詞が並んでいる。空所は文頭にあり、空所後には関係詞 who があり、who enroll in 〜となっている。enroll が原形であることから空所に入る語は複数の人を表し、かつ主語となることから、これを満たす (B) が正解となる。Those who 〜で「〜する人々」という不特定多数の人を意味する。(D) は they と特定の人物を指す代名詞だが、誰を指すかわからないため、ここでは不正解。

Those who enroll in such courses will still have direct access / to our team of instructors.
S　　S　　V　　　O　　　　V　　　O

---

42. ★★★★☆

(A) There is more detailed information about the options on our Web site.
(B) Thank you for your interest in employment opportunities at our institution.
(C) Please contact me if you wish to withdraw from any of these classes.
(D) Your application for enrollment in the class is now being processed.

(A) このオプションの詳細は当校のウェブサイトに掲載しております。
(B) 当校の採用情報にご関心をお寄せいただき、ありがとうございます。
(C) これらのクラスの受講を取りやめる場合は、私に連絡してください。
(D) 現在、お客様のこのクラスの受講申込書の事務処理をしているところです。

選択肢には文が並んでおり、空所は文章の最後にある。空所の前では、「特に忙しい方のためのオンラインクラスもあり、こちらのコースに登録しても当校の講師たちと直接コンタクトを取ることができる」と、オンラインクラスという別の受講方法についての言及がなされている。ここから、このオンラインクラスの選択に関する内容に関係しているものが空所に入ることがわかる。よって、正解は (A)。ほかの選択肢は、(B) 採用情報への関心、(C) クラス受講の辞退、(D) クラスの申し込みに関する状況の報告、で文意が通らないため、いずれも不正解。

□interest in 〜への関心　□employment opportunity 雇用の機会　□application for 〜の申し込み
□enrollment in 〜の受講　□be being processed 手続き中である

Questions 39-42 refer to the following letter.

June 7

Ms. Felizia Wolfmeier
31 Maylor Hill Road
Buckley CH7 3PL

Dear Ms. Wolfmeier,

❶ Thank you for contacting Prescott School of Art & Design to inquire about our evening classes. ❷ Allow me to give you details of our courses, specifically ones that we run every week on Mondays and Wednesdays, ___39 as___ you requested. ❸ First, there is our Beginner Oil Painting class, which provides instruction on basic techniques and emphasizes the importance of color. ❹ Second, there is our Technical Drawing class, which is designed for those interested in engineering and architecture. ❺ 40 Unfortunately, these are the only weekday classes that we currently run in the evenings. ❻ However, we do offer various online classes for individuals who have particularly busy schedules. ❼ 41 Those who enroll in such courses will still have direct access to our team of instructors. ❽ 42 There is more detailed information about the options on our Web site.

Yours sincerely,

David Gadhavy, Student Services Manager
Prescott School of Art & Design

問題 39-42 は次の手紙に関するものです。

6月7日

Felizia Wolfmeier 様
31 Maylor Hill Road
Buckley CH7 3PL

Wolfmeier 様

❶この度は、Prescott School of Art & Design の夜間クラスについてお問い合わせいただき、ありがとうございます。❷ご要望のあった（通り）、特に、毎週月曜日と水曜日に開講しているコースについて、詳しくご説明いたします。❸まず、基本的なテクニックを学び、色彩の重要性を強調する初級油絵のクラスがあります。❹2つ目は、工学や建築に興味のある方を対象としたテクニカル・ドローイングのクラスです。❺残念ながら、現在、平日の夜間に開講しているのは、これらのクラスのみになります。❻ただし、特に忙しい方のために、さまざまなオンラインクラスも用意しております。❼こちらのコースに登録された方でも、当校の講師と直接コンタクトを取ることができます。❽このオプションの詳細は当校のウェブサイトに掲載しております。

敬具

学生サービスマネジャー David Gadhavy
Prescott School of Art & Design

□contact ～に連絡する　□inquire about ～について問い合わせる　□allow me to *do* ～させてください　□detail 詳細
□specifically 特に　□run 行っている　□oil painting 油絵　□provide instruction on ～に関する教育を行う
□emphasize ～を強調する　□designed for ～向けの　□those interested in ～に興味のある人　□architecture 建築
□various さまざまな　□for individuals 個人向けの　□enroll in ～に参加登録する、入学する
□direct access to ～に直接連絡すること　□instructor 講師

Questions 43-46 refer to the following information.

We at Hackney Art Supplies do our utmost every day to make sure our customers' orders arrive on time and in perfect condition. If you have not yet received your items, please ------- the following points. Shipping times vary from 5 days to 7 weeks, ------- the
    43   **44**
delivery method you choose during checkout. -------. Although we strive to offer the most
                                                45
accurate estimate possible, some orders may take longer to be delivered. In the event of a significant delay in delivery, please give us a call. We will attempt to track your order then contact you with information regarding the ------- of your delivery.
                                                             46

43. (A) send
(B) note
(C) arrange
(D) demand

44. (A) following
(B) for the purpose of
(C) depending on
(D) until

45. (A) Visit us online for more details about new painting equipment we are offering.
(B) Our customer service agents are trained to answer your questions in a timely manner.
(C) Refunds will not be issued for items that have been discounted.
(D) Customers will automatically receive an expected delivery date when a purchase is made.

46. (A) status
(B) existence
(C) consultation
(D) appearance

43. ★★★★☆

(A) send
(B) note
(C) arrange
(D) demand

(A) 動 ～を送る
(B) 動 ～に注意を払う
(C) 動 ～を整える
(D) 動 ～を要求する

選択肢には意味の異なる動詞が並んでいる。空所を含む文の意味は「以下の点に……するように」となっている。この次の文を見ると、配送にかかる日数の情報が書かれている。つまり、配送日数の見込みをよく考慮してほしいことを伝えたいとわかる。以上より、正解は **(B)**。

If you have not yet received your items, / please note the following points.
　S　　　　　V　　　　　　　O　　　　命令文　V　　　　　O
（副詞節［条件］）

---

44. ★★★★☆

(A) following
(B) for the purpose of
(C) depending on
(D) until

(A) 前 ～に次いで
(B) ～の目的のために
(C) ～次第で
(D) 前 ～まで

選択肢には意味の異なる前置詞や接続表現などが並んでいる。空所はカンマの直後にあり、「ご精算時にお選びいただいた配送方法……、配送にかかる日数が異なる」となっている。ここから、配送方法によって到着日数が異なる、とすると文意が通ることがわかる。以上より、正解は「～次第で」を意味する **(C)**。

Shipping times vary / from 5 days to 7 weeks, /
　　　　　　S　　　V

depending on the delivery method / (that) you choose during checkout.
～次第で（副詞句）　　　　　　　　　　　　　O　　S　　　V

45. ★★★★☆

(A) Visit us online for more details about new painting equipment we are offering.
(B) Our customer service agents are trained to answer your questions in a timely manner.
(C) Refunds will not be issued for items that have been discounted.
(D) Customers will automatically receive an expected delivery date when a purchase is made.

(A) 当社が提供している新しい塗装機器の詳細については、当社のウェブサイトをご覧ください。
(B) 当社の顧客サービス担当者は、お客様の質問に迅速にお答えするための訓練を受けています。
(C) 割引が適用された商品については、払い戻しは致しません。
(D) お客様のご購入手続きが完了した時点で、自動的に配送予定日が通知されます。

🔍 選択肢には文が並んでいる。空所前後の文を読んでいくと、「配送日数は、配送方法により異なる」➡（空所）➡「正確な配送予定日をお知らせするよう努めているが、配達に時間がかかることもある」、というつながりになっている。ここから空所には、「配送日に関する情報を提供する」という内容を入れると、文意が成立する。以上から、**(D)** が正解。

✏️ □detail 詳細 □painting equipment 塗装用具、設備 □customer service agent 顧客サービス係
□trained 教育を受けて □in a timely manner 迅速に、タイミングよく □issue refunds 払い戻しを行う
□automatically 自動的に □expected delivery date 配送予定日 □purchase 購入

46. ★★★★☆

(A) status
(B) existence
(C) consultation
(D) appearance

(A) 名 状態
(B) 名 存在
(C) 名 相談
(D) 名 外観

🔍 選択肢には意味の異なる名詞が並んでいる。空所を含む文の意味は「注文された商品の追跡を行い、配送……について連絡する」となっている。ここから、商品を追跡して得られるものは、配送の状況であることがわかる。以上より、正解は **(A)**。

🧠 We will attempt to track your order / then contact you /
　　S　　　　V¹　　　　　　O　　それから　V²　　O
with information / regarding the status of your delivery.
　　　　　　　　　　～に関する

Questions 43-46 refer to the following information.

❶ We at Hackney Art Supplies do our utmost every day to make sure our customers' orders arrive on time and in perfect condition. ❷ If you have not yet received your items, please <u>**43** note</u> the following points. ❸ Shipping times vary from 5 days to 7 weeks, <u>**44** depending on</u> the delivery method you choose during checkout. ❹ <u>**45** Customers will automatically receive an expected delivery date when a purchase is made.</u> ❺ Although we strive to offer the most accurate estimate possible, some orders may take longer to be delivered. ❻ In the event of a significant delay in delivery, please give us a call. ❼ We will attempt to track your order then contact you with information regarding the <u>**46** status</u> of your delivery.

問題 43-46 は次のインフォメーションに関するものです。

❶ Hackney Art Supplies 社では、お客様のご注文の商品が時間通りに、完璧な状態で届くよう、日々最善を尽くしています。❷ まだ商品をお受け取りになっていない場合は、以下の点にご注意ください。❸ 配送にかかる日数は、ご精算時にお選びいただいた配送方法により、5 日～ 7 週間の間で変動します。❹ お客様のご購入手続きが完了した時点で、自動的に配送予定日が通知されます。❺ 可能な限り正確な予定日をお知らせするよう努めておりますが、一部のご注文についてはお届けに時間がかかる場合があります。❻ 配送に大幅な遅れが生じた場合は、お電話にてご連絡ください。❼ ご注文いただいた商品の追跡を行い、配送状況についてご連絡いたします。

□ do one's utmost 最善を尽くす □ in perfect condition 完全な状態で □ not yet まだ～ではない
□ the following point 以下の点 □ vary 変わる、変化する □ delivery method 配送方法 □ checkout 精算、会計
□ strive to *do* ～しようとする □ the most accurate estimate possible 可能な限り正確な予測
□ take longer もっと時間がかかる □ significant delay 大幅な遅れ □ attempt to *do* ～しようとする
□ track ～を追跡する □ regarding ～に関する

Test 6

Questions 31-34 refer to the following notice.

Energosound portable music player has been manufactured after numerous strict tests to satisfy the highest standards of quality. However, if at any time your music player malfunctions ------- the warranty period, which extends for 90 days after the date of
31
purchase, you can mail it to an authorized Energosound service center and get a replacement free of charge. The music player ------- in a strong cardboard box with plenty
32
of packing material to protect the device from any damage not covered by the warranty. Please be aware that the Energosound is not responsible for merchandise lost in -------.
33
Therefore we strongly recommend that you use one of the shipping companies in partnership with us. You can find a list of them on our Web site. -------.
34

31. (A) within
(B) since
(C) between
(D) above

32. (A) has been placed
(B) may place
(C) should be placed
(D) will be placing

33. (A) transit
(B) condition
(C) supply
(D) location

34. (A) There is a flat shipping rate of $10 for any orders under $100.
(B) We will never share your information with outside parties.
(C) They all offer competitive rates and a free tracking service.
(D) All expenses for repair work will be charged to your account.

31. ★★★☆☆

(A) within
(B) since
(C) between
(D) above

(A) 前 ～以内に
(B) 前 ～以来
(C) 前 ～の間に
(D) 前 ～の上に

選択肢には前置詞が並んでいる。空所を含む文の意味は「購入日から 90 日間の保証期間……に故障した場合は、無償交換を受けることができる」となっている。ここから、「保証期間内に故障した場合は…」とすると文意が成立することがわかる。以上より、正解は **(A)**。

However, if at any time your music player malfunctions /
　　　　　(副詞節 [条件])　　　　　　　S　　　　　　　V
within the warranty period, / which extends for 90 days / after the date of purchase, /
　　　　　　　　　　　　　　　　S　　　　V　　　　　O　　　　　(副詞句 [時])
　　　　　　　(補足説明)
you can mail it to an authorized Energosound service center /
　S　　V　O
and get a replacement / free of charge.
　　　V　　　O

---

32. ★★★☆☆

(A) has been placed
(B) may place
(C) should be placed
(D) will be placing

(A) ～が置かれた
(B) ～を置くかもしれない
(C) ～が置かれるべきだ
(D) ～を置く予定だ

選択肢には動詞 place が時制を変えたり、助動詞と結びついたりして並んでいる。空所を含む文の意味は「破損は保証の対象外なので、破損から本体を保護するために梱包材を十分に詰めた丈夫な段ボール箱に音楽プレーヤーを入れ……」となっている。ここから、対象の音楽プレーヤーを保護するために記載されている内容を遵守しなくてはいけないことがわかる。主語も music player とモノになっていることから、義務の助動詞かつ受け身の形になっている **(C)** が正解。

The music player should be placed / in a strong cardboard box / with plenty of packing material /
　　S　　　　　　V
to protect the device from any damage / not covered by the warranty.
to 不定詞 (副詞句)　protect A from B

33. ★★★★☆

(A) transit
(B) condition
(C) supply
(D) location

(A) 名 運送
(B) 名 状態
(C) 名 供給
(D) 名 場所

〈命令文〉

Please be aware / that the Energosound is not responsible for merchandise lost in transit.
　　V　　O (that 節)　　S　　　　　　　　V　　　　　　　O

---

34. ★★★★☆

(A) There is a flat shipping rate of $10 for any orders under $100.
(B) We will never share your information with outside parties.
(C) They all offer competitive rates and a free tracking service.
(D) All expenses for repair work will be charged to your account.

(A) 100 ドル未満のご注文の場合、送料は一律 10 ドルです。
(B) お客様の情報を外部の第三者と共有することは決してありません。
(C) 提携会社はいずれも、お得な運送料と無料の追跡サービスを提供しています。
(D) 修理にかかる費用はすべてお客様の口座に請求いたします。

□flat 一律の　□shipping rate 送料　□outside party 第三者、部外者　□competitive rate お得な料金
□tracking service 追跡サービス　□charge ～を課金する

Questions 31-34 refer to the following notice.

❶ Energosound portable music player has been manufactured after numerous strict tests to satisfy the highest standards of quality. ❷ However, if at any time your music player malfunctions **31 within** the warranty period, which extends for 90 days after the date of purchase, you can mail it to an authorized Energosound service center and get a replacement free of charge. ❸ The music player **32 should be placed** in a strong cardboard box with plenty of packing material to protect the device from any damage not covered by the warranty. ❹ Please be aware that the Energosound is not responsible for merchandise lost in **33 transit**. ❺ Therefore we strongly recommend that you use one of the shipping companies in partnership with us. ❻ You can find a list of them on our Web site. ❼ **34 They** all offer competitive rates and a free tracking service.

問題 31-34 は次のお知らせに関するものです。

❶ Energosound 社の携帯音楽プレーヤーは、高い品質基準を満たすために、数々の厳しいテストを経て製造されています。❷ただし、購入日から 90 日間の保証期間内に故障した場合は、Energosound 社の正規サービスセンターにご郵送いただければ、無償で交換いたします。❸破損は保証の対象外ですので、破損から本体を保護するために、梱包材を十分に詰めた丈夫な段ボール箱に音楽プレーヤーを入れるようにしてください。❹輸送中の紛失については、Energosound 社は責任を負いかねますのでご了承ください。❺そのため、当社と提携している運送会社のご利用を強くお勧めします。❻リストは当社のウェブサイトでご覧いただけます。❼提携会社はいずれも、お得な運送料と無料の追跡サービスを提供しています。

□portable 携帯できる □manufacture ～を製造する □numerous 数多くの □strict 厳格な □satisfy ～を満たす
□the highest standards of quality 最高の品質基準 □at any time いつでも □malfunction 故障する
□warranty period 保証期間 □extend for ～にわたる、及ぶ □authorized 正規の □replacement 交換品
□free of charge 無料で □cardboard box 段ボール箱 □plenty of たくさんの □packing material 包装資材
□protect ～を保護する □device 装置、用具 □cover ～を補償する □be aware that ～ということを知っている
□merchandise lost 商品の紛失 □shipping company 配送会社 □in partnership with ～と提携して

Questions 35-38 refer to the following letter.

Dear Ms. Marlowe,

We greatly appreciate your interest in our organizing committee. Here are the details that you requested about the Whitehaven New Year Festival. We think this would be a great ------- for you to become involved, should you wish to volunteer your time to help with this
35
event.

The event will begin on Saturday, February 7th at 3 P.M. and conclude on Sunday, February 8th at 5 P.M. You can volunteer for as much time as you like, although we prefer at least a six-hour commitment. Your main responsibility will be to assist with crowd control. There are several locations ------- the food court, the Wooshu demonstration area, the children's play
36
ground and the yo-yo competition zone. -------.
37

You will be expected to attend an ------- event on Friday, February 6th at 6 P.M.
38

Please let me know if you would like to volunteer.

Sincerely,

Chris Kerrigan
Volunteer Coordinator

35. (A) idea
(B) suggestion
(C) contribution
(D) opportunity

36. (A) whereas
(B) such as
(C) seeing that
(D) by then

37. (A) The winner of the yo-yo competition will receive a $50 voucher.
(B) You may be asked to move between locations.
(C) Most volunteers say it was great experience to attend this event.
(D) You will learn about the origin of the Whitehaven New Year.

38. (A) environmental
(B) international
(C) orientation
(D) accounts

35. ★★★☆☆

(A) idea
(B) suggestion
(C) contribution
(D) opportunity

(A) 名 考え
(B) 名 提案
(C) 名 寄付
(D) 名 機会

We think / (that) this would be a great opportunity / for you / to become involved,
  S   V   S   V   C   あなたが関わるという（機会）
         O (that 節)

should you wish to volunteer your time / to help with this event.
   S   V   O
（副詞節 [条件]）＝ If you should

---

36. ★★★☆☆

(A) whereas
(B) such as
(C) seeing that
(D) by then

(A) 接 ところが
(B) 〜のような
(C) 〜であることを考えると
(D) その時までに

〈There is 構文〉

There are several locations / such as the food court, the Wooshu demonstration area,
  V   S   例えば〜のような such as A, B, C and D
the children's play ground and the yo-yo competition zone.

37. ★★★☆☆

(A) The winner of the yo-yo competition will receive a $50 voucher.
(B) You may be asked to move between locations.
(C) Most volunteers say it was great experience to attend this event.
(D) You will learn about the origin of the Whitehaven New Year.

(A) ヨーヨー競技の優勝者は50ドル分のクーポンを受け取ることができます。
(B) それらのエリア間で移動していただくこともあります。
(C) ほとんどのボランティアが、このイベントに参加したことは素晴らしい経験だったと言っています。
(D) Whitehaven新年祭の由来を知ることができます。

選択肢には文が並んでおり、空所は第2パラグラフの最後にある。空所より前の箇所を読んでいくと、「主な仕事は、混み具合を調整することで、複数の場所がある」➡（空所）、というつながりになっている。ここから、空所には仕事と複数の場所に関連したことが入ると考えられる。以上より、正解は**(B)**。

□voucher 金券、クーポン　□origin 発祥、由来

---

38. ★★★☆☆

(A) environmental
(B) international
(C) orientation
(D) accounts

(A) 形 環境の
(B) 形 国際的な
(C) 名 説明会
(D) 名 口座

選択肢には意味の異なる形容詞、名詞が並んでいる。空所を含む文の意味は「2月6日（金）午後6時に行う……に出席してもらう」となっている。この2月6日は、前のパラグラフからイベントの前日であることがわかる。ここから、空所にはイベントの前日にボランティアとして参加する人向けに行われるものが入ると考えられる。以上より、正解は**(C)**。orientation event は複合名詞で、「説明会」という意味になる。

You will be expected to attend an orientation event / on Friday, February 6th at 6 P.M.
S　　V (be expected to *do*)　　　　　　　O
　　　　〜するのを期待される

---

35. (D)　36. (B)　37. (B)　38. (C)

Questions 35-38 refer to the following letter.

Dear Ms. Marlowe,

❶ We greatly appreciate your interest in our organizing committee. ❷ Here are the details that you requested about the Whitehaven New Year Festival. ❸ We think this would be a great 35 opportunity for you to become involved, should you wish to volunteer your time to help with this event.

❹ The event will begin on Saturday, February 7th at 3 P.M. and conclude on Sunday, February 8th at 5 P.M. ❺ You can volunteer for as much time as you like, although we prefer at least a six-hour commitment. ❻ Your main responsibility will be to assist with crowd control. ❼ There are several locations 36 such as the food court, the Wooshu demonstration area, the children's play ground and the yo-yo competition zone. ❽ 37 You may be asked to move between locations.

❾ You will be expected to attend an 38 orientation event on Friday, February 6th at 6 P.M.

❿ Please let me know if you would like to volunteer.

Sincerely,

Chris Kerrigan
Volunteer Coordinator

問題 35-38 は次の手紙に関するものです。

Marlowe 様

❶私どもの組織委員会にご関心をお寄せいただき、誠にありがとうございます。❷ご要望のあった Whitehaven 新年祭についての詳細は下記のとおりです。❸Marlowe 様がこのイベントのボランティアに参加をご希望であれば、とても素晴らしい機会になると思います。

❹イベントは 2 月 7 日（土）午後 3 時に始まり、2 月 8 日（日）午後 5 時に終了する予定です。❺ボランティアはお好きな時間だけ参加できますが、最低でも 6 時間以上ご参加いただければ幸いです。❻主な仕事は、混み具合を調整することです。❼フードコート、Wooshu の実演エリア、子供たちの遊び場、ヨーヨー競技ゾーンなど、いくつかのエリアがあります。❽それらのエリア間で移動していただくこともあります。

❾2 月 6 日（金）午後 6 時に行う説明会に出席をお願いいたします。

❿ボランティアにご参加いただける場合は、ご一報ください。

敬具

Chris Kerrigan
ボランティア・コーディネーター

□interest in ～への関心 □organizing committee 組織委員会 □detail 詳細 □involved 関与して
□should you wish to *do* もし～することを望むのであれば □volunteer ～を捧げる □conclude 終わる
□as much time as you like 好きなだけの時間 □prefer ～を好む □commitment 従事 □assist 補佐する
□crowd 混雑 □demonstration 実演 □competition zone 競技エリア

Questions 39-42 refer to the following article.

Local News

EDGBASTON (August 11)— -------. The theater has long been an important part of
                                39
Edgbaston's cultural life. Numerous successful, well-reviewed plays have been staged at
the venue, although it has not held a performance ------- October last year.
                                                        40

Because of a lack of funding and the worsening condition of the building, a decision was
made to close it down, prompting many residents to show their support for the theater.
------- their fundraising efforts, the theater will be able to stage a farewell show on
  41
September 1st, when a local drama group will perform a production of Swarovski's Black
Swan.

Admission will cost only seven dollars, and all ------- from the performance will go to
                                                  42
Mr. Oliver Stockton, the owner of the theater, who has worked tirelessly for over twenty
years to bring exceptional plays to the people of Edgbaston.

39. (A) Next month, the Ellison Theater, one of
        our city's treasures, will put on its
        final performance.
   (B) Local residents are flocking to the
       renovated Ellison Theater.
   (C) The Ellison Theater has just
       announced a new series of
       performances.
   (D) Theater critics have been praising the
       recent play at the Ellison Theater.

41. (A) Whether
   (B) As a result of
   (C) Moreover
   (D) Instead of

42. (A) expenses
   (B) reviews
   (C) proceeds
   (D) advantages

40. (A) by
   (B) around
   (C) during
   (D) since

39. ★★★★☆

(A) Next month, the Ellison Theater, one of our city's treasures, will put on its final performance.
(B) Local residents are flocking to the renovated Ellison Theater.
(C) The Ellison Theater has just announced a new series of performances.
(D) Theater critics have been praising the recent play at the Ellison Theater.

(A) 来月、この街の宝の一つである Ellison 劇場が最後の公演を行うことになった。
(B) 地元の住民が、改装された Ellison 劇場に押し寄せている。
(C) Ellison 劇場はシリーズの公開を発表したところだ。
(D) 演劇評論家たちが、Ellison 劇場で最近上演された作品を絶賛している。

🔍 選択肢には文が並んでおり、空所は文書の冒頭にある。空所より後を読んでいくと、「この劇場は、長い間、Edgbaston の文化活動の重要な部分を担ってきた」、「多くの演劇が上演されたが、現在は公演が行われていない」となっている。さらに、次のパラグラフで閉鎖が決定しているとあることから、この劇場の閉館に関する内容が入ることが考えられる。以上より、正解は **(A)**。

✎ □put on a performance 公演を行う □flock to ～に押し寄せる □renovated 改修された □critic 批評家
□praise ～をほめる

---

40. ★★★☆☆

(A) by
(B) around
(C) during
(D) since

(A) 前 ～までに
(B) 前 およそ
(C) 前 ～の間に
(D) 前 ～以来

🔍 選択肢には前置詞が並んでいる。空所を含む文は「これまでで数多くの演劇が上演され、好評を博してきたが、昨年10月……、公演は行われていない」という意味で、現在完了形の文となっている。ここから、昨年のある段階から今まで公演を行っていない、とすると文意が通る。以上より、正解は **(D)**。

🎧 Numerous successful, well-reviewed plays have been staged at the venue, /
　　　　　　　　S　　　　　　　　　　　　　　　　V
although it has not held a performance / since October last year .
　　　　　S　　V　　　　　O　　　　　～以来（副詞句）
（副詞節 [譲歩]）

41. ★★★☆☆

(A) Whether
(B) As a result of
(C) Moreover
(D) Instead of

(A) 接 ～かどうか
(B) ～の結果として
(C) 副 さらに
(D) ～の代わりに

 選択肢には副詞や接続表現が並んでいる。空所を含む文の意味は「その支援活動の……、9月1日にお別れ公演を行えることになった」となっている。次に、この空所の前の文を見ると「多くの市民が劇場への支援を呼びかけた」とあるため、市民による支援活動の結果としてお別れ公演が行われる、とすると文意が通ることがわかる。以上より、正解は **(B)**。

As a result of their fundraising efforts, /
～の結果として (副詞句)

the theater will be able to stage a farewell show on September 1st, /
　　　S　　　　　　V　　　　　　　　O

when a local drama group will perform a production of Swarovski's Black Swan.
(9月1日に)　　　S　　　　　　　V　　　　　　　　　O

----

42. ★★★☆☆

(A) expenses
(B) reviews
(C) proceeds
(D) advantages

(A) 名 費用
(B) 名 批評
(C) 名 収益
(D) 名 利点

 選択肢には意味の異なる名詞が並んでいる。空所を含む文の意味は「入場料はわずか7ドルで、この公演の……はすべて、劇場オーナーの Oliver Stockton 氏に贈られる」となっている。ここから、空所は公演の入場料で得たお金を表すものが入ることがわかる。以上より、正解は「収益金」を意味する **(C)** となる。

Admission will cost only seven dollars, /
　　S　　　V　　　　　　O

and all proceeds from the performance will go to Mr. Oliver Stockton,
　　　　S　　　　　　　　　　　V　　　O

the owner of the theater, / who has worked tirelessly for over twenty years /
= Mr. Oliver Stockton　　　　S　　　V

to bring exceptional plays to the people of Edgbaston.
to 不定詞 (副詞句) bring A to B

🚩 39. (A)　40. (D)　41. (B)　42. (C)

Questions 39-42 refer to the following article.

Local News
EDGBASTON (August 11)— ❶ **39** Next month, the Ellison Theater, one of our city's treasures, will put on its final performance. ❷ The theater has long been an important part of Edgbaston's cultural life. ❸ Numerous successful, well-reviewed plays have been staged at the venue, although it has not held a performance **40** since October last year.

❹ Because of a lack of funding and the worsening condition of the building, a decision was made to close it down, prompting many residents to show their support for the theater. ❺ **41** As a result of their fundraising efforts, the theater will be able to stage a farewell show on September 1st, when a local drama group will perform a production of Swarovski's Black Swan.

❻ Admission will cost only seven dollars, and all **42** proceeds from the performance will go to Mr. Oliver Stockton, the owner of the theater, who has worked tirelessly for over twenty years to bring exceptional plays to the people of Edgbaston.

問題 39-42 は次の記事に関するものです。

地域のニュース
EDGBASTON（8 月 11 日）—❶来月、この街の宝の一つである Ellison Theater が最後の公演を行うことになった。❷この劇場は、長い間、Edgbaston の文化活動の重要な部分を担ってきた。❸これまで数多くの演劇が上演され、好評を博してきたが、昨年 10 月以降、公演は行われていない。

❹資金不足と建物の老朽化により、閉館が決定すると、多くの市民が劇場への支援を呼びかけた。❺その支援活動の結果、9 月 1 日にお別れ公演を行えることになり、地元の演劇グループがスワロフスキーの「ブラック・スワン」を上演する。

❻入場料はわずか 7 ドルで、この公演の収益はすべて、20 年以上にわたって Edgbaston の人々に優れた演劇を提供するために精力的に活動してきた劇場のオーナー、Oliver Stockton 氏に贈られることになっている。

☑ □cultural life 文化活動 □numerous 数多くの □well-reviewed 好評の □stage 〜を上演する □venue 会場 □a lack of 〜の不足 □funding 資金 □worsening condition 悪化した状態 □close down 〜を閉鎖する □prompt 人 to do 人が〜するようにしむける □fundraising 資金集めの □effort 努力 □farewell お別れの □work tirelessly 精力的に働く、活動する □exceptional 素晴らしい

Questions 43-46 refer to the following e-mail.

To: Vivian Tulio <tovivian@yoomail.com>
From: Drawbridge Customer Service <cs@drawbridge.net>
Date: October 12, 11:45 A.M.
Subject: Transfer #52403

Dear Ms. Tulio,

We are contacting you regarding your recent transfer on October 11 at 11:26 A.M. We are afraid that the transfer was not able to be made. This may be because the bank account number you gave was -------. The transfer was supposed to be sent to a foreign account
　　　　　　　　　　　　　　43
under the name of Ms. Sally Witham. Please check the account number again, including

------- branch code, and contact us as soon as possible. The remaining information you
44
have registered seems to be in order, so we can proceed with the transfer immediately after

------- the missing information. -------. Instead, contact me at 723-999-1483 (extension
45　　　　　　　　　　　　　46
number 459).

43. (A) inconsiderate
    (B) uncertain
    (C) incomplete
    (D) unwilling

44. (A) her
    (B) his
    (C) its
    (D) their

45. (A) receive
    (B) received
    (C) to receive
    (D) receiving

46. (A) The transfer fee was added to the invoice on October 11.
    (B) We are very sorry for the error we have made.
    (C) It will take about one day to retrieve all the missing items.
    (D) If you'd like to resolve this situation right now, please do not reply to this e-mail.

43. ★★★☆☆

(A) inconsiderate
(B) uncertain
(C) incomplete
(D) unwilling

(A) 形 思いやりのない
(B) 形 不確実な
(C) 形 不完全な
(D) 形 いやいやながらの

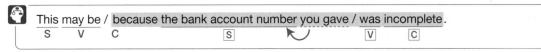

選択肢には意味の異なる形容詞が並んでいる。空所を含む文の意味は「これはご指定の口座番号が……だったためと思われる」となっている。次にこの前の文を見ると「振り込みができなかった」とある。ここから、指定した口座番号に何らかの間違いがあったと考えられる。以上より、正解は **(C)**。

> This may be / because the bank account number you gave / was incomplete.
> S   V   C   S   V   C

---

44. ★★★☆☆

(A) her
(B) his
(C) its
(D) their

(A) 彼女の
(B) 彼の
(C) その
(D) それらの

選択肢にはさまざまな所有格代名詞が並んでいる。空所を含む文の意味は「もう一度……の支店コードを確認してほしい」となっている。また、この前の文では「今回の振込先はSally Witham 様名義の海外口座」だと言及している。ここから、空所にはその海外口座を表すものを入れると文意が成立することがわかる。以上より、正解は **(C)**。

〈命令文〉

> Please check the account number again, / including its branch code, /
>   V¹   O   〜を含めて
> and contact us / as soon as possible.
>   V²   O

45. ★★☆☆☆

(A) receive
(B) received
(C) to receive
(D) receiving

(A) 動 ～を受け取る
(B) 過去分詞
(C) to不定詞
(D) 動名詞

 選択肢には動詞 receive が形を変えて並んでいる。空所の前後を見ると、前置詞 after＋（空所）＋the missing information となっていることから、前置詞と結びつき、目的語を導くことのできる動名詞にすると文法的に当てはめることができるとわかる。以上から、正解は **(D)**。

The remaining information / (that) you have registered seems to be in order, /
　　　　　　S　　　　　　　　　　　O　　S　　　V　　　　　　　V　　　　C

so we can proceed with the transfer immediately / after receiving the missing information.
　　S　　V　　　　　　　　O　　　　　　　　　　　　（副詞句［時］）

46. ★★★★☆

(A) The transfer fee was added to the invoice on October 11.
(B) We are very sorry for the error we have made.
(C) It will take about one day to retrieve all the missing items.
(D) If you'd like to resolve this situation right now, please do not reply to this e-mail.

(A) 10月11日付の、請求書に振込手数料が追加されていました。
(B) 私どものミスをおわび申し上げます。
(C) すべての紛失物を回収するには、約1日かかります。
(D) 今すぐこの問題を解決するために、このメールには返信しないでください。

 選択肢には文が並んでいる。空所前後の文を読んでいくと、「不足している情報をいただいた後、すぐに振込手続きを行う」➡（空所）➡「代わりに指定する番号に電話してほしい」、というつながりになっている。空所後に代わりの連絡手段が入っていることから、空所には代わりとなる連絡先を知らせた理由となる内容が入ると考えられる。以上から、**(D)** が正解。

Questions 43-46 refer to the following e-mail.

To: Vivian Tulio <tovivian@yoomail.com>
From: Drawbridge Customer Service <cs@drawbridge.net>
Date: October 12, 11:45 A.M.
Subject: Transfer #52403

Dear Ms. Tulio,

❶ We are contacting you regarding your recent transfer on October 11 at 11:26 A.M. ❷ We are afraid that the transfer was not able to be made. ❸ This may be because the bank account number you gave was __43 incomplete__. ❹ The transfer was supposed to be sent to a foreign account under the name of Ms. Sally Witham. ❺ Please check the account number again, including __44 its__ branch code, and contact us as soon as possible. ❻ The remaining information you have registered seems to be in order, so we can proceed with the transfer immediately after __45 receiving__ the missing information. ❼ __46 If you'd like to resolve this situation right now, please do not reply to this e-mail.__ ❽ Instead, contact me at 723-999-1483 (extension number 459).

問題 43-46 は次の E メールに関するものです。

宛先： Vivian Tulio <tovivian@yoomail.com>
差出人： Drawbridge カスタマーサービス <cs@drawbridge.net>
日付： 10 月 12 日午前 11 時 45 分
件名： お振込み #52403

Tulio 様

❶ 10 月 11 日午前 11 時 26 分に行われたお振込みについてご連絡いたします。❷ 申し訳ございませんが、お振込みができませんでした。❸ これは、ご指定の口座番号に間違いがあったためと思われます。❹ 今回のお振込みは、Sally Witham 様名義の海外口座へのお振込みとなっておりました。❺ お振込み先の支店コードも含め、もう一度口座番号をご確認の上、至急ご連絡ください。❻ ご登録いただいたそのほかの情報には問題がないようですので、不足している情報をいただき次第、すぐに振込手続きを行います。❼ 今すぐこの問題を解決するためには、このメールには返信しないでください。❽ 代わりに、723-999-1483（内線番号 459）に連絡してください。

□contact ～に連絡する □regarding ～について □transfer 振込み □bank account number 銀行口座番号
□be supposed to *do* ～することになっている □foreign account 外国の口座 □under the name of ～の名義の
□include ～を含む □remaining 残りの □register ～を登録する □in order 問題がない □proceed with ～を進める
□immediately after ～の後すぐに □missing information 不足している情報 □instead 代わりに
□extension number 内線番号

Test 7

Questions 31-34 refer to the following article.

Mayfield Valley to get Metro Station!!!

VANCOUVER (October 17)—Mayor Manning announced today a plan to build a new metro station in the Mayfield Valley, estimated to cost three million dollars. The new station will be built on the corner of Pinetree Street and Vancouver Hill. According to the Mayor's Office, the project is expected to break ground on July 1st and will be completed in one year.

The area is long ------- for a new metro station. However, residents are mixed about the
       31
project. Some residents complain about the cost, while others are concerned about the potential traffic problems which could occur during the construction.

------- alleviate some of these fears, Mayor Manning said that road closings would be kept
32
to a minimum. -------. The mayor hopes citizens will focus on the huge benefits of the
       33
project. ------- completed, the new station will reduce commuting time to the downtown
    34
area by 30 minutes at least.

Alex Harper
Transportation News

---

31. (A) quick
(B) overdue
(C) continual
(D) eventual

32. (A) Refusing to
(B) Because of
(C) Together with
(D) In an effort to

33. (A) Please pay attention to the detour signs to get to City Hall.
(B) For the summer peak season, all local businesses are preparing for the tourists.
(C) Most stages of construction will be done outside peak hours.
(D) Natural gas buses will be bought to substitute old ones.

34. (A) Once
(B) Because
(C) As if
(D) As long as

31. ★★★★★

(A) quick
(B) overdue
(C) continual
(D) eventual

(A) 形 素早い
(B) 形 久しく待ち望まれている
(C) 形 頻繁に起こる
(D) 形 いつかは起こる

選択肢には意味の異なる形容詞が並んでいる。空所を含む文の意味は「この地域には、長い間新しい地下鉄の駅が……」となっている。次にこの空所を含む文の前後を見ていくと、空所より前のパラグラフには新しい地下鉄駅の工事に関する内容があり、空所後には however（しかしながら）という逆説の表現に続けて、地下鉄の駅の工事に対する懸念の声について述べられている。ここから、空所には懸念の声とは反対の表現が入ると考えることができる。以上より、正解は **(B)**。long overdue ～で、「長い間待ち焦がれていた、待望の～」という意味になる。

 The area is long overdue / for a new metro station.
　　　　　 S　　 V　　　　C

---

32. ★★★☆☆

(A) Refusing to
(B) Because of
(C) Together with
(D) In an effort to

(A) ～することを拒否して
(B) ～の理由で
(C) ～と共に
(D) ～するために

選択肢には意味の異なる接続表現が並んでいる。空所を含む文の意味は「こうした不安を解消する……、Manning 市長は、道路の閉鎖を最小限にとどめたいと述べた」となっている。ここから、カンマ以降の道路の閉鎖を最小限にとどめることは、不安を解消するための解決策であることがわかる。以上から、不定詞の形で目的を意味する **(D)** が正解となる。

 In an effort to alleviate some of these fears, /
　　　　 ～しようと努力して（副詞句）

Mayor Manning said / that road closings would be kept to a minimum .
　　　　 S　　　　　　 V　O（that 節）　⬚S　　　　 ⬚V

33. ★★★★☆

(A) Please pay attention to the detour signs to get to City Hall.
(B) For the summer peak season, all local businesses are preparing for the tourists.
(C) Most stages of construction will be done outside peak hours.
(D) Natural gas buses will be bought to substitute old ones.

(A) 市役所へ行くときは、迂回路の標識に注意してください。
(B) 夏のピークシーズンに向けて、すべての地元企業は観光客を受け入れる準備をしている。
(C) 工事のほとんどの段階は、ピーク時間帯を外して行われる予定だとのことだ。
(D) 古いバスと入れ替えるため、天然ガスで走るバスを購入する予定である。

🔍 選択肢には文が並んでいる。空所前後の文を読んでいくと、「市長は、道路閉鎖は最小限にとどめたい」➡（空所）➡「市長は、市民がこのプロジェクトのメリットに目を向けることを望んでいる」というつながりになっている。ここから、空所には道路閉鎖もしくはプロジェクトの利点に関係するような内容が入ることが考えられる。以上から、**(C)** が正解となる。

✏️ □pay attention to 〜に注意を払う　□detour 迂回路　□peak season 混雑する季節　□natural gas 天然ガス
□substitute 〜を入れ替える

34. ★★★☆☆

(A) Once
(B) Because
(C) As if
(D) As long as

(A) 接 いったん（〜すれば）
(B) 接 なぜなら
(C) まるで〜であるかのように
(D) 〜する間は

🔍 選択肢には意味の異なる接続表現が並んでいる。空所を含む文の意味は「完成される……、通勤時間が短縮されるだろう」となっている。ここから、「駅が完成➡通勤時間が短縮」と考えると、空所には時や条件を表す副詞節を作る表現が入るとわかる。以上から、その機能を持つ **(A)** が正解となる。この問題はカンマより前の部分が、Once (the new station is) completed, のように主節と同じ主語を省略していることも意識して解くようにしよう。

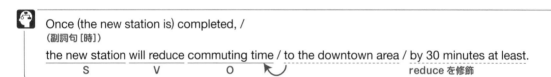

🚗 Once (the new station is) completed, /
（副詞句[時]）

the new station will reduce commuting time / to the downtown area / by 30 minutes at least.
　　　S　　　　　　V　　　　　O　　↰　　　　　　　　　　　　　　reduce を修飾

🚩 31. (B)　32. (D)　33. (C)　34. (A)

Questions 31-34 refer to the following article.

Mayfield Valley to get Metro Station!!!

VANCOUVER (October 17)— ❶ Mayor Manning announced today a plan to build a new metro station in the Mayfield Valley, estimated to cost three million dollars. ❷ The new station will be built on the corner of Pinetree Street and Vancouver Hill. ❸ According to the Mayor's Office, the project is expected to break ground on July 1st and will be completed in one year.

❹ The area is long **31** overdue for a new metro station. ❺ However, residents are mixed about the project. ❻ Some residents complain about the cost, while others are concerned about the potential traffic problems which could occur during the construction.

❼ **32** In an effort to alleviate some of these fears, Mayor Manning said that road closings would be kept to a minimum. ❽ **33** Most stages of construction will be done outside peak hours. ❾ The mayor hopes citizens will focus on the huge benefits of the project. ❿ **34** Once completed, the new station will reduce commuting time to the downtown area by 30 minutes at least.

Alex Harper
Transportation News

問題 31-34 は次の記事に関するものです。

Mayfield Valley に地下鉄の駅ができる !!

バンクーバー（10 月 17 日）—❶ Manning 市長は本日、Mayfield Valley に 300 万ドルをかけて新しい地下鉄の駅を建設する計画を発表した。❷新駅は、Pinetree Street と Vancouver Hill の角に建設される予定だ。❸市長室によると、7 月 1 日に着工し、1 年後に完成する予定だ。

❹この地域には、長い間、新しい地下鉄の駅が待ち望まれていた。❺しかしながら、このプロジェクトについて、住民の意見はさまざまだ。❻費用について不満を持つ住民もいれば、工事期間中に起こりうる交通の問題を懸念する住民もいる。

❼こうした不安を解消するために、Manning 市長は、道路の閉鎖は最小限にとどめたいと述べた。❽工事のほとんどの段階は、ピークの時間帯を外して行われる予定だ。❾市長は、市民がこのプロジェクトの大きなメリットに目を向けてくれることを望んでいる。❿新駅が完成すれば、ダウンタウン地区への通勤時間は少なくとも 30 分短縮される。

Alex Harper
交通ニュース

□metro station 地下鉄駅 □according to ～によると □be expected to *do* ～する予定である □break ground （建築に）着工する □resident 住人 □mixed 入り混じった □complain about ～について不平を言う □be concerned about ～について心配して □potential 可能性のある □occur 発生する □alleviate ～を和らげる □fear 不安 □road closing 道路の閉鎖 □citizen 市民 □focus on ～に集中する □huge 巨大な □benefit 利益 □commuting time 通勤時間

Questions 35-38 refer to the following e-mail.

To: Sean Dalton <sdalton@daltonmedtech.com>
From: Herrietta Brown <hrtbr@miles.nsw.org>
Date: March 23
Subject: Collaboration with Dalton Med-Tech Inc.

Dear Mr. Dalton,

Thank you for taking time to visit us last Wednesday. It was a pleasure for me to have an opportunity to talk with you and get familiar with the ------- of Dalton Med-Tech. I
                                                                        35
especially enjoyed hearing about the work you are doing with small lasers and their -------
                                                                                      36
for the surgical field.

-------. Therefore, I believe that working with Dalton Med-Tech would be beneficial for Miles
 37
Hospital. I spoke to the board of directors and they have agreed that we should proceed
with the proposed collaboration. Please let me know when you ------- a meeting with the
                                                               38
board. I look forward to working together with you.

Sincerely,

Herrietta Brown
Chief Medical Officer
Miles Hospital

35. (A) challenges
(B) employees
(C) expectations
(D) projects

36. (A) implicate
(B) implicated
(C) implications
(D) implicating

37. (A) I wish you the best of luck in your future research.
(B) High technology in the medical field is crucial to our future.
(C) Adjustments to these lasers has led to enhanced performance.
(D) Such cutting-edge devices would be of little use to our surgeons.

38. (A) attended
(B) could attend
(C) must attend
(D) have attended

35. ★★★★☆

(A) challenges
(B) employees
(C) expectations
(D) projects

(A) 名 課題
(B) 名 従業員
(C) 名 期待
(D) 名 プロジェクト

 選択肢には意味の異なる名詞が並んでいる。空所を含む文の意味は「この度は、Dalton Med-Tech 社の……について、話を聞けてよかった」となっている。次にこの文より後の内容を見てみると、第2パラグラフで、Dalton Med-Tech 社との協力や共同研究といった内容も含まれていることがわかる。以上より、空所には協働で取り組む案件という意味が含まれたものが入ると文章が成立する。よって、正解は **(D)**。(A) は困難な課題を意味するが、この取り組みが相当困難なものかどうかという記載がないことから根拠がなく、ここでは不正解。

It was a pleasure for me to have an opportunity / to talk with you /
仮S V　　　C　to have の S　　　真S¹

and (to) get familiar with the projects of Dalton Med-Tech.
真S²

---

36. ★★☆☆☆

(A) implicate
(B) implicated
(C) implications
(D) implicating

(A) 動 ～の関与を明らかにする
(B) 過去分詞
(C) 名 影響
(D) 現在分詞

 選択肢には動詞 implicate の形を変えたものや派生語が並んでいる。空所前後を見ると、所有格代名詞＋（空所）＋前置詞という組み合わせになっているため、空所には名詞が入ることがわかる。以上から、正解は **(C)**。

I especially enjoyed hearing about the work / you are doing with small lasers /
S　　　　　V　　　　　　　O　S　　V

and their implications for the surgical field.
　　　O

37. ★★★★☆

(A) I wish you the best of luck in your future research.
(B) High technology in the medical field is crucial to our future.
(C) Adjustments to these lasers has led to enhanced performance.
(D) Such cutting-edge devices would be of little use to our surgeons.

(A) あなたの今後の研究の成功を祈っています。
(B) 医療分野の高度な技術は、我々の未来にとって非常に重要です。
(C) これらのレーザーを調整したため、性能は向上しています。
(D) このような最先端のデバイスは、当院の外科医にはほとんど役に立たないでしょう。

選択肢には文が並んでおり、空所は第2パラグラフの冒頭にある。空所前後の文を読んでいくと、「Dalton Med-Tech 社の小型レーザーと外科分野に関する話を聞けた」➡（空所）➡「それゆえ、Dalton Med-Tech 社との協力は、Miles 病院にとって有益だ」というつながりになっている。空所後の文の冒頭にある順接の接続副詞 therefore をヒントに、これと合致するような内容が含まれる文を選ぶ。以上から、正解は **(B)**。

□medical field 医療分野　□adjustment 調整　□enhance 〜を強化する　□cutting-edge 最新の　□device 装置
□of use 役に立つ　□surgeon 外科医

38. ★★★☆☆

(A) attended
(B) could attend
(C) must attend
(D) have attended

(A) 出席した
(B) 出席できそうだ
(C) 出席しなければならない
(D) 出席した

選択肢には動詞 attend が助動詞や時制を変えて並んでいる。空所を含む文の意味は「理事会との会合にいつ……なのか教えてほしい」となっている。ここから、空所を含む文は、これから会合の日取りを決めるアポ取りの内容だとわかる。以上より、正解は「出席できる、出席しうる」という意味の **(B)**。ここでの could は仮定法のニュアンスもあり、「もしかしたら出席できるような日」と少し丁寧な意味が含まれていることにも注目しておこう。

〈命令文〉
Please let me know / when you could attend a meeting with the board.
　　　 V　O　C　 （名詞節）[S]　　　　[V]　　　　　　　　　 [O]
　　　　　　　　　　 know（〜を教える）の目的語

To: Sean Dalton <sdalton@daltonmedtech.com>
From: Herrietta Brown <hrtbr@miles.nsw.org>
Date: March 23
Subject: Collaboration with Dalton Med-Tech Inc.

Dear Mr. Dalton,

❶ Thank you for taking time to visit us last Wednesday. ❷ It was a pleasure for me to have an opportunity to talk with you and get familiar with the **35** projects of Dalton Med-Tech. ❸ I especially enjoyed hearing about the work you are doing with small lasers and their **36** implications for the surgical field.

❹ **37** High technology in the medical field is crucial to our future . ❺ Therefore, I believe that working with Dalton Med-Tech would be beneficial for Miles Hospital. ❻ I spoke to the board of directors and they have agreed that we should proceed with the proposed collaboration. ❼ Please let me know when you **38** could attend a meeting with the board. ❽ I look forward to working together with you.

Sincerely,

Herrietta Brown
Chief Medical Officer
Miles Hospital

PART
6

問題 35-38 は、次のメールに関するものです。

宛先： 　Sean Dalton <sdalton@daltonmedtech.com>
差出人： 　Herrietta Brown <hrtbr@miles.nsw.org>
日付： 　3 月 23 日
件名： 　Dalton Med-Tech 社との協力について

Dalton 様

❶先週の水曜日は時間を割いていただき、ありがとうございました。❷この度は、Dalton Med-Tech 社のプロジェクトについて、お話を伺う機会を頂き、詳しく知ることができましたので、大変嬉しく思っております。❸特に、貴社が小型レーザーで取り組んでいることとそれが外科分野に与える影響についてお聞きできて、とても楽しかったです。

❹医療分野の高度な技術は、我々の未来にとって非常に重要です。❺そのため、Dalton Med-Tech 社と協力することは、Miles 病院にとって有益であると確信しています。❻理事会に話したところ、ご提案いただいた共同研究を進めることに同意を得られました。❼理事会との会合にご出席になれる日にちを教えてください。❽ご一緒にお仕事ができることを楽しみにしています。

敬具

Herrietta Brown
医長
Miles 病院

TEST
7

□ Thank you for taking time to ～にお時間をいただきありがとうございます　□ opportunity 機会
□ get familiar with ～を詳しく知る　□ laser レーザー　□ surgical field 外科分野　□ beneficial 有益な
□ proceed with ～を進める　□ proposed 提案のあった　□ collaboration 協力、連携

Questions 39-42 refer to the following article.

A Final Farewell to the Jeremy Burton Radio Hall

ATLANTA (April 17)—Plans were announced yesterday to permanently close down the Jeremy Burton Radio Hall later this year, ------- the city council's resolution. This -------
                                                              39   **40**
will come as a shock to music lovers, as the concert hall is one of the city's oldest and most popular cultural institutions.

Singer Zoe Blank, one of the performers who made a name for herself on Radio Hall's stage, said, "It's a shame that the public are not attending concerts as frequently as they used to. I'll be sad to say goodbye." She ------- that a group of artists had been campaigning to
                                            41
keep the concert hall open, but in vain. However, it was announced that a gala party celebrating the history of this famous venue will be held on Tuesday, June 26. -------. To
                                                                                                              42
buy tickets for this special event, log on to www.jeremyburtonrh.org.

---

39. (A) following
(B) barring
(C) including
(D) notwithstanding

40. (A) apology
(B) performance
(C) investigation
(D) decision

41. (A) avoided
(B) submitted
(C) added
(D) supported

42. (A) Construction will resume on Friday, June 29.
(B) Formal invitations have already been sent out to interested residents.
(C) All proceeds have been donated to the Jeremy Burton Foundation.
(D) All who wish to say a last goodbye are welcome to attend.

39. ★★★★☆

(A) following
(B) barring
(C) including
(D) notwithstanding

(A) 前 〜の結果
(B) 前 〜がなければ
(C) 前 〜を含めて
(D) 前 〜にもかかわらず

 選択肢には前置詞が並んでいる。空所を含む文の意味は「Jeremy Burton Radio Hall が、市議会の決議……、今年末に永久に閉鎖することになったと発表された」となっている。ここから、該当のホールが閉鎖されるのは、決議によって決定したものとわかる。以上より、正解は「〜の結果、〜に基づき」という意味になる **(A)**。ここでの following は as a results of（〜の結果として）と同じような意味合いになる。

Plans were announced yesterday /
　S　　　　V

to permanently close down / the Jeremy Burton Radio Hall later this year, /
close down（〜を閉鎖する）という plans（計画）

following the city council's resolution.
〜の後で・結果

---

40. ★★★☆☆

(A) apology
(B) performance
(C) investigation
(D) decision

(A) 名 謝罪
(B) 名 上演
(C) 名 調査
(D) 名 決定

 選択肢には意味の異なる名詞が並んでいる。空所を含む文の意味は「この……は音楽ファンにとって衝撃的なものだろう」となっている。この空所以前の文がホールの閉鎖の発表という内容であることから、空所はこの閉鎖を決定したことを意味していると考えられる。以上より、正解は **(D)**。

This decision will come as a shock / to music lovers, /
　S　　　　　　V　　　　O

as the concert hall is one of the city's oldest and most popular cultural institutions.
（副詞節［理由]) S　　　　V　　　　　　　　　　　　　　　　　C

41. ★★★☆☆

(A) avoided
(B) submitted
(C) added
(D) supported

(A) 動 ～を避ける（過去形）
(B) 動 ～を提出する（過去形）
(C) 動 ～を付け加える（過去形）
(D) 動 ～を支持する（過去形）

 選択肢には意味の異なる動詞の過去形が並んでいる。空所を含む文の意味は「彼女（Blank さん）はアーティストの団体がコンサートホールの存続のために運動をしてきたが、無駄だったと……」となっている。Blank さんはこの空所を含む文の直前に「一般の人々がコンサートに足を運ばなくなって残念」とコメントを寄せていることから、このコメントに付け加えて発言したと考えられる。以上より、正解は「～を付け加えた」という意味になる **(C)**。

She added / that a group of artists had been campaigning /
　S　　V　O（that 節）　　⬜S　　　　　　　　⬜V

to keep the concert hall open, / but in vain.
　（V）　　　（O）　　　（C）
to 不定詞（前の ⬜V を修飾）

---

42. ★★★★★

(A) Construction will resume on Friday, June 29.
(B) Formal invitations have already been sent out to interested residents.
(C) All proceeds have been donated to the Jeremy Burton Foundation.
(D) All who wish to say a last goodbye are welcome to attend.

(A) 工事は 6 月 29 日（金）に再開する予定だ。
(B) 正式な招待状は、関心を示した住民へ、すでに発送されている。
(C) 収益金はすべて、Jeremy Burton 財団に寄付された。
(D) 最後のお別れをしたい方は、誰でも参加できる。

 選択肢には文が並んでいる。空所前後の文を読んでいくと、「このホールの歴史を祝うパーティーの開催日が発表された」➡（空所）➡「イベントのチケット購入はウェブサイトへ」、というつながりになっている。ここから空所には、このイベントへの参加に関する内容が入ると文意が通る。以上から、正解は **(D)**。

□resume 再開する　□invitation 招待（状）　□send out ～を送付する　□interested 興味のある　□proceeds 収益金
□be donated to ～に寄付される

Questions 39-42 refer to the following article.

A Final Farewell to the Jeremy Burton Radio Hall

ATLANTA (April 17)— ❶ Plans were announced yesterday to permanently close down the Jeremy Burton Radio Hall later this year, **39** following the city council's resolution. ❷ This **40** decision will come as a shock to music lovers, as the concert hall is one of the city's oldest and most popular cultural institutions.

❸ Singer Zoe Blank, one of the performers who made a name for herself on Radio Hall's stage, said, "It's a shame that the public are not attending concerts as frequently as they used to. I'll be sad to say goodbye." ❹ She **41** added that a group of artists had been campaigning to keep the concert hall open, but in vain. ❺ However, it was announced that a gala party celebrating the history of this famous venue will be held on Tuesday, June 26. ❻ **42** All who wish to say a last goodbye are welcome to attend. ❼ To buy tickets for this special event, log on to www.jeremyburtonrh.org.

問題 39-42 は次の記事に関するものです。

Jeremy Burton Radio Hall に最後の別れを告げる

アトランタ (4 月 17 日) ―❶昨日、市議会の決議により Jeremy Burton Radio Hall を今年末をもって永久に閉鎖することになったと発表された。❷同ホールは、同市で最も古く、最も人気のある文化施設の一つであるため、この決定は音楽ファンにとって衝撃的なものになるだろう。

❸Radio Hall のステージで名を馳せた演奏家の一人である歌手の Zoe Blank 氏は、「一般の人々が以前ほど頻繁にコンサートに足を運ばなくなったのは残念だ。ホールとのお別れは悲しい」と述べた。❹さらに、「アーティストの団体がコンサートホールの存続のために運動をしてきたが、無駄だった」と付け加えた。❺ただ、この有名なホールの歴史を祝う特別なパーティーが 6 月 26 日 (火) に開催されることが発表された。❻最後のお別れをしたい方は、誰でも参加できる。❼この特別イベントのチケットは、www.jeremyburtonrh.org にログインすれば購入できる。

□farewell お別れ　□permanently 永久に　□close down ～を閉鎖する　□city council 市議会　□resolution 決議
□come as a shock to ～にとって驚きである　□cultural institution 文化施設
□It's a shame that ～であることは残念だ　□as frequently as S used to　S が以前と同じくらい頻繁に
□campaign 活動する　□in vain 無駄に　□gala party 特別なパーティー　□celebrate ～を祝う　□venue 会場
□log on to ～にログインする

Questions 43-46 refer to the following e-mail.

To: Kurt Bondell <kbondell23@hmail.net>
From: Grant German Fan Club <fanclub@grantfc.org>
Subject: Record Store Shows
Date: March 21

Dear Mr. Bondell,

It is my great pleasure to inform you of the upcoming record store shows that Grant's management is organizing for ------- fan club members. Grant is expected to perform
    43
about twenty songs, both old and new. These record store shows will offer an opportunity for fans to joyfully experience a Grant German performance in a small, intimate setting.
-------, they will be able to meet with their favorite pop singer during an autograph session,
  44
which will immediately follow his performance. Copies of Grant's new record will be available for purchase, and fans can also have these signed during the autograph session.
Tickets will be ------- priced and may be bought online. The record store concerts will take
         45
place between April 15 and June 8, and the exact tour schedule will be posted on www.grantgerman.com within the next few days. -------.
                                46

Kindly,

Shawna Powar, Secretary
Grant German Fan Club

---

43. (A) valuing
(B) value
(C) valuation
(D) valued

44. (A) Afterward
(B) In advance
(C) Instead
(D) Even though

45. (A) exceptionally
(B) respectively
(C) plentifully
(D) affordably

46. (A) You will receive your free tickets within a week.
(B) The first show will be held at the end of the month.
(C) You don't want to miss this chance to see Grant in person.
(D) Thank you for your recent inquiry about Grant German.

43. ★★★☆☆

(A) valuing
(B) value
(C) valuation
(D) valued

(A) 現在分詞
(B) 動 ～を評価する
(C) 名 評価
(D) 過去分詞

 選択肢には動詞 value の形を変えたものや派生語が並んでいる。空所前後を見ると、for＋(空所)＋fan club members となっており、空所にはこの「ファンクラブ会員」を修飾する表現が入ることがわかる。以上から、分詞の形で、「価値のある、貴重な」を意味する (D) が正解。value は他動詞であり、現在分詞 valuing にすると「～を評価すること」と目的語を伴わないと成立しないため、(A) はここでは不正解。

It is my great pleasure / to inform you of the upcoming record store shows /
仮S V   C   真S   inform A of B (A に B を知らせる)

that Grant's management is organizing / for valued fan club members.
O = shows   S   V

---

44. ★★★☆☆

(A) Afterward
(B) In advance
(C) Instead
(D) Even though

(A) 副 その後
(B) 先に
(C) 副 その代わりに
(D) ～ではあるが

 選択肢にはさまざまな副詞、接続表現が並んでいる。空所は直後にカンマがあるため、前後の意味を取っていくと、「レコード店での演奏は、ファンにとって楽しく体験できる機会だ」➡(空所)➡「演奏終了後に行われるサイン会で、Grant German に直接会うことができる」というつながりになっている。ここから、時系列でいうと、レコード店での演奏会の後にサイン会、ということがわかる。以上から、空所には「その後」を意味する副詞の (A) を入れると文意が成立する。

Afterward, / they will be able to meet with their favorite pop singer /
          S   V   O

during an autograph session, / which will immediately follow his performance.
～の間に (副詞句)   S = session   V   O
              (補足説明)   A follow B (B → A の順)

45. ★★★☆☆

(A) exceptionally
(B) respectively
(C) plentifully
(D) affordably

(A)	副	例外的に
(B)	副	それぞれ
(C)	副	たくさん
(D)	副	手ごろに

 選択肢には意味の異なる副詞が並んでいる。空所を含む文の意味は「チケットは……価格が付けられており、オンラインで購入可能」となっている。ここから、空所は動詞のbe priced を修飾する副詞となるため、値付けに関して修飾できる語だとわかる。以上より、正解は **(D)**。be affordably priced で、「手ごろな値段である」という慣用表現なので、この表現で押さえておこう。

Tickets will be affordably priced and may be bought online.
　　 S 　　　　　　 V¹ 　　　　　　　　　 V²

---

46. ★★★★☆

(A) You will receive your free tickets within a week.
(B) The first show will be held at the end of the month.
(C) You don't want to miss this chance to see Grant in person.
(D) Thank you for your recent inquiry about Grant German.

(A) 1週間以内に無料でチケットをお受け取りいただけます。
(B) 最初の公演は月末に行われる予定です。
(C) Grant を生で見ることができるこの機会をお見逃しなく。
(D) Grant German についてお問い合わせいただき、ありがとうございました。

選択肢には文が並んでおり、空所は文章の最後にある。空所前の内容を読みながら整理すると、「Grant がレコード店での演奏とサイン会を実施して、ファンとの交流を開催」、「チケットはオンラインで購入可能」➡ (空所) というつながりになっている。ここから空所には、イベント情報の紹介に関連したもの、もしくは参加を呼びかけるような締めくくりの表現が適切だと考えられる。以上から、正解は **(C)**。(B) は公演の日程はすでに知らされているので不正解。

□first show 初回公演　□miss this chance この機会を見逃す　□inquiry 問い合わせ

43. (D)　44. (A)　45. (D)　46. (C)

Questions 43-46 refer to the following e-mail.

To: Kurt Bondell <kbondell23@hmail.net>
From: Grant German Fan Club <fanclub@grantfc.org>
Subject: Record Store Shows
Date: March 21

Dear Mr. Bondell,

❶ It is my great pleasure to inform you of the upcoming record store shows that Grant's management is organizing for ―43― valued fan club members. ❷ Grant is expected to perform about twenty songs, both old and new. ❸ These record store shows will offer an opportunity for fans to joyfully experience a Grant German performance in a small, intimate setting. ❹ ―44― Afterward, they will be able to meet with their favorite pop singer during an autograph session, which will immediately follow his performance. ❺ Copies of Grant's new record will be available for purchase, and fans can also have these signed during the autograph session. ❻ Tickets will be ―45― affordably priced and may be bought online. ❼ The record store concerts will take place between April 15 and June 8, and the exact tour schedule will be posted on www.grantgerman.com within the next few days. ❽ ―46― You don't want to miss this chance to see Grant in person.

Kindly,

Shawna Powar, Secretary
Grant German Fan Club

問題 43-46 は次の E メールに関するものです。

宛先： Kurt Bondell <kbondell23@hmail.net>
差出人： Grant German ファンクラブ <fanclub@grantfc.org>
件名： レコード店での演奏
日付： 3 月 21 日

Bondell 様

❶この度、Grant の事務所が大切なファンクラブ会員のために企画した、レコード店での演奏についてお知らせいたします。❷ Grant は、新旧合わせて、約 20 曲を演奏する予定です。❸このようなレコード店のイベントでは、ファンの皆さまに、小規模でくつろいだ環境の中で Grant German の演奏を楽しく体験していただけます。❹その後、演奏終了後に行われるサイン会で、Grant German に直接会うことができます。❺サイン会では、Grant の新譜を購入して、それにサインしてもらうことができます。❻チケットはお手ごろな価格で、オンラインで購入できます。❼レコード店での公演は、4 月 15 日から 6 月 8 日の間に行われる予定で、詳しいツアースケジュールは数日中に www.grantgerman.com に掲載されます。❽ Grant を生で見ることができるこの機会をお見逃しなく。

どうぞよろしくお願いします。

Shawna Powar
Grant German ファンクラブ事務局

□inform A of B　A に B のことを知らせる　□upcoming 来たるべき　□be expected to *do* ～する見込みである
□opportunity 機会　□intimate setting 形式張らない気楽な環境　□favorite 好きな　□autograph session サイン会
□immediately すぐに　□available for purchase 購入可能な　□take place 開催される　□exact 正確な
□post ～を掲載する

Test 8

Questions 31-34 refer to the following e-mail.

To: Adam Mooregrave, Simi Industries <adamm@simii.org>
From: Mike Fitzgerald <info@cwsa.gov>
Date: October 25
Subject: RE: Applying for CWSA Certification

Dear Mr. Mooregrave

We appreciate your contacting the Canadian Workplace Safety Association. In order to

apply for CWSA quality control certification, there are certain ------- that your factory must
                                                                    31

meet. Employees must comply with federal safety standards through completion of various

workplace safety courses. If your employees have not undergone this training yet, CWSA

centers throughout the country ------- new applicants this month. As your company deals
                               32

with hazardous chemicals, we need to verify that your waste disposal systems, ------- air
                                                                              33

and water purification methods, comply with our strict standards. -------.
                                                                 34

To download a full list of available CWSA certifications, or to schedule an inspection of your

factory, please visit www.cwsa.gov.

Best regards,

Mike Fitzgerald
Canadian Workplace Safety Association

---

31. (A) requirements
(B) officials
(C) examinations
(D) colleagues

32. (A) were accepted
(B) to accept
(C) are accepting
(D) have accepted

33. (A) along with
(B) only if
(C) referring to
(D) saying this

34. (A) This involves arranging a visit to your plant by our inspectors.
(B) Education materials will be offered free of charge to all participating retirees.
(C) We really appreciate your considerable efforts to reduce pollution.
(D) Please comply with our safety regulations when touring our factory.

31. ★★★☆☆

(A) requirements
(B) officials
(C) examinations
(D) colleagues

(A) 名 要件
(B) 名 （上級）公務員
(C) 名 検査
(D) 名 同僚

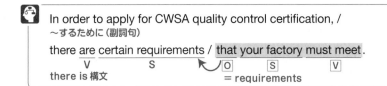
選択肢には意味の異なる名詞が並んでいる。空所を含む文の意味は「CWSA 品質管理認証の申請には、貴社の工場が満たすべき一定の……がある」となっている。そして、この次の文では具体的に満たすべき内容が書かれていることから、空所には「要件、必要となる条件」という意味合いの語が入ることがわかる。以上より、正解は **(A)**。

In order to apply for CWSA quality control certification, /
～するために（副詞句）

there are certain requirements / that your factory must meet.
V   S   O   S   V
there is 構文   = requirements

32. ★★★★★

(A) were accepted
(B) to accept
(C) are accepting
(D) have accepted

(A) 動 ～を受け付ける
     受動態
(B) to 不定詞
(C) 現在進行形
(D) 現在完了形

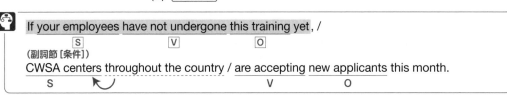
選択肢には動詞 accept（～を受け付ける）が形を変えて並んでいる。空所を含む文の意味は「訓練を受けていない場合、全国の CWSA センターでは今月から新規の申請者を……」となっている。ここから、空所は目的語を取る述語動詞となり、「今月から」という未来の時制になりうる動詞を選ぶ必要がある。以上より、正解は **(C)**。

If your employees have not undergone this training yet, /
         S   V   O
（副詞節［条件］）

CWSA centers throughout the country / are accepting new applicants this month.
    S   V   O

33. ★★★☆☆

(A) along with
(B) only if
(C) referring to
(D) saying this

(A) ～に加えて
(B) ～する場合にかぎり
(C) ～を参照して
(D) こう言って

選択肢にはさまざまな接続表現が並んでいる。空所を含む文の意味は「貴社は化学物質を扱っているため、空気や水の浄化方法に……、廃棄物処理システムが当協会の基準に適合しているか確認が必要」となっている。ここから、空気・水の浄化方法と、廃棄物処理システムは並列の情報の関係であることがわかる。以上により、「～と共に、～に加えて」と追加・並列を意味することのできる表現の **(A)** が正解。

As your company deals with hazardous chemicals, /
(副詞節 [理由]) S　　　V　　　　O

we need to verify / that your waste disposal systems, along with air and water purification methods,
S　V　　O (that 節)　　　　　　　　　　　　　　　　　　　　S

comply with our strict standards .
V　　　　　O

---

34. ★★★★☆

(A) This involves arranging a visit to your plant by our inspectors.
(B) Education materials will be offered free of charge to all participating retirees.
(C) We really appreciate your considerable efforts to reduce pollution.
(D) Please comply with our safety regulations when touring our factory.

(A) そのために、当協会の検査員による貴社工場への訪問を手配する場合があります。
(B) 参加される退職者の皆さまには、無料で教材を提供させていただきます。
(C) 汚染物質削減のための多大な努力に感謝します。
(D) 工場見学の際は、当社の安全規則を遵守してください。

選択肢には文が並んでおり、空所は第1パラグラフの最後にある。このパラグラフ内の空所より前の文を読んでいくと、「いくつかの方法、システムが基準に適合しているか確認が必要」➡ (空所) というつながりになっている。ここから空所には、基準の適合に関係する内容が入ることが考えられる。以上により、前の文を this と受け、確認には検査員も含まれることを意図している **(A)** が正解。

□involve ～を含む　□arrange a visit 訪問を手配する　□inspector 検査官　□education material 教材
□free of charge 無料で　□participating 参加する　□retiree 退職者　□considerable かなりの　□pollution 汚染
□safety regulation 安全規制　□tour a factory 工場を見学する

🚩 **31.** (A)　**32.** (C)　**33.** (A)　**34.** (A)

Questions 31-34 refer to the following e-mail.

To: Adam Mooregrave, Simi Industries <adamm@simii.org>
From: Mike Fitzgerald <info@cwsa.gov>
Date: October 25
Subject: RE: Applying for CWSA Certification

Dear Mr. Mooregrave

❶ We appreciate your contacting the Canadian Workplace Safety Association. ❷ In order to apply for CWSA quality control certification, there are certain ³¹ requirements that your factory must meet. ❸ Employees must comply with federal safety standards through completion of various workplace safety courses. ❹ If your employees have not undergone this training yet, CWSA centers throughout the country ³² are accepting new applicants this month. ❺ As your company deals with hazardous chemicals, we need to verify that your waste disposal systems, ³³ along with air and water purification methods, comply with our strict standards. ❻ ³⁴ This involves arranging a visit to your plant by our inspectors .

❼ To download a full list of available CWSA certifications, or to schedule an inspection of your factory, please visit www.cwsa.gov.

Best regards,

Mike Fitzgerald
Canadian Workplace Safety Association

問題 31-34 は次の E メールに関するものです。

宛先： 　 Adam Mooregrave, Simi Industries <adamm@simii.org>
差出人： 　Mike Fitzgerald <info@cwsa.gov>
日付： 　　10 月 25 日
件名： 　　RE: CWSA 認証の申請について

Mooregrave 様

❶ カナダ労働安全協会にご連絡いただき、ありがとうございます。❷ CWSA 品質管理認証の申請には、貴社の工場が満たすべき一定の要件があります。❸ 従業員は、さまざまな職場安全コースの研修を修了し、連邦の安全基準を遵守する必要があります。❹ 従業員がまだこのトレーニングを受けていない場合は、全国の CWSA センターで今月から新規の受講希望者を受け付けています。❺ 貴社は危険な化学物質を扱っているため、空気や水の浄化方法に加えて、廃棄物処理システムが当協会の厳しい基準に適合していることを確認する必要があります。❻ そのために、当協会の検査員による貴社の工場への訪問を手配する場合があります。

❼ 利用可能な CWSA 認証の全リストをダウンロードする場合や、貴社の工場の検査を予約する場合は、www.cwsa.gov にアクセスしてください。

よろしくお願いします。

Mike Fitzgerald
カナダ労働安全協会

□ appreciate ～を感謝する 　□ contact ～に連絡する 　□ in order to *do* ～するために 　□ certification 認証、証明書
□ certain 一定の 　□ comply with ～を遵守する 　□ federal safety standards 連邦の安全基準 　□ completion 修了
□ workplace safety course 職場安全講習 　□ undergo ～を経験する 　□ applicant 応募者 　□ deal with ～を扱う
□ hazardous 危険な 　□ chemical 化学物質 　□ verify ～を検証する 　□ waste disposal 廃棄物処理
□ air and water purification 空気および水の浄化 　□ strict 厳格な 　□ inspection 調査、検査

Questions 35-38 refer to the following letter.

Dear Hudson Telecom Customer:

-------. Hudson Telecom has been providing the finest satellite dishes in the region for over
    35
three decades. As part of our commitment to our customers, we always make sure that you

know how to ------- our products.
                36

Hudson satellite dishes are ------- to damage or displacement from storms, strong winds,
                            37
or other inclement weather. Therefore, we strongly recommend a sturdy base such as your

roof or balcony to prevent severe damage. Additionally, we suggest that you make use of

our offer to have a Hudson Telecom worker perform a free maintenance check of your dish

on the one-year anniversary of your purchase. Attention to the enclosed instructions and

------- available on our Web site will ensure an extended life for your new satellite dish.
    38

Thank you for choosing Hudson to meet your satellite dish needs.

---

35. (A) You must have an eye for good
        products.
    (B) Thank you for your inquiry about
        extended warranties.
    (C) You must submit proof of purchase
        along with the serial number of your
        product.
    (D) Congratulations on buying a new
        Hudson satellite dish for your home.

36. (A) pick up
    (B) care for
    (C) turn down
    (D) put off

37. (A) adjacent
    (B) frequent
    (C) incompatible
    (D) susceptible

38. (A) they
    (B) there
    (C) those
    (D) which

35. ★★★☆☆

(A) You must have an eye for good products.
(B) Thank you for your inquiry about extended warranties.
(C) You must submit proof of purchase along with the serial number of your product.
(D) Congratulations on buying a new Hudson satellite dish for your home.

(A) 良い商品を見抜く力が必要です。
(B) 延長保証についてお問い合わせいただきありがとうございます。
(C) お客様がお持ちの商品のシリアル番号と一緒に購入を証明できるものをご提出いただく必要がございます。
(D) ご自宅用に Hudson 社の衛星放送受信アンテナを新しくご購入いただき、ありがとうございます。

選択肢には文が並んでおり、空所は文書の冒頭にある。空所後の文を読んでいくと、「Hudson Telecom 社はこの地域で衛星放送アンテナの提供をしてきたこと」、「お客様へのサービスについての記載」となっていることから、空所には Hudson Telecom 社の製品、とりわけ衛星放送アンテナに関するお客様へのメッセージのようなものが入るとわかる。以上より、正解は **(D)**。文章の一番最後にも同様の表現があり、「弊社をお選びいただき」となっているので、ここもヒントになっていることも押さえておこう。

□eye for ～を見抜く目　□inquiry about ～に関する問い合わせ　□extended 延長された　□warranty 保証
□proof of purchase 購入証明　□along with ～と共に　□serial number 製品番号

36. ★★★★☆

(A) pick up
(B) care for
(C) turn down
(D) put off

(A) 動 ～を受け取る
(B) 動 ～を手入れする
(C) 動 ～を折りたたむ
(D) 動 ～を延期する

選択肢には意味の異なる句動詞が並んでいる。空所を含む文の意味は「お客様に弊社製品の……方法をお知らせしている」となっている。次に空所を含む文以降のパラグラフを読んでいくと、「頑丈な土台設置」や「購入後の無料点検」など、購入製品の手入れについてのアドバイスやサービスが書かれている。以上から、手入れやメンテナンスに関する内容が空所に入ることがわかる。よって、正解は **(B)**。

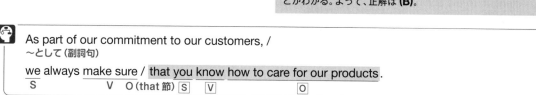

As part of our commitment to our customers, /
～として（副詞句）

we always make sure / that you know how to care for our products.
　S　　　　V　O（that 節）⎡S⎤ ⎡V⎤　　　　　　⎡O⎤

37. ★★★★★

(A) adjacent
(B) frequent
(C) incompatible
(D) susceptible

(A) 形 隣接した
(B) 形 頻繁な
(C) 形 相いれない
(D) 形 受けやすい

 選択肢には意味の異なる形容詞が並んでいる。空所を含む文の意味は「Hudson 社の衛星放送用アンテナは、嵐、強風、そのほかの悪天候で損傷したり設置位置がずれたり……」となっている。そして、この次の文で「頑丈に土台を置くように」とアドバイスがあることから、このアンテナは嵐や強風の影響による損傷などを受けやすいことがわかる。以上より、**(D)** が正解。susceptible to はやや難語だが、subject to や vulnerable to と並んで、「～に影響されやすい、～を受けやすい」という意味なので、上級者はしっかり押さえておこう。

 Hudson satellite dishes are susceptible to damage or displacement /
　　　　　　S　　　　　　　V　　　　　　　O

from storms, strong winds, or other inclement weather.
O を修飾　from A, B, or C

38. ★★★★☆

(A) they
(B) there
(C) those
(D) which

(A) 彼ら
(B) そこ
(C) それら
(D) どれ

 選択肢には代名詞、関係詞が並んでいる。空所を含む文の意味は「同封の説明書および弊社ウェブサイトで利用できる …… は、」となっている。ここから問われているのは available on our Web site が修飾する代名詞で、この説明書 (instructions)、かつウェブサイトで入手できる同一内容の説明書のことを指すとわかる。よって、同封の説明書およびウェブサイトで利用できる「それらの説明書」とすると文意が成立する。以上より、正解は **(C)**。(A) にも「それら」という意味があるが、この場合同封した説明書のことを指してしまうため、ここでは不正解。

 Attention to the enclosed instructions and those available on our Web site /
　　　　　S

will ensure an extended life for your new satellite dish.
　　　V　　　O

Dear Hudson Telecom Customer:

❶ **35** Congratulations on buying a new Hudson satellite dish for your home . **❷** Hudson Telecom has been providing the finest satellite dishes in the region for over three decades. **❸** As part of our commitment to our customers, we always make sure that you know how to **36** care for our products.

❹ Hudson satellite dishes are **37** susceptible to damage or displacement from storms, strong winds, or other inclement weather. **❺** Therefore, we strongly recommend a sturdy base such as your roof or balcony to prevent severe damage. **❻** Additionally, we suggest that you make use of our offer to have a Hudson Telecom worker perform a free maintenance check of your dish on the one-year anniversary of your purchase. **❼** Attention to the enclosed instructions and **38** those available on our Web site will ensure an extended life for your new satellite dish.

❽ Thank you for choosing Hudson to meet your satellite dish needs.

問題 35-38 は次の手紙に関するものです。

Hudson Telecom のお客様

❶ ご自宅用に Hudson 社の衛星放送受信アンテナを新しくご購入いただき、ありがとうございます。**❷** Hudson Telecom 社は、30 年以上にわたり、この地域で最高品質の衛星放送用アンテナを提供してまいりました。**❸** お客様に対するサービスの一つとして、弊社は常にお客様に弊社製品のお手入れ方法をお知らせしております。

❹ Hudson 社の衛星放送用アンテナは、嵐、強風、そのほかの悪天候で損傷したり設置位置がずれたりしやすくなっています。**❺** したがって、大きな損傷を防ぐために、屋根やバルコニーなどの頑丈な土台に設置することを強くお勧めします。**❻** また、ご購入後 1 年経過した時点で、Hudson Telecom の社員によるアンテナの無料点検のサービスをご利用になることをお勧めいたします。**❼** 同封の説明書および弊社ウェブサイトで閲覧できる説明書をお読みになれば新しい衛星放送受信アンテナを長くお使いになれます。

❽ このたびは、Hudson 社にお客様の衛星放送受信アンテナをご用命いただき、誠にありがとうございます。

□satellite dish 衛星放送受信アンテナ □region 地域 □commitment 約束 □make sure ～となるようにする □displacement 位置のずれ □inclement weather 悪天候 □sturdy 頑丈な □base 土台 □prevent ～を防ぐ □severe 厳しい、ひどい □make use of ～を利用する □enclosed 同封している □instruction 説明書 □ensure ～を保証する □extended life (製品等の) 伸びた寿命

Questions 39-42 refer to the following article.

Yesterday, Burton Air Industries announced a fire accident and the recall of its air conditioner, Fresh Wind model of 2018. According to an incident investigation report, a house fire accident occurred last June. -------.
                                                                              39

The report also says that a few consumers have witnessed sparks flying out of the machine when it has been in use for longer than four hours. ------- a thorough examination,
                                                                              40
engineers have found that when the Fresh Wind Air Conditioner is left running for an extended period of time, a buildup of moisture can cause a malfunction in the system.

Burton has claimed that this issue has been dealt with in their latest model, which has been subjected to ------- testing prior to its public release. -------, an official apology was
                   41   **42**
issued by Burton last month.

39. (A) It has the capacity to cool down 100 square feet in an hour.
(B) It has led to some cases of dangerous overheating.
(C) You will be contacted later this month for customer feedback.
(D) We offer a variety of payment options for appliances costing more than $300.

40. (A) After
(B) Since
(C) When
(D) Until

41. (A) failed
(B) logical
(C) rigorous
(D) following

42. (A) Adversely
(B) Consequently
(C) Alternatively
(D) Furthermore

39. ★★★★☆

(A) It has the capacity to cool down 100 square feet in an hour.
(B) It has led to some cases of dangerous overheating.
(C) You will be contacted later this month for customer feedback.
(D) We offer a variety of payment options for appliances costing more than $300.

(A) 1時間で100平方フィートを冷やす能力があります。
(B) それは危険なオーバーヒートの発生につながりました。
(C) 感想を伺うため今月末にお客様にご連絡します。
(D) 300ドルを超える製品にはさまざまな支払い方法を提供します。

🔍 選択肢には文が並んでおり、空所は第1パラグラフの最後にある。空所より前を読んでいくと、「Burton Air Industries が火災事故と商品のリコールについて謝罪」、「昨年6月に住宅の火災事故が発生」➡(空所)、というつながりになっている。ここから、空所には事故に関連した情報が入ることがわかる。以上より、事故につながるほかの事例について述べている **(B)** が正解。

🔧 □capacity 能力 □cool down 〜を冷却する □case 事例 □overheating 過熱 □contact 〜に連絡する
□customer feedback お客さんからの意見、感想 □a variety of 多様な □payment option 支払い方法
□appliance 機器 □cost 〜の費用がかかる

PART 6

40. ★★★☆☆

(A) After
(B) Since
(C) When
(D) Until

(A) 前 〜の後で
(B) 接 〜以来
(C) 接 〜の時
(D) 前 〜まで

🔍 選択肢には前置詞や接続詞が並んでいる。空所を含む文の意味は「徹底的に調査した……、エンジニアは原因となった不具合を突きとめた」となっている。ここから、エンジニアが徹底的に調査した後に原因が判明した」とすると文意が成立することがわかる。以上より、正解は **(A)**。

After a thorough examination, / engineers have found / that
（副詞句［時］）　　　　　　　　　　S　　　V　　　O (that 節)

《when the Fresh Wind Air Conditioner is left running / for an extended period of time》, /
（副詞節［時］）　　　　　　　　S　　　　　　　V　　C
　　　　　　　　　　　　　　　　leave + O + doing（…を〜のままにしておく）

a buildup of moisture can cause a malfunction in the system.
　　S　　　　　　　　　V　　　　O

41. ★★★☆☆

(A) failed
(B) logical
(C) rigorous
(D) following

(A) 形 失敗した
(B) 形 論理的な
(C) 形 厳格な
(D) 形 次の

Burton has claimed / that this issue has been dealt with in their latest model, /
　　S　　　V　　O (that 節) 　S　　　　　　V

which has been subjected to rigorous testing / prior to its public release.
　S = latest model V　　　　　　　　O　　　　　～の前に (副詞句)
（補足説明）

---

42. ★★★☆☆

(A) Adversely
(B) Consequently
(C) Alternatively
(D) Furthermore

(A) 副 逆に
(B) 副 その結果
(C) 副 あるいは
(D) 副 さらに

Furthermore, / an official apology was issued / by Burton last month.
　　　　　　　　　　　S　　　　　　V

🚩 39. (B)　40. (A)　41. (C)　42. (D)

Questions 39-42 refer to the following article.

❶ Yesterday, Burton Air Industries announced a fire accident and the recall of its air conditioner, Fresh Wind model of 2018. ❷ According to an incident investigation report, a house fire accident occurred last June. ❸ **39** It has led to some cases of dangerous overheating.

❹ The report also says that a few consumers have witnessed sparks flying out of the machine when it has been in use for longer than four hours. ❺ **40** After a thorough examination, engineers have found that when the Fresh Wind Air Conditioner is left running for an extended period of time, a buildup of moisture can cause a malfunction in the system.

❻ Burton has claimed that this issue has been dealt with in their latest model, which has been subjected to **41** rigorous testing prior to its public release. ❼ **42** Furthermore, an official apology was issued by Burton last month.

問題 39-42 は次の記事に関するものです。

❶昨日、Burton Air Industries 社が、火災事故とエアコンの Fresh Wind 2018 年モデルのリコールについて発表しました。❷事故調査報告書によると、昨年 6 月に住宅の火災が発生したとのことです。❸それは危険なオーバーヒートの発生につながりました。

❹また、同報告書によると、機械を 4 時間以上使用した際に、火花が飛び散るのを目撃した消費者が数名いるとのことです。❺徹底的に調査した結果、エンジニアは、Fresh Wind エアコンを長時間稼働させたままにしておくと、水滴がたまってシステムに不具合が生じることがあることを突きとめました。

❻ Burton 社は、この問題は、発売の前に厳格なテストを行った最新モデルで対処済みであるとしています。❼なお、先月、Burton 社から公式の謝罪文が発表されました。

□public apology for ～に関する公式謝罪　□fire accident 火事　□recall 回収　□according to ～によると
□incident investigation report 事故調査報告書　□occur 発生する　□witness ～を目撃する　□spark 発火
□fly out of ～から飛散する　□in use for ～の間使用されて　□thorough examination 徹底的な調査
□be left running 作動しっぱなしにされる　□an extended period of time 長時間　□buildup 蓄積　□moisture 水滴
□cause ～の原因になる　□malfunction 故障　□claim ～と主張する　□latest 最新の　□be subjected to ～を受ける
□prior to ～に先立って

Questions 43-46 refer to the following notice.

Kiley Elementary School is currently seeking an individual to serve as a school bus driver. ------- our community's children safely to and from school is a job of huge responsibility. In
43
addition to working during normal school hours, you will occasionally be asked to be on duty for after school activities, such as sporting events, school band and choir performances, and educational field trips.

During the first three months, all drivers, ------- how much experience they have, are hired
44
on a probationary basis. ------- we will hire them as full-time employees if there are no
45
problems.

Please join us for an information day on August 27. -------.
46

43. (A) Transporting
    (B) Guiding
    (C) Touring
    (D) Performing

44. (A) instead of
    (B) according to
    (C) regardless of
    (D) owing to

45. (A) Thereafter
    (B) Unless
    (C) Whenever
    (D) Suddenly

46. (A) A determination on your exact bus
        route will be made at that time.
    (B) Your paycheck will be deposited into
        the bank account you designate.
    (C) You are insured by the car insurance
        company we have a contract with.
    (D) More information about the job
        openings will be provided at that
        time.

43. ★★★☆☆

(A) Transporting
(B) Guiding
(C) Touring
(D) Performing

(A) ～を運ぶこと
(B) ～を案内すること
(C) ～を周遊すること
(D) ～を行うこと

選択肢には意味の異なる動詞の動名詞が並んでいる。空所を含む文の意味は「地域の子どもたちを安全に……は、大きな責任を伴う仕事だ」となっている。これより前の文に、スクールバスのドライバーの募集について述べられていることから、空所には「～送迎する」というような意味が入ることがわかる。以上より、正解は **(A)**。

Transporting our community's children / safely to and from school /
　　　　　　　　S　　　　　　　　　　　　　　transporting を修飾

is a job of huge responsibility.
V　　　　　　C

---

44. ★★★☆☆

(A) instead of
(B) according to
(C) regardless of
(D) owing to

(A) ～のかわりに
(B) ～によると
(C) ～にかかわらず
(D) ～のために

選択肢にはさまざまな接続表現が並んでいる。空所を含む文の意味は「最初の 3 カ月間は、経験の年数……、すべてのドライバーが試用期間として雇用」となっている。ここから、空所には経験値に関係なく、という意味が入ることがわかる。以上より、正解は「～にかかわらず」という意味の **(C)**。

During the first three months, /
～の間（副詞句）

all drivers, / regardless of how much experience they have, / are hired on a probationary basis.
　　S　　　　　～にかかわらず（名詞節）　　　O　　　　　S　　V　　　V
　　　　　　　　（前置詞句）

45. ★★★★☆

(A) Thereafter
(B) Unless
(C) Whenever
(D) Suddenly

(A) 副 その後
(B) 接 ～ではないかぎり
(C) ～するときはいつでも
(D) 副 突然

選択肢には接続詞や副詞が並んでいる。空所を含む文の意味は「……、問題がなければ正社員として雇用する」となっている。次にこの前の文を見ると、「採用者は3カ月間は試用期間である」という意味になっている。ここから、試用期間の後に問題なければ、とすると文意が成立することがわかる。以上より、接続副詞として前の文を受け、「その後」という意味になる (A) が正解。

Thereafter we will hire them / as full-time employees / if there are no problems.
　　　S　　V　　　O　　　　　　　　　　　　　　　　　　　(副詞節 [条件]) V 　　　S

46. ★★★★☆

(A) A determination on your exact bus route will be made at that time.
(B) Your paycheck will be deposited into the bank account you designate.
(C) You are insured by the car insurance company we have a contract with.
(D) More information about the job openings will be provided at that time.

(A) 正確なバス路線はその時に決定されます。
(B) あなたの給与小切手は、あなたが指定した銀行口座に預けられます。
(C) 当校が契約している自動車保険会社の保険をあなたにかけています。
(D) 求人情報の詳細については、その時にお知らせします。

選択肢には文が並んでおり、空所は文章の最後にある。この文章は冒頭からスクールバスの送迎ドライバーの求人に関することが述べられており、空所の前の文では、「8月27日の説明会にご参加ください」とあることから、空所にはこの求人の説明会に関連した内容が入ることがわかる。以上から、正解は (D)。(A) や (C) はバスというキーワードから連想される bus route や car insurance といった語を使っている。安易に考えず、文意が通るかをきちんと確認するように注意しよう。

□determination 決定 □bus route バス路線 □at that time その時に □paycheck 給与小切手
□be deposited into the bank account 銀行口座に預けられる □designate ～を指定する
□insure ～に保険をかける □car insurance 自動車保険 □contract 契約 □job opening 求人

🚩 **43. (A)　44. (C)　45. (A)　46. (D)**

Questions 43-46 refer to the following notice.

❶ Kiley Elementary School is currently seeking an individual to serve as a school bus driver. ❷ **43** Transporting our community's children safely to and from school is a job of huge responsibility. ❸ In addition to working during normal school hours, you will occasionally be asked to be on duty for after school activities, such as sporting events, school band and choir performances, and educational field trips.

❹ During the first three months, all drivers, **44** regardless of how much experience they have, are hired on a probationary basis. ❺ **45** Thereafter we will hire them as full-time employees if there are no problems.

❻ Please join us for an information day on August 27. ❼ **46** More information about the job openings will be provided at that time.

問題 43-46 は次のお知らせに関するものです。

❶ Kiley 小学校では現在、スクールバスのドライバーとして働いてくださる方を募集しています。❷地域の子どもたちを安全に送迎することは、大きな責任を伴う仕事です。❸通常の授業時間内だけでなく、スポーツイベント、スクールバンドや合唱団の演奏、社会科見学など、課外活動の業務もお願いすることがあります。

❹最初の 3 カ月間は、経験年数にかかわらず、すべてのドライバーが試用期間として雇用されます。❺その後、問題がなければ正社員として雇用します。

❻ 8 月 27 日の説明会にご参加ください。❼求人情報の詳細については、その時にお知らせします。

□elementary school 小学校 □seek 〜を募集する □individual 個人 □serve as 〜として働く □huge 大きな □responsibility 責任 □in addition to 〜に加えて □occasionally 時折 □after school activity 学校活動 □educational field trip 社会科見学 □probationary 試用の □full-time employee 正社員

GO ON TO THE NEXT TEST!

Test

1

1. While Mary Visconti is out of the office next month, she will make sure that she checks her e-mails from me -------.

(A) evenly
(B) exactly
(C) regularly
(D) timely

2. ------- a report in the *Saline County News*, Ethan Investment Co. posted a net profit of 30 million dollars, 20% higher than that of last year.

(A) As if
(B) Nevertheless
(C) Even though
(D) According to

3. To celebrate its grand opening, Hannah's Food will give out complimentary samples of meats and cheeses to visitors ------- the store opens at ten o'clock on Friday morning.

(A) as soon as
(B) whether
(C) along with
(D) as much as

4. There has been a lot of ------- that Mike Travel Magazine will go out of business at the end of the year because of its declining number of subscribers.

(A) speculation
(B) to speculate
(C) speculated
(D) speculators

5. You are cordially invited to stay for the ------- being held in honor of Courtney Woods, the retiring president.

(A) celebration
(B) progress
(C) approval
(D) encouragement

6. ------- employee interested in attending the workshop should contact Jacky Lee to reserve a seat in advance.

(A) All
(B) Any
(C) Both
(D) Few

7. Ms. Moore is planning a conference ------- the customers to discuss their specific requests for the construction of new office space.

(A) above
(B) until
(C) around
(D) with

8. The first step that you have to take in preparing for an ------- presentation is to choose a proper topic.

(A) inform
(B) informer
(C) informative
(D) information

9. It is suggested that the general manager ------- the new workers with operating the cash registers.

(A) assist
(B) assists
(C) assisted
(D) assisting

10. Jesse's Shoe Store is going to make ------- room for its new summer collection after the seasonal clearance sale ends on May 31.

(A) sufficient
(B) accurate
(C) communicative
(D) competent

11. During its repair, the untidy appearance of the May Housing Complex has not ------- potential renters from calling to inquire about the availability of units.

(A) argued
(B) interfered
(C) evaded
(D) discouraged

12. ------- setting up your new Rose Spring Office desk, please make sure you keep the instructions in the manual sent along with the product.

(A) When
(B) How
(C) In case
(D) Unless

13. Although Tera Nixon considered herself just a consultant, her coworkers were ------- more dependent on her intelligence than she had thought.

(A) highly
(B) so
(C) only
(D) somewhat

14. Danny Smoltz ------- profound articles for many influential local newspapers until he retired.

(A) write
(B) writes
(C) wrote
(D) written

15. Please keep in mind that you should ------- all safety regulations when using the pool and fitness facilities in this building.

(A) dedicate
(B) comply
(C) observe
(D) adhere

16. To place your order, completely fill out the enclosed order form and return it, ------- your payment, in the response envelope provided.

(A) as long as
(B) otherwise
(C) not only
(D) along with

17. The antique fair in the commercial district, which the citizens are eagerly awaiting, is expected to ------- in April.

(A) commence
(B) transmit
(C) revolve
(D) prolong

18. The board of directors has finally reached a decision about ------- operations in Jacksonville.

(A) suspend
(B) suspends
(C) suspending
(D) to suspend

19. Purchases that you bought in our shop can be returned or refunded ------- accompanied with an original receipt.

(A) since
(B) until
(C) only if
(D) in full

20. ------- you need any further help during your first year, please refer to your employee guide or visit the personnel office.

(A) Than
(B) Should
(C) What
(D) Having

21. Mr. Columbus, the director of the general affairs department, will forward an ------- from minutes of last month's meeting to board members.

(A) exertion
(B) excitement
(C) excerpt
(D) expedition

22. The Golden Prize will be granted to Mr. Damon, from *Northern New Zealand Morning Post*, ------- photographs leave a deep impression.

(A) that
(B) whose
(C) which
(D) who

23. It seems that the readers' response to the updated print layout has been ------- negative.

(A) overwhelm
(B) overwhelmed
(C) overwhelming
(D) overwhelmingly

24. All workers have to shut down their computers before leaving for the day unless instructed -------.

(A) meanwhile
(B) accordingly
(C) otherwise
(D) indeed

25. Hera's Fashion Shop can be found in five ------- in the city for the convenience of its customers.

(A) locations
(B) moments
(C) executives
(D) appointments

26. As per your request, I am writing to confirm that the briefcase left in bus number 615 on July 28 is -------.

(A) myself
(B) mine
(C) your
(D) yourselves

27. Excursions to the island's most celebrated historical sites should be reserved two weeks ------- your departure.

(A) because of
(B) together with
(C) prior to
(D) as for

28. Individuals who stay at our hotel will be given three-day ------- to the weight room and swimming pool.

(A) access
(B) accessed
(C) accessing
(D) accesses

29. Ms. Anderson was honored for ------- missing a day of work at Dally's Accounting Firm during the last three years.

(A) still
(B) even
(C) quite
(D) never

30. Savannah Inc. has endeavored to build partnerships with various companies ------- the nation.

(A) everywhere
(B) somewhat
(C) moreover
(D) throughout

PART5
TOKIMAKURE!

Test

1. Starting next month, Ethan Institution ------- free lunches to all of its staff members to keep them motivated.

   (A) has provided
   (B) will be providing
   (C) will have provided
   (D) has been providing

2. ------- the repairperson come earlier this morning, the customer database server would now be fixed.

   (A) If
   (B) Had
   (C) Should
   (D) Did

3. The city has contracted Wales Design to ------- the historical Edison Museum to its original condition.

   (A) restore
   (B) regain
   (C) resume
   (D) replace

4. Sales figures for the last quarter will be ------- to the public before the end of the week.

   (A) assured
   (B) requested
   (C) convinced
   (D) announced

5. We have encountered ------- problems such as system errors since installing the latest version of Saline Scheduling software.

   (A) supportive
   (B) numerous
   (C) exclusive
   (D) voluntary

6. Next week, the citizens ------- will take place in the convention center of the Stoltz Hotel.

   (A) assembly
   (B) assemble
   (C) assembles
   (D) assembled

7. Columbus Motors' contract clearly stipulates that the final delivery of automotive components will be postponed ------- the remainder of the payment has been made.

   (A) then
   (B) next
   (C) by
   (D) until

8. Patrick Jackson will be the leader of the consulting team at Bonner Chemistry, ------- in April.

   (A) begins
   (B) beginning
   (C) began
   (D) begun

9. ------- the spring music festival is over, the temporary concession stands at the park will be packed up and taken away.

   (A) Owing to
   (B) In particular
   (C) Even so
   (D) Now that

10. In an effort to expand its international presence, Demian Holdings, originally based in Macau, is planning to ------- foreign branches in Taipei and Singapore.

    (A) grant
    (B) demolish
    (C) establish
    (D) name

11. Due to a shortage of qualified graduates in San Remo City, we are having a hard time finding someone with suitable skills and ------- qualifications.

(A) similar
(B) appropriate
(C) relative
(D) alternative

12. Rainfall amounts in the northeastern region of the country this year have been ------- lower than those of last year.

(A) notices
(B) noticing
(C) notice
(D) noticeably

13. -------, it was Dr. Judy Waters who was selected to serve as the new chief surgeon at Eugene General Hospital.

(A) Timely
(B) Ultimately
(C) Permanently
(D) Realistically

14. ------- who believe in the growth potential of solar power are increasingly investing in alternative energy sources.

(A) Ours
(B) Anyone
(C) These
(D) Those

15. The Mayor, Mr. Upton, was formerly an actor who had ------- major roles in various movies and TV series.

(A) made
(B) brought
(C) served
(D) had

16. Some of the apartment complexes in the older neighborhoods of Tempa are in need of ------- remodeling.

(A) extend
(B) extension
(C) extensively
(D) extensive

17. The location of the ceremony was not decided officially, ------- was given oral approval by the chairperson of the planning board.

(A) nor
(B) but
(C) which
(D) or

18. All employees who work in the payroll office at the cosmetic company have been prevented from signing ------- paychecks.

(A) themselves
(B) them
(C) their own
(D) theirs

19. During her meeting at the corporate headquarters, Ms. Yasmin said that the company would go bankrupt ------- cutting costs drastically.

(A) further
(B) without
(C) considering
(D) against

20. Information that we have collected over the last year will be first categorized according to location and ------- in alphabetical order.

(A) since
(B) there
(C) then
(D) largely

21. Student academic progress should be reviewed at the end of each academic year for programs lasting ------- 4 years.

(A) as much
(B) by then
(C) at least
(D) in case

22. The construction industry in Manila is experiencing substantial growth ------- the increasing number of newcomers.

(A) in that
(B) as for
(C) prior to
(D) due to

23. As discussed at today's conference, Richmond's newly elected mayor is taking a ------- fresh approach to improving the city's transit system.

(A) decided
(B) decision
(C) decidedly
(D) deciding

24. We are searching for trained actors who have the skills to communicate ------- with various kinds of audiences.

(A) effect
(B) effective
(C) effectiveness
(D) effectively

25. The main buildings of the state government are closed to the general public ------- Friday evening to Monday morning every week.

(A) of
(B) in
(C) from
(D) only

26. The ------- of the lease agreement with Dally Condominiums can be renegotiated every two years.

(A) locations
(B) records
(C) views
(D) terms

27. Successful applicants should have at least three years of relevant experience, ------- in the online advertising field.

(A) inclusively
(B) ideally
(C) completely
(D) mutually

28. Quantum Bank takes every ------- to protect your personal information by requiring all users to enter a unique login ID and password whenever they want to access their account.

(A) advice
(B) recommendation
(C) precaution
(D) suggestion

29. Staff members ------- reimbursement of travel expenses for their business trips must submit an expense report with the approval of their managers.

(A) seeking
(B) struggling
(C) returning
(D) aiming

30. ------- her dedication and commitment to trying to reach solutions, I am sure that Ms. Hartford will be a great asset to your company.

(A) Given
(B) Between
(C) Namely
(D) Regardless

PART5
TOKIMAKURE!

Test ③

1. Since customer satisfaction is our number one priority, we ------- conduct a brief survey to learn more about our customers' needs.

   (A) routinely
   (B) vastly
   (C) approximately
   (D) considerably

2. Today's staff meeting will begin late ------- some of the sales department employees are meeting with a customer right now.

   (A) until
   (B) because
   (C) in case of
   (D) so that

3. Candidates for accounting positions ------- to possess at least five years of experience and three or more letters of reference.

   (A) require
   (B) are required
   (C) have required
   (D) requiring

4. Mr. Russel said he will draft the yearly advertising budget proposal ------- because most of his colleagues are away attending a conference.

   (A) he
   (B) himself
   (C) his
   (D) him

5. Hexagon Industrial Support provides ------- workwear and full safety training to all employees.

   (A) protection
   (B) protective
   (C) protectively
   (D) protect

6. With annual rainfall decreasing substantially in the North Sydney area in recent years, the ------- of groundwater is now well below normal.

   (A) reinforcement
   (B) jeopardy
   (C) accumulation
   (D) consideration

7. Nora Johns Express will be ------- its delivery operations into three more countries in April.

   (A) choosing
   (B) expanding
   (C) reserving
   (D) cooperating

8. The ------- employees at Gateway Ski Resort create a welcoming and comfortable atmosphere for its visitors.

   (A) except
   (B) exception
   (C) exceptionally
   (D) exceptional

9. Although staff members are satisfied with the proposed salary and benefits, some object to ------- to the new overseas branch at short notice.

   (A) relocated
   (B) relocate
   (C) relocating
   (D) relocates

10. ------- printed on the label, these dairy products must not be sold after their expiration date.

    (A) As
    (B) Since
    (C) Unless
    (D) While

11. Some reviewers said Jessica Bradley's new drama was ------- boring because of its weak storyline.

(A) still
(B) rather
(C) worse
(D) merely

12. In Fulton County, the discount coupons of One Mart are mailed to participating customers on a monthly -------.

(A) base
(B) basis
(C) based
(D) basing

13. As a benefit of being a newly registered member, any purchase of more than $500 ------- for free shipping within three months of registration.

(A) equips
(B) qualifies
(C) arranges
(D) schedules

14. Almost everyone considered Ms. Mogan's plan to be -------, but she believes it is simple to implement.

(A) inaudible
(B) unconcerned
(C) impractical
(D) unavoidable

15. ------- the shocking news that Mill Lane Investments had filed for bankruptcy aired, most of its stakeholders sold their stocks at a loss.

(A) Already
(B) So
(C) Once
(D) Along

16. ------- up to twenty-four hours for our customer satisfaction center to reply to your e-mail before you send a new inquiry.

(A) Allowed
(B) Allow
(C) Allowing
(D) Allows

17. ------- a power failure, the crisis management department recommends that each state government should operate backup generators immediately.

(A) Only if
(B) For example
(C) In case of
(D) In contrast

18. With just five days remaining before Albam's annual festival, the coordinator has ------- to determine the parade route.

(A) finally
(B) yet
(C) seldom
(D) already

19. The many ------- listed on her résumé suggest that no one will be better qualified for the job than Audrey Breeding.

(A) accomplish
(B) accomplishes
(C) accomplishing
(D) accomplishments

20. The report that Mr. Stevenson has submitted does not only contain a technical ------- of the problem, but also a possible solution.

(A) attention
(B) intelligence
(C) information
(D) description

21. To ensure that your order is ------- efficiently, please fill in the order form completely and return it in the envelope provided.

(A) provided
(B) processed
(C) promised
(D) persisted

22. People on the mailing list of Hampshire Shopping Mall receive text alerts ------- new sales promotions begin.

(A) whenever
(B) therefore
(C) unless
(D) whatever

23. To satisfy all our customers, every cup of coffee at Williams Restaurant is prepared with gourmet beans ------- from Columbia.

(A) imports
(B) imported
(C) import
(D) importing

24. The White Tiger Football team ended its season with a remarkable winning record ------- even the most ambitious goal of the coaching staff.

(A) into
(B) excluding
(C) beyond
(D) though

25. Kirt Motors Co. has been using Sheena Promotions to increase the company's ------- in foreign markets.

(A) recognized
(B) recognizing
(C) recognition
(D) recognize

26. To confirm how capable you are at solving problems, the recruiter will ask you for an example of the ------- you showed in a past project.

(A) revision
(B) initiative
(C) requirement
(D) suspension

27. Melies Inc. is celebrating after being announced as one of the firms to ------- a government contract on the new highway construction.

(A) reserve
(B) order
(C) secure
(D) record

28. The boss ------- disagrees with his financial advisor about the company's growth potential.

(A) thoroughness
(B) thorough
(C) thoroughly
(D) most thorough

29. ------- slow wage growth in the last year, consumer confidence is stronger than experts previously expected.

(A) Despite
(B) Nonetheless
(C) Although
(D) So

30. The Fall Concert Series this year features musical performances by ------- of the finest bands in the region.

(A) little
(B) some
(C) any
(D) every

PART5

TOKIMAKURE!

Test

4

1. While Mr. Oliver's job application is -------, we are looking for someone with an accounting qualification.

    (A) impresses
    (B) impression
    (C) impressive
    (D) impressively

2. ------- the environmental organization has limited funds, it has managed to put together a number of informative seminars.

    (A) Despite
    (B) Meanwhile
    (C) Whether
    (D) Although

3. The food stands which operate on Patrick Street must be at least twenty feet -------.

    (A) apart
    (B) between
    (C) beyond
    (D) far

4. Mr. McGuire, spokesman of Sammy Electronics, said that it will establish one manufacturing plant in Queensland and ------- in Perth by the end of this year.

    (A) each other
    (B) one another
    (C) another
    (D) other

5. When ------- the protective film from the screen, be careful not to scratch the glass.

    (A) removes
    (B) removing
    (C) remove
    (D) removed

6. To succeed in today's highly competitive environment where online reviews have real influence, manufacturers must focus on the ------- of their products.

    (A) reliability
    (B) dependence
    (C) obligation
    (D) determination

7. Special meals can be ------- for passengers with food allergies when notified in advance.

    (A) collected
    (B) aligned
    (C) compensated
    (D) arranged

8. Classroom assistants at Simane Art School perform many routine tasks ------- teachers can give more attention to the students.

    (A) just as
    (B) rather than
    (C) so that
    (D) as if

9. Applicants are asked to send official transcripts ------- their degree from an accredited educational institution.

    (A) verified
    (B) verification
    (C) verifiable
    (D) verifying

10. ------- next week, the municipal library will lend newly released books to users for six days only.

    (A) As of
    (B) At
    (C) Behind
    (D) Since

11. All the software programs you see on this Web site are now ------- free of charge for both commercial and non-commercial use.

(A) completely
(B) extremely
(C) exclusively
(D) continually

12. A store gift card will be sent to you upon ------- of your customer questionnaire.

(A) receive
(B) receiving
(C) recipient
(D) receipt

13. The reception party will begin at 6:30 P.M. and will be ------- by the opening remarks of the CEO, Todd Critcher.

(A) advanced
(B) followed
(C) finalized
(D) permitted

14. The president of Macro World Iron attributed the recent success in developing new alloys ------- its hard-working and dedicated employees.

(A) to
(B) for
(C) as
(D) by

15. Due to overwhelming customer demand, orders for new office equipment ------- take at least five business days to process.

(A) quickly
(B) totally
(C) specially
(D) generally

16. This year's distinguished service award went to an individual ------- volunteer work totaled more than 200 hours.

(A) whom
(B) what
(C) who
(D) whose

17. EBS Airlines, which operates out of Taipei, canceled more flights ------- any other small-scale international airline.

(A) as
(B) to
(C) while
(D) than

18. Mr. Anderson, who ------- works part-time from 2 to 6 P.M. at the local public library, used to be a well-known graphic artist.

(A) precisely
(B) currently
(C) commonly
(D) academically

19. Beginning next year, ------- to *Trinity Monthly Magazine* may sometimes include special offers from trusted partner companies.

(A) subscribe
(B) subscribed
(C) subscriber
(D) subscriptions

20. Viet-Jet Air's ------- is to make international air travel accessible to a large number of people through low fares.

(A) structure
(B) inquiry
(C) transfer
(D) objective

21. ------- did the items arrive two weeks late, but they also were in a severely damaged condition.

(A) Hardly
(B) Never
(C) Neither
(D) Not only

22. Before the merger deal was announced to the public, Kissmer Services ------- redesigning the company logo to reflect its new name, Kissmer-Musk, Inc.

(A) had begun
(B) will begin
(C) begins
(D) having begun

23. A government commission will be set up tasked with finding ways to minimize the time it takes ------- from economic recessions.

(A) to recover
(B) will recover
(C) be recovered
(D) has recovered

24. ------- other employees, front desk clerk Katie Weinberg has worked at the Joey Inn for more than ten years.

(A) Unlike
(B) Rather
(C) Similarly
(D) Altogether

25. Mr. Simon was assigned to ------- the emergency exits during the next building maintenance.

(A) admit
(B) guarantee
(C) inspect
(D) extinguish

26. Every moment on an Addam Elegance Cruise is filled with ------- onboard events and activities.

(A) reimbursed
(B) amused
(C) stimulating
(D) exchanging

27. Hankins Studio spent more than ------- to enhance the quality of its recent design project, and the client was completely satisfied.

(A) particular
(B) ready
(C) probable
(D) usual

28. In spite of the clear need to focus on long-term sustainability, most companies have been ------- concerned with short-term profits.

(A) excessive
(B) excess
(C) excessively
(D) excesses

29. Based on safety laws, green neon exit signs should be installed ------- every door of the movie theater.

(A) up
(B) until
(C) along
(D) above

30. ------- it may be difficult to avoid natural disasters such as earthquakes, the damage can be minimized by thorough preparation.

(A) Despite
(B) Since
(C) While
(D) However

PART5

TOKIMAKURE!

Test

5

1. The purpose of today's presentation is to show how ------- our advertising campaigns perform.

(A) effect
(B) effective
(C) effectively
(D) effectiveness

2. Any ------- payments must be received within two weeks of initial notice.

(A) prominent
(B) extraordinary
(C) tremendous
(D) outstanding

3. *Siobhan Magazine*'s revised guide to Prague has caused some confusion ------- the readers due to some wrong information.

(A) among
(B) after
(C) against
(D) besides

4. If the items you purchased was defective, we will either send you a new one or refund you the ------- of the item.

(A) worthlessness
(B) fee
(C) fare
(D) value

5. Vicksburg Design Firm stated that it will ------- open a new branch office in Cleveland.

(A) soon
(B) recently
(C) once
(D) newly

6. The sales team event will be ------- until Wednesday afternoon at 5:00 in Indigo Banquet Hall.

(A) abbreviated
(B) postponed
(C) terminated
(D) scheduled

7. In spite of the takeover, the new management has decided to ------- the former company's production line.

(A) practice
(B) persist
(C) cooperate
(D) retain

8. Waterfront Purifier Co. strongly recommends its customers to get their filters cleaned -------.

(A) frequently
(B) frequent
(C) frequency
(D) frequencies

9. Johnson Theater Group's ------- performances call attention to important social issues currently facing the people of this country.

(A) innovator
(B) innovative
(C) innovation
(D) innovated

10. Our expenses policy requires truck drivers to submit road toll receipts ------- were issued out of state.

(A) whether
(B) that
(C) if
(D) what

11. ------- surpassed the quarterly goal for lumber sales, all employees in Randy Harper's sales department received a bonus check.

(A) Having
(B) To have
(C) Being
(D) To be

12. Drysdale's Interior shelving units need to be fully assembled ------- delivery at your retail branch.

(A) next
(B) afterward
(C) about
(D) upon

13. According to our new policy, thirty hours of training in machine operation is a ------- for new product assemblers at Butterfly Electronics.

(A) requirement
(B) require
(C) requiring
(D) required

14. The municipal housing authority announced that limited financial ------- would be given to first-time home buyers.

(A) assistance
(B) division
(C) association
(D) statement

15. A late fee is ------- for books and magazines returned after the date indicated on your library card.

(A) allotted
(B) gratified
(C) imposed
(D) dismissed

16. In order to meet the demand for its products, Onomu Inc. will expand its international operations ------- by establishing a center in Singapore.

(A) over
(B) closely
(C) jointly
(D) further

17. After thorough investigation and analysis, Sheffield Property Services has decided to expand its business ------- the New Jersey market.

(A) include
(B) included
(C) to include
(D) includes

18. Every employee has scheduled appointments this week, so Ms. Vanderbilt has to travel by -------.

(A) she
(B) her
(C) hers
(D) herself

19. The previous mayor, Ms. Franklin, believed that opening the Alabaster Hearts wholesale market was her ------- accomplishment.

(A) most gratifying
(B) more gratified
(C) gratify
(D) gratifyingly

20. Thomas Electronics' salespeople ------- skip any features when giving on-site product demonstrations.

(A) since
(B) seldom
(C) clearly
(D) afterward

21. Child care center workers are told to keep a first aid kit in every room in an ------- location in case of emergency.

(A) expert
(B) attentive
(C) extraordinary
(D) accessible

22. Those ------- office supplies should first obtain permission from their immediate supervisor.

(A) order
(B) ordered
(C) ordering
(D) will order

23. The maintenance crew will replace the air conditioning unit ------- cleaning out the air ducts throughout the building.

(A) as well as
(B) so that
(C) as for
(D) in order that

24. ------- you're purchasing or selling a house, be sure to contact Chicago Real Estate to receive the most competitive prices.

(A) That
(B) So
(C) If
(D) Due to

25. If you have yet to turn in your self-evaluation form to your manager, please do ------- by the end of the week.

(A) one
(B) so
(C) which
(D) them

26. ------- displaying the time, the Delight watch is also a fashionable accessory that matches both casual and formal attire.

(A) Consisting of
(B) Aside from
(C) In view of
(D) Seeing that

27. Lynn Underwear is involved in the manufacture, sale, and ------- of its clothing products.

(A) distribution
(B) exception
(C) repetition
(D) accreditation

28. Due to unexpectedly high ------- for organic goods, we must quickly expand production.

(A) occurrence
(B) percentage
(C) demand
(D) amount

29. The main goal of the Austin Charity Foundation is to build a free medical clinic in ------- major city in the state of Texas.

(A) every
(B) all
(C) first
(D) many

30. Please enter another e-mail address ------- which you can be reached while you are away.

(A) at
(B) for
(C) in
(D) to

PART5
TOKIMAKURE!

Test 6

1. The new payroll system for part-time workers was ------- than management had originally hoped.

   (A) so efficiently
   (B) as efficient
   (C) most efficiently
   (D) more efficient

2. It is essential to provide your outdoor pets with plenty of water to drink once summer -------.

   (A) arrived
   (B) arrives
   (C) will arrive
   (D) is arriving

3. Develyn Natural Cafe gives all visitors the chance to enjoy an exquisite ------- experience at a reasonable price.

   (A) dine
   (B) dines
   (C) dined
   (D) dining

4. In spite of the increased fares, analysts expect a rise in public transport use in Fort Worth ------- the next five years.

   (A) upon
   (B) over
   (C) by
   (D) against

5. All staff members who will attend this experiment should download and print laboratory handbooks for quick -------.

   (A) reference
   (B) procedure
   (C) measure
   (D) indication

6. The formal launch of the new comprehensive tax self-assessment program was postponed because of a problem that ------- when it was tested.

   (A) connected
   (B) emerged
   (C) revealed
   (D) reacted

7. Maintenance records suggest that tools ordered from Granderson Products are more ------- than those ordered from Sanford's Wholesale Store.

   (A) dependability
   (B) depend
   (C) dependably
   (D) dependable

8. We have now realized that most tourists are ------- to reserve an unfamiliar hotel before consulting online reviews.

   (A) reluctant
   (B) detached
   (C) sensitive
   (D) provisional

9. A river cleanup campaign is one of the ------- activities that the NGO launched to fight pollution in their district.

   (A) excessive
   (B) voluntary
   (C) competitive
   (D) aggressive

10. Ms. Turner and her colleagues are planning to give a presentation on consumer patterns, but outside consultants should join ------- to add in-depth knowledge.

    (A) they
    (B) their
    (C) them
    (D) themselves

11. In light of new safety regulations, you must refrain from using your cellular phone while ------- the aircraft.

(A) across
(B) into
(C) beyond
(D) aboard

12. Ms. Timber will represent Marybell Homes at the local real estate conference since she knows commercial property law better than -------.

(A) most
(B) whichever
(C) usual
(D) each

13. Employees in the sales department are required to ------- regular meetings every Wednesday.

(A) register
(B) enroll
(C) attend
(D) participate

14. The area manager told Mr. Mathers that the accounting figures from the Kanemone branch office need to be regularly verified for -------.

(A) requirement
(B) complaint
(C) suggestion
(D) accuracy

15. The selection committee of the Auckland Writing Competition created detailed evaluation criteria, and all the submissions will be judged -------.

(A) purposely
(B) chiefly
(C) persistently
(D) accordingly

16. A new location for Sakae Bakery is under construction at the corner of Bingham Avenue and Machado Street, ------- the old courthouse used to be.

(A) where
(B) next to
(C) when
(D) across

17. ------- accommodations in the small town of Bakersfield, there are only two bed-and-breakfasts and a mountain lodge.

(A) For example
(B) Because
(C) In terms of
(D) Whereas

18. ------- those interns who perform well in their assigned tasks will be permitted to apply for permanent positions.

(A) Ever
(B) If
(C) Only
(D) When

19. After ------- considering the options, Ms. Craig was finally ready to resign from her job and run her own business.

(A) care
(B) caring
(C) careful
(D) carefully

20. Newly elected mayor Clara Hightower expressed her ------- to everyone who supported her campaign.

(A) publicity
(B) gratitude
(C) abundance
(D) replication

21. Emergency exit signs and maps of fire escape routes are ------- posted in every guest room at the Clint Hotel.

(A) harshly
(B) prominently
(C) forcefully
(D) cooperatively

22. Ms. Hilton has to use public transportation to get to the airport ------- her car is being repaired.

(A) neither
(B) why
(C) that
(D) as

23. Mr. O'Reilly intends ------- his laptop computer from his office before leaving for the business trip.

(A) retrieve
(B) retrieved
(C) to retrieve
(D) being retrieved

24. Even mileage club members will need to pay almost double the normal fare for flying ------- peak times.

(A) while
(B) during
(C) when
(D) about

25. Our employees, in ------- with management, have identified ways to reduce costs by 10 percent.

(A) cooperate
(B) cooperated
(C) cooperation
(D) cooperates

26. The director of the human resource department made a ------- presentation on features of the newly announced employee benefits package.

(A) deserved
(B) subtle
(C) brief
(D) strict

27. The 19th Annual Accounting Conference was the highest attended conference ever ------- in Hong Kong.

(A) stayed
(B) referred
(C) gone
(D) held

28. The heads of the marketing division ------- endorsed Mr. Blackstone's innovative advertising approach.

(A) enthusiastic
(B) enthusiast
(C) enthusiasm
(D) enthusiastically

29. Ziozia Conference Center is ------- larger than the Ozawa Auditorium, making it more appropriate for big events.

(A) such
(B) still
(C) very
(D) fairly

30. Please submit any questions or concerns in writing to the office of admissions, and then ------- fax or mail them using the contact details below.

(A) either
(B) neither
(C) both
(D) whether

PART5
TOKIMAKURE!

Test

1. Ms. Alves ------- her employees that the Dancer-S1 music player will be discontinued because of poor sales.

   (A) announced
   (B) informed
   (C) complied
   (D) verified

2. ------- for the work efficiency seminars have been sent at regular intervals throughout the year to all workers.

   (A) Invitations
   (B) Invitation
   (C) Invite
   (D) Inviting

3. To make our new textbook easier to understand, we eliminated some illustrations that we thought were too -------.

   (A) distract
   (B) distracting
   (C) distraction
   (D) distractedly

4. The survey will determine ------- the new manufacturing plant in Bay Canou will have a significant impact on energy consumption.

   (A) whatever
   (B) whether
   (C) whichever
   (D) what

5. Valley Spring City Authority announced that Highway 12 will be temporarily closed ------- flooding from the nearby Redcliff River.

   (A) owing to
   (B) instead of
   (C) ahead of
   (D) besides

6. Shine Airline is planning to upgrade its fleet of aircraft over the next ------- years.

   (A) of
   (B) each
   (C) some
   (D) few

7. Housing associations and construction firms in partnership with the city planning committee will host a state conference on new affordable housing -------.

   (A) develop
   (B) developers
   (C) developmental
   (D) development

8. Putting his own ------- aside, Bradley Plummer agreed to approve the office redesign favored by the majority of his staff.

   (A) compensation
   (B) preference
   (C) reminder
   (D) permission

9. Over the last two decades, there has been ------- little change in the gender balance in some of the most common occupations.

   (A) remark
   (B) remarkably
   (C) remarking
   (D) remarked

10. To ensure quality service is provided, Danson Satellite Ltd. reviews all technical support calls ------- the customer requests that the call not be recorded.

    (A) unless
    (B) without
    (C) against
    (D) despite

11. The director of the Personnel Department recommended that all employees should regularly ------- basic medical checkups.

(A) postpone
(B) undergo
(C) dissolve
(D) display

12. As Mr. Steinbeck had already been through the programming course, he offered to help his colleague finish -------.

(A) she
(B) her
(C) hers
(D) herself

13. The new security guidelines mean users who ------- installed unapproved software will be punished.

(A) know
(B) knowledge
(C) knowingly
(D) knowledgeable

14. The magazine's readership has risen almost 30 percent ------- its online promotion.

(A) aboard
(B) quickly
(C) straight
(D) through

15. College clerical staff need to ------- their parking permits on their front windshields when using campus parking.

(A) display
(B) print
(C) commit
(D) state

16. The price of Cavendar watermelons is ------- according to the size of that year's harvest.

(A) empathetic
(B) variable
(C) portable
(D) infrequent

17. ------- himself with new working practices and overcoming difficulties in communication were Mr. Rumelos' priorities in Korea.

(A) Familiarize
(B) Being familiarized
(C) Familiarizes
(D) Familiarizing

18. ------- the difficulty the event planners initially had with the sound system, the concert was a huge success.

(A) On the other hand
(B) As a matter of fact
(C) Although
(D) Notwithstanding

19. Anyone working on site must return their identification badge ------- leaving the office building.

(A) upon
(B) to
(C) than
(D) among

20. All restaurant wait staff are required to wear uniforms for the entire duration of their ------- unless instructed otherwise.

(A) challenge
(B) position
(C) shift
(D) gathering

21. ------- Fregonea Castle is twenty miles outside of the city, it is one of the most visited tourist attractions in the area.

(A) For
(B) Until
(C) How
(D) Although

22. The appointment of Dr. Jim Trump as director will ------- Walterson Trust's position as one of the finest research institutions in Canada.

(A) administer
(B) solidify
(C) accomplish
(D) incline

23. The attached document details ------- changes to the existing billing procedure that all staff members should be aware of as soon as possible.

(A) proposed
(B) proposes
(C) to proposing
(D) propose

24. The flight reservations ------- Mr. Campbell's trip to Tokyo have just been confirmed by Peach Fly.

(A) by
(B) about
(C) in
(D) for

25. Had Gaspa Television not hired Ms. Lucas as a general manager, we ------- her the same position with us.

(A) should offer
(B) will be offering
(C) would have offered
(D) has offered

26. At Greyhaven Mall, business owners will likely see an ------- in sales shortly after the completion of the second parking lot.

(A) array
(B) effort
(C) increase
(D) insert

27. Whether shopping for an economy car or a luxury vehicle, every customer who visits Kovac Auto Sales ------- high quality service.

(A) deserves
(B) awards
(C) manages
(D) relates

28. After weeks of research, Kalama Presence Analysts reported that consumers reacted ------- to how content was presented on Murphy Coffee House's Web site.

(A) unlikely
(B) potentially
(C) unfavorably
(D) probably

29. To promote healthy living, Moop Beverages creates its products using all-natural ingredients ------- food additives.

(A) on account of
(B) rather than
(C) in that
(D) however

30. The number of entrants to the Delmonse Fitness Competition was expected to be lower than last year, but it was ------- much higher.

(A) strongly
(B) broadly
(C) actually
(D) particularly

PART 5

TOKIMAKURE!

Test 8

1. Savings accounts are gaining ------- with many individuals as interest rates continue to rise.

   (A) elevation
   (B) mobility
   (C) risk
   (D) popularity

2. After receiving favorable feedback from customers, Presley Carpet Cleaning Service is justifiably ------- about its business outlook.

   (A) optimistic
   (B) exciting
   (C) sufficient
   (D) dedicated

3. Some canned dog food made by Navi Pet Supply is formulated ------- for large adult dogs over 20 kg, so please avoid feeding it to small dogs.

   (A) incompletely
   (B) jointly
   (C) exclusively
   (D) alternatively

4. Our warehouse staff all agree that the HG-5 bar code scanner is more reliable than ------- they have used.

   (A) last
   (B) others
   (C) who
   (D) ever

5. For your convenience, Sally-B's Web site lists prices of products and gives information ------- shipping options in our place.

   (A) on
   (B) into
   (C) until
   (D) along

6. Most residents who attended the municipal conference shared some ------- that were related to traffic problems in the downtown area.

   (A) worries
   (B) worried
   (C) worrying
   (D) worrisome

7. Lindon Bistro Co. is joining the organizers of Dextra Automobile Expo ------- an official catering partner.

   (A) against
   (B) during
   (C) as
   (D) below

8. The Wilpont Associate Council is now ------- applications for the position of program director to begin in August.

   (A) accepting
   (B) advising
   (C) renovating
   (D) running

9. The company's policy regarding the salary payment schedule and health benefits is ------- outlined in the staff handbook.

   (A) passionately
   (B) elusively
   (C) equally
   (D) explicitly

10. The ------- document should be signed and returned to Mallory Business Publishers before a manuscript can be considered for publication.

    (A) surrounded
    (B) confined
    (C) stationed
    (D) enclosed

11. Every survey respondent is required ------- to the guidelines listed in the manual, and failure to do so may invalidate the survey.

(A) adhere
(B) adhering
(C) have adhered
(D) to adhere

12. Murdoch Electronics is closely following the trend ------- interactive games, which allow users to play and chat together.

(A) onto
(B) beside
(C) toward
(D) along

13. Remington General Hospital has been meeting the health care ------- of the greater Fosberg area for nearly fifteen years.

(A) to need
(B) has needed
(C) needing
(D) needs

14. Watson Studios of Hampton is seeking a marketing agent to ------- publicity campaigns for three new movies that will premiere this spring.

(A) inform
(B) participate
(C) emerge
(D) launch

15. The task of restructuring the finance and administration should take ------- over all other work in the coming weeks.

(A) resolve
(B) priority
(C) credit
(D) standard

16. Chase Foodmarkets has seen only ------- profit growth and so may start an expansion program.

(A) margin
(B) marginal
(C) marginally
(D) marginalize

17. Salespeople who will be involved in the sales campaign targeting senior citizens must take the training course on effective -------.

(A) communication
(B) communicate
(C) communicated
(D) communicatively

18. The report by Roseville City on population growth strategies ------- data from the past forty years.

(A) observes
(B) arrives
(C) believes
(D) contains

19. Advancements in the field of agriculture over the last decade have increased ------- to such an extent that surplus produce is now exported abroad.

(A) location
(B) preparation
(C) output
(D) rules

20. Larson's new range features cell phone cases that are both ------- and heat resistant.

(A) durably
(B) durability
(C) durable
(D) durableness

21. Although the latest software is expensive, its implementation will greatly ------- the performance of the company's accounting system.

(A) adapt
(B) improve
(C) reimburse
(D) reward

22. Oscar Copeland's job appraisal stated that he is more efficient when working ------- than as a team member.

(A) substantially
(B) independently
(C) jointly
(D) dramatically

23. Food items containing milk or eggs are more ------- to spoiling when there is an increase in temperature.

(A) obtainable
(B) sensational
(C) vulnerable
(D) compatible

24. Last month, ------- of the new workers was officially invited to participate in the welcome reception held by the company's president.

(A) most
(B) all
(C) every
(D) each

25. At the tourist information counter, officials hand out guide maps and brochures featuring regional attractions to ------- requests them.

(A) whoever
(B) whatsoever
(C) whenever
(D) whichever

26. Our company ------- its overall sales grow by 20 percent since Sylvia Ritter joined the sales force.

(A) sees
(B) can see
(C) seeing
(D) has seen

27. The more Ann Ruiz's clients dealt with her, the more ------- they became with her customer service and attention to detail.

(A) impressed
(B) impression
(C) impress
(D) impresses

28. The sign warns that ------- is allowed to enter Stevenage Forest without written permission from its owner.

(A) anything
(B) somebody
(C) each other
(D) no one

29. The findings from new research show that in most industries, novice workers spend at least twice ------- hours as experienced workers finishing the same tasks.

(A) much more
(B) more than
(C) as many
(D) very long

30. According to market analysts, the price of gasoline is expected to increase -------, so drivers are encouraged to fill up their gas tanks now.

(A) mainly
(B) ever
(C) anxiously
(D) soon

GO ON TO THE NEXT TEST!

PART 6 TOKIMAKURE!

Test 1

Questions 31-34 refer to the following e-mail.

To: Nikki Douglas <nkdgs@online.net>
From: Chris Richmond <chris_r@tdo.org>
Date: March 8
Subject: Workshop

Dear Ms. Douglas,

As the chairman of the Tylor Development Organization, I am writing to inform you about the commercial development workshop we are organizing for ------- members. As a long-time TDO member, you will be aware that our workshops provide a fantastic opportunity for our members to easily ------- a deep and wide comprehension of various business concepts and strategies. -------, they can use the workshops as a convenient way to network with other businesspeople, which may in turn lead to profitable collaborations in the future. The workshops will take place throughout May, and many famous, successful individuals will be leading the sessions, so the tickets for the events are expected to sell out soon. This is why I am contacting our long-time members to let them know about the workshops in advance. -------.

Best regards,

Chris Richmond
Chairman, Tylor Development Organization

---

31. (A) register
(B) registered
(C) registering
(D) registration

32. (A) participate
(B) appoint
(C) develop
(D) strive

33. (A) As well as
(B) Nevertheless
(C) In contrast
(D) Moreover

34. (A) Allow me to explain the revised schedule to them.
(B) Her session is certain to be a well-attended event.
(C) This workshop has been rescheduled for April.
(D) I anticipate that you will not miss this great opportunity.

Questions 35-38 refer to the following article.

Dr. Eva Wilson ------- the visiting professor at the Maple Ocean Institute of Technology.
35
After completing a Bachelor's degree in engineering, Dr. Wilson went on to pursue a Ph.D. in
physics at the prestigious Notty University of Applied Sciences. -------. She then spent
36
twelve years as a Roswell University Professor. During her ------- there, she authored five
37
books on the physical changes undergone by rockets in space.

Her invitation was a delightful surprise to many in the institute's science department. Some
even suggest that she might be asked to stay on permanently after her term is up, due to
the ------- retirement of the Science Chair, Professor Anderson.
38

Anything is possible with her impressive credentials. We look forward to seeing what kind of
a contribution Dr. Wilson will make during her time at the institute.

35. (A) has named
(B) is naming
(C) has been named
(D) will have named

36. (A) Many ideas and concepts were
developed into prototypes.
(B) After that she spent six years working
at the Jumbo Propulsion Institute in
Germany.
(C) There was a long negotiation between
her and the university.
(D) She is operating her own company
which supplies various chemicals.

37. (A) tenure
(B) status
(C) consultation
(D) appearance

38. (A) plan
(B) planned
(C) planning
(D) planner

Zelda's Coat Factory
153 Ford Drive
Saskatoon, SK S8M

Dear regular customer,

Are you ready for winter? Meteorologists are predicting one of the ------- winters we've
39
ever seen in this region. At Zelda's Coat Factory, we don't want you to freeze! We ------- a
40
special sale throughout the month of November this year. Come to see us for a new coat.

With discounts of up to 50% off, you can't miss this great opportunity! -------. Thank you
41
for your ------- and we look forward to welcoming you back in our store this November.
42

Your Neighborhood Coat Store,
Zelda's Coat Factory
Marketing Team

---

39. (A) cold
(B) colder
(C) coldest
(D) coldly

40. (A) held
(B) are held
(C) are holding
(D) will have held

41. (A) You will receive your order in five
business days.
(B) This is our last big sale to make room
for the spring collection.
(C) You deserve to enjoy being warm
inside and cool outside.
(D) Many celebrities have endorsed our
products.

42. (A) patience
(B) contribution
(C) donation
(D) patronage

Questions 43-46 refer to the following notice.

Attention!!!

Sweeney Apartments Residents:

Please, note that the annual cleaning of the central air conditioning system and ventilation shafts has been rescheduled from June 24 to June 26. The maintenance will start at 10:00 A.M. and will end by 4:00 P.M., if no complex problem is ------- . We prohibit the use

43

of water during this time. ------- . We apologize for any inconvenience this may ------- you.

44

45

It will help maintain good indoor air quality through adequate ventilation and provide a comfortable environment during the ------- summer.

46

Thank you for your cooperation.

Karen Hicks, Manager

---

43. (A) solved
(B) happened
(C) detected
(D) brought

44. (A) Moreover, there will be coin laundries around the area.
(B) Therefore, you can't have access to the laundry equipment in the basement.
(C) Consequently, you can purchase drinking water from the local shops.
(D) Nevertheless, average water usage has risen a lot.

45. (A) cause
(B) include
(C) bear
(D) contain

46. (A) impulsive
(B) previous
(C) advisory
(D) upcoming

PART **6**

TOKIMAKURE!

Test **2**

Questions 31-34 refer to the following e-mail.

To: Jesse Lundgard
From: Martin Kerr
Date: 20 October
Subject: Resignation Notice

Dear Ms. Lundgard

This e-mail is to ------- notify you that I will resign from my position as an assistant
         31

accountant with Rydell Pharmaceuticals. -------. I think that one month will be sufficient
                    32

time for you to find and train my successor. I really appreciate the opportunity I have been

given at such a wonderful company. I worked for five years in the general administration

department before receiving accounting training and being placed in my current

department. There is no proper way to thank you for the knowledge and experience I have

gained while ------- for you.
       33

If there is anything I can do to help you during this -------, then please don't hesitate to ask.
                            34

I wish you and Rydell Pharmaceuticals every success in the future.

Best regards,

Martin Kerr

---

31. (A) form
(B) forming
(C) formal
(D) formally

32. (A) You are responsible for a full-time
     position.
(B) November 23 should be my last day at
     the company.
(C) According to the contract, I should
     work until next year.
(D) Kindly tell me what steps you have
     taken.

33. (A) work
(B) works
(C) working
(D) worked

34. (A) transition
(B) conference
(C) promotion
(D) session

Questions 35-38 refer to the following memo.

To: All staff members
From: Kelly Douglas, Employee Training Manager
Date: April 5
Subject: Spreadsheet Software Training Classes

Many staff members have expressed an interest in ------- more skilled in the use of our
                                                 35
spreadsheet software. So next week we will hold four training classes given by software

specialists from the Richmond Tech Advisory Group. They will provide a simple yet effective

training program for users at different ------- of ability.
                                        36

-------. Participants in this class are ------- to have some prior experience in using the
37   **38**
spreadsheet software as well as basic knowledge of all its features. For staff members who

are not familiar with or have had little practice in using the spreadsheet software, a class for

beginners will be held next Tuesday, April 13.

35. (A) becoming
    (B) to become
    (C) become
    (D) have become

36. (A) levels
    (B) ideas
    (C) plans
    (D) actions

37. (A) New software will be installed within
       the next month.
    (B) The company will not provide private
       classes.
    (C) Please contact me if you wish to
       cancel your appointment.
    (D) The first class is designed for those of
       medium ability.

38. (A) expect
    (B) expects
    (C) expected
    (D) expecting

Questions 39-42 refer to the following article.

Reaching the Masses in the Digital Age

"I think that the best route to success in business is to enter the online market and use Web advertisements," says Garry Ford. He is a businessman who has been operating a jewelry shop on Main Street for almost fifteen years. As he was starting his business, he believed that having eye-catching print advertisements and an -------- packaging style was enough
                                                                                                              39
to ensure product marketability and exposure.

However, his -------- changed considerably a few years ago. "An increasing number of
              40
customers suggested that I make my merchandise available online and advertise it on popular local Web sites. --------, I decided that an online store was becoming necessary."
                                          41
Mr. Ford now makes over 50 percent of his sales through his Web site. --------.
                                                                        42

---

39. (A) attracts
    (B) attracted
    (C) attraction
    (D) attractive

40. (A) location
    (B) outlook
    (C) income
    (D) appearance

41. (A) Eventually
    (B) Typically
    (C) Likewise
    (D) Comparatively

42. (A) Market analysts suggest that online shopping statistics are wrong.
    (B) He is trying to launch a massive sales campaign in major jewelry shops.
    (C) Lower prices have attracted more customers to his business.
    (D) His story shows the power of Internet marketing.

Questions 43-46 refer to the following letter.

September 12

Mr. Howard King
428 Cleary Avenue
Brownsburg, IN 46112

Dear Mr. King,

Thank you for contacting us about the vacant Head Computer Programmer position here at Double Gate Games Inc. ------- our evaluation of your skills and experience, we believe
                                43
you are a strong candidate for the position. We would like to talk with you in person about the job. If it is convenient for you, we would like you to visit our headquarters at 2 P.M. on Wednesday, September 17.

At the meeting, you ------- to go into further detail about your strengths, and to describe
                       44
your contributions to projects you have worked on in the past. If we feel that you would fit well into our team here at Double Gate Games Inc., we will then place ------- on a shortlist
                                                                                    45
for the final round of interviews. Please call me at 999-5637 to let me know if the meeting date and time are agreeable to you. -------.
                                                    46

Sincerely,

Doug Goertz
Human Resources Manager
Double Gate Games Inc.

43. (A) Accordingly
    (B) So that
    (C) Based on
    (D) Prior to

44. (A) would have asked
    (B) were asked
    (C) will be asked
    (D) had asked

45. (A) us
    (B) you
    (C) him
    (D) myself

46. (A) Thank you for your interest in our company.
    (B) I'm very pleased to work with you.
    (C) I'm so sorry that the meeting will be postponed.
    (D) I'd like to put you on our waiting list for future positions.

PART 6

TOKIMAKURE!

Test

③

Questions 31-34 refer to the following letter.

August 16

Ross Swan
Order Fulfillment Manager

Reynard Distribution, Ltd.
887 Sawyer Street
Boston, MA 02205

Dear Mr. Swan,

Thank you for enrolling in the 8th Logistics in Action Conference. In my ------- as chairman
                                                                        31
of the conference, I make every effort to contact those who might add significant value to
the discussion on areas of logistics at the conference. I would like you ------- in one of our
                                                                           32
discussion panels on either September 10 or 11. I will try to contact you by phone next
week. -------.
       33

I would also appreciate it if you could e-mail me some details about yourself such as your
full name, department, educational background and ------- companies so that I can place
                                                     34
this information on our conference Web site.

Sincerely,

Chairman, Logistics in Action Conference
Yann Koeman

---

31. (A) demonstration
(B) capacity
(C) guidance
(D) origin

32. (A) participation
(B) participating
(C) for participators
(D) to participate

33. (A) Committee members will vote on who
should speak.
(B) You do not need to pay until after the
conference.
(C) We will send the information to your
mailing address.
(D) I hope to hear soon which day is more
convenient for you.

34. (A) affiliated
(B) competed
(C) altered
(D) detect

Questions 35-38 refer to the following memo.

To: Evans Industries Staff Members
From: Ryan Fabian
Subject: Next month's training

I am pleased to invite you to our next training session ------- will show how to improve your
                                                         35
communication skills in the business world. Evans Industries' products and brand names
are well known all over the world. But our success is measured not just by our presence in
the business market but also by the ------- process of developing professional
                                      36
relationships. Liam Baird, senior executive of business partnerships, is an authority in the
area of business communication.

This training session will address a crucial point of how to communicate ------- with other
                                                                         37
professionals. -------. You can learn about many cases, from training new staff members to
               38
working with other corporations.

Lunch will be served to all who attend.

35. (A) what
　　 (B) whose
　　 (C) so
　　 (D) which

36. (A) extensive
　　 (B) extend
　　 (C) extensively
　　 (D) extension

37. (A) confidently
　　 (B) alternatively
　　 (C) immaturely
　　 (D) handsomely

38. (A) It may be moved indoors depending
　　　　 on the weather.
　　 (B) Mr. Baird has worked for the company
　　　　 for fifteen years.
　　 (C) Please send your completed feedback
　　　　 forms to my inbox.
　　 (D) He will share his own experience of
　　　　 various types of problems and
　　　　 solutions.

Questions 39-42 refer to the following e-mail.

To: All plant workers
From: Jolene Ratzenberger
Date: November 26
Sub: Trouble with the Equipment

Yesterday it was reported that a pressure regulation button on the machinery we use to attach lids to our sauce jars was not working ------- . The capping machine was applying a
                                          39
lower force than ------- the regulation button setting was showing. ------- .
               40   **41**

An engineer is scheduled to come by this morning to examine the button and pump of the machine. ------- , please inspect all the jars extra carefully before transferring them to the
          42
labeling department. If you notice any loosely sealed jars or other errors, please remove them from the assembly line and place them in the rejection bin.

Sincerely,

Jolene Ratzenberger, Production Supervisor

---

39. (A) appropriately
(B) currently
(C) faithfully
(D) tightly

40. (A) that
(B) what
(C) how
(D) why

41. (A) Employees are asked to attend the training seminar to become familiar with the new machine.
(B) The instruction manual we have is very old.
(C) The expert suggested that we revise the safety guidelines.
(D) However, the equipment had been operating without issue for many years.

42. (A) Furthermore
(B) Conversely
(C) Besides
(D) Meanwhile

Questions 43-46 refer to the following letter.

11 April
3877 Pen Street
Jefferson City, MO 65109

Dear Mr. Routhier,

-------. These sessions are designed to help companies to cut down on absenteeism
43
resulting from high levels of stress and to maintain efficient productivity. Seminar

participants learn to ------- the latest stress reduction and relaxation techniques. Our
44
sessions will teach the staff members of your organization practical and simple methods to

minimize and stop the stress response before it has a chance to build up.

Our seminars are run at our downtown location, ------- we can also arrange for them to be
45
conducted at your place of business if you prefer. I have enclosed some information -------
46
available seminars and dates for you to review at your convenience.

For more details, please contact me directly at 777-4338.

Best regards,

Ken Gupta
Stress Control Seminars

43. (A) We are planning to sign up for your
new series of seminars.
(B) We are sure that you will hold our
workplace safety seminar.
(C) We have decided to offer our staff
members free medical help for
job-related stress.
(D) Thank you for your keen interest in our
stress control seminar.

44. (A) apply
(B) appeal
(C) resist
(D) partition

45. (A) so
(B) even
(C) however
(D) but

46. (A) at
(B) in
(C) on
(D) to

PART 6

TOKIMAKURE!

Test

4

Questions 31-34 refer to the following letter.

Kidman Utility Services

401 Minto Avenue
Cleveland, OH 44115

Dear Mr. Beltram,

Thank you for using our services. We issued a bill for your monthly utilities on November 3. And, according to our records, you have not paid the bill. The amount due is $57.69. If you have already sent your payment, then please ------- this part of the letter. But, if you have
                                                    31
not yet made a payment, then please send it as soon as possible.

Kidman Utility Services would also like to make you ------- of some other resources which
              32
may be useful to you. If you are having trouble paying your bill, then you can call our customer service hotline, 777-0573. -------. For those who need more convenience, we
              33
offer automatic withdrawal from your bank account with your written consent.

Please be advised that if we do not receive your payment by December 3, then you may experience an interruption in your utility services.

Thank you again for ------- Kidman Utility Services.
              34

31. (A) modify
    (B) discontinue
    (C) complain
    (D) disregard

32. (A) obvious
    (B) impressed
    (C) aware
    (D) satisfied

33. (A) You can get more information about our services on our Web site.
    (B) A late fee will be added to your next bill.
    (C) Please contain your account number in the e-mail.
    (D) Our representatives will explain the various payment options available.

34. (A) choosing
    (B) chosen
    (C) choice
    (D) to choose

August 22

Dear Valued Clients,

Dantona Crafts was established with the vision to offer our clients the means to sell their handmade goods in a secure online environment. Through our continued efforts ------- our 35 clients, we are pleased to announce a revamped Web site to facilitate your trading.

Up to now, the service was only available in the U.S., but we have now made it available worldwide. -------. In addition to this, customers can also perform ------- in their native 36 37 languages.

Simply choose the language you want in the setting menu and the site will do the rest. Of course, you can return to the menu and ------- your language preference at any time. The 38 Web site will always remember your choice. This is just another example of how we are trying to satisfy our clients.

Annalise Woods
President
Dantona Crafts

35. (A) on behalf of
    (B) in honor of
    (C) by means of
    (D) with regard to

36. (A) An instruction manual was sent to you
        by e-mail.
    (B) We ask you to set up an online
        account.
    (C) You will be charged $100 every month.
    (D) Now five languages are available
        including Spanish, Chinese, and
        Korean.

37. (A) advertisements
    (B) presentations
    (C) options
    (D) transactions

38. (A) compare
    (B) alter
    (C) repeat
    (D) continue

Questions 39-42 refer to the following article.

Doubts Over Keyboard Benefits

TORONTO (September 1)— -------. The computer keyboards and mice in the latest MM5
_____39_____
series are advertised as preventing tiredness and pain. However, their benefits may be much

fewer than the manufacturers claim on television and in newspapers. According to a

recently published study, these specially designed devices do little to alleviate muscle or

joint pain.

Dr. Norman Johnson conducted a six-month study involving one hundred office workers

who regularly experience pain in their hands or wrists when typing. Half of the participants

used a standard keyboard and mouse for the first three months, ------- the other half used
_____40_____
MM5 models. After three months, the groups switched devices. At the end of the study,

neither group reported any notable changes after switching models.

This news may be useful to consumers who are considering buying MM5 models. This

series of keyboards ------- cost around 80 dollars, which is about 1.5 times higher than
_____41_____
their standard counterparts. Now that Dr. Johnson's findings have been made public,

keyboard manufacturers may find it difficult to ------- such a high retail price.
_____42_____

39. (A) Specially designed devices are to be
recalled because of a design fault.
(B) A survey show a decrease in demand
for computer accessories.
(C) New technology has improved the
health of office employees.
(D) Consumers are recommended to think
again when buying new computer
gadgets.

40. (A) while
(B) during
(C) as
(D) in order to

41. (A) individually
(B) typically
(C) exclusively
(D) particularly

42. (A) pay
(B) allow
(C) justify
(D) advertise

14 Snyder Court
Winnipeg R3C 0H8

Dear Mr. Jake Warren,

We are writing to inform you that our insurance rates have recently been ------- to keep up
43
with current market levels. This means that there will be an increase of $5.00 in your

monthly bill. These changes are necessary ------- we can continue to provide you with the
44
best coverage on the market. If you have any ------- inquiries about our prices or policies,
45
please do not hesitate to contact us. We will strive to continue to provide you with

high-quality insurance. -------.
46

Best regards,

Kevin Qualls
Reva Insurance Customer Services

43. (A) adjusted
(B) waived
(C) exchanged
(D) omitted

44. (A) only if
(B) because
(C) so that
(D) whenever

45. (A) specify
(B) specific
(C) specifically
(D) specification

46. (A) Your car will be fully insured beginning
on January 1 next year.
(B) We would appreciate your
understanding of this change.
(C) Thank you for reporting this billing
error promptly.
(D) Please make use of this perfect
opportunity for your family.

PART **6**

TOKIMAKURE!

Test **5**

Questions 31-34 refer to the following e-mail.

To: All employees <employees@westernvirginia.org>
From: Dana Ausbrook, Senior Manager <dnab@westernvirginia.org>
Date: May 15
Subject: A New Office

To all Western Virginia employees,

The purpose of this e-mail is to remind you of our upcoming relocation. As you know, in order to cut costs Western Virginia Law Firm will be moving ------- a new office building
31
next week. Employees need to be aware that there will be some disruptions in work schedules on May 20 because of this -------. The move is expected to last about eight
32
hours. Beginning at 9:00 A.M., we ask that you clean out your desks and place your documents and items in the cardboard boxes -------. -------.
33   **34**

Thank you,

Dana Ausbrook
Senior Manager
Western Virginia Law Firm

---

31. (A) into
(B) onto
(C) toward
(D) forward

32. (A) renovation
(B) change
(C) absence
(D) mistake

33. (A) provide
(B) provision
(C) providing
(D) provided

34. (A) Some movers are waiting on the first floor, so please hurry up.
(B) Take special care with important items such as contracts and keys.
(C) The moving company came last week to estimate costs.
(D) We will attempt to solve some scheduling conflicts before the weekend.

Questions 35-38 refer to the following e-mail.

To: John Principle
From: Nancy Arnott
Date: October 14
Re: Inquiries

Dear Mr. Principle,

Thank you for your e-mail inquiring about the estate listing number #76412, which is a two-bedroom bungalow on Halbrooke Lane. To answer your questions, you are very welcome to come and ------- the house. In line with the owner's request, the house can be
                                         35
entered only at certain times. Please call me to arrange an -------, which I will then confirm
                                                              36
with the owner. I usually work from 9 A.M. to 6 P.M. on weekdays. -------.
                                                                    37

Additionally, the asking price for this property is fixed. It is not -------. If there are any other
                                                                      38
questions, please call our office or my cellular phone at 0202-555-0347.

Kindly,

Nancy Arnott
Patel Solutions, Inc.

35. (A) repair
(B) purchase
(C) remodel
(D) view

36. (A) interview
(B) expansion
(C) appointment
(D) adjustment

37. (A) If needed, I could make myself available on weekends.
(B) It is only for rent, not for sale.
(C) It is well-furnished, including a king-sized bed.
(D) The owner is absent for business purposes.

38. (A) transferable
(B) comparable
(C) negotiable
(D) reasonable

Questions 39-42 refer to the following letter.

June 7

Ms. Felizia Wolfmeier
31 Maylor Hill Road
Buckley CH7 3PL

Dear Ms. Wolfmeier,

Thank you for contacting Prescott School of Art & Design to inquire about our evening classes. Allow me to give you details of our courses, specifically ones that we run every week on Mondays and Wednesdays, ------- you requested. First, there is our Beginner Oil
                                                    39
Painting class, which provides instruction on basic techniques and emphasizes the importance of color. Second, there is our Technical Drawing class, which is designed for those interested in engineering and architecture. -------, these are the only weekday
                                                          40
classes that we currently run in the evenings. However, we do offer various online classes for individuals who have particularly busy schedules. ------- who enroll in such courses will
                                                              41
still have direct access to our team of instructors. -------.
                                                      42

Yours sincerely,

David Gadhavy, Student Services Manager
Prescott School of Art & Design

39. (A) so
(B) would
(C) what
(D) as

40. (A) Suddenly
(B) Unfortunately
(C) Alternatively
(D) Finally

41. (A) Ours
(B) Those
(C) He
(D) They

42. (A) There is more detailed information about the options on our Web site.
(B) Thank you for your interest in employment opportunities at our institution.
(C) Please contact me if you wish to withdraw from any of these classes.
(D) Your application for enrollment in the class is now being processed.

Questions 43-46 refer to the following information.

We at Hackney Art Supplies do our utmost every day to make sure our customers' orders arrive on time and in perfect condition. If you have not yet received your items, please ------- the following points. Shipping times vary from 5 days to 7 weeks, ------- the
43   44
delivery method you choose during checkout. -------. Although we strive to offer the most
                                              45
accurate estimate possible, some orders may take longer to be delivered. In the event of a significant delay in delivery, please give us a call. We will attempt to track your order then contact you with information regarding the ------- of your delivery.
                                              46

43. (A) send
   (B) note
   (C) arrange
   (D) demand

44. (A) following
   (B) for the purpose of
   (C) depending on
   (D) until

45. (A) Visit us online for more details about new painting equipment we are offering.
   (B) Our customer service agents are trained to answer your questions in a timely manner.
   (C) Refunds will not be issued for items that have been discounted.
   (D) Customers will automatically receive an expected delivery date when a purchase is made.

46. (A) status
   (B) existence
   (C) consultation
   (D) appearance

PART 6

TOKIMAKURE!

Test

6

Questions 31-34 refer to the following notice.

Energosound portable music player has been manufactured after numerous strict tests to satisfy the highest standards of quality. However, if at any time your music player malfunctions ------- the warranty period, which extends for 90 days after the date of
31
purchase, you can mail it to an authorized Energosound service center and get a replacement free of charge. The music player ------- in a strong cardboard box with plenty
32
of packing material to protect the device from any damage not covered by the warranty. Please be aware that the Energosound is not responsible for merchandise lost in -------.
33
Therefore we strongly recommend that you use one of the shipping companies in partnership with us. You can find a list of them on our Web site. -------.
34

---

31. (A) within
(B) since
(C) between
(D) above

32. (A) has been placed
(B) may place
(C) should be placed
(D) will be placing

33. (A) transit
(B) condition
(C) supply
(D) location

34. (A) There is a flat shipping rate of $10 for any orders under $100.
(B) We will never share your information with outside parties.
(C) They all offer competitive rates and a free tracking service.
(D) All expenses for repair work will be charged to your account.

Questions 35-38 refer to the following letter.

Dear Ms. Marlowe,

We greatly appreciate your interest in our organizing committee. Here are the details that you requested about the Whitehaven New Year Festival. We think this would be a great ------- for you to become involved, should you wish to volunteer your time to help with this event.

35

The event will begin on Saturday, February 7th at 3 P.M. and conclude on Sunday, February 8th at 5 P.M. You can volunteer for as much time as you like, although we prefer at least a six-hour commitment. Your main responsibility will be to assist with crowd control. There are several locations ------- the food court, the Wooshu demonstration area, the children's play

36
ground and the yo-yo competition zone. -------.

37

You will be expected to attend an ------- event on Friday, February 6th at 6 P.M.

38

Please let me know if you would like to volunteer.

Sincerely,

Chris Kerrigan
Volunteer Coordinator

35. (A) idea
    (B) suggestion
    (C) contribution
    (D) opportunity

36. (A) whereas
    (B) such as
    (C) seeing that
    (D) by then

37. (A) The winner of the yo-yo competition will receive a $50 voucher.
    (B) You may be asked to move between locations.
    (C) Most volunteers say it was great experience to attend this event.
    (D) You will learn about the origin of the Whitehaven New Year.

38. (A) environmental
    (B) international
    (C) orientation
    (D) accounts

Questions 39-42 refer to the following article.

Local News

EDGBASTON (August 11)— -------. The theater has long been an important part of
                                  39
Edgbaston's cultural life. Numerous successful, well-reviewed plays have been staged at
the venue, although it has not held a performance ------- October last year.
                                                        40

Because of a lack of funding and the worsening condition of the building, a decision was
made to close it down, prompting many residents to show their support for the theater.
------- their fundraising efforts, the theater will be able to stage a farewell show on
  41
September 1st, when a local drama group will perform a production of Swarovski's Black
Swan.

Admission will cost only seven dollars, and all ------- from the performance will go to
                                                    42
Mr. Oliver Stockton, the owner of the theater, who has worked tirelessly for over twenty
years to bring exceptional plays to the people of Edgbaston.

39. (A) Next month, the Ellison Theater, one of
        our city's treasures, will put on its
        final performance.
    (B) Local residents are flocking to the
        renovated Ellison Theater.
    (C) The Ellison Theater has just
        announced a new series of
        performances.
    (D) Theater critics have been praising the
        recent play at the Ellison Theater.

40. (A) by
    (B) around
    (C) during
    (D) since

41. (A) Whether
    (B) As a result of
    (C) Moreover
    (D) Instead of

42. (A) expenses
    (B) reviews
    (C) proceeds
    (D) advantages

Questions 43-46 refer to the following e-mail.

To: Vivian Tulio <tovivian@yoomail.com>
From: Drawbridge Customer Service <cs@drawbridge.net>
Date: October 12, 11:45 A.M.
Subject: Transfer #52403

Dear Ms. Tulio,

We are contacting you regarding your recent transfer on October 11 at 11:26 A.M. We are afraid that the transfer was not able to be made. This may be because the bank account number you gave was -------. The transfer was supposed to be sent to a foreign account
43
under the name of Ms. Sally Witham. Please check the account number again, including
------- branch code, and contact us as soon as possible. The remaining information you
44
have registered seems to be in order, so we can proceed with the transfer immediately after
------- the missing information. -------. Instead, contact me at 723-999-1483 (extension
45   **46**
number 459).

---

43. (A) inconsiderate
(B) uncertain
(C) incomplete
(D) unwilling

44. (A) her
(B) his
(C) its
(D) their

45. (A) receive
(B) received
(C) to receive
(D) receiving

46. (A) The transfer fee was added to the invoice on October 11.
(B) We are very sorry for the error we have made.
(C) It will take about one day to retrieve all the missing items.
(D) If you'd like to resolve this situation right now, please do not reply to this e-mail.

PART **6** TOKIMAKURE!

Test

7

Questions 31-34 refer to the following article.

Mayfield Valley to get Metro Station!!!

VANCOUVER (October 17)—Mayor Manning announced today a plan to build a new metro station in the Mayfield Valley, estimated to cost three million dollars. The new station will be built on the corner of Pinetree Street and Vancouver Hill. According to the Mayor's Office, the project is expected to break ground on July 1st and will be completed in one year.

The area is long ------- for a new metro station. However, residents are mixed about the
      31
project. Some residents complain about the cost, while others are concerned about the potential traffic problems which could occur during the construction.

------- alleviate some of these fears, Mayor Manning said that road closings would be kept
  32
to a minimum. --------. The mayor hopes citizens will focus on the huge benefits of the
              33
project. ------- completed, the new station will reduce commuting time to the downtown
        34
area by 30 minutes at least.

Alex Harper
Transportation News

---

31. (A) quick
(B) overdue
(C) continual
(D) eventual

32. (A) Refusing to
(B) Because of
(C) Together with
(D) In an effort to

33. (A) Please pay attention to the detour signs to get to City Hall.
(B) For the summer peak season, all local businesses are preparing for the tourists.
(C) Most stages of construction will be done outside peak hours.
(D) Natural gas buses will be bought to substitute old ones.

34. (A) Once
(B) Because
(C) As if
(D) As long as

Questions 35-38 refer to the following e-mail.

To: Sean Dalton <sdalton@daltonmedtech.com>
From: Herrietta Brown <hrtbr@miles.nsw.org>
Date: March 23
Subject: Collaboration with Dalton Med-Tech Inc.

Dear Mr. Dalton,

Thank you for taking time to visit us last Wednesday. It was a pleasure for me to have an opportunity to talk with you and get familiar with the ------- of Dalton Med-Tech. I
                                                                                35
especially enjoyed hearing about the work you are doing with small lasers and their -------
                                                                                          36
for the surgical field.

-------. Therefore, I believe that working with Dalton Med-Tech would be beneficial for Miles
   37
Hospital. I spoke to the board of directors and they have agreed that we should proceed
with the proposed collaboration. Please let me know when you ------- a meeting with the
                                                                38
board. I look forward to working together with you.

Sincerely,

Herrietta Brown
Chief Medical Officer
Miles Hospital

35. (A) challenges
(B) employees
(C) expectations
(D) projects

36. (A) implicate
(B) implicated
(C) implications
(D) implicating

37. (A) I wish you the best of luck in your
future research.
(B) High technology in the medical field is
crucial to our future.
(C) Adjustments to these lasers has led to
enhanced performance.
(D) Such cutting-edge devices would be
of little use to our surgeons.

38. (A) attended
(B) could attend
(C) must attend
(D) have attended

Questions 39-42 refer to the following article.

A Final Farewell to the Jeremy Burton Radio Hall

ATLANTA (April 17)—Plans were announced yesterday to permanently close down the Jeremy Burton Radio Hall later this year, ------- the city council's resolution. This ------- **40** will come as a shock to music lovers, as the concert hall is one of the city's oldest and most popular cultural institutions.

Singer Zoe Blank, one of the performers who made a name for herself on Radio Hall's stage, said, "It's a shame that the public are not attending concerts as frequently as they used to. I'll be sad to say goodbye." She ------- that a group of artists had been campaigning to **41** keep the concert hall open, but in vain. However, it was announced that a gala party celebrating the history of this famous venue will be held on Tuesday, June 26. -------. To **42** buy tickets for this special event, log on to www.jeremyburtonrh.org.

39. (A) following
(B) barring
(C) including
(D) notwithstanding

40. (A) apology
(B) performance
(C) investigation
(D) decision

41. (A) avoided
(B) submitted
(C) added
(D) supported

42. (A) Construction will resume on Friday, June 29.
(B) Formal invitations have already been sent out to interested residents.
(C) All proceeds have been donated to the Jeremy Burton Foundation.
(D) All who wish to say a last goodbye are welcome to attend.

Questions 43-46 refer to the following e-mail.

To: Kurt Bondell <kbondell23@hmail.net>
From: Grant German Fan Club <fanclub@grantfc.org>
Subject: Record Store Shows
Date: March 21

Dear Mr. Bondell,

It is my great pleasure to inform you of the upcoming record store shows that Grant's

management is organizing for ------- fan club members. Grant is expected to perform
              43

about twenty songs, both old and new. These record store shows will offer an opportunity

for fans to joyfully experience a Grant German performance in a small, intimate setting.

-------, they will be able to meet with their favorite pop singer during an autograph session,
  44

which will immediately follow his performance. Copies of Grant's new record will be

available for purchase, and fans can also have these signed during the autograph session.

Tickets will be ------- priced and may be bought online. The record store concerts will take
                45

place between April 15 and June 8, and the exact tour schedule will be posted on

www.grantgerman.com within the next few days. -------.
                                                46

Kindly,

Shawna Powar, Secretary
Grant German Fan Club

43. (A) valuing
    (B) value
    (C) valuation
    (D) valued

44. (A) Afterward
    (B) In advance
    (C) Instead
    (D) Even though

45. (A) exceptionally
    (B) respectively
    (C) plentifully
    (D) affordably

46. (A) You will receive your free tickets within
        a week.
    (B) The first show will be held at the end
        of the month.
    (C) You don't want to miss this chance to
        see Grant in person.
    (D) Thank you for your recent inquiry
        about Grant German.

PART **6**

TOKIMAKURE!

Test **8**

Questions 31-34 refer to the following e-mail.

To: Adam Mooregrave, Simi Industries <adamm@simii.org>
From: Mike Fitzgerald <info@cwsa.gov>
Date: October 25
Subject: RE: Applying for CWSA Certification

Dear Mr. Mooregrave

We appreciate your contacting the Canadian Workplace Safety Association. In order to apply for CWSA quality control certification, there are certain ------- that your factory must

31
meet. Employees must comply with federal safety standards through completion of various workplace safety courses. If your employees have not undergone this training yet, CWSA centers throughout the country ------- new applicants this month. As your company deals

32
with hazardous chemicals, we need to verify that your waste disposal systems, ------- air

33
and water purification methods, comply with our strict standards. -------.

34

To download a full list of available CWSA certifications, or to schedule an inspection of your factory, please visit www.cwsa.gov.

Best regards,

Mike Fitzgerald
Canadian Workplace Safety Association

---

31. (A) requirements
(B) officials
(C) examinations
(D) colleagues

32. (A) were accepted
(B) to accept
(C) are accepting
(D) have accepted

33. (A) along with
(B) only if
(C) referring to
(D) saying this

34. (A) This involves arranging a visit to your plant by our inspectors.
(B) Education materials will be offered free of charge to all participating retirees.
(C) We really appreciate your considerable efforts to reduce pollution.
(D) Please comply with our safety regulations when touring our factory.

Dear Hudson Telecom Customer:

-------. Hudson Telecom has been providing the finest satellite dishes in the region for over
35
three decades. As part of our commitment to our customers, we always make sure that you

know how to ------- our products.
36

Hudson satellite dishes are ------- to damage or displacement from storms, strong winds,
37
or other inclement weather. Therefore, we strongly recommend a sturdy base such as your

roof or balcony to prevent severe damage. Additionally, we suggest that you make use of

our offer to have a Hudson Telecom worker perform a free maintenance check of your dish

on the one-year anniversary of your purchase. Attention to the enclosed instructions and

------- available on our Web site will ensure an extended life for your new satellite dish.
38

Thank you for choosing Hudson to meet your satellite dish needs.

35. (A) You must have an eye for good
     products.
  (B) Thank you for your inquiry about
     extended warranties.
  (C) You must submit proof of purchase
     along with the serial number of your
     product.
  (D) Congratulations on buying a new
     Hudson satellite dish for your home.

36. (A) pick up
  (B) care for
  (C) turn down
  (D) put off

37. (A) adjacent
  (B) frequent
  (C) incompatible
  (D) susceptible

38. (A) they
  (B) there
  (C) those
  (D) which

Yesterday, Burton Air Industries announced a fire accident and the recall of its air conditioner, Fresh Wind model of 2018. According to an incident investigation report, a house fire accident occurred last June. -------.
                                                                    39

The report also says that a few consumers have witnessed sparks flying out of the machine when it has been in use for longer than four hours. ------- a thorough examination,
                                                                    40
engineers have found that when the Fresh Wind Air Conditioner is left running for an extended period of time, a buildup of moisture can cause a malfunction in the system.

Burton has claimed that this issue has been dealt with in their latest model, which has been subjected to ------- testing prior to its public release. -------, an official apology was
                  41   **42**
issued by Burton last month.

39. (A) It has the capacity to cool down 100 square feet in an hour.
  (B) It has led to some cases of dangerous overheating.
  (C) You will be contacted later this month for customer feedback.
  (D) We offer a variety of payment options for appliances costing more than $300.

40. (A) After
  (B) Since
  (C) When
  (D) Until

41. (A) failed
  (B) logical
  (C) rigorous
  (D) following

42. (A) Adversely
  (B) Consequently
  (C) Alternatively
  (D) Furthermore

Questions 43-46 refer to the following notice.

Kiley Elementary School is currently seeking an individual to serve as a school bus driver. ------- our community's children safely to and from school is a job of huge responsibility. In
43
addition to working during normal school hours, you will occasionally be asked to be on duty for after school activities, such as sporting events, school band and choir performances, and educational field trips.

During the first three months, all drivers, ------- how much experience they have, are hired
44
on a probationary basis. ------- we will hire them as full-time employees if there are no
45
problems.

Please join us for an information day on August 27. -------.
46

43. (A) Transporting
    (B) Guiding
    (C) Touring
    (D) Performing

44. (A) instead of
    (B) according to
    (C) regardless of
    (D) owing to

45. (A) Thereafter
    (B) Unless
    (C) Whenever
    (D) Suddenly

46. (A) A determination on your exact bus
        route will be made at that time.
    (B) Your paycheck will be deposited into
        the bank account you designate.
    (C) You are insured by the car insurance
        company we have a contract with.
    (D) More information about the job
        openings will be provided at that
        time.

PART 5 Answer

No.	TEST 1	TEST 2	TEST 3	TEST 4
1	C	B	A	C
2	D	B	B	D
3	A	A	B	A
4	A	D	B	C
5	A	B	B	B
6	B	A	C	A
7	D	D	B	D
8	C	B	D	C
9	A	D	C	D
10	A	C	A	A
11	D	B	B	A
12	A	D	B	D
13	D	B	B	B
14	C	D	C	A
15	C	D	C	D
16	D	D	B	D
17	A	B	C	D
18	C	C	B	B
19	C	B	D	D
20	B	C	D	D
21	C	C	B	D
22	B	D	A	A
23	D	C	B	A
24	C	D	C	A
25	A	C	C	C
26	B	D	B	C
27	C	B	C	D
28	A	C	C	C
29	D	A	A	D
30	D	A	B	C

PART 5 Answer

TEST 5

No.	ANSWER (A B C D)		No.	ANSWER (A B C D)
1	C		28	C
2			29	A
3	A		30	A
4	D			
5	A			
6	B			
7	A			
8	A			
9				
10				
11	A			
12				
13				
14				
15	A			
16	C			
17	C			
18				
19	D			
20				
21	C			
22				
23	C			
24				
25	C			
26				
27	A			

TEST 6

No.	ANSWER (A B C D)		No.	ANSWER (A B C D)
1	D		28	D
2	B		29	D
3			30	A
4	B			
5	A			
6				
7	A			
8				
9				
10	B			
11				
12	A			
13				
14				
15	B			
16	B			
17	A			
18				
19				
20				
21				
22	C			
23				
24				
25	C			
26	B			
27				

TEST 7

No.	ANSWER (A B C D)		No.	ANSWER (A B C D)
1	B		28	C
2	A		29	C
3			30	C
4				
5	A			
6				
7				
8				
9				
10	A			
11				
12				
13	C			
14				
15	A			
16				
17				
18				
19	A			
20				
21				
22				
23	A			
24				
25				
26				
27	A			

TEST 8

No.	ANSWER (A B C D)		No.	ANSWER (A B C D)
1			28	D
2	B		29	C
3	B		30	D
4				
5	B			
6	A			
7	B			
8	B			
9				
10				
11				
12	C			
13	B			
14				
15	B			
16	A			
17	B			
18				
19	C			
20				
21				
22				
23	B			
24	D			
25	A			
26				
27	A			

PART 6 Answer

TEST 1	No.	A	B	C	D
	31				
	32			●	
	33			●	
	34				●
	35				●
	36			●	
	37	●			
	38		●		
	39			●	
	40			●	
	41			●	
	42			●	
	43		●		
	44				
	45	●			
	46				●

TEST 2	No.	A	B	C	D
	31				●
	32		●		
	33			●	
	34	●			
	35	●			
	36	●			
	37			●	
	38			●	
	39				●
	40				●
	41	●			
	42				●
	43			●	
	44				
	45				
	46	●			

TEST 3	No.	A	B	C	D
	31				●
	32				●
	33				●
	34	●			
	35				●
	36	●			
	37	●			
	38				●
	39	●			
	40				●
	41				●
	42				●
	43				●
	44	●			
	45				●
	46			●	

TEST 4	No.	A	B	C	D
	31				●
	32			●	
	33				●
	34	●			
	35	●			
	36				●
	37		●		
	38				●
	39				●
	40	●			
	41		●		
	42			●	
	43	●			
	44			●	
	45		●		
	46		●		

PART 6 Answer

TEST 5

No.	ANSWER
	A B C D
31	A
32	B
33	A
34	A
35	D
36	B
37	A
38	C
39	D
40	A
41	B
42	A
43	B
44	C
45	D
46	A

TEST 6

No.	ANSWER
	A B C D
31	A
32	C
33	A
34	C
35	D
36	B
37	A
38	C
39	A
40	D
41	B
42	C
43	C
44	B
45	D
46	D

TEST 7

No.	ANSWER
	A B C D
31	B
32	D
33	C
34	A
35	D
36	B
37	A
38	A
39	A
40	D
41	C
42	D
43	D
44	A
45	D
46	C

TEST 8

No.	ANSWER
	A B C D
31	D
32	C
33	A
34	A
35	D
36	B
37	D
38	C
39	A
40	A
41	C
42	D
43	A
44	C
45	A
46	D

大里秀介　Shusuke Osato

TOEIC L&Rテスト990点、TOEIC S&Wテスト ライティング200点満点取得の経験を持つ現役サラリーマン。2006年から英語学習を開始して、2007年スコア730点を突破、社内選考でイギリス留学を経験する。2012年からカナダに駐在勤務し、北米間の大ビジネスプロジェクトをTOEICで磨いた英語力を駆使して成功に導く。著書に『3週間で攻略 TOEIC L&Rテスト900点！』(アルク)、『TOEIC テスト新形式完全攻略模試』(学研プラス)、『TOEIC L&Rテスト壁越えトレーニングPart 7』『TOEIC L&Rテスト 壁越え模試 リーディング』(旺文社)、『極めろ！ TOEIC L&R TEST 990点 リーディング特訓』(スリーエーネットワーク)などがある。

装幀・本文デザイン	斉藤 啓(ブッダプロダクションズ)
制作協力	Testing Contents Service
編集協力	渡邉真理子
翻訳協力	河野伸治

解きまくれ！ リーディングドリル TOEIC® L&R TEST PART 5&6

2022年12月23日　初版第1刷発行

著 者	大里秀介
発行者	藤嵜政子
発行所	株式会社　スリーエーネットワーク
	〒102-0083 東京都千代田区麹町3丁目4番 トラスティ麹町ビル2F
	電話：03-5275-2722 [営業]　03-5275-2726 [編集]
	https://www.3anet.co.jp/
印刷・製本	萩原印刷株式会社

©2022 Shusuke Osato
Printed in Japan
ISBN 978-4-88319-895-5 C0082

PART 5
Answer Sheet

TEST 1 /30

TEST 2 /30

TEST 3 /30

TEST 4 /30

TEST 1

No.	ANSWER	No.	ANSWER
---	A B C D	---	A B C D
1	A B C D	28	A B C D
2	A B C D	29	A B C D
3	A B C D	30	A B C D
4	A B C D		
5	A B C D		
6	A B C D		
7	A B C D		
8	A B C D		
9	A B C D		
10	A B C D		
11	A B C D		
12	A B C D		
13	A B C D		
14	A B C D		
15	A B C D		
16	A B C D		
17	A B C D		
18	A B C D		
19	A B C D		
20	A B C D		
21	A B C D		
22	A B C D		
23	A B C D		
24	A B C D		
25	A B C D		
26	A B C D		
27	A B C D		

TEST 2

No.	ANSWER	No.	ANSWER
---	A B C D	---	A B C D
1	A B C D	28	A B C D
2	A B C D	29	A B C D
3	A B C D	30	A B C D
4	A B C D		
5	A B C D		
6	A B C D		
7	A B C D		
8	A B C D		
9	A B C D		
10	A B C D		
11	A B C D		
12	A B C D		
13	A B C D		
14	A B C D		
15	A B C D		
16	A B C D		
17	A B C D		
18	A B C D		
19	A B C D		
20	A B C D		
21	A B C D		
22	A B C D		
23	A B C D		
24	A B C D		
25	A B C D		
26	A B C D		
27	A B C D		

TEST 3

No.	ANSWER	No.	ANSWER
---	A B C D	---	A B C D
1	A B C D	28	A B C D
2	A B C D	29	A B C D
3	A B C D	30	A B C D
4	A B C D		
5	A B C D		
6	A B C D		
7	A B C D		
8	A B C D		
9	A B C D		
10	A B C D		
11	A B C D		
12	A B C D		
13	A B C D		
14	A B C D		
15	A B C D		
16	A B C D		
17	A B C D		
18	A B C D		
19	A B C D		
20	A B C D		
21	A B C D		
22	A B C D		
23	A B C D		
24	A B C D		
25	A B C D		
26	A B C D		
27	A B C D		

TEST 4

No.	ANSWER	No.	ANSWER
---	A B C D	---	A B C D
1	A B C D	28	A B C D
2	A B C D	29	A B C D
3	A B C D	30	A B C D
4	A B C D		
5	A B C D		
6	A B C D		
7	A B C D		
8	A B C D		
9	A B C D		
10	A B C D		
11	A B C D		
12	A B C D		
13	A B C D		
14	A B C D		
15	A B C D		
16	A B C D		
17	A B C D		
18	A B C D		
19	A B C D		
20	A B C D		
21	A B C D		
22	A B C D		
23	A B C D		
24	A B C D		
25	A B C D		
26	A B C D		
27	A B C D		

PART 5
Answer Sheet

TEST 5

No.	A	B	C	D
1	Ⓐ	Ⓑ	Ⓒ	Ⓓ
2	Ⓐ	Ⓑ	Ⓒ	Ⓓ
3	Ⓐ	Ⓑ	Ⓒ	Ⓓ
4	Ⓐ	Ⓑ	Ⓒ	Ⓓ
5	Ⓐ	Ⓑ	Ⓒ	Ⓓ
6	Ⓐ	Ⓑ	Ⓒ	Ⓓ
7	Ⓐ	Ⓑ	Ⓒ	Ⓓ
8	Ⓐ	Ⓑ	Ⓒ	Ⓓ
9	Ⓐ	Ⓑ	Ⓒ	Ⓓ
10	Ⓐ	Ⓑ	Ⓒ	Ⓓ
11	Ⓐ	Ⓑ	Ⓒ	Ⓓ
12	Ⓐ	Ⓑ	Ⓒ	Ⓓ
13	Ⓐ	Ⓑ	Ⓒ	Ⓓ
14	Ⓐ	Ⓑ	Ⓒ	Ⓓ
15	Ⓐ	Ⓑ	Ⓒ	Ⓓ
16	Ⓐ	Ⓑ	Ⓒ	Ⓓ
17	Ⓐ	Ⓑ	Ⓒ	Ⓓ
18	Ⓐ	Ⓑ	Ⓒ	Ⓓ
19	Ⓐ	Ⓑ	Ⓒ	Ⓓ
20	Ⓐ	Ⓑ	Ⓒ	Ⓓ
21	Ⓐ	Ⓑ	Ⓒ	Ⓓ
22	Ⓐ	Ⓑ	Ⓒ	Ⓓ
23	Ⓐ	Ⓑ	Ⓒ	Ⓓ
24	Ⓐ	Ⓑ	Ⓒ	Ⓓ
25	Ⓐ	Ⓑ	Ⓒ	Ⓓ
26	Ⓐ	Ⓑ	Ⓒ	Ⓓ
27	Ⓐ	Ⓑ	Ⓒ	Ⓓ
28	Ⓐ	Ⓑ	Ⓒ	Ⓓ
29	Ⓐ	Ⓑ	Ⓒ	Ⓓ
30	Ⓐ	Ⓑ	Ⓒ	Ⓓ

TEST 6

No.	A	B	C	D
1	Ⓐ	Ⓑ	Ⓒ	Ⓓ
2	Ⓐ	Ⓑ	Ⓒ	Ⓓ
3	Ⓐ	Ⓑ	Ⓒ	Ⓓ
4	Ⓐ	Ⓑ	Ⓒ	Ⓓ
5	Ⓐ	Ⓑ	Ⓒ	Ⓓ
6	Ⓐ	Ⓑ	Ⓒ	Ⓓ
7	Ⓐ	Ⓑ	Ⓒ	Ⓓ
8	Ⓐ	Ⓑ	Ⓒ	Ⓓ
9	Ⓐ	Ⓑ	Ⓒ	Ⓓ
10	Ⓐ	Ⓑ	Ⓒ	Ⓓ
11	Ⓐ	Ⓑ	Ⓒ	Ⓓ
12	Ⓐ	Ⓑ	Ⓒ	Ⓓ
13	Ⓐ	Ⓑ	Ⓒ	Ⓓ
14	Ⓐ	Ⓑ	Ⓒ	Ⓓ
15	Ⓐ	Ⓑ	Ⓒ	Ⓓ
16	Ⓐ	Ⓑ	Ⓒ	Ⓓ
17	Ⓐ	Ⓑ	Ⓒ	Ⓓ
18	Ⓐ	Ⓑ	Ⓒ	Ⓓ
19	Ⓐ	Ⓑ	Ⓒ	Ⓓ
20	Ⓐ	Ⓑ	Ⓒ	Ⓓ
21	Ⓐ	Ⓑ	Ⓒ	Ⓓ
22	Ⓐ	Ⓑ	Ⓒ	Ⓓ
23	Ⓐ	Ⓑ	Ⓒ	Ⓓ
24	Ⓐ	Ⓑ	Ⓒ	Ⓓ
25	Ⓐ	Ⓑ	Ⓒ	Ⓓ
26	Ⓐ	Ⓑ	Ⓒ	Ⓓ
27	Ⓐ	Ⓑ	Ⓒ	Ⓓ
28	Ⓐ	Ⓑ	Ⓒ	Ⓓ
29	Ⓐ	Ⓑ	Ⓒ	Ⓓ
30	Ⓐ	Ⓑ	Ⓒ	Ⓓ

TEST 7

No.	A	B	C	D
1	Ⓐ	Ⓑ	Ⓒ	Ⓓ
2	Ⓐ	Ⓑ	Ⓒ	Ⓓ
3	Ⓐ	Ⓑ	Ⓒ	Ⓓ
4	Ⓐ	Ⓑ	Ⓒ	Ⓓ
5	Ⓐ	Ⓑ	Ⓒ	Ⓓ
6	Ⓐ	Ⓑ	Ⓒ	Ⓓ
7	Ⓐ	Ⓑ	Ⓒ	Ⓓ
8	Ⓐ	Ⓑ	Ⓒ	Ⓓ
9	Ⓐ	Ⓑ	Ⓒ	Ⓓ
10	Ⓐ	Ⓑ	Ⓒ	Ⓓ
11	Ⓐ	Ⓑ	Ⓒ	Ⓓ
12	Ⓐ	Ⓑ	Ⓒ	Ⓓ
13	Ⓐ	Ⓑ	Ⓒ	Ⓓ
14	Ⓐ	Ⓑ	Ⓒ	Ⓓ
15	Ⓐ	Ⓑ	Ⓒ	Ⓓ
16	Ⓐ	Ⓑ	Ⓒ	Ⓓ
17	Ⓐ	Ⓑ	Ⓒ	Ⓓ
18	Ⓐ	Ⓑ	Ⓒ	Ⓓ
19	Ⓐ	Ⓑ	Ⓒ	Ⓓ
20	Ⓐ	Ⓑ	Ⓒ	Ⓓ
21	Ⓐ	Ⓑ	Ⓒ	Ⓓ
22	Ⓐ	Ⓑ	Ⓒ	Ⓓ
23	Ⓐ	Ⓑ	Ⓒ	Ⓓ
24	Ⓐ	Ⓑ	Ⓒ	Ⓓ
25	Ⓐ	Ⓑ	Ⓒ	Ⓓ
26	Ⓐ	Ⓑ	Ⓒ	Ⓓ
27	Ⓐ	Ⓑ	Ⓒ	Ⓓ
28	Ⓐ	Ⓑ	Ⓒ	Ⓓ
29	Ⓐ	Ⓑ	Ⓒ	Ⓓ
30	Ⓐ	Ⓑ	Ⓒ	Ⓓ

TEST 8

No.	A	B	C	D
1	Ⓐ	Ⓑ	Ⓒ	Ⓓ
2	Ⓐ	Ⓑ	Ⓒ	Ⓓ
3	Ⓐ	Ⓑ	Ⓒ	Ⓓ
4	Ⓐ	Ⓑ	Ⓒ	Ⓓ
5	Ⓐ	Ⓑ	Ⓒ	Ⓓ
6	Ⓐ	Ⓑ	Ⓒ	Ⓓ
7	Ⓐ	Ⓑ	Ⓒ	Ⓓ
8	Ⓐ	Ⓑ	Ⓒ	Ⓓ
9	Ⓐ	Ⓑ	Ⓒ	Ⓓ
10	Ⓐ	Ⓑ	Ⓒ	Ⓓ
11	Ⓐ	Ⓑ	Ⓒ	Ⓓ
12	Ⓐ	Ⓑ	Ⓒ	Ⓓ
13	Ⓐ	Ⓑ	Ⓒ	Ⓓ
14	Ⓐ	Ⓑ	Ⓒ	Ⓓ
15	Ⓐ	Ⓑ	Ⓒ	Ⓓ
16	Ⓐ	Ⓑ	Ⓒ	Ⓓ
17	Ⓐ	Ⓑ	Ⓒ	Ⓓ
18	Ⓐ	Ⓑ	Ⓒ	Ⓓ
19	Ⓐ	Ⓑ	Ⓒ	Ⓓ
20	Ⓐ	Ⓑ	Ⓒ	Ⓓ
21	Ⓐ	Ⓑ	Ⓒ	Ⓓ
22	Ⓐ	Ⓑ	Ⓒ	Ⓓ
23	Ⓐ	Ⓑ	Ⓒ	Ⓓ
24	Ⓐ	Ⓑ	Ⓒ	Ⓓ
25	Ⓐ	Ⓑ	Ⓒ	Ⓓ
26	Ⓐ	Ⓑ	Ⓒ	Ⓓ
27	Ⓐ	Ⓑ	Ⓒ	Ⓓ
28	Ⓐ	Ⓑ	Ⓒ	Ⓓ
29	Ⓐ	Ⓑ	Ⓒ	Ⓓ
30	Ⓐ	Ⓑ	Ⓒ	Ⓓ

PART 6
Answer Sheet

TEST 1

No.	ANSWER
	A B C D
31	Ⓐ Ⓑ Ⓒ Ⓓ
32	Ⓐ Ⓑ Ⓒ Ⓓ
33	Ⓐ Ⓑ Ⓒ Ⓓ
34	Ⓐ Ⓑ Ⓒ Ⓓ
35	Ⓐ Ⓑ Ⓒ Ⓓ
36	Ⓐ Ⓑ Ⓒ Ⓓ
37	Ⓐ Ⓑ Ⓒ Ⓓ
38	Ⓐ Ⓑ Ⓒ Ⓓ
39	Ⓐ Ⓑ Ⓒ Ⓓ
40	Ⓐ Ⓑ Ⓒ Ⓓ
41	Ⓐ Ⓑ Ⓒ Ⓓ
42	Ⓐ Ⓑ Ⓒ Ⓓ
43	Ⓐ Ⓑ Ⓒ Ⓓ
44	Ⓐ Ⓑ Ⓒ Ⓓ
45	Ⓐ Ⓑ Ⓒ Ⓓ
46	Ⓐ Ⓑ Ⓒ Ⓓ

TEST 2

No.	ANSWER
	A B C D
31	Ⓐ Ⓑ Ⓒ Ⓓ
32	Ⓐ Ⓑ Ⓒ Ⓓ
33	Ⓐ Ⓑ Ⓒ Ⓓ
34	Ⓐ Ⓑ Ⓒ Ⓓ
35	Ⓐ Ⓑ Ⓒ Ⓓ
36	Ⓐ Ⓑ Ⓒ Ⓓ
37	Ⓐ Ⓑ Ⓒ Ⓓ
38	Ⓐ Ⓑ Ⓒ Ⓓ
39	Ⓐ Ⓑ Ⓒ Ⓓ
40	Ⓐ Ⓑ Ⓒ Ⓓ
41	Ⓐ Ⓑ Ⓒ Ⓓ
42	Ⓐ Ⓑ Ⓒ Ⓓ
43	Ⓐ Ⓑ Ⓒ Ⓓ
44	Ⓐ Ⓑ Ⓒ Ⓓ
45	Ⓐ Ⓑ Ⓒ Ⓓ
46	Ⓐ Ⓑ Ⓒ Ⓓ

TEST 3

No.	ANSWER
	A B C D
31	Ⓐ Ⓑ Ⓒ Ⓓ
32	Ⓐ Ⓑ Ⓒ Ⓓ
33	Ⓐ Ⓑ Ⓒ Ⓓ
34	Ⓐ Ⓑ Ⓒ Ⓓ
35	Ⓐ Ⓑ Ⓒ Ⓓ
36	Ⓐ Ⓑ Ⓒ Ⓓ
37	Ⓐ Ⓑ Ⓒ Ⓓ
38	Ⓐ Ⓑ Ⓒ Ⓓ
39	Ⓐ Ⓑ Ⓒ Ⓓ
40	Ⓐ Ⓑ Ⓒ Ⓓ
41	Ⓐ Ⓑ Ⓒ Ⓓ
42	Ⓐ Ⓑ Ⓒ Ⓓ
43	Ⓐ Ⓑ Ⓒ Ⓓ
44	Ⓐ Ⓑ Ⓒ Ⓓ
45	Ⓐ Ⓑ Ⓒ Ⓓ
46	Ⓐ Ⓑ Ⓒ Ⓓ

TEST 4

No.	ANSWER
	A B C D
31	Ⓐ Ⓑ Ⓒ Ⓓ
32	Ⓐ Ⓑ Ⓒ Ⓓ
33	Ⓐ Ⓑ Ⓒ Ⓓ
34	Ⓐ Ⓑ Ⓒ Ⓓ
35	Ⓐ Ⓑ Ⓒ Ⓓ
36	Ⓐ Ⓑ Ⓒ Ⓓ
37	Ⓐ Ⓑ Ⓒ Ⓓ
38	Ⓐ Ⓑ Ⓒ Ⓓ
39	Ⓐ Ⓑ Ⓒ Ⓓ
40	Ⓐ Ⓑ Ⓒ Ⓓ
41	Ⓐ Ⓑ Ⓒ Ⓓ
42	Ⓐ Ⓑ Ⓒ Ⓓ
43	Ⓐ Ⓑ Ⓒ Ⓓ
44	Ⓐ Ⓑ Ⓒ Ⓓ
45	Ⓐ Ⓑ Ⓒ Ⓓ
46	Ⓐ Ⓑ Ⓒ Ⓓ

TEST 1 ___/16

TEST 2 ___/16

TEST 3 ___/16

TEST 4 ___/16

PART 6
Answer Sheet

TEST 5				
No.	\multicolumn{4}{c	}{ANSWER}
	A	B	C	D
31	Ⓐ	Ⓑ	Ⓒ	Ⓓ
32	Ⓐ	Ⓑ	Ⓒ	Ⓓ
33	Ⓐ	Ⓑ	Ⓒ	Ⓓ
34	Ⓐ	Ⓑ	Ⓒ	Ⓓ
35	Ⓐ	Ⓑ	Ⓒ	Ⓓ
36	Ⓐ	Ⓑ	Ⓒ	Ⓓ
37	Ⓐ	Ⓑ	Ⓒ	Ⓓ
38	Ⓐ	Ⓑ	Ⓒ	Ⓓ
39	Ⓐ	Ⓑ	Ⓒ	Ⓓ
40	Ⓐ	Ⓑ	Ⓒ	Ⓓ
41	Ⓐ	Ⓑ	Ⓒ	Ⓓ
42	Ⓐ	Ⓑ	Ⓒ	Ⓓ
43	Ⓐ	Ⓑ	Ⓒ	Ⓓ
44	Ⓐ	Ⓑ	Ⓒ	Ⓓ
45	Ⓐ	Ⓑ	Ⓒ	Ⓓ
46	Ⓐ	Ⓑ	Ⓒ	Ⓓ

TEST 6				
No.	\multicolumn{4}{c	}{ANSWER}
	A	B	C	D
31	Ⓐ	Ⓑ	Ⓒ	Ⓓ
32	Ⓐ	Ⓑ	Ⓒ	Ⓓ
33	Ⓐ	Ⓑ	Ⓒ	Ⓓ
34	Ⓐ	Ⓑ	Ⓒ	Ⓓ
35	Ⓐ	Ⓑ	Ⓒ	Ⓓ
36	Ⓐ	Ⓑ	Ⓒ	Ⓓ
37	Ⓐ	Ⓑ	Ⓒ	Ⓓ
38	Ⓐ	Ⓑ	Ⓒ	Ⓓ
39	Ⓐ	Ⓑ	Ⓒ	Ⓓ
40	Ⓐ	Ⓑ	Ⓒ	Ⓓ
41	Ⓐ	Ⓑ	Ⓒ	Ⓓ
42	Ⓐ	Ⓑ	Ⓒ	Ⓓ
43	Ⓐ	Ⓑ	Ⓒ	Ⓓ
44	Ⓐ	Ⓑ	Ⓒ	Ⓓ
45	Ⓐ	Ⓑ	Ⓒ	Ⓓ
46	Ⓐ	Ⓑ	Ⓒ	Ⓓ

TEST 7				
No.	\multicolumn{4}{c	}{ANSWER}
	A	B	C	D
31	Ⓐ	Ⓑ	Ⓒ	Ⓓ
32	Ⓐ	Ⓑ	Ⓒ	Ⓓ
33	Ⓐ	Ⓑ	Ⓒ	Ⓓ
34	Ⓐ	Ⓑ	Ⓒ	Ⓓ
35	Ⓐ	Ⓑ	Ⓒ	Ⓓ
36	Ⓐ	Ⓑ	Ⓒ	Ⓓ
37	Ⓐ	Ⓑ	Ⓒ	Ⓓ
38	Ⓐ	Ⓑ	Ⓒ	Ⓓ
39	Ⓐ	Ⓑ	Ⓒ	Ⓓ
40	Ⓐ	Ⓑ	Ⓒ	Ⓓ
41	Ⓐ	Ⓑ	Ⓒ	Ⓓ
42	Ⓐ	Ⓑ	Ⓒ	Ⓓ
43	Ⓐ	Ⓑ	Ⓒ	Ⓓ
44	Ⓐ	Ⓑ	Ⓒ	Ⓓ
45	Ⓐ	Ⓑ	Ⓒ	Ⓓ
46	Ⓐ	Ⓑ	Ⓒ	Ⓓ

TEST 8				
No.	\multicolumn{4}{c	}{ANSWER}
	A	B	C	D
31	Ⓐ	Ⓑ	Ⓒ	Ⓓ
32	Ⓐ	Ⓑ	Ⓒ	Ⓓ
33	Ⓐ	Ⓑ	Ⓒ	Ⓓ
34	Ⓐ	Ⓑ	Ⓒ	Ⓓ
35	Ⓐ	Ⓑ	Ⓒ	Ⓓ
36	Ⓐ	Ⓑ	Ⓒ	Ⓓ
37	Ⓐ	Ⓑ	Ⓒ	Ⓓ
38	Ⓐ	Ⓑ	Ⓒ	Ⓓ
39	Ⓐ	Ⓑ	Ⓒ	Ⓓ
40	Ⓐ	Ⓑ	Ⓒ	Ⓓ
41	Ⓐ	Ⓑ	Ⓒ	Ⓓ
42	Ⓐ	Ⓑ	Ⓒ	Ⓓ
43	Ⓐ	Ⓑ	Ⓒ	Ⓓ
44	Ⓐ	Ⓑ	Ⓒ	Ⓓ
45	Ⓐ	Ⓑ	Ⓒ	Ⓓ
46	Ⓐ	Ⓑ	Ⓒ	Ⓓ

TEST 5 /16

TEST 6 /16

TEST 7 /16

TEST 8 /16